THE ROLE OF THE SOLICITOR-GENERAL

Behind every government there is an impressive team of hard-working lawyers. In Australia, the Solicitor-General leads that team. A former Attorney-General once said, 'The Solicitor-General is next to the High Court and God.' And yet the role of government lawyers in Australia, and specifically the Solicitor-General as the most senior of government lawyers, is under-theorised and under-studied.

The Role of the Solicitor-General: Negotiating Law, Politics and the Public Interest goes behind the scenes of government—drawing from interviews with over 45 government and judicial officials—to uncover the history, theory and practice of the Australian Solicitor-General. The analysis reveals a role that is of fundamental constitutional importance to ensuring both the legality and the integrity of government action, thus contributing to the achievement of rule-of-law ideals. The Solicitor-General also works to defend government action and prosecute government policies in the court, and thus performs an important role as messenger between the political and judicial branches of government.

But the Solicitor-General's position, as both an internal integrity check on government and an external warrior for government, gives rise to competing pressures: between the law, politics and the public interest. The office of the Solicitor-General in Australia has evolved many characteristics across the almost two centuries of its history in an attempt to navigate these tensions. These pressures are not unique to the Australian context. The understanding of the Australian position provided by this book is informed by, and will inform, comparative analysis of the role of government lawyers across the world.

The Role of the Solicitor-General

Negotiating Law, Politics and the Public Interest

Gabrielle Appleby

•HART•

OXFORD • LONDON • NEW YORK • NEW DELHI • SYDNEY

HART PUBLISHING
Bloomsbury Publishing Plc
Kemp House, Chawley Park, Cumnor Hill, Oxford, OX2 9PH, UK

HART PUBLISHING, the Hart/Stag logo, BLOOMSBURY and the Diana logo are
trademarks of Bloomsbury Publishing Plc
First published in Great Britain 2016

First published in hardback, 2016
Paperback edition, 2018

A catalogue record for this book is available from the British Library.

Library of Congress Cataloging-in-Publication Data

Names: Appleby, Gabrielle, author.

Title: The role of the solicitor-general : negotiating law, politics and the public interest / Gabrielle Appleby.

Description: Oxford ; Portland, Oregon : Hart Publishing, 2016. | Includes bibliographical references and index.

Identifiers: LCCN 2016005224 (print) | LCCN 2016006131 (ebook) | ISBN 9781849467124 (hardback : alk. paper) | ISBN 9781509903955 (Epub)

Subjects: LCSH: Australia. Solicitor General. | Government attorneys—Australia.

Classification: LCC KU3428 .A67 2016 (print) | LCC KU3428 (ebook) | DDC 353.4/22930994—dc23

LC record available at http://lccn.loc.gov/2016005224

ISBN: PB: 978-1-50992-472-1
HB: 978-1-84946-712-4
ePDF: 978-1-50990-396-2
ePub: 978-1-50990-395-5

Typeset by Compuscript Ltd, Shannon

PREFACE

My ongoing interest in the role of the Solicitor-General can be traced back to my early work with Justice Patrick Keane. As Solicitor-General for the State of Queensland, Pat inspired a young articled clerk to understand more about our constitutional system, to venture beyond the words of the constitutional text and judicial exegesis, and investigate the offices and people who make the system work.

This book draws greatly from my doctoral research: *The Constitutional Role of the Solicitor-General: An Historical, Legal and Lived Portrait*. For their encouragement, support and confidence in that endeavour, I am forever grateful to my supervisors, John Williams, Clem Macintyre and the aforementioned Justice Keane.

I must reserve a special thank you for all of my interview participants. Without them I would never have been able to achieve the objective of the book, to look at one small dimension of our working constitution with richness and depth. Many of my interviewees gave up hours of their time to assist me. Each one of them answered my questions with a level of candour for which I am extremely grateful. Many also attended, and contributed to, a symposium on the role of the Solicitor-General that I co-organised in April 2011 and that resulted in the publication *Public Sentinels: A Comparative Analysis of Australian Solicitors-General* (Ashgate Publishing, 2014).

I was supported in this project by many other wonderful people. To Suzanne Le Mire, Adam Webster, Stephanie Wilkins, Alison John, Peter Burdon, Alex Reilly, Shih-Ning Then, Andrew McGee, Anna Olijnyk, Dale Stephens, Andrew Lynch, David Collins, Matthew Windsor, Jeffrey Jowell, Anthony Bradley, Graham Gee, Robert Hazell and Benjamin Yong, thank you for variously reading my work, offering insightful comments and suggestions for further research, debating my ideas and disagreeing with me when necessary. Thank you to Paolo Buchberger, Secretary of the Special Committee of Solicitors-General, for help, advice, wisdom and friendship throughout the project. I would also like to thank Peter Bailey who generously provided me with consent to access the manuscripts of his father, former Commonwealth Solicitor-General Sir Kenneth Bailey, at the National Library of Australia.

Lastly, I would like to thank Bill Asquith and Annie Mirza at Hart Publishing for their ongoing enthusiasm for the project as it worked towards its final form.

CONTENTS

Part II: The Australian Solicitor-General

LIST OF ACRONYMS

ABA	Australian Bar Association
AGD	Attorney-General's Department (Commonwealth)
AGS	Australian Government Solicitor
ACTGS	Australian Capital Territory Government Solicitor
APS	Australian Public Service
DFAT	Department of Foreign Affairs and Trade (Commonwealth)
DPP	Director of Public Prosecutions
GBE	Government Business Enterprise
GLS	Government Legal Service
ICAC	Independent Commission Against Corruption (New South Wales)
LCCSC	Law, Crime and Community Safety Council
MP	Member of Parliament
OIL	Office of International Law (Commonwealth, Attorney-General's Department)
OLC	Office of Legal Counsel (US)
OLSC	Office of Legal Services Coordination (Commonwealth, Attorney-General's Department)
OPC	Office of Parliamentary Counsel
OSG	Office of Solicitor-General (United States)
SCAG	Standing Committee of Attorneys-General
SCLJ	Standing Council on Law and Justice
SCSG	Special Committee of Solicitors-General
SFO	Serious Fraud Office (UK)
UK	United Kingdom
UNCITRAL	United Nations Commission on International Trade Law
UNCLOS III	United Nations Convention on the Law of the Sea III
US	United States
VGSO	Victorian Government Solicitor's Office

TABLE OF CASES

TABLE OF STATUTES

Australia

New Zealand

United Kingdom

Part I

Introducing the Solicitor-General

1

The Solicitor-General and the Constitution

A constitution does not work itself; it has to be worked by men [and women].
Ivor Jennings (1959)[1]

I. The Working Constitution

The study of the Solicitor-General undertaken in this book is underpinned by a broader objective: to seek a better understanding of the 'working',[2] or 'complete',[3] form of constitutional systems. Arguably, the study of constitutional law has been excessively focused upon the constituting document (where one exists) and judicial interpretation of it.[4] At times it appears that constitutional law is coextensive with the constitutional text and judicial doctrine. But myopic focus upon these institutions is 'hopelessly misdescriptive'[5] and has led to the undervaluing, and therefore the understudying, of other key constitutional institutions. Because of Australia's Westminster heritage, there is a wide acceptance that its constitution transcends the text and judicial pronouncements to include those political understandings and rules of practice known as constitutional conventions. Once conventions are accepted as fundamental facets of our constitutional system, it is clear that the focus on text and judicial interpretation is insufficient. The necessity arises for a broader definition of the Constitution.

[1] I Jennings, *The Law and the Constitution* (University of London Press, 5th edn, 1959) 82. That Jennings had referred only to men is telling. In Australia, only two female Solicitors-General have been appointed: Mary Gaudron as Solicitor-General of New South Wales in 1981 and Pamela Tate as Solicitor-General of Victoria in 2003.

[2] This is the terminology preferred by Karl Llewellyn: K Llewellyn, 'The Constitution as Institution' (1934) 34 *Columbia Law Review* 1, 6.

[3] This is the terminology introduced by Matthew Palmer: see, eg, MSR Palmer, 'Using Constitutional Realism to Identify the Complete Constitution: Lessons from an Unwritten Constitution' (2006) 54 *The American Journal of Comparative Law* 587.

[4] Llewellyn referred to this as 'orthodox constitutional theory': Llewellyn, above n 2, 3–4. See also R Posner, *Frontiers of Legal Theory* (Harvard University Press, 2001) 18. In the Australian context, this focus has also been identified: see, eg, J McMillan, 'Rethinking the Separation of Powers' (2010) 38 *Federal Law Review* 423; J McMillan, 'The Ombudsman and the Rule of Law' (2006) 44 *AIAL Forum* 1.

[5] Llewellyn, above n 2, 4.

Martin Loughlin proposed that 'public law' must include those other mechanisms beyond the constitutional text that facilitate the governance of a community: 'The assemblage of rules, principles, canons, maxims, customs, usages, and manners that condition, sustain and regulate the activity of governing.'[6] Loughlin's definition introduces the possibility of a second definition of the Constitution, one that includes not simply rules but also their *usage*.[7] Loughlin further argued that public law scholarship ought first to explore this usage before drawing conclusions about the nature of the law behind it.[8]

For Karl Llewellyn, a legal institution is 'in first instance a set of ways of living and doing. It is not, in first instance, a matter of words or rules.'[9] Drawing extensively on Llewellyn's work, Matthew Palmer introduced the concept of 'constitutional realism': to understand the 'complete' constitution, Palmer suggested that we must understand 'what factors affect the exercise of power and how'.[10] Similarly, Mark Tushnet referred to 'constitutional orders' or 'regimes' rather than constitutions, meaning 'a reasonably stable set of institutions through which a nation's fundamental decisions are made over a sustained period, and the principles that guide those decisions'.[11] Tushnet also postulated that a constitutional order will be constructed and transformed over time.[12] At any moment, a constitutional order contains residues of the past and hints of the future.

In Australia and elsewhere, there is a normative expectation that those in government will act legally, constrained by the limitations placed on them by the law. This is the fundamental tenet of the rule of law, and reflects an embedded norm of constitutionalism. It is this tenet that places on the Executive an obligation to first interpret, and then obey, the law. In a system that operates under the separation of powers, many see the task of interpreting the law as it limits government power as residing with the Judiciary.[13] This is, in the last instance, undeniably correct: the existence of an independent judicial branch is one of the

[6] M Loughlin, *The Idea of Public Law* (Oxford University Press, 2003) 115. See also M Loughlin, *Foundations of Public Law* (Oxford University Press, 2010) 11.

[7] See also MJ Detmold, *The Australian Commonwealth: A Fundamental Analysis of its Constitution* (Law Book Co, 1985) 5; S Ratnapala, *Australian Constitutional Law: Foundations and Theory* (Oxford University Press, 2007) 4.

[8] Loughlin, *The Idea of Public Law*, above n 6, 44.

[9] Llewellyn, above n 2, 17. See also KN Llewellyn, *The Bramble Bush: The Classic Lectures on the Law and Law School* (Oxford University Press, 1930, 1960 reprint) 4, 7, 16, 79; KN Llewellyn, *The Theory of Rules* (University of Chicago Press, 2011) 63.

[10] MSR Palmer, 'What is New Zealand's Constitution and Who Interprets It? Constitutional Realism and the Importance of Public Office-Holders' (2006) 17 *Public Law Review* 133, 134. See also Palmer, above n 3, 589.

[11] M Tushnet, *A New Constitutional Order* (Princeton University Press, 2003) 1.

[12] ibid, 2.

[13] The famous pronouncement of Marshall CJ in *Marbury v Madison* (1803) 1 Cranch 137, 177, that '[i]t is, emphatically, the province and duty of the judicial department to say what the law is', while not expressly adopted by the Australian framers, has been embraced by the Court as 'axiomatic' (*Australian Communist Party v Commonwealth* (1951) 83 CLR 1, 262 (Fullagar J)). See also McMillan, 'The Ombudsman and the Rule of Law', above n 4, 1.

bulwarks on which governance under the rule of law rests. The perception of the 'great powers'[14] of the Judiciary has meant that there is much concern over, and therefore consideration of, this institution's independence and impartiality.[15] However, if interpretation were left only to the Judiciary, constitutional systems would have stalled at their inception. 'After-the-fact' judicial review alone does not explain how constitutionalism is achieved.[16]

Thomas Hobbes observed that '[a]ll laws, written, and unwritten, have need of Interpretation'.[17] Words consistently prove to be imperfect vehicles to convey unambiguous meaning, and this is particularly the case with those words that form part of a constitutional text, forged from political compromise.[18] If the court has not considered (or in rare instances, cannot consider) a question of interpretation, the words of the Constitution and other laws must still be given meaning. Those with the mandate of administering and implementing the Constitution and the laws have been bestowed with a constant task of interpretation and adjudication.[19] Often the Executive receives no guidance from the courts in this endeavour. Sanford Levinson explained:

> Because courts can view only a very small percentage of official acts, it is crucial to the maintenance of a constitutional order that individuals believe themselves obligated to be conscientious adjudicators even in the absence of coercive constraints provided by courts.[20]

Further, according to David Luban there is still 'indeterminacy in legal doctrine' with which administrators must grapple despite courts' assistance in the interpretation of statutes.[21] Sometimes judicial attempts to inject clarity into statutory language can result in further ambiguity. Similarly, indeterminacy will often plague common law doctrines. To understand how our Constitution and laws are practised, it is necessary to study and understand many more institutions in the system than simply the Judiciary.[22]

[14] Sir Ninian Stephen, 'Southey Memorial Lecture 1981: Judicial Independence—A Fragile Bastion' (1982) 13 *Melbourne University Law Review* 334, 338.

[15] This has led to detailed analysis of the structural and other mechanisms that exist to protect these traits. Judicially, this concern was evident from the inception of the Commonwealth and has continued in its Chapter III jurisprudence.

[16] DE Johnsen, 'Faithfully Executing the Laws: Internal Legal Constraints on Executive Power' (2007) 54 *UCLA Law Review* 1559, 1564.

[17] T Hobbes, *Leviathan* (Penguin Books Ltd, 1651, 1968 reprint) pt II, ch 26, 322.

[18] D Luban, *Legal Ethics and Human Dignity* (Cambridge University Press, 2007) 196; Llewellyn, *The Theory of Rules*, above n 9, 42.

[19] See, eg, J Quick and R Garran, *The Annotated Constitution of the Australian Commonwealth* (Legal Books, 1901, 1976 reprint) 791; CTL Pillard, 'The Unfulfilled Promise of the Constitution in Executive Hands' (2005) 103 *Michigan Law Review* 676, 687.

[20] S Levinson, *Constitutional Faith* (Princeton University Press, 1988) 50; see also P Brest, 'The Conscientious Legislator's Guide to Constitutional Interpretation' (1975) 90 *Harvard Law Review* 585.

[21] Luban, above n 18, 197.

[22] Palmer, 'What is New Zealand's Constitution', above n 10; See also M Tushnet, 'Non-Judicial Review' (2003) 40 *Harvard Journal on Legislation* 453, 492 and fn 228.

A. The Constitutional Role of Government Lawyers

The central character of this book is one of the major actors in the contemporary Australian constitutional order: the Solicitor-General.[23] Before providing an introduction to that specific office's role, the role of government lawyers requires some explanation. To apply constitutional rules (written and otherwise) the Executive needs assistance from those skilled in understanding the law to interpret them. It is the *understanding* of the constitutional text and judicial pronouncements held by public officials (elected and appointed) that guides their actions. Often, it is legal advice they receive that forms the basis of their understanding. Luban argued that 'the most significant actors are not judges, not … officials more generally, but lawyers'.[24] It is through the lawyer–client interface that 'law in books becomes the law in action'.[25] AH Dennis claimed that the government lawyer constitutes 'a link between the law and the Executive'.[26] Similarly, Cornell Clayton observed:

> Today, most government action takes place in a twilight zone that exists between what the clear commands of law authorize and what they prohibit. Within this zone, custom, convention, professional norms, and institutional cultures merge to authorize and constrain discretionary conduct. It is the work of government attorneys, … to construct and define these informal understandings and to assist their political superiors in navigating through them.[27]

Comprehension of a working constitution therefore requires considered study of those actors who guide the conduct of government officials by providing them with an understanding of the constitutional text, other laws and judicial pronouncements. It is the officials' understanding, combined with their conduct, that eventually becomes accepted as constitutional convention, particularly in light of the requirement for normative-based practice.[28] The advice of government lawyers assists in keeping governments within the law, and also facilitates the adaptation of legal frameworks in a climate of evolving social needs and political ideas.[29]

Government lawyers are key components in achieving constitutionalism.[30] They can act as guards against tyranny and abuse within government. Indeed, in many

[23] In 1964, the seminal work on the English Law Officers said they comprised 'integral parts of our constitution': JLJ Edwards, *The Law Officers of the Crown: A Study of the Offices of the Attorney-General and Solicitor-General of England with an Account of the Office of the Director of Public Prosecutions of England* (Sweet & Maxwell, 1964) 11.

[24] Luban, above n 18, 131. See also ibid, 140.

[25] ibid.

[26] AH Dennis, 'The Official Lawyers' Place in the Constitution' (1925) 41 *Law Quarterly Review* 378, 379. See also ibid, 380.

[27] CW Clayton, 'Introduction: Politics and the Legal Bureaucracy' in CW Clayton (ed), *Government Lawyers: The Federal Legal Bureaucracy and Presidential Politics* (University Press of Kansas, 1995) 1, 13.

[28] Jennings, above n 1, 135.

[29] See, in the context of conventions, ibid, 101.

[30] American scholarship has recognised the idea that a significant part is played by non-judicial actors (including government legal officers) in the operation of the Constitution, and there has been

unstable fledgling democracies, government legal officers are quickly targeted by those leading revolutionary coups, or despotic leaders.[31] It is the rule of law and the striving for constitutionalism that serves to explain and provide the rationale for the constitutional role of government legal officers, including in Australia the primary legal officer, the Solicitor-General.[32]

II. The Australian Solicitor-General

Across the Australian jurisdictions, the Solicitor-General provides legal advice to the Executive on significant constitutional and public law matters, and otherwise legally or politically important issues. The Solicitor-General also defends the position of the government in the superior courts, including the High Court of Australia. The office is a relatively modern statutory one, with roots in the antiquity of the English Law Officers (the Attorney-General and the Solicitor-General). The contemporary Australian Solicitor-General is a constitutional specialist, although this has not always been the case.

Today, the role of Solicitor-General is *central* to the regulation of public power in every Australian jurisdiction. While the function of day-to-day legal adviser to the government is filled by a vast number of legal professionals both within and outside government, at the apex of these sits the Solicitor-General. Subject only to a future contrary judicial ruling, the office provides the final word on significant legal questions within the Executive. In a system of separation of powers between the federal Judiciary and the Executive, the office also provides an important conduit between these branches. It is the combination of these functions that makes the Solicitor-General unique among statutory officeholders in Australia. The office both ensures the integrity of the exercise of government power by actors within government, and defends the exercise of government power from external legal challenge. The Solicitor-General is, then, an important link in the chain between simply having rules and achieving effective constitutionalism. And yet the role of the Solicitor-General in Australia's constitutional system has gone largely

increasingly concerted study of these actors. See, eg, Tushnet, above n 22; M Tushnet, *Taking the Constitution away from the Courts* (Princeton University Press, 1999); Pillard, above n 19; MJ Gerhardt, 'Non-Judicial Precedent' (2006) 61(3) *Vanderbilt Law Review* 713; MJ Gerhardt, *The Power of Precedent* (Oxford University Press, 2011) ch 4.

[31] See, eg, the analysis of the coup in Fiji of December 2006 in P Larmour, *Guarding the Guardians: Accountability and Anticorruption in Fiji's Cleanup Campaign*, Pacific Island Policy 4 (Honolulu, East–West Centre, 2008) and of the government of Prime Minister Manasseh Sogavare in the Solomon Islands in C Moore, 'Unchartered Pacific Waters: The Soloman Islands Constitution and the Government of Prime Minister Manassah Sogavare' (2008) 6(2) *History Compass* 488, 498.

[32] B Selway, *The Constitution of South Australia* (Federation Press, 1997) iii.

unstudied.[33] The role of lawyers in government has been discussed more generally in some Australian literature, although the scholarship is still relatively sparse.[34]

There have been some, largely historical, pieces written on the Solicitor-General.[35] There are also some brief sketches of the position outlined in speeches delivered, or papers written, by officeholders.[36] These accounts provide a generally uncritical description of the office, often peppered with interesting anecdotes, rather than offering any robust analysis of it. This, of course, is understandable. Officeholders must be cognisant of the need to maintain the integrity and independence of the office. Detailed consideration in general constitutional texts is also lacking, often overlooked in the abundance of analysis of the constitutional documents and judicial interpretations. State constitutional texts, which have tended to focus more on the workings of government and the exercise of public power than their federal counterparts, give some consideration to the role.[37] In the 1980s two volumes of selected opinions from the (Commonwealth) Attorney-General, Solicitor-General and Attorney-General's Department were compiled,[38] providing

[33] A similar conclusion was reached in a survey of the Australian position conducted in C Goff-Gray, 'The Solicitor-General in Context: A Tri-Jurisdictional Study' (2011) 23 *Bond Law Review* 48, 82–83. Note the recent publication of G Appleby, P Keyzer and J Williams (eds), *Public Sentinels: A Comparative Analysis of Australian Solicitors-General* (Ashgate Publishing, 2014), and the contributions contained therein.

[34] Three works stand out: L Curtis and G Kolts, 'The Role of the Government Lawyer in the Protection of Citizens' Rights' (1975) 49 *Australian Law Journal* 335; M Sexton and LW Maher, *The Legal Mystique: The Role of Lawyers in Australian Society* (Angus & Robertson Publishers, 1982) ch 6; and B Selway, 'The Duties of Lawyers Acting for Government' (1999) 10 *Public Law Review* 114.

[35] K Mason, 'The Office of Solicitor General for New South Wales' (Autumn 1988) *Bar News* 22; MG Sexton, 'The Role of the Solicitor General' in G Lindsay (ed), *No Mere Mouthpiece: Servants of All, Yet of None* (LexisNexis Butterworths, 2002) 86; T Kass, *A Brief History of the Attorney-General's Department* (Attorney-General's Department, 1996). See also *Solicitor-General v Wylde* (1945) 46 SR (NSW) 83, 91–92 (Jordan CJ); Crown Law, *In My Opinion: The History of Crown Law Queensland 1859–2009* (Department of Justice and Attorney-General, 2009). JLJ Edwards, *The Attorney General, Politics and the Public Interest* (Sweet & Maxwell, 1984) 367–88, also provided a brief and largely historical description of the Australian Law Officers. More recently see K Mason, 'Aspects of the History of the Solicitor-General in Australia' in Appleby, Keyzer and Williams (eds), above n 33, 23; and G Appleby, 'The Evolution of a Public Sentinel: Australia's Solicitor-General' (2012) 63(3) *Northern Ireland Legal Quarterly* 397, which contains much of the research that has informed ch 3 of this book.

[36] See, eg, P Tate, 'The Role of the Solicitor-General for Victoria' (Speech Delivered at the University of Melbourne, 12 November 2003); R Meadows, '"Perhaps the Most to Be Desired" The Role of the Solicitor-General in Western Australia' (Paper presented at the Western Australia Bar Association Conference, Perth, 2009); Sexton, 'The Role of the Solicitor General', above n 35; G Griffith, 'Solicitors-General' in M Coper, T Blackshield and G Williams (eds), *Oxford Companion to the High Court of Australia* (Oxford University Press, 2001, 2007 online edition); J Gleeson, *The Role of the Solicitor-General* (Speech to Seven Wentworth Chambers, 27 February 2014). There is also some discussion in memoirs, papers and interviews of former officeholders and tributes to them. See, eg, RR Garran, *Prosper the Commonwealth* (Angus and Robertson, 1958); National Library of Australia, 'Papers of Sir Maurice Byers' (1975–99); D Connell, Interview with Maurice Byers (Law in Australian Society Oral History Project, 10 January 1997).

[37] See, eg, A Twomey, *The Constitution of New South Wales* (Federation Press, 2004) 714–15; B Selway, *The Constitution of South Australia* (Federation Press, 1997) 81, 156–57; G Taylor, *The Constitution of Victoria* (Federation Press, 2006) 187–89.

[38] P Brazil, *Opinions of Attorneys-General of the Commonwealth of Australia, with opinions of Solicitors-General and the Attorney-General's Department: Volume 1 (1901–1914)* (Australian

a valuable insight into the breadth of the advisory function of the federal office in the early twentieth century.[39] A third volume was published in 2013,[40] and in 2015 there was a further digital release,[41] extending the published range of opinions from 1901 to 1950. Later opinions lie in archival storage, contemporaneous public release by governments being the exception rather than the norm.[42]

Many reasons exist for the lack of analytical, or generalised,[43] study of the Australian Solicitor-General. Consistent with the narrow focus of orthodox constitutional study upon the role, independence and doctrinal reasoning of the courts,[44] the opinions of government legal advisers have been largely overlooked. There is greater difficulty in accessing Solicitor-General opinions compared with publicly accessible judicial decisions, although they are gradually released under archival requirements, and some are voluntarily released by the government contemporaneously. Nonetheless, for the most part, they stand unscrutinised,[45] either for their legal reasoning or as part of a broader analysis of the office's involvement in the government system.[46]

Government Publishing Service, 1981); P Brazil, *Opinions of Attorneys-General of the Commonwealth of Australia, with opinions of Solicitors-General and the Attorney-General's Department: Volume 2 (1914–23)* (Australian Government Publishing Service, 1988).

[39] John Farquharson, Interview with Pat Brazil (Law in Australian Society Oral History Project, 12 and 26 September, 26 October 1995 and 27 February and 20 March 1997) 12–14.

[40] *Opinions of Attorneys-General of the Commonwealth of Australia, with opinions of Solicitors-General and the Attorney-General's Department: Volume 3 (1923–1945)* (Australian Government Solicitors, 2013).

[41] *Opinions of Attorneys-General of the Commonwealth of Australia, with opinions of Solicitors-General and the Attorney-General's Department: Volume 3 (1946–1950)* (2015), available online at <http://legalopinions.ags.gov.au>.

[42] For example, the release of the Solicitor-General's advice after the dismissal of Prime Minister Whitlam in 1975: Opinion from Kep Enderby and Maurice Byers, 4 November 1975; the tabling of advice to Parliament during the controversy over whether the actions of Justice Murphy were sufficient to justify removal: E Campbell and HP Lee, *The Australian Judiciary* (Cambridge University Press, 2001) 102–03; and more recent releases, eg, Letter of advice from Stephen Gageler SC, *In the Matter of the Office of the Speaker of the House of Representatives*, 22 September 2010.

[43] In the sense of going beyond the individual recollections or descriptions by officeholders.

[44] See also JL Pierce, *Inside the Mason Court Revolution: The High Court of Australia Transformed* (Carolina Academic Press, 2006) 15; R Gray, *The Constitutional Jurisprudence of the High Court of Australia: The Dixon, Mason and Gleeson Eras* (Presidian Legal Publications, 2008) 4; C Saunders, 'Oration: Sir Daryl Dawson' (1998) 20 *Adelaide Law Review* 1, 7; J Williams, 'The Australian Constitution and the Challenge of Theory' in C Sampford and T Round (eds), *Beyond the Republic: Meeting the Global Challenges to Constitutionalism* (Federation Press, 2001) 119, 119.

[45] Although Solicitor-General advices released more recently (2009–13) have been subjected to some scrutiny. See, eg, critiques in Memorandum of Advice from Peter Hanks QC, Debbie Mortimer SC, Associate Professor Kristen Walker and Graeme Hill, *On the Justiciability of Social and Economic Rights under a Commonwealth Human Rights Act*, 8 December 2009; Australian Capital Territory Economic, Social and Cultural Rights Research Project, 'Final Report' (Australian National University, September 2010), 132–33; J Allan, 'Stephen Gageler too risk-averse in his advice on Nauru option', *The Australian* (Sydney) (16 September 2011), available at <http://www.theaustralian.com.au/business/legal-affairs/stephen-gageler-too-risk-averse-in-his-advice-on-nauru-option/story-e6frg97x-1226138211343>; A Twomey, 'Advice to the Governor-General on the Appointment of Kevin Rudd as Prime Minister' (2014) 24 *Public Law Review* 289.

[46] Similar observations have been made in the British context, see KA Kyriakides, 'The Advisory Functions of the Attorney-General' (2003) 1 *Hertfordshire Law Journal* 73.

There is also a difficulty because the study of the role of Solicitor-General straddles the disciplines of both law and political science.[47] In America, much of the literature on government lawyers has come from political scientists. In Australia, however, political scientists have generally left the study of the law and the courts to the lawyers.[48] Political scientists have even observed that general study of the working of the executive system of government in Australia is slim, lacking in original fieldwork and devoid of theory.[49]

In Britain and America, much of the scholarship on the Law Officers was generated after public outcry over overt political interference with officeholders. In contrast, in Australia there have been no significant public scandals raising allegations that Solicitors-General have failed to fulfil the appropriate or desirable functions of the office.[50] There has therefore been little sustained impetus for the dedicated study of the office in Australia. Even the Solicitor-General's role in the highly controversial dismissal of Prime Minister Gough Whitlam by the Governor-General in 1975 was given only passing attention,[51] overshadowed by the events themselves and other difficult constitutional questions they raised. On occasion there have been concerns voiced in Parliament about the independence, accountability and integrity of the office, but in the absence of significant media or public interest, Solicitors-General have been left to perform the office's fundamental tasks within the government structure subject to little public understanding, scrutiny or consternation.

Historically, the Australian Attorney-General has received much greater attention than the Solicitor-General. The Attorney-General's role was firmly

[47] CW Clayton, 'Introduction: Politics and the Legal Bureaucracy' in CW Clayton (ed), *Government Lawyers: The Federal Legal Bureaucracy and Presidential Politics* (University Press of Kansas, 1995) 1, 21. See also similar comments in relation to the somewhat similar position in England of the Lord Chancellor: G Gee, 'What are Lord Chancellors For?' [2014] *Public Law* 11.

[48] Pierce, above n 44, 15; B Galligan, *Politics of the High Court: A Study of the Judicial Branch of Government in Australia* (University of Queensland Press, 1987) 3.

[49] P Weller, 'Investigating Power at the Centre of Government Surveying Research on the Australian Executive' (2005) 64 *Australian Journal of Public Administration* 35; RAW Rhodes and J Wanna, 'The Core Executive' in RAW Rhodes (ed), *The Australian Study of Politics* (Palgrave Macmillan, 2009) 119. Note, however, recent empirical contributions on the role of ministerial advisers: RAW Rhodes and A Tiernan, *Lessons in Governing: A Profile of Prime Ministers' Chiefs of Staff* (Melbourne University Press, 2014); RAW Rhodes and A Tiernan, *The Gatekeepers: Lessons From Prime Ministers' Chief of Staff* (Melbourne University Press, 2014).

[50] There have been small-scale scandals that have generated localised interest. Many of these are canvassed in the remainder of the book. Attention has materialised mostly in parliamentary debate, with only limited media coverage. This has been negligible compared to the public outcry following the release of the 'Torture Memos' in the United States, or the revelations of the pressure placed on the English Attorney-General in relation to the Iraq War advice.

[51] See, eg, Interview of Robert Ellicott by Kel Richards, *AM Broadcast*, 17 November 1975. At the State level there has been some discussion of the Solicitor-General's role in these circumstances: Twomey, above n 37, 635; A Twomey, 'The Governor-General's Role in the Formation of Government in a Hung Parliament' (2011) 22 *Public Law Review* 52, 60; M Sexton, 'The Role of Solicitors-General in Advising the Holders of Vice Regal Officers' in Appleby, Keyzer and Williams (eds), above n 33, 91; A Twomey, 'Advice to Vice-Regal Officers by Crown Law Officers and Others' (2015) 26 *Public Law Review* 193.

thrust into the public spotlight in the 1990s,[52] and it was in this period that the predominance of scholarly debate over the role emerged. Comments of the then Shadow Attorney-General, Daryl Williams, that any convention that the office acted independently of the political Executive in Australia was 'erroneous or at least eroded', sparked the debate.[53] He highlighted the departure of Australia from the British traditions.[54] Additional comments made by Williams doubting the Attorney-General's constitutional duty to defend the courts from political attacks[55] caused outcry among the Judiciary and its supporters.[56]

Scholars clambered aboard the brewing controversy, and interest developed regarding the balance that is, or ought to be, struck in the Australian legal paradigm between the office's obligations to politics, law and the public interest.[57] Divisions were most evident over whether Australia had accepted, or ought to

[52] Although note commentary on it in Queensland earlier: Commission of Inquiry into Possible Illegal Activities and Associated Police Misconduct, 'Report of a Commission of Inquiry Pursuant to Orders in Council ("Fitzgerald Report")' (1989) 138. See also Electoral and Administrative Review Commission, 'Report on Review of the Independence of the Attorney-General' (1993).

[53] D Williams, 'Who Speaks for the Courts?' (1994) *AIJA* 183, 192.

[54] ibid, 191–92.

[55] ibid; D Williams, 'The Role of the Attorney-General' (2002) 13 *Public Law Review* 252. Australia has never had an office of Lord Chancellor, and it was generally considered that the role of defending the Judiciary's independence in the Australian constitutional arrangements fell on the Attorney-General.

[56] See G Brennan, 'The State of the Judicature Address' (Paper presented at the 30th Australian Legal Convention, Melbourne, 19 September 1997) 30; A Mason, 'No Place in a Modern Democratic Society for a Supine Judiciary' (1997) 35(11) *Law Society Journal* 51.

[57] See, eg, G Carney, 'Comment—The Role of the Attorney-General' (1997) 9 *Bond Law Review* 1; a conference was held in Melbourne on the Attorney-General's role, and many of the papers were subsequently published: B Selway, 'The Different Role of an Australian Attorney-General' (2002) 13 *Public Law Review* 263; R McColl, 'Reflections on the Role of the Attorney-General' (2003) 14 *Public Law Review* 20; T Abbott, 'Reflections on the Role of the Attorney-General' (2002) 13 *Public Law Review* 273. See also B Heraghty, 'Defender of the Faith? The Role of the Attorney-General in Defending the High Court' (2002) 28(2) *Monash Law Review* 209; D Bennett, 'The Roles and Functions of the Attorney-General of the Commonwealth' (2002) 23 *Australian Bar Review* 61; A McCarthy, 'The Evolution of the Role of the Attorney-General' (2004) 11(4) *Murdoch University Electronic Journal of Law* 30; C Mantziaris, 'The Federal Division of Public Interest Suits by an Attorney-General' (2004) 25 *Adelaide Law Review* 211; G Griffith, 'The Office of Attorney General in New South Wales' (2007) 11 *Legal History* 79; F Hanlon, *An Analysis of the Office of Attorney General in Australia and Directions for the Future* (PhD, University of Melbourne, 2007); F Hanlon, 'Death of the Rule of Law? The Attorney General—First Law Officer of the Crown, Political Guardian of the Rule of Law, or just Another Politician?—An Historical Assessment of the Office in Australia and Directions for the Future' (Paper presented at the Twelfth Annual Public Law Weekend, National Museum of Australia, Canberra, 9–10 November 2007); P Keyzer, *Open Constitutional Courts* (Federation Press, 2010) ch 4. The scholarly literature has been supplemented by the views of officeholders: see, eg, LJ King, 'The Attorney-General, Politics and the Judiciary' (2000) 74 *Australian Law Journal* 444; B Debus, 'Maintaining the Rule of Law: The Role of the Attorney General' (Winter 2006) *Bar News* 5; J Hatzistergos, 'The evolving office of the New South Wales Attorney General' (2012) 86 *Australian Law Journal* 197. And also a number of government-commissioned reports during the 1990s that investigated the provision of legal services to government in the context of the inter-governmental commitment to the National Competition Policy: see, eg, B Logan, D Wicks and S Skehill, *Report of the Review of the Attorney-General's Legal Practice* (March 1997); M Byers and M Gill, 'Review of Legal Services to Government' (New South Wales Attorney General's Department, 1993). The reports have been drawn on in academic works, but the material they contain is generally informative about, rather than critical of, the Attorney-General's role.

accept, a doctrine of independent judgement (that is, whether the Attorney-General's legal and public interest functions ought to be carried out independently from the Cabinet).[58] Bradley Selway confronted two fundamental differences between the English Attorney-General and the office that has developed in Australia, noting, first, the Australian office's intimate involvement with Cabinet and, secondly, the office's responsibility for and control of the provision of legal services to the *whole of government*. While sacrificing some independence from politics, Selway argued that the Australian office's advantage lies in a more engaged and influential Attorney-General, capable of monitoring and ensuring compliance with the rule of law.[59] A number of academics noted the vague definition of the role in Australia. Ben Heraghty observed that the nature of the office in Australia is 'left open to wide interpretation and is therefore interpreted by the particular officeholders themselves'.[60]

Australian academic scholarship on the role of the Attorney-General can be broadly described as reactive and focused upon the influence of the senior Law Officer's *political* position on the office's other functions, particularly the exercise of prosecutorial discretion, the conduct of public interest litigation and the defence of the Judiciary. Scholars have engaged in analysis of the extent to which British traditions are of continuing relevance in Australia.

In this context, scholars have at times also raised the question of the proper role of the Solicitor-General,[61] but this has not developed into comprehensive or systematic study of the office. While much of the scholarship's focus has little direct relevance to the Australian Solicitor-General, it raises pertinent questions about how this office can negotiate the tensions between politics, the law and the public interest in an environment where the Attorney-General has evolved toward the political. The creation of the modern Solicitor-General in Australia was intended to defuse many of the debates surrounding the 'independence' of the senior Law Officer by creating an independent, non-political office to assist the Attorney-General in the fulfilment of the legal services functions. The time is ripe for a full analysis of the Solicitor-General to consider the office's effectiveness in doing so.

This book undertakes an investigation of both the history and law underpinning the role of the Solicitor-General, and the operation of the role in its richness, depth, nuance, context and complexity. It includes an analysis of the historical, legal, political and cultural position of the office to determine its normative and behavioural characteristics. The design of the project tends towards the

58 For example, King, above n 57, 449, 451; Hanlon, *An Analysis of the Office of Attorney General*, above n 57; contra McColl, above n 57; G Griffith, above n 57, 98–104.

59 Selway, 'The Different Role of an Australian Attorney-General', above n 57, 271. See also Selway, 'The Duties of Lawyers Acting for Government', above n 34.

60 Heraghty, above n 57, 220.

61 See, eg, Hanlon, *An Analysis of the Office of Attorney General*, above n 57, 249–50; Electoral and Administrative Review Commission, above n 52, 14, 16–17; Byers and Gill, above n 57, ch 4; Logan, Wicks and Skehill, above n 57, 59.

transdisciplinary, although the initial analyses are delineated into historical and legal. The last part, however, brings these dimensions of the investigation together in a focused, holistic study of the Solicitor-General, drawing on several different sources to provide a description of its culture.[62] 'Culture' is a notoriously difficult and ambiguous concept. In this book, I draw from Clifford Geertz's explanation of the interpretative nature of culture:

> Believing, with Max Weber, that man is an animal suspended in webs of significance he himself has spun, I take culture to be those webs, and the analysis of it to be therefore not an experimental science in search of law, but an interpretative one in search of meaning.[63]

My analysis of the Solicitor-General's 'cultural' position therefore researches the practices, relationships, norms and customs that surround the office. By not only drawing on traditional historical and legal methodology but also undertaking a qualitative analysis of the views of officeholders, the book provides a portrait of the office in practice, rather than simply theorising the role in its abstract form.

This book explores how individuals perform the role of Solicitor-General, and the extent to which that is influenced by the role perceptions of those individuals and others who interact with the office. The book thus contains a description of the office's status, the 'collection of rights and duties', and also a more complex exploration of the *role*, 'the dynamic aspect of a status'.[64] To understand the dynamic aspect of the Solicitor-General requires an examination of the 'norms, attitudes, contextual demands, negotiation, and the evolving definition of the situation' as understood by officeholders and those interacting with them.[65] It requires an examination of the 'actual workings of the office and the traditions and conventions' around it.[66] Compiling a 'thick description'[67] of the lived experience of the Solicitor-General in this way is driven by the objective of lifting the veil on the true nature of an office that, through its advising and advocacy, has enormous potential to influence the normative framework of government. This orientation for the research in the book is congruent with the principles on which constitutional realism has been founded, with its emphasis on 'multi-causal, non-linear, reciprocating, recursive interactions between law, the environment in which it works and the ideas that people have about it'.[68]

[62] J Klein, 'A Taxonomy of Interdisciplinarity' in R Frodeman (ed) *The Oxford Handbook of Interdisciplinarity* (Oxford University Press, 2010).

[63] C Geertz, 'Thick Description: Toward an Interpretative Theory of Culture' in C Geertz (ed), *The Interpretation of Cultures* (Basic Books, 1973) 5.

[64] R Linton, *The Study of Man: An Introduction* (Appleton-Century, 1936) 113–14.

[65] BJ Biddle, 'Recent Development in Role Theory' (1986) 12 *Annual Review of Sociology* 67, 72.

[66] HM Seervai, 'The Legal Profession and the State: The Place of Law Officers and Ministers of Justice' (1977) 22 *Journal of the Law Society of Scotland* 265, 266.

[67] Geertz, above n 63.

[68] Palmer, above n 3, 593. See also the growth of the idea of 'New Legal Realism': *New Legal Realism: Empirical Law and Society*, available at < www.newlegalrealism.org>.

III. The Rest of this Book

Part I of the book commences with this chapter, introducing the office of Solicitor-General and its role within the Australian constitutional system. Chapter two provides an historical and comparative base, tracing the history and literature from which the remaining analysis of the Australian Solicitor-General is conducted. Chapter two considers the generally comparable offices[69] in Britain (the Attorney-General and the Solicitor-General of England and Wales, which in this book will be referred to as the English Law Officers; Scotland has its own Advocate-General), the United States (the Attorney-General, the Office of Solicitor-General (OSG) and the Office of Legal Counsel (OLC)) and New Zealand (the Solicitor-General).[70] It provides an extended historical introduction to the Law Officers as they developed in England, from which the Law Officers in Australia, the United States and New Zealand all evolved.

In John Edwards' influential work on the English Law Officers, he raised the importance of comparative endeavour to understanding the different aspects of, influences on and tensions within the Law Officers' roles.[71] Exploration of the operation of offices in Britain, the US and New Zealand provides an opportunity to reflect on how to understand, and perhaps improve, the framework and functioning of the offices not only in Australia, but also in these other jurisdictions. As with any comparative endeavour, it is fundamental to remember that the constitutional system in which the Solicitor-General operates is necessarily underpinned by the philosophical basis, history, traditions, values and other traits (political, social, legal and economic) of the particular community.[72] Nonetheless, a comparative endeavour is worthwhile where, as is the case for the Law Officers, different jurisdictions have experimented with different governmental structures to address many of the enduring tensions in the role.

Part II of the book turns to Australia. Chapter three develops an understanding of the origins of the contemporary Australian Solicitor-General and the reasons and theories that governed its creation. This chapter chronicles the evolution of the colonial position that led to the development of the modern Solicitor-General in the States, Territories and the Commonwealth. In chapter four, an analysis of

[69] A rough 'functionality' test of comparability was applied in identifying these offices: K Zweigert and H Kötz, *Introduction to Comparative Law 2*, T Weir trans(Oxford University Press, 3rd edn, 1998); M Tushnet, 'The Possibilities of Comparative Constitutional Law' (1999) 108 *Yale Law Journal* 1225, 1238.

[70] The hyphenation of Attorney-General and Solicitor-General varies between jurisdictions. In Australia and New Zealand, it is more commonly hyphenated, while in England and the US it is not. For consistency, this book will adopt the hyphenation.

[71] Edwards, *The Attorney General*, above n 35, 61–62.

[72] C Saunders, 'Towards a Global Constitutional Gene Pool' (2009) 4 *National Taiwan University Law Review* 1, 9–11; O Kahn-Freund, 'On Uses and Misuses of Comparative Law' (1974) 37 *Modern Law Review* 1, 7.

the legal position builds from the historical chapter, considering whether 'insights of history' persist, or whether the position has moved so far from its origins as to be a completely new office.[73] With the creation of the modern statutory position, much of the framework that governs the office is now legislative. But to understand the legal position of the office requires the stark legislative provisions to be supplemented with professional ethical obligations and residual common law duties of the Law Officers to the public interest.

The description of the legal boundaries of the office provides a necessary but thin introduction to the office itself. The legal structures are certainly 'central to understanding of the present state of affairs, the exercise of power and in visions of possible futures'.[74] However, they are necessarily limited. The South Australian Solicitor-General, Martin Hinton, recounted the story that after his appointment, and reading the legislation governing his new role, he was dismayed. He was left with no great guidance as to what was expected of him.[75] The current federal Solicitor-General, Justin Gleeson, explained:

> The statute tells you what you may do and what you may not do. What you actually end up doing, within the confines of the legally possible, depends very much on what you wish to make of the role and how you choose to relate to those with whom you have to deal.[76]

The last part of the book moves to a 'thick description' of the role of the Solicitor-General and tells the stories of how the office is practised.[77] These narratives are constructed by investigating individuals' perceptions of, and experiences in, the role. The practical manifestation of the Solicitor-General's role is greatly influenced by the views, understandings, interpretations and perspectives of that role held by the Solicitor-General and others closely associated with the office.[78]

In this last part, I am not attempting to provide a universal description of the role but rather a contextual study of its 'social practice', a study of the history, theory and social factors that influence the realisation of the office.[79] This study provides no single ideal model or set of criteria for 'what is to be done' by an

[73] MM Siems, 'Legal Originality' (2008) 28(1) *Oxford Journal of Legal Studies* 147, 150.

[74] B Murphy and J McGee, 'Phronetic Legal Inquiry: An Effective Design for Law and Society Research?' (2015) 24 *Griffith Law Review* 288, 307.

[75] M Hinton, 'The Courts, the Executive and the Solicitor-General' in Appleby, Keyzer and Williams (eds), above n 33, 67.

[76] J Gleeson, *The Role of the Solicitor-General* (Speech to Seven Wentworth Chambers, 27 February 2014) 13.

[77] Geertz, above n 63.

[78] This is an assumption 'endemic' in most versions of role theory (BJ Biddle, 'Recent Development in Role Theory' (1986) 12 *Annual Review of Sociology* 67) and underpins much qualitative research relying upon the interview method: J Mason, *Qualitative Researching* (Sage Publications, 2002) 63. See also MB Miles and AM Huberman, *Qualitative Data Analysis: An Expanded Sourcebook* (Sage Publications, 3rd edn1994) 4.

[79] B Flyvbjerg, *Making Social Science Matter: Why Social Inquiry Fails and How it can Succeed Again* (Cambridge University Press, 2001) 2. See also Murphy and McGee, above n 74.

officeholder when particular circumstances arise. Indeed, the description of the practice of the role provided in the final part of the book provides a context-dependent description, intentionally free from value judgement (although not analysis).[80] It reveals, within the same statutory context, the different ways in which the office has been practised and its tensions negotiated, by different people, in different social and political circumstances. It is offered so that future actors may deliberate on their own role, taking from the narratives offered what wisdom they can, testing them against their own experiences, practices and perceptions.[81]

Part III draws on extensive interviews with current and former Solicitors-General and those closely associated with the office (including Attorneys-General, judges and other government legal professionals: n=47), and on analysis of memoirs, oral histories, government reports and Cabinet papers, manuscript collections, legal opinions (where available) and biographies. Further details of the methodology are provided in the introduction to Part III, and the research design, including the sampling and recruitment of interview participants, development and conduct of interviews, and analysis, is set out in detail in Appendix A to the book.

Chapter five illustrates that the *advisory* function of the Solicitor-General was viewed by participants as the function most significant to the broader constitutional system. However, the effectiveness of the Solicitor-General's advisory function rests on a number of assumptions, including that the Executive will seek the Solicitor-General's advice and treat it as determinative of the legal issue; and that the Solicitor-General will provide objective advice 'independently' of the desires of the government. The chapter also explores the extent to which the Solicitor-General does, and whether participants thought it ought to, provide advice to the Executive beyond strictly legal issues.

Chapter six examines the Solicitor-General's other significant function: advocacy for the Executive in the courts. The analysis in this chapter explores the extent to which the Solicitor-General exercises *de facto* independence as government advocate. The chapter also explores the relationship between the Solicitor-General and the court, particularly when the officeholder acts as an interface between the Judiciary and the Executive.

Chapter seven returns then to the central idea of 'independence', and canvasses the views of the participants on the extent and protection of the Solicitor-General's independence in the different jurisdictions. What this research reveals is that, even with Australia's specific legislative arrangements designed to provide structural safeguards for independence, the office's independence still rests upon the professional integrity and ethics of the officeholder. The chapter traces two approaches to how participants saw independence in the context of the Solicitor-General's overall role. Some participants perceived the independence of the office as so vital for government that it must be protected from all political interference,

[80] Flyvbjerg, above n 79, 59.

[81] ibid, at 139, referring to RN Bellah et al, *Habits of the Heart: Individualism and Commitment in American Life* (Harper & Row, 1985) 307.

removing the Solicitor-General somewhat from the Executive, even at the expense of engagement in all matters in which the Solicitor-General's advice ought to be sought. This I refer to as the 'autonomous expert' approach. Others regarded the independence of the Solicitor-General as existing for an overarching constitutional purpose, and that it must be balanced against the objective of ensuring that during the development of policy the government is provided with high quality legal advice. This may, at times, undermine the autonomy of the Solicitor-General as the officeholder becomes closer to government and the subtle pressures associated with that, but it comes with the benefit of ensuring greater integrity across the broader spectrum of government action. This I refer to as the 'team member' approach.

The conclusion in chapter eight draws together the findings about the historical moment of the Solicitor-General's development, the legal framework in which individuals must operate and the actual manifestations of the role. The framers of the modern statutes might have sought to compartmentalise the legal responsibilities of the Solicitor-General from politics and insulate the office from political influences. However, the continuing close relationship between the Solicitor-General and the Crown has meant politics and ideals relating to the public interest continue to influence, inform and antagonise the office.

2

The Law Officers: An Historical and Comparative Introduction

> When Mr Dunning was Solicitor-General ... he went on a Vacation to Prussia. The King, understanding him to be a Military General, invited him to a great Review of his Troops, and mounted him, as an eminent Military Person, upon one of his finest Chargers. The Charger carried the Solicitor-General thro' all the Evolutions of the Day, the General in every Movement being in a most dreadful Fright, and the Horse's duty never allowing him to dismount, he was so terrified and distressed by this great Compliment that he never would go abroad again as a General of any Sort.[1]

An Australian Solicitor-General is positioned at the intersection of law, politics and the public interest. Officeholders must negotiate these at times conflicting dimensions of the role. Understanding these tensions starts with tracing their development back to their roots in the English Law Officers. Australia, together with other common law systems, has adopted a modified version of these Officers.[2] Through the English Law Officers, the first origins of the modern Australian Solicitor-General can be traced back to the King's Solicitor, an office developed in thirteenth-century England to assist the King's Attorney defend the royal interests in the royal courts. The Officers' functions and obligations have undergone significant changes since that date in both the United Kingdom (UK) and then Australia. As Edwards observed, while the modern Law Officers might bear a resemblance to these ancient ones, it is not necessarily a 'close' one.[3]

Despite the scale of difference between the modern form of the Law Officers and these medieval offices, developing an understanding of the reasons for the

[1] ALJ Lincoln and RL McEwen (eds), *Lord Eldon's Anecdote Book* (Stevens & Sons Ltd, 1960) 21.

[2] AB Keith, *Responsible Government in the Dominions*, vol I (Clarendon Press, 1912) 311. This chapter considers Britain, the US and New Zealand. Investigation and scholarship do exist in relation to the Law Officers of other jurisdictions: see, eg, HM Seervai, 'The Legal Profession and the State: The Place of Law Officers and Ministers of Justice' (1977) 22 *Journal of the Law Society of Scotland* 265 (India); K Roach, 'Not Just the Government's Lawyer: The Attorney General as Defender of the Rule of Law' (2006) 31 *Queen's Law Journal* 598 (Canada).

[3] JLJ Edwards, *The Law Officers of the Crown: A Study of the Offices of the Attorney-General and Solicitor-General of England with an Account of the Office of the Director of Public Prosecutions of England* (Sweet & Maxwell, 1964) 3. See also WS Holdsworth, 'The Early History of the Attorney and Solicitor General' (1918–19) 13 *Illinois Law Review* 604; W Holdsworth, *A History of English Law*, vol VI (Methuen & Co Ltd, Sweet and Maxwell, 1924, 1937 reprint) 457.

changes in the office informs our comprehension of its modern functions and responsibilities. It can explain how and why the modern tensions in the office between the legal, political and public interest functions have arisen. And perhaps most importantly, it may reveal whether, how and with what success attempts have been made historically to allay these tensions, either through an individual officeholder's practice or through changes to the institutional design of the office itself.

The development of the Australian Solicitor-General from the tradition of the English Law Officers is chronicled in chapter three. This chapter traces the development of the English Law Officers from their roles as King's Attorney and King's Solicitor to their current position as ministerial Law Officers. It will introduce some of the controversies and attempts at reform that have accompanied the practice of the role as it persists in England. It is apparent that the ongoing debates over reform of the English offices would be greatly assisted by a more complete understanding of the development and practice of the roles in Australia, as well as other former British colonies. The last section of the chapter briefly introduces the Law Officers in the two additional jurisdictions that will be employed as comparative examples for the analysis in the remainder of this book: the United States (US) and New Zealand.

I. An Introduction to the History of the English Law Officers

In debates over the Australian Law Officers, many Australian scholars have focused their inquiries on whether the British traditions aimed at protecting the independence of the Law Officers from political influences were brought across to, or have evolved autonomously in, Australia. Almost all of the existing Australian literature on the Attorney-General is informed by the two leading works of John Edwards on the English Law Officers.

Although Edwards' work on the English Law Officers was seminal, some historical accounts and expositions by officeholders preceded it.[4] His first volume (published

[4] See, eg, JW Norton-Kyshe, *The Law and Privileges Relating to the Attorney-General and Solicitor-General of England: With a history from the earliest periods, and a series of King's Attorneys and Attorneys and Solicitors-General from the reign of Henry III to the 60th of Queen Victoria* (Stevens and Haynes, 1897); GS Robertson, *The Law and Practice of Civil Proceedings by and against The Crown and Departments of the Government: with numerous forms and precedents* (Stevens & Sons, 1908) 9–16; HHL Bellot, 'The Origin of the Attorney-General' (1909) 25 *Law Quarterly Review* 400; Holdsworth, *A History of English Law*, above n 3, 457–80; Holdsworth, 'The Early History' above n 3; H Shawcross, *The Office of the Attorney General* (The Law Society, 1953); RW Cooley, 'Predecessors of the Federal Attorney General: The Attorney General in England and the American Colonies' (1958) 2 *American Journal of Legal History* 304. See also an early account of the role of the Attorney-General provided in *R v Wilkes* (1768) Wilm 320; 97 ER 123, 327–30, 332 (Wilmot CJ).

in 1964) provided what has become an authoritative account of the historical transformation of the English office to that date,[5] and is heavily referenced in any discussion of the Law Officers. His historical analysis is supplemented by detailed consideration of the practice of the English Law Officers. Edwards stressed the need to better understand the tightrope walked by Law Officers between the law, the public interest and politics.[6]

A. The First Role of the Law Officers: Representing the King in Court

The ancient offices that evolved into the Law Officers emerged in the thirteenth century. The precursors to the modern Law Officers were the King's Serjeants, the King's Attorneys and the King's Solicitor. At this time these officers were primarily focused on bringing complaints on behalf of the King, and otherwise representing the King's interests, in the courts. The other legal (advisory), political, parliamentary and public interest dimensions of the Law Officer's role were created centuries later.

The role of bringing complaints on behalf of the King was initially performed not by the Attorney-General but a number of officials, including the King's procurators and the King's Serjeants. It was in the mid-thirteenth century that Lawrence Del Brok appeared as the first King's Attorney, although he did not appear under the title *attornatus regis* but as *sequitur pro rege.*[7] During the thirteenth century, it was not uncommon for more than one attorney to hold the title *attornatus regis* at the same time. King's Attorneys were commonly given limited appointments: for particular courts, for particular localities, or for particular causes.[8]

Theoretically, the King was always present in the courts. To make this constitutional fiction work, a person had to be appointed to *actually* be present.[9] Holdsworth explained that a person so appointed

> must see that the rights of his theoretically present but actually absent principal did not suffer; and the court must see that all the procedural advantages given to the king by his prerogative were given to his attorney.[10]

So the extraordinary position of the King before the royal courts gave special status and seniority to the King's representatives. The prerogatives enjoyed by

[5] See, eg, E Jones, 'The Office of Attorney General' (1969) 27 *Cambridge Law Journal* 43, 43. While Edwards draws on the earlier sources, he does note that these have been plagued by much 'conjectural effort', and warns against making absolute analogies between modern and ancient offices: Edwards, above n 3, 13.

[6] Edwards, above n 3, ix.

[7] Bellot, above n 4, 406

[8] See examples provided in Holdsworth, 'The Early History', above n 3, 604–05; Holdsworth, *A History of English Law*, above n 3, 459–60.

[9] Robertson, above n 4, 9.

[10] Holdsworth, 'The Early History', above n 3, 613.

the King—and through him, his representatives—included the power to bring *ex officio* indictments, intervene in matters on behalf of the public interest, take over prosecutions, request a trial at bar and choice of venue, the right to begin and the right to the last word.[11] Today many, although not all, of these ancient prerogatives have fallen into disuse.

During these nascent years of the Law Officers, the English constitutional system was still developing. The judges were expected not just to hear and determine matters, but also protect the King's interests in the courts. While it may offend modern senses of the separation of powers, there are recorded instances of judges being appointed *attornatus regis* and of King's Attorneys taking on judicial roles.[12] It appears that it was only when a judge of the King's Bench attempted to adjudicate a case in which he had appeared as the King's Attorney that concerns were raised about the potential for a conflict.[13]

The year 1461 was an important one in the history of the Law Officers. John Herbert, for the first time under the title Attorney-General—*attornatus generalis in Anglia*[14]—was given the right to appear for the King in *all* the courts of England. Herbert was also given the power to appoint deputies. It was also in this year that Richard Fowler was appointed to be King's Solicitor 'in all matters, pleas, suits, and quarrels affecting us within our realm of England'.[15]

There is a dispute among historians as to the reason for Fowler's appointment as 'Solicitor'.[16] These go to the nature of the role as it was originally conceived. Bellot claimed that the office was called 'Solicitor', but in practice Fowler was actually acting as deputy for the King's Attorney. Bellot claimed the title 'Solicitor' was used because of Fowler's expertise in chancellery.[17] Holdsworth disputed this, asserting, rather, that Fowler would have filled a role similar to that which a solicitor filled at the time, assisting the litigant and the attorney. Holdsworth claimed it was 'natural' that the deputy of the Attorney-General 'should take the title solicitor'.[18] Edwards questioned whether the King's Solicitor was intended to be the Attorney's deputy, or whether this rather evolved to be the case.[19]

In 1515 the title of Solicitor-General appeared: John Fort was appointed *Solicitator Generallis domini Regis*.[20] It was around this time that it came to be generally accepted that the office of Solicitor-General would be a 'stepping stone' to the role of senior Law Officer.[21]

[11] See examination of these traditional privileges in Robertson, above n 4, 10.
[12] Edwards, above n 3, 17–18.
[13] ibid.
[14] ibid, 27.
[15] ibid, 27–28.
[16] See, eg, Norton-Kyshe, above n 4, 4–5, fn 2.
[17] Bellot, above n 4, 410.
[18] Holdsworth, 'The Early History', above n 3, 615.
[19] Edwards, above n 3, 29.
[20] Although note this his name is sometimes recorded as 'Port': Norton-Kyshe, above n 4, vi.
[21] ibid 29; note the slightly different date provided by Holdsworth, 'The Early History', above n 3, 608.

Holdsworth explained that by the sixteenth century, the King's Attorney had become 'the most important person in the legal department of the state and the chief representative of the crown in the courts'.[22] In 1814 the Attorney-General and Solicitor-General were recognised, formally by direction of the King, as the heads of the bar.[23] Why was it the Law Officers in whom the government's legal power consolidated, and not the historically more senior King's Serjeants? At a time when Britain's trade and commerce were expanding, activity was increasing in the colonies and the administration more generally was growing, the King needed legal generalists whom he could trust.[24] The King's Attorneys were elevated because of their broader legal experience (Serjeants had specialised practices in the common law courts), thus being better able to meet the 'new needs of the modern state'.[25] The Law Officers had also developed a greater political awareness (the Law Officers were becoming the trusted legal advisers to and then members of Parliament). Holdsworth explained:

> [The King] required also lawyers who were conversant with the political problems of the day. The need for lawyers who had had a political as well as a legal training grew greater as the contests of jurisdiction between rival courts grew fiercer, and as the constitutional differences between king and Parliament became more bitter. If the Stuart kings found it necessary to choose judges who would take their view of the constitutional questions of the day, much more did they find it necessary to choose legal advisers whose politics they could trust. But the serjeants, because they were pure Common lawyers, could not be trusted to see eye to eye with the king on many of these political questions. They were too well read in that medieval common law which taught that the law should be supreme in the state, and that Parliament had powers and privileges which could not be overridden.[26]

The Law Officers were not promoted to their position as leaders of the Bar because of the robust independence and fidelity to the rule of law, but because the King could trust that they would undertake their responsibilities in the courts sympathetically and with a grasp of the political interests and costs at play.

In 1768, a rare case expounding the role of the Law Officers was delivered. *Wilkes v The King* explained the historical primacy of the Law Officers in bringing prosecutions on behalf of the King.[27] Mr John Wilkes challenged informations filed against him by the Solicitor-General. Wilkes was charged with seditious libel against the King in his publication *The North Briton*, and for obscene libel for the publication of *Essay on Woman*. The Solicitor-General had filed the informations

[22] Holdsworth, 'The Early History', above n 3, 606.

[23] *The Order of the Precedency of the Attorney- and Solicitor-General* (1816) 6 Taunt 424, 128 ER 1099.

[24] R Pound, *The Lawyer From Antiquity to Modern Times* (West Publishing Co, 1953) 114. See also Holdsworth, 'The Early History', above n 3, 616–17.

[25] Holdsworth, *A History of English Law*, above n 3, 471.

[26] Holdsworth, 'The Early History', above n 3, 617.

[27] *R v Wilkes* (1768) Wilm 322; on appeal *R v Wilkes* (1770) 4 Burr 2527. See also *Attorney-General of Prince of Wales v Sir J St Aubyn* (1811) Wight 169.

as the office of Attorney-General had been vacant. Sir Eardley Wilmot, Lord Chief Justice of the Court of Common Pleas, explained that the title of King's Attorney 'means no more than the person generally employed to sue and defend for the King'.[28] The Attorney-General himself held no constitutional powers; rather, he exercised the constitutional powers held by the King:

> The arguing that the Attorney General only, and no other officer, was entrusted by the constitution to sue for the King, either civilly or criminally, is a fundamental mistake. The Attorney General is entrusted by the King, and not by the Constitution; it is the King who is entrusted by the Constitution.
>
> The great abilities of the persons appointed to this office have made it figure high in the imagination, and annexed ideas to it which do not belong to it; for he is but an attorney, though to the King, and in no other or different relation to him than every other attorney is to his employer ...[29]

In this constitutional arrangement, Wilmot CJ explained that the Solicitor-General performed the role of '*secundarius attornatus*': 'as the Courts take notice judicially of the Attorney General, when there is one, they take notice of the Solicitor General, as standing in his place, when there is none'.[30] 'But', Wilmot CJ again emphasised, 'whether it be the one or the other, they only echo the King's complaint, and his application to the Court to act upon it'.[31]

The relationship between the Law Officers as explained by Wilmot CJ was codified in statute in the *Law Officers Act 1944*, after some confusion arose as to whether the position was maintained with respect to the Attorney-General's statutory powers. That Act provided that the Solicitor-General was authorised to perform the Attorney-General's statutory functions in the event of the office of Attorney-General being vacant, the Attorney-General being unable to act because of absence or illness, or where the Attorney-General authorised the Solicitor-General to act.[32] This position was amended in 1997 to avoid the need for individual delegations, so that the statute now provides, 'Any function [statutory or otherwise] of the Attorney General may be exercised by the Solicitor General'.[33] The 1997 Act permits 'the Attorney and the Solicitor to agree a general division of labour between them and then the work can be distributed without the need for further formality'.[34]

The commentary provided in *Wilkes* on the relationship between the Attorney-General and Solicitor-General represents the extent to which the junior UK Law

[28] *R v Wilkes* (1768) Wilm 322, 328.

[29] ibid, 327–28.

[30] This conclusion was confirmed in *R v Wilkes* (1770) 4 Burr 2527, 98 All ER 327, by Lord Chief Justice Mansfield, 'there is nothing so certain, as that the whole business and authority of the Attorney devolves upon the Solicitor-General'.

[31] *R v Wilkes* (1768) Wilm 322, 329–30.

[32] *Law Officers Act 1944*, s 1 (repealed).

[33] *Law Officers Act 1997*, s 1.

[34] HL Deb, Series 5, Vol 580, 16 June 1997, cols 1074–78 (Lord Falconer QC (Solicitor-General)).

Officer has received separate attention—either in the courts or in the academic commentary. The roles of the senior and junior Law Officers are essentially those of primary and deputy. Unlike the office that evolved in Australia, New Zealand and the US, in England there was insufficient distinction between the roles of the Law Officers for there to be any sustained analysis of the role of Solicitor-General.[35]

The early reputation of the English Law Officers as counsel for the sovereign was that they were 'always zealous and subservient in the interests of the Crown'.[36] Writing in 1819, an anonymous author said of the Law Officers that they are 'pretty sure to be charged with having ascended by the usual steps of political fawning and judicial servility'.[37] The vitriolic prosecution of Sir Walter Raleigh by the Attorney-General Sir Edward Coke has become infamous. David Mallett, in his biography of Sir Francis Bacon, observed that the men who filled the roles of Attorney- and Solicitor-General 'acted at the bar as if they thought themselves, by the duty of their places, absolved from all obligations of truth, honour and decency'.[38] The officeholders were known as 'prerogative lawyers'[39] and, more disparagingly, 'bloodhounds of the Crown'.[40] It was widely believed that the Attorney-General used the prerogative to bring *ex officio* indictments for criminal libel and treason for political reasons. In this respect the junior Law Officer managed to avoid such a poor reputation.[41] Queen Elizabeth I, however, expressed the opposing sentiment: her Attorney-General was not so much retained *Pro Domina Regina* as *Pro Domina Veritate* (although this does not appear to have manifested in practice, given the conduct of Sir Edward Coke as her Attorney).[42]

It was in the nineteenth century that officeholders managed to turn around the office's tarnished reputation. Descriptions of Attorneys-General during this period start to resemble language that we associate with modern representatives of the Crown. For example, Attorney-General Thomas Denman was described as conducting prosecutions with a 'humane, temperate, yet firm and dignified demeanour'.[43] The King saw the benefit to himself and his interests of this more balanced approach. His private secretary wrote to the Attorney:

> His Majesty is quite sensible, from all he hears, that there has been no relaxation of zeal and attention in the able discharge of your duties, and he feels that a tone has been given by your proceedings which must have a useful and important effect upon the public mind ...[44]

[35] T Daintith and A Page, *The Executive in the Constitution: Structure, Autonomy and Internal Control* (Oxford University Press, 1999) 233.
[36] Edwards, above n 3, 54.
[37] Amicus Curiae, *Criticisms on the Bar* (1819), see extract in ibid, 58–59.
[38] D Mallett, *Life of Francis Bacon* (A Millar, 1760) xix.
[39] Edwards, above n 3, 57.
[40] Shawcross, above n 4, 3.
[41] ibid 127.
[42] Norton-Kyshe, above n 4, 18–19, fn 1.
[43] ibid, 61.
[44] ibid.

Nonetheless, the role of the Law Officers remained to defend the prerogatives of the Crown and, later, Parliament. This was apparent when criticisms arose of the conduct of Attorney-General Rufus Isaacs in a case brought against the Admiralty by the father of a cadet wrongly expelled from naval college. Isaacs had pleaded a technical defence: that no claim could be maintained against the Crown for the exercise of its prerogative in the dismissal of one of its servants. Unusually, Isaacs gave a full explanation to the House for his conduct of the trial. He explained the Attorney-General's role in protecting the Crown and its prerogative, 'In administering the law, I was bound, until Parliament expressed a different view, to maintain the Crown prerogative, and it was simply in accordance with that view that I took the point and argued it.'[45]

The role of the Law Officers as the primary and most senior representatives of the sovereign in the courts led to the practice of officeholders being appointed to high judicial office. This then led to some commentators arguing that a practice of 'judicial preferment' had emerged (some officeholders made similar claims, although these were often self-serving statements).[46] The belief in judicial preferment was supported on several grounds: that it was a 'reward' for good service as a Law Officer (which was accepted as being at times a trying position); that it would induce the best lawyers to accept appointment as Law Officers; and that it would increase the status of the Law Officers. However, Edwards strongly opposed the idea that preferment may have developed into a custom or convention. He claimed that it was, more simply, a result of the professional characteristics of the individuals appointed to the office. The similar nature of the roles meant that they were likely to attract similar candidates for appointment; further, once a barrister was appointed as Law Officer, he would be given more opportunity to gain experience in cases that would make him attractive for judicial appointment.[47] Since the Law Officers' ministerial and parliamentary responsibilities have increased, judicial appointment has been less frequent,[48] lending weight to Edwards' arguments.

B. The Law Officers Attend and Enter Parliament

In 1460, the Duke of York put forward a claim to the throne. The House of Lords called the judges and King's Serjeants, and for the first time the King's Attorney, to them to give advice.[49] After this date, the King's Attorney was regularly called to the Lords to advise on points of law, and to draft and advise on government Bills. He would act as an agent between the Houses. By 1509 the Solicitor-General

[45] HC Deb 6 April 1911, vol 23, cols 2466–70.

[46] Holdsworth, 'The Early History' above n 3, 608.

[47] Edwards, above n 3, 319.

[48] R Brazier, *Constitutional Practice: The Foundations of British Government* (Oxford University Press, 3rd edn, 1999) 273.

[49] Holdsworth, 'The Early History', above n 3, 606; ibid, 27.

was also called to the Lords to attend and advise. Probably by 1700, and certainly by 1742, while the call was still made, the Law Officers no longer answered it.[50] From this date, the Law Officers appeared before the Lords only in their capacity as counsel, never to attend and advise.

While the Attorney-General acted as an agent between the Houses, he was very much seen as the King's man by the Commons, and thus was viewed with distrust. There was a concern that if the Attorney-General were allowed to sit in the Commons, the influence of the Crown in the House would be dangerously enhanced.[51] However, as Holdsworth explained, '[i]t was obviously desirable that the legal advisers of the government should be able to explain to the House the legal bearings of the government measures before it'.[52] While the strong relationship between the Attorney-General and the House of Lords marred that office's relationship with the House of Commons, the Solicitor-General, in contrast, was perceived as the less political, having had a shorter affiliation with the Lords. In 1566, the Queen's Solicitor, Richard Onslow, was elected to the House of Commons: Elizabeth I expressed a desire that he be made Speaker, to which the House happily agreed. This became a regular practice, if not a convention. But the Commons remained reluctant to allow the Attorney to take a seat in the House.

In 1606, Henry Hobart, the Solicitor-General, was elevated to the position of Attorney. The Commons referred the question of whether Hobart could continue to sit in the Commons to the Committee of Privileges, although the resolution of the issue in relation to Hobart is unclear. In 1614, Sir Francis Bacon was elevated to the office of Attorney-General. His political connections and ambitions made the Commons nervous. Not being able to bring themselves to remove Bacon from the House, they resolved that the present Attorney-General could sit in the Commons, but not future holders of the office. Holdsworth said that 'This rule, though illogical, was followed for some time.'[53]

Edwards too commented on the paradox of this position: the Commons could have garnered great advantage by availing themselves of the skills and expertise of the senior Law Officer. As the Commons became the more constitutional significant house, these potential advantages increased.[54] But historic distrust continued, and the Commons remained highly suspicious of the individuals who held the office of Attorney-General. It was not until a number of individuals of perceived high integrity took office, and demonstrated that in providing advice on points of law and legislation they acted independently, that the necessary trust developed. Edwards observed that the eventual increase in involvement and trust could be traced back to the 'political acuteness and forensic ability' of individual

[50] Edwards, above n 3, 34.

[51] TFT Plucknett, *A Concise History of the Common Law* (Butterworth & Co, 5th edn,1956) 229.

[52] Holdsworth, *A History of English Law*, above n 3, 464.

[53] Holdsworth, 'The Early History', above n 3, 610.

[54] Edwards, above n 3, 34–35.

Attorneys-General and Solicitors-General.[55] After 1673, with only some exceptions, the Attorney-General joined the Solicitor-General in the Commons.

The advent of the Law Officers sitting in the House of Commons created tensions in the role, particularly when a Law Officer was asked to provide legal advice to the House on Bills and other issues.[56] Edwards explained:

> Whereas a Minister is normally expected to make a controversial speech, when a Law Officer participates in a Commons debate involving any questions of law he is generally expected to assume an attitude of some independence and to speak as a lawyer, not as a politician bent on defending the position adopted by the government.[57]

The responsibility of the Law Officers to Parliament also introduced a form of accountability for the exercise of the officeholders' independent responsibility for decisions in the public interest in the courts.[58]

During the nineteenth century, the parliamentary and ministerial work of the Law Officers was increasing. This fundamentally changed the nature of the roles. Edwards argued that the changing roles can be understood by tracing the debates over the size and nature of their remuneration. As is explored in chapter three, the correlation between the changing nature of the roles and the debates over the structure of the offices' remuneration can also be observed in the development of the Australian Law Officers.

Initially, King's Serjeants were paid what amounted to annual retainers of £20 per year and King's Attorneys £10. The King's Serjeants engaged in private practice, but King's Attorneys did so only irregularly.[59] By the seventeenth century both Law Officers earned substantial sums from private fees, far more than their annual salaries. In the nineteenth century, the question emerged of how to remunerate the Law Officers now that they were no longer counsel for the King in the courts but expected to play a more significant role as ministers and parliamentary advisers?

An 1871 Treasury Minute records the salaries of the Law Officers as follows:

> 1. The Attorney-General shall receive £7000 a year for non-contentious business, and the Solicitor-General £6000 a year.
> 2. All fees payable for non-contentious business shall be paid into the Exchequer.
> 3. The law officers shall receive fees for contentious business, and for opinions connected with it according to the ordinary professional scale.
> 4. The salaries above mentioned shall be voted by the House of Commons.[60]

At this point, with a more substantial annual salary paid to the Law Officers, the Commons and government departments started to think of the Law Officers as in

55 ibid, 48.
56 ibid, ch 3.
57 ibid, 51.
58 ibid, ch 12.
59 ibid, 70.
60 ibid, 80.

their exclusive employ. Dissatisfaction arose over the Law Officers' unavailability for government work because of the demands of their (often extensive) private practices. Sir William Harcourt alleged that the Law Officers' great private practices meant that they had 'to "pack away" the public business of the country into those nooks and corners of time which a large or moderate private practice may leave undisposed of'.[61]

However, the lucrative private practice that the position of Attorney-General attracted was considered one of the 'rewards' of the office.[62] Edwards described the growing tension:

> On the one hand, there were the Law Officers vigorously maintaining their traditional independence and prestige as leaders of the Bar, which they believed was enhanced by the old system of fees for professional services rendered to the government, and, on the other, an increasing tendency for the government to regard the Attorney-General and Solicitor-General as Ministers whose services, by reason of the salary paid, were at the beck and call of any other state department in matters involving legal advice and representation.[63]

The official duties of the Law Officers—ministerial and legal—were growing steadily (although there was also some consternation that the departments were *abusing* the Law Officers now that they were providing them with a regular salary, seeking their advice on trivial matters and occupying 'a great deal of their time unnecessarily').[64] The matter came to a head and was resolved in 1892 against private practice,[65] after increasing unease emerged over the appearance of conflicts in the Law Officers' private and public roles.[66] In 1894 this prohibition was extended and made absolute.

At the same time as the right to private practice was removed, the remuneration of the Law Officers was changed. The Attorney-General was paid £10,000 and the Solicitor-General £9,000, to 'cover all business of whatever sort done by the Law Officers, as such, for or on the instructions of any department of government, including the contentious business as defined in the Treasury Minute of December 5, 1892'.[67] In 1895, fees for contentious work were reintroduced. The new Treasury Minute now specified in what work the Law Officers should be instructed to appear:

(a) cases in which directions to that effect shall be given by the head of any government department;
(b) any case in which, in the opinion of the Solicitor to the Treasury, or of the solicitor of any government department, it is desirable, in the public interest, that a Law Officer should appear;

[61] Extracted, ibid, 92.
[62] ibid, 63.
[63] ibid, 82.
[64] Evidence of Sir William Harcourt to the Jessel Committee, extracted, ibid, 85.
[65] ibid, 98.
[66] ibid, 93–96.
[67] ibid, 100.

(c) cases concerning prolongation of patents in the Privy Council;
(d) informations on the Crown side and Customs cases;
(e) cases in the Revenue Paper; and
(f) cases in the Court of Appeal, House of Lords and Privy Council.

In addition, 'In all other cases a Law Officer shall not be instructed unless, in the opinion of the Attorney-General for the time being, it is necessary, in the interest of the public service, that a Law Officer should appear.'[68] Leaving the power with the Attorney to determine whether the Law Officers should be involved as counsel in particular matters removed the possibility that the Law Officers would be avoided, whether for cost or other reasons. This practice continues to the present day.[69]

In 1901, AJ Balfour, First Lord of the Treasury, noted the two-fold benefits of returning to a scheme of payment for contentious work. First was that, by fixing the positions' salaries at a level on a par with that of the private bar, top barristers would be attracted to the positions. Second was that, by retaining fees for contentious work, the Law Officers were encouraged to appear in court themselves and not delegate that role to junior officers. This ensured the Law Officers would stay in touch with the courts and thus enhance their capacity to perform their other roles. Balfour thus emphasised the desirability of the Law Officers' remaining active across the different dimensions of their roles.

In two parliamentary inquiries in 1920 and 1930 into whether the salaries paid to the Law Officers ought to be reduced, concerns were raised that such a move would reduce the likelihood of attracting the best candidates to the positions. Mr Lloyd George responded:

> When someone tells me that you will not get first-class lawyers to take the honourable office of the Attorney-General or the Solicitor-General unless you give them something which approximates to what they are earning at the present moment, it is absurd. I do not believe any lawyer would refuse to accept the post, if you said to him: 'You will get £7000 and the headship of your profession', and a sort of practical guarantee that the highest promotions are open to them if there is a vacancy during their term of office. I am perfectly certain they would accept it … There is only one thing to do. That is, give them a fixed salary, and you will find that you will get the best lawyers at the Bar who will be delighted to take the office for the honour of the position.[70]

The Prime Minister was more cautious. He noted the importance of the Law Officers to government, and the need to attract 'the very best of legal talent'.[71]

[68] Extracted, ibid, 103.

[69] Cabinet Office, *Ministerial Code* (May 2010), Rules 7.16 and 7.17; and see also discussion in R Brazier, *Ministers of the Crown* (Clarendon Press, 1997) 220.

[70] *Report from the Select Committee on Ministers' Remuneration, Together with the proceedings of the committee, minutes of evidence, appendices and index*, HC Paper 170 of 1930 p 25 Q 233.

[71] ibid p 33 Q 294 and p 39 Q 345.

Debates over the Law Officers' remuneration continued. In 1937, Sir Stafford Cripps observed:

> Until a decision has been arrived at as to whether a Law Officer is really a Minister, and is to be paid and regarded as a Minister, or whether he is half Minister and half practising lawyer, no satisfactory conclusion will be arrived at as regards his salary.[72]

In 1946 a fixed salary for the Law Officers was reintroduced. A single, all-inclusive salary of £10,000 for the Attorney-General and £7,000 for the Solicitor-General was to cover instructions received by government departments. Fees for briefs to appear were set off against these salaries.

Until the end of the nineteenth century, the Law Officers were supported only by their personal clerks and legal assistance in the form of a 'devil'.[73] In 1893, in recognition of their increased parliamentary responsibilities and the restrictions imposed on their right to private practice, they were given the assistance of their own department, set up in the Royal Courts of Justice. Initially, it was staffed only by secretarial support services. It was not until into the twentieth century that they gained professional staff and moved out of the courts building.

There was much debate in England—and even before that in the colonies[74]—over whether the Law Officers were to be included in the Cabinet. This debate highlighted arguments about whether the Law Officers' obligations to the law and the public interest overrode their political obligations. In Britain, at least since the early twentieth century, as a general rule neither the Attorney-General nor the Solicitor-General has been appointed to Cabinet.[75]

In 1872, Attorney-General Sir John Duke Coleridge expressed concern that this placed Law Officers in the position where they might not have seen Bills until they were asked to support them in Parliament. Further, a seat in Cabinet would provide the Law Officers with a platform to recommend and explain law reform measures. Edwards noted that '[a]t the time when Coleridge was expressing the concern of the Law Officers regarding their being by-passed in the preparation of new Bills, personality factors were very much to the fore.'[76] Generally, there appears to have been a convention that the Law Officers would be consulted on government Bills, even though they did not sit in Cabinet. Edwards' explanation that the circumstances complained of by Coleridge were driven by the personalities involved highlights, rather than reduces, the issue Coleridge raised. It demonstrates that under a system where the Attorney is not required to be briefed and privy to all Cabinet deliberations, there is a danger that Law Officers may be bypassed if personality conflicts arise.

[72] HC Deb 3 June 1937, Series 5, Vol 324, col 1208.

[73] Norton-Kyshe, above n 4, 12–13.

[74] See, eg, discussion in ch 3 of Justice Benjamin Boothby's concerns about including the Law Officers in the Cabinet in South Australia.

[75] Edwards, above n 3, 174–75.

[76] ibid, 149.

In 1924, the following Cabinet instruction was issued:

> [A]ll memoranda, draft Bills and other constituents of the Agenda will be sent to the Cabinet Secretariat for circulation only *after* their subject matter has been fully examined between the Departments from which they emanate, the Treasury, the Law Officers where contentious Bills are involved, and any other Department concerned, and these documents will bear on the face of them a specific statement that this examination has taken place.[77]

The concern about bringing the Attorney-General into Cabinet appeared to be twofold. Edwards explained the concern by reference to the potential for inclusion to compromise the Attorney's ability to discharge his obligations in relation to the bringing of criminal prosecutions and other actions that might require him to act independently of the Government in determine questions in the public interest. The second concern was whether the Attorney, when called upon to provide his legal opinion to Cabinet, might be compromised because of his involvement in the development of the policies, therefore having too close an understanding of the politics and political consequences of the legal advice. As Viscount Simon explained:

> The Cabinet from time to time needs the legal advice of the Attorney-General on some aspect of an urgent and complicated political question, either international or domestic, and this advice often requires research and reflection. If the Attorney-General is a party to the earlier deliberations of the Cabinet out of which the need for technical guidance has arisen, it may be difficult for him to approach the problem ultimately presented to him as a lawyer with an entirely open mind.[78]

Against these arguments were those that the Law Officers ought to be included in Cabinet because if they were not, they might not be consulted on important legal issues. Further, they were, in effect, increasingly operating as the ministerial heads of their departmental administrations, not in the more independent tradition of the Law Officers, and there was thus little to distinguish between them and other Cabinet ministers.

The colonies responded to these tensions in far more novel ways than England. For example, New Zealand experimented in 1866 with an entirely non-political Attorney-General: the *Attorney-General Act 1866* (NZ) stated that the Attorney was to be removed from the ministry altogether, appointed during good behaviour, only to be removed by address of Parliament. This experiment was short-lived. The *Attorney-General Act 1876* (NZ) gave the Governor the choice to appoint the Attorney-General as a permanent and non-political officer, or as a political officer 'during pleasure'. In Australia, the Law Officers were initially both included in Cabinet. This led to the increased politicisation of the Attorney-General, and eventually to the depoliticisation of the Solicitor-General.

77 Treasury Circular No 11/24 April 28 1924, extracted, ibid, 146.
78 Viscount Simon, *The Memoirs of the Rt Hon Viscount Simon* (Hutchnison, 1952) 89–90.

Temporary change occurred in the UK in 1912, when the Attorney-General was made a member of Cabinet (no Solicitor-General has ever been included within Cabinet).[79] This appears to have been largely driven by the personalities and ambition of individual officeholders, with a position in Cabinet offered to a disappointed Attorney-General, Sir Rufus Isaacs, who had thought he would be appointed Lord Chancellor but had been overlooked.[80] By 1928, the practice stopped, and has not been followed again.

II. The Modern English Law Officers: Negotiating Politics, Law and the Public Interest

The roles of the Law Officers are no longer limited to being the sovereign's representative in the courts, or the ministerial head of the Law Officers' Department. In the annexure to the 2007 government consultation paper on the role of the Attorney-General, 42 separate statutory, common law and customary-based roles were listed.[81] Terence Daintith and Alan Page referred to them as a 'bewildering range of roles'.[82] This section of the chapter outlines the modern form of the Law Officers' primary roles—as advisers to government, as parliamentarians and ministers—and their public interest responsibilities, including for initiating criminal and civil litigation, before turning to explain some of the recent controversies that enveloped the position, the debates these have triggered and the 2007–08 attempts to reform the offices.

A. Adviser to Government and the Queen

Since the 2005 changes to the constitutional role of Lord Chancellor, the Law Officers are the only ministers in government required to be legally qualified (at least by convention).[83] The Law Officers are the legal advisers on the most important and contentious issues confronting government. They do not necessarily handle the legal questions that are referred to them in person, but rather will often mobilise legal expertise within government and from outside counsel.[84] The Law Officers are ultimately responsible for the provision of legal advice to

[79] ibid, 165, fn 29.

[80] ibid, 170–71.

[81] *The Governance of Britain: A Consultation on the Role of the Attorney General* (The Stationery Office Limited, 2007) Appendix A, 25–26.

[82] Daintith and Page, above n 35, 232.

[83] House of Commons Constitutional Affairs Committee, *Constitutional Role of the Attorney General*, Fifth Report of Session 2006–07 (HC306).

[84] JLJ Edwards, *The Attorney General, Politics and the Public Interest* (Sweet & Maxwell, 1984) 188.

government by the lawyers within the Government Legal Service (GLS), although the Treasury Solicitor oversees the daily administration of the GLS. Members of the GLS can access the Law Officers who act as a 'final Court of Appeal'.[85] In 1953, Lord Shawcross described the matters on which advice of the Law Officers is sought:

> The advice of the Law Officers is ordinarily only sought where some problem arises which is of special importance, perhaps because of its legal difficulty, very often because of considerations of policy or public relations which arise in connection with it, or possibly because there is a very large amount at stake, and the department concerned does not want to take any risks and be told afterwards when it has lost the case that it ought to have consulted the Law Officers before it embarked upon it. Very often there arise matters of a constitutional nature or matters affecting international relations on which the Attorney-General is asked to advise either the Cabinet or the Prime Minister.[86]

The breadth of the modern advice function remains similar. A very brief description of the matters that must be brought to the Law Officers' attention is provided in the Ministerial Code. The current Code, published May 2010, states 'The Law Officers must be consulted in good time before the Government is committed to critical decisions involving legal considerations.'[87] The Code also provides:

> [2.11] By convention, written opinions of the Law Officers, unlike other ministerial papers, are generally made available to succeeding Administrations.
>
> [2.12] When advice from the Law Officers is included in correspondence between Ministers, or in papers for the Cabinet or Ministerial Committees, the conclusions may if necessary be summarised but, if this is done, the complete text of the advice should be attached.
>
> [2.13] The fact that the Law Officers have advised or have not advised and the content of the advice must not be disclosed outside Government without their authority.

The current Code is a much briefer version than that released in 1997 under the Blair Administration (the briefer version is actually an earlier version, reintroduced by Prime Minister Gordon Brown in 2007).[88] The 1997 Code provided:

> [22] The Law Officers must be consulted in good time before the Government is committed to critical decisions involving legal considerations. It will normally be appropriate to consult the Law Officers in cases where:
>
> a. The Legal consequences of action by the Government might have important repercussions in the foreign, European Union or domestic field;
> b. A Departmental Legal Adviser is in doubt concerning
>   (i) the legality or constitutional propriety of legislation which Government proposes to introduce; or

[85] ibid, 185.
[86] Shawcross, above n 5, 6.
[87] Cabinet Office, *Ministerial Code* (May 2010), available at <www.gov.uk/government/publications/ministerial-code>, [2.10] 5.
[88] See Edwards, above n 84, 187.

(ii) the vires of proposed administrative action; or

(iii) the legality of proposed administrative action, particularly where that action might be subject to challenge in the courts by means of application for judicial review; or

c. Ministers, or their officials, wish to have the advice of the Law Officers on questions involving legal considerations, which are likely to come before the Cabinet or Cabinet Committee;

d. There is a particular legal difficulty which may raise political aspects of policy;

e. Two or more Departments disagree on legal questions and wish to seek the view of the Law Officers.

As the Code makes clear, the Law Officers' advice is treated confidentially, to the extent that the fact that advice has been given will not be disclosed. Further, unlike with ordinary claims for legal professional privilege, the legal advisers, that is the Law Officers themselves, have to consent to the release of the advice.[89] In 1865, then Prime Minister Lord Palmerston explained this was because 'the Law Officers would be more cautious in expressing an opinion if they knew that it was to be laid before Parliament and the public'.[90] In 2015, Attorney-General Jeremy Wright explained why the Attorney-General's opinion would not be released:

> I'm part of an obligation to ensure that legal advice is taken by government, and that legal advice is as full and as frank as it possibly can be when it is given to government … I also think that it's important when you are talking about Law Officers' advice to take account of the collective responsibility issues that apply to cabinet government. As we've discussed, I attend Cabinet meetings, I do that at least in part so that Cabinet can hear legal advice. And it's important that that legal advice is part and parcel of the decisions that Cabinet takes.[91]

The confidentiality of the Law Officers' opinions is reinforced by section 35(1) of the *Freedom of Information Act 2000*, which provides that 'the provision of advice by any of the Law Officers or any request for the provision of such advice' is exempt material. This reflects what Edwards described as the 'Law Officers' Convention'.[92]

The Government may *choose* to lay the Law Officers' opinions before Parliament (or otherwise release them),[93] although the Code makes it clear this must be with the authority of the Law Officers themselves. Failure to adhere to the convention

[89] Daintith and Page, above n 35, 310.

[90] HC Deb, 17 February 1865, vol 177, col 354.

[91] Evidence to the House of Commons Justice Select Committee, 15 September 2015 (Jeremy Wright), available at <http://www.parliament.uk/business/committees/committees-a-z/commons-select/justice-committee/news-parliament-20151/work-of-the-attorney-general-ev-session/>; see also report of evidence and context in O Bowcott, 'Syria Drone Strikes, UK Attorney-General refuses to disclose advice' *Guardian* (15 September 2015), available at <http://www.theguardian.com/politics/2015/sep/15/syria-drone-strikes-uk-attorney-general-refuses-to-disclose-advice>.

[92] Edwards, above n 3, 257; See further KA Kyriakides, 'The Advisory Functions of the Attorney-General' (2003) 1 *Hertfordshire Law Journal* 73; Daintith and Page, above n 35, 309–15.

[93] See also M Jack (ed) *Erskine May's Treatise on The Law, Privileges, Proceedings and Usage of Parliament* (24th edn, LexisNexis, 2011) 447.

has, in the past, led to ministerial resignation.[94] In 2009, the English High Court acknowledged that 'there are only five occasions in the 40 years before 2008 when the government of the day decided that the public interest favoured disclosure of such advice'.[95]

In addition to being the chief legal adviser to the Government, the Attorney-General is also Her Majesty's Attorney-General, and fills the role of legal adviser to the Queen.[96]

It was once customary for a Law Officer, as the Crown's legal representative, to lead the Crown in court in cases involving serious constitutional considerations or public order, and in criminal prosecutions for treason. How much court work Law Officers do will depend on the individual and the time he or she is able to find for court appearances. More often, the advocacy role is performed by Treasury Counsel. The Attorney-General may also represent the UK in regional and international courts and tribunals, such as the International Court of Justice and the European Court of Human Rights.

B. Parliamentary and Ministerial Roles

The English Law Officers continue to sit in Parliament and are the ministerial heads of the Law Officers' Department responsible to Parliament for the agencies within their remit. While neither Law Officer sits in Cabinet, it is generally accepted that there is a need to keep the Attorney fully apprised of Cabinet deliberations and decisions so that he or she can advise if there is a need. The practice today is that the Attorney-General is privy to all Cabinet papers, and is routinely invited to *attend* all meetings[97] without being a *member* of Cabinet. The Attorney also sits on the Domestic Affairs Committee and the Legislative Programs Committee of Cabinet. The intimacy of the Law Officers' involvement in Cabinet arose as a contentious aspects of current practice during the 2007 08 reviews of the office, returned to in section II.D.iii. below.

The modern Attorney-General still predominantly sits in the House of Commons, although for periods has been selected from the Lords, usually on the

[94] AW Bradley, KD Ewing and CJS Knight, *Constitutional and Administrative Law* (Pearson, 16th edn, 2015) 346.

[95] *HM Treasury v Information Commissioner* [2010] QB 563 [9].

[96] *The Governance of Britain: A Consultation on the Role of the Attorney General* (The Stationery Office Limited, 2007) Annex A.

[97] House of Lords Constitution Committee, *Reform of the Office of Attorney General* (HL 2007–08, 93), available at <http://www.publications.parliament.uk/pa/ld200708/ldselect/ldconst/93/93.pdf>, evidence of Baroness of Scotland, 34; Evidence to the House of Commons Justice Select Committee, 15 September 2015 (Jeremy Wright), available at <http://www.parliament.uk/business/committees/committees-a-z/commons-select/justice-committee/news-parliament-20151/work-of-the-attorney-general-ev-session/>.

basis of the most qualified candidates.[98] The Solicitor-General has, generally, also remained in the Commons.

In Parliament, the Law Officers advise on Bills, as well as undertaking functions relating to the privileges of Parliament and the conduct and discipline of Members of Parliament (MPs).[99] Former Solicitor-General Edward Garnier explained that the Law Officers' Department is briefed by Parliamentary Counsel as Bills are drafted, and Parliamentary Counsel will alert the Law Officers to Bills that raise matters of legal policy and those that affect the rule of law.[100] The Law Officers sit on the Parliamentary Business Committee and review and advise the Committee regarding the departmental memoranda on compliance with the *Human Rights Act 1998*.[101] The Law Officers have a right to take part in the deliberations of other committees but do not vote.[102] Legislation that has an expedited commencement date (the general practice is for legislation to commence two months after it receives the Royal Assent) and legislation that operates retrospectively are introduced only with the consent of the Law Officers.[103] Garnier explained that consent is not given automatically, and that the Law Officers will weigh the unfairness that may be caused by expedited commencement or retrospective operation against other public interest considerations.[104] The Law Officers also have a role in representing Parliament before the courts.[105]

The Law Officers' roles in Parliament continue to be a focal point for misunderstanding. In 1984, Edwards explained:

> Understandably, the task of separating the different roles expected of the Attorney-General and Solicitor-General as, first, the government's chief legal advisers, secondly,

[98] Note the times he or she sat in the House of Lords—Lord Williams of Mostyn (29 July 1999–11 June 2001); Lord Goldsmith (11 June 2001–27 June 2007), Baroness Scotland of Asthal (27 June 2007–11 May 2010). Since then, the Attorney-General has returned to the Commons.

[99] See explanation of the role in Law Officers' Department files, letter from Sam Silkin to the Chairman of the Select Committee on Trade and Industry, extracted in Edwards, above n 84, 219.

[100] E Garnier, *The Law Officers and Legislative Procedure* (Speech to ALBA Summer Conference, 17 July 2010) 8.

[101] ibid 10. The Law Officers also appear to have a role in the preparation of s 19 certificates and memoranda. See further Lord Goldsmith, 'Government and the Rule of Law in the Modern Age', Paper delivered to London School of Economics and Clifford Chance Lectures Series on Rule of Law, 22 February 2006 <http://www.lse.ac.uk/publicEvents/pdf/20060222-Goldsmith.pdf> 15.

[102] M Jack (ed), *Erskine May's Treatise on The Law, Privileges, Proceedings and Usage of Parliament* (LexisNexis, 24th edn, 2011) 861.

[103] Garnier, above n 100, 11.

[104] ibid.

[105] See, eg, *Pepper v Hart* [1993] AC 593, where the Attorney-General argued on behalf of the Clerk of the House of Commons that recourse to Hansard by the courts would breach parliamentary privilege. Note more recently the controversy over the application of parliamentary privilege to MPs' expenses, where the Attorney-General argued in Parliament to allow the courts to determine whether the matter fell within parliamentary privilege, but did not appear in court to represent Parliament's interests. See *R v Chaytor* [2010] UKSC 52, where the Court itself made reference to the absence of an argument from Parliament that oversight of expenses was within its exclusive jurisdiction. See further the comments of D Howarth, 'Joint Seminar with UK Constitutional Law Group on Parliamentary Privilege, 12 October 2011', available at <www.studyofparliament.org.uk/privilege.htm>. See also S Lipscombe and A Horne, 'Parliamentary Privilege and the Criminal Law' in A Horne, G Drewry and D Oliver (eds), *Parliament and the Law* (Hart Publishing, 2013) 67, 86–87.

> as ministerial colleagues assisting in piloting measures through the House of Commons, and thirdly, as servants of the House in their capacity as legal advisers to Parliament, is apt to confuse parliamentarians and non-parliamentarians alike, to say nothing of the ability of the Law Officers themselves to maintain the essential qualities attached to the respective roles.[106]

Despite their continuing obligations to Parliament, the Law Officers are no longer the sole, nor often the most respected, source of legal advice to Parliament.[107] Writing in 2014, Andrew Kennon explained that this may be attributable to the reduced pool of MPs with well-established professional legal careers from whom the Law Officers can be drawn, and the appointment of Attorneys-General from the House of Lords between 1997–2010, without 'the political experience to carry weight in the Commons'.[108]

C. Public Interest Responsibilities, Including for Criminal and Civil Litigation

The prosecutorial responsibilities form one of the most important dimensions of the English Law Officers' 'public interest' role. The Law Officers continue to have responsibilities for some prosecutorial decisions (initiating certain prosecutions, appealing unduly lenient sentences and referring points of law to the Court of Appeal if there is an acquittal, and submitting a *nolle prosequi*), as well as for 'superintending' the prosecution service of the UK. This encompasses a combination of oversight, accountability and, more controversially, direction, but does not extend to day-to-day responsibility for running the organisation.[109] Law Officers are responsible for decisions about administration and policies of the prosecution service, and they have a right to be consulted and informed in difficult, sensitive and high-profile cases. The prosecution service includes the Crown Prosecution Service (CPS, which now incorporates the Revenue and Customs Prosecution Service), the Serious Fraud Office (SFO), and the Army, Royal Navy and Royal Air Force Prosecutions Authority. Following the Government's consultation about possible reform of the role in 2007–08, which was largely motivated by concerns over prosecutorial independence, a protocol has been introduced that outlines the exceptional instances where the Attorney will give a direction about prosecutorial decisions.[110]

[106] Edwards, above n 84, 215.

[107] A Kennon, 'Legal Advice to Parliament' in Horne, Drewry and Oliver (eds), above n 105, 121, 126.

[108] ibid, 126.

[109] See *The Governance of Britain: A Consultation on the Role of the Attorney General* (The Stationery Office Limited, 2007) 7. See also discussion in Daintith and Page, above n 35, 287–95.

[110] See further Protocol between the Attorney-General and the Prosecuting Departments (July 2009), available at <https://www.gov.uk/government/uploads/system/uploads/attachmentdata/file/15197/ProtocolbetweentheAttorneyGeneralandtheProsecutingDepartments.pdf>.

In addition to their responsibilities for criminal matters, the English Law Officers continue to have the power to bring actions to defend public rights, for contempt of court and against vexatious litigants, and to supervise and intervene in charity proceedings. They have a role in appointing advocates of the court (previously *amicus curiae*) and a statutory role in appointing special advocates in national security cases.[111] (For a period the Law Officers also appeared in Tribunals of Inquiry as counsel assisting the Tribunal in pursuit of the public interest, but this role has lapsed.)[112] Some of these public interest powers are conferred by statute and others continue to rely on the common law responsibilities of the Law Officers as guardians of the public interest.[113]

D. The Controversies of the Modern English Law Officers

The varied responsibilities of the modern English Law Officers have given rise to occasions of great and ongoing controversy across their public interest and advisory functions.

i. The Prosecutorial and Other Public Interest Functions

Much of the debate around the roles of the Law Officers, and how an individual may negotiate the different pressures that the different roles exert, has centred around the 'independence' that needs to be exercised in the 'public interest functions': the prosecutorial function and the closely related function of granting a fiat for bringing cases to protect public rights. That public and political debate should centre on the prosecutorial function is understandable. A number of high-profile cases arose that brought into question the proper exercise of these Law Officer powers in the late twentieth and twenty-first centuries. The main question that appeared unresolved was whether the Law Officers act under the direction of the Cabinet in making prosecutorial decisions, whether they have an obligation to consult Cabinet but the final determination remains theirs alone, or whether they must make the decisions on their own and entirely free from Cabinet influence and even advice.

In 1951, after attracting criticism for his decision to prosecute a number of gas workers under the *Conditions of Employment and National Arbitration Order 1940* for taking prohibited strike action, the Attorney-General, Sir Hartley Shawcross, set out what would come to be a long-standing practice for the exercise of the prosecutorial discretion. Edwards referred to his detailed parliamentary

[111] *Special Immigration Appeals Commission Act 1997*, s 6.

[112] Edwards, above n 84, 302.

[113] See explanation of the Attorney-General's public interest obligations in the courts in *Attorney-General v Blake* [1998] Ch 439 (Lord Woolf MR).

statement as 'the modern exposition of the constitutional position of the Attorney-General':[114]

> I think the true doctrine is that it is the duty of an Attorney-General, in deciding whether or not to authorise the prosecution, to acquaint himself with all the relevant facts, including, for instance, the effect which the prosecution, successful or unsuccessful as the case may be, would have upon public morale and order, and with any other consideration affecting public policy. In order so to inform himself, he may, although I do not think he is obliged to, consult with any of his colleagues in the government, and indeed, as Lord Simon once said, he would in some cases be a fool if he did not. On the other hand, the assistance of his colleagues is confined to informing him of particular considerations which might affect his own decision, and does not consist, and must not consist, in telling him what that decision ought to be. The responsibility for the eventual decision rests with the Attorney-General, and he is not to be put, and is not put, under pressure by his colleagues in the matter. Nor, of course, can the Attorney-General shift his responsibility for making the decision on to the shoulders of his colleagues. If political considerations which in the broad sense that I have indicated affect government in the abstract arise it is the Attorney-General, applying his judicial mind, who has to be the sole judge of those considerations.[115]

A number of events arose during the tenure of Sam Silkin as Attorney-General (1974–79) that also drew criticism.[116] In *Gouriet v Union of Post Office Workers*, the Attorney-General's discretion to grant a fiat in a relator action was challenged in the courts and ultimately before the House of Lords. The case concerned the refusal of Silkin to grant Mr Gouriet a fiat to bring relator proceedings for an injunction against the Union of Post Office Workers. The Union had resolved to place an anti-apartheid boycott on the handling of mail to South Africa, allegedly in breach of the *Post Office Act 1953* and the *Telegraph Act 1863*. Having had his request for a fiat denied, Gouriet issued a writ in his own name, which was initially dismissed. Gouriet appealed to the Court of Appeal, where he also challenged the Attorney-General's decision as improper and wrongful. Silkin, representing himself, claimed that he was accountable for his prerogative responsibilities to Parliament and not the courts.

By majority (Lawton LJ and Ormrod LJ), the Court of Appeal held that the discretion was non-justiciable; Lord Denning MR held that it was indirectly reviewable. By the time the case reached the House of Lords, this question had been dropped: 'The Attorney-General's decision is accepted as, in the courts, unassailable. The prerogatives of his office are no longer attacked.'[117] The case then turned to whether Mr Gouriet had standing to bring the claim for injunctive relief.

Another controversy arose, not in relation to Silkin's public interest discretions but in connection with his parliamentary responsibilities and his support of indemnity legislation in the Clay Cross councillors affair. During Labour's time

[114] Edwards, above n 84, 223.
[115] HC Deb 29 January 1951, vol 483, col 682.
[116] See separate section in Edwards, above n 84, dedicated to his tenure, at 334–53.
[117] *Gouriet v Union of Post Office Workers* [1978] AC 435, 476 (Lord Wilberforce).

in opposition, the Clay Cross Council had refused to enforce provisions of the Conservative Government's *Housing Finance Act 1972* that required it to increase rents on public housing. The councillors were charged with making good the losses incurred by the Government through their wilful disobedience of the law, and were disqualified from sitting as councillors. Labour sought the views of its Shadow Solicitor-General, Silkin, on the question of whether Labour could reimburse the trade unions or councillors. Silkin provided strident advice:

> I know of no example of legislation by a Parliament to recompense persons or organisations for financial penalties incurred in consequence of refusing to obey the requirements of legislation passed by a preceding Parliament. An Act of Indemnity passed for this purpose would, in my opinion, contravene all constitutional practice and would set a dangerous precedent. … It is my opinion that no Law Officer of the Crown, of any political party, would be likely to advise the Government of which he was a member to initiate such legislation.[118]

On taking office in 1974, Labour introduced the *Housing Finance (Special Provisions) Bill*. The legislation did not recompense the Clay Cross councillors for financial penalties already incurred, but it prevented further surcharges from arising out of the *Housing Finance Act 1972*. It also reversed the Clay Cross councillors' disqualifications.[119] Silkin was trenchantly criticised for supporting the Bill in Parliament as Attorney-General. He defended himself, claiming that the surcharges had been left in place, and that a compromise had been reached after balancing the rule of law with the public interest in compassionate leniency to those who acted unlawfully but in the belief that they were asked to administer a bad and unfair law against their own democratic mandates. As Edwards' observed, Silkin seemed to have been satisfied that he had fulfilled his obligation 'to modify any indemnity legislation in the direction of moderation'.[120]

Following these events, Edwards' 1984 volume outlined three 'philosophic' approaches[121] that had been proposed by various officeholders, current and former. One approach put forward was that of Lord Rawlinson: the doctrine of 'independent aloofness'. An independently aloof Attorney-General does not engage too closely in government policy, political debates and party politicking.[122] The second approach is Sam Silkin's doctrine of 'intimate but independent involvement'. Silkin explained:

> I regard it as the Law Officer's duty to learn as much as he can of his colleague's policies, their intentions, their wishes, their methods, indeed their very temperaments and characters. I believe that only so can he give them the best possible advice, not merely as to what they cannot lawfully do, or should not with propriety do, but also as to how they can achieve their aims by means which are both lawful and proper. … The Law Officer

118 Extracted in Edwards, above n 84, 345.
119 This provision was ultimately deleted from the Bill.
120 Edwards, above n 84, 350.
121 SC Silkin, 'The Office of Attorney-General' (1980) 4 *Trent Law Journal* 21, 24.
122 P Rawlinson, 'A Vital Link in the Machinery of Justice' (1977) 74 *Guardian Gazette* 798, 799.

> must know the colleague he is dealing with and the colleague he is dealing with must know the Law Officer, and know him well enough to be able to place his trust in his experience, his wisdom, and his full-hearted desire to achieve the governmental objectives which unite them in a common Ministry.[123]

This doctrine recognises a number of benefits from a more politically involved, but still independent, officeholder.[124] In assessing these two competing philosophies, Edwards warned of the 'disproportionate' cost of Silkin's approach, being 'a further erosion in the public's perception of an independent Attorney General'.[125]

Lord Shawcross proposed a third approach: a non-elected, non-political, public-service model to achieve absolute independence from the political milieu.[126] Shawcross explained:

> [T]he enforcement of the rights of the public and the rule of law would then be given not only the reality (which I hope it still has) but also the appearance (which it now lacks) of complete detachment from party politics.[127]

Edwards, however, considered that Shawcross' approach suffered from a fundamental weakness: the removal of the office from the line of accountability.[128]

Controversy continues to dog the English Law Officers, and particularly but not exclusively their prosecutorial function, into the twenty-first century. A number of more recent controversies formed the catalyst for the House of Commons Select Committee on the Constitution to commence an inquiry into reform of the constitutional role of the Attorney-General in 2007, and for the Government to engage in its own extensive consultation on the question.

On 14 December 2006, the Attorney-General, Lord Goldsmith, announced that the SFO was discontinuing its investigations into BAE Systems over allegations that the company had bribed Saudi officials to extend a large defence contract. The SFO was investigated for breaches of the *Anti-terrorism, Crime and Security Act 2001*. It is subject to the superintendence of the Attorney-General under section 1(2) of the *Criminal Justice Act 1987*. Based on the announcement made by Lord Goldsmith, there were concerns that political pressure had been applied to the SFO Director to stop the investigation.

In a later judicial review of the Director's decision in the House of Lords—ultimately dismissed—their Lordships explained that the dropping of the investigation had been preceded by a 'Shawcross exercise':

> On 2 December 2005 the Attorney General and the Director decided that it would be appropriate to invite the views of other Government ministers, in order to acquaint

[123] SC Silkin, 'The Functions and Position of the Attorney-General in the United Kingdom' (1978) 59 *The Parliamentarian* 149, 156.

[124] ibid; see also Silkin, above n 123.

[125] Edwards, above n 84, 75.

[126] Lord Shawcross's proposal is in a letter to *The Times* (1977), extracted, ibid, 63–64.

[127] ibid.

[128] ibid, 66–67. See also Silkin, above n 123, 157.

> themselves with all the relevant considerations, so as to enable them to assess whether it was contrary to the public interest for the investigation to succeed.[129]

In January 2006, both the Director and the Attorney had concluded that it would be in the public interest to continue the investigation, despite representations that had been made to the contrary by the Cabinet Secretary with the support of the Prime Minister, the Foreign Secretary and the Defence Secretary. Further representations—by the Prime Minister and also the UK Ambassador to Saudi Arabia—were made to the Director and the Attorney-General in late 2006. On 13 December, the Director indicated that he had reached a view that the public interest (national and international security) might dictate a discontinuation of the investigation, even though he was satisfied that there was sufficient evidence to continue. An initial judicial review was successful on the ground that the Director had inappropriately discontinued the investigation in response to a threat, but the House of Lords overturned the initial decision, holding that the discretion had been properly exercised.

The second controversy was the so-called 'cash for honours' scandal. It was revealed in 2006–07 that individuals who had made large loans had been offered peerages, in possible breach of the *Honours (Prevention of Abuses) Act 1925*. The police and the CPS investigated the claims. Ultimately, the Attorney-General had to determine whether to prosecute the MPs over the scandal—including MPs from his own party. To allay some of the controversy, then Attorney-General, Lord Goldsmith, indicated that he would make public all advice he took on the issue. His successor, Baroness Scotland, indicated she would not be involved in the prosecutorial decisions at all. On 20 July 2008, the CPS announced that there would be no prosecution as it could not prove that there had been an agreement that the loans had been made in return for the peerages.

ii. The Advisory Function

The advisory function is a less publicly-known aspect of the Law Officers' role, and as such it has historically been less usual for controversy to arise as to its proper exercise. Yet, as Edwards observes, 'No less important is the appreciation by everyone concerned as to the scope of the Law Officers' authority and the degree of independence with which the Attorney-General and the Solicitor-General discharge their advisory functions.'[130]

In the last few years, concerns about the level of independence exercised by government lawyers in their advisory function has increased. In 2004, scandals broke in the US when the 'Torture Memos' were released, and questions were raised about the quality and independence of advice provided by the Office of Legal Counsel. Following these revelations, in 2005 in the UK, controversy would

[129] *R (On the Application of Corner House Research and Ors) v Director of the Serious Fraud Office* [2008] UKHL 60 [6].

[130] Edwards, above n 84, 189.

arise over alleged political pressure that had been brought to bear on the Attorney-General when he was asked to advise on the legality of Britain's entry into the Iraq war without a further UN Security Council resolution.

On 17 March 2003, in response to a parliamentary question, Attorney-General Lord Goldsmith tabled a statement that was unequivocal about the legality of the action.[131] The Government refused to table the full advice, relying on the 'Law Officers' Convention'.[132] However, it was revealed in 2005 that the 17 March advice had been preceded by a piece of advice to the Prime Minister dated 7 March 2003. In that advice, the Attorney-General was far more cautious, indicating that it would be better if a further resolution was obtained. Questions were raised as to whether the Attorney-General changed his advice after pressure was placed on him by the then Foreign Secretary, Jack Straw.[133] The episode raised questions not only about the independence of the exercise of the Law Officers' advisory function, but also about whether advice ought to be released to Parliament for scrutiny.[134]

iii. The 2007–08 Inquiries into Reforming the English Law Officers

As controversy over the proper exercise of the Law Officers' functions continued into the twenty-first century, in 2007 Prime Minister Gordon Brown announced that the Attorney-General's role would be reviewed to ensure that public confidence in the position was retained.[135] The announcement was followed by an extensive report on the Attorney-General's role by the House of Commons Constitutional Affairs Select Committee.[136] That Committee was concerned over the modern Attorney-General's capacity to provide independent legal advice as well as exercise independence in the office's prosecutorial and other public interest functions. The Committee acknowledged that the tensions that arose in the Attorney-General's functions between the law, politics and the public interest were not new, however, it argued, 'it is time that these issues were addressed'.[137]

Ultimately, the Committee recommended drastic changes to the office through a division in responsibility: the purely legal functions (legal decisions in

[131] HL Deb, Series 6, Vol 646, 17 March 2003, col 2WA.

[132] See statement of Prime Minister in Question Time: HC Deb, Series 6, Vol 401, 14 March 2003, col 482W.

[133] These allegations are part of the investigation being undertaken by the 'Iraq Inquiry', led by Chairman Sir John Chilcot: see <http://www.iraqinquiry.org.uk>.

[134] House of Commons Constitutional Affairs Committee, *Constitutional Role of the Attorney General*, Fifth Report of Session 2006–07 (HC306) [49] 21. See also Kyriakides, 'The Advisory Functions of the Attorney-General', above n 92, and KA Kyriakides, 'The Law Officers of the Crown and the Rule of Law in the United Kingdom' in G Appleby, P Keyzer and J Williams (eds), *Public Sentinels: A Comparative Study of Australian Solicitors-General* (Ashgate Publishing, 2014) 185.

[135] Prime Minister and Secretary of State for Justice and Lord Chancellor, *The Governance of Britain* (July 2007), available at <https://www.gov.uk/government/uploads/system/uploads/attachment_data/file/228834/7170.pdf>.

[136] House of Commons Constitutional Affairs Committee, *Constitutional Role of the Attorney General*, Fifth Report of Session 2006–07 (HC306).

[137] ibid, 23.

prosecutions and the provision of legal advice) should be carried out by an official outside party political life; the ministerial duties should be carried out by a minister in the Ministry of Justice. The Secretary of State for Justice might still instruct the head of prosecutions on public interest matters, but must be accountable to Parliament for any instruction.[138] The proposal largely mirrored Shawcross's earlier proposal to create a non-political Attorney-General (see section II.D.i. above). As had Shawcross, the Committee emphasised the importance of public *perception* of the office's capacity to exercise the different functions with independence and propriety, regardless of how well individuals negotiated the tensions in the role.[139]

Following the House of Commons Committee's report, the Government released a consultation paper seeking submissions on a number of issues, including: Whether the position of chief legal adviser ought to be separated from that of government minister and, if so, who should exercise the role? Whether the legal opinions provided to government should be published and, if so, in what circumstances? Whether changes to the role of the Attorney-General in relation to criminal proceedings (including the role as superintending minister for the prosecuting authorities) were needed?[140]

Perhaps surprisingly, the Government's consultations revealed very little concern about the current structure of the Attorney-General's role.[141] The Government's response to the House of Commons' Committee stated:

> The Government notes that neither the Committee nor the vast majority of respondents considered that any Attorney General had in recent years actually exercised his or her functions in an improper or partisan manner. The Government agrees with those respondents who took the view that 'mistaken perception is a weak foundation on which to base reform'. (Lord Lloyd of Berwick).[142]

The House of Lords Constitution Committee also issued a report,[143] but no recommendation, choosing rather to set the arguments out for and against reforming the different aspects of the Attorney-General's role.[144] The report was supported by evidence from Anthony Bradley, broadly against substantial reform of the office, Sir Jeffrey Jowell, in favour of reform akin to that proposed by the House of

[138] ibid, 4, 41–42.

[139] ibid, 26.

[140] *The Governance of Britain: A Consultation on the Role of the Attorney General* (The Stationery Office Limited, 2007).

[141] See summary of consultations in Ministry of Justice, *The Governance of Britain: Constitutional Renewal* (March 2008) 16–18 and Ministry of Justice, *The Governance of Britain—Analysis of Consultations* (2008, CM 7342-3).

[142] UK, 'The Government's Response to the Constitutional Affairs Select Committee Report on the Constitutional Role of the Attorney General' (The Stationary Office Limited, April 2008, CM 7355) [44] 6.

[143] House of Lords Constitution Committee, *Reform of the Office of Attorney General* (HL 2007–08, 93), available at <http://www.publications.parliament.uk/pa/ld200708/ldselect/ldconst/93/93.pdf>.

[144] ibid, 5.

Commons Committee,[145] and evidence provided by the then Attorney-General, Baroness Scotland, who was also against substantive reform of the office in light of the results of the Government's consultations.

The Government ultimately accepted a number of objections to the House of Commons' proposal that had been advanced in the course of the consultations, and also in the evidence before the parliamentary committees.[146] These were, first, that it was important to have a lawyer 'at the heart of government' as a vital constitutional safeguard.[147] Secondly, that the Attorney-General as a political minister ensured accountability for the functions of the office. Baroness Scotland had said, 'No-one has got over the difficulty about there not being anyone accountable to Parliament at the despatch box.'[148] This echoes the concerns expressed by Edwards, when he said, 'it is my belief that the principle of accountability to Parliament is of no less importance than the principle of independence now recognised as operating before the institution and during the continuance of a criminal prosecution'.[149] Thirdly, the need for the Attorney-General to have a strong understanding of the system of government, the wider considerations in which the advice is sought and how policy is formulated. Fourthly, that a ministerial Law Officer was more likely to command confidence, in the form of authority and respect, in the Cabinet than a non-political officer. This was related to the third point, in that ministers would be confident that they were receiving advice from a lawyer who understood the full context of the request. As Peter Archer explained in 1978, advice from the Attorney reflects a professional politician's

> understanding of the problems confronting the politicians whom they are advising and the need to pursue a coherent policy, the tactical problems of introducing legislation to deal with a technical snag and the need to express advice in a way which can be passed on intelligibly to the public.[150]

Lastly, that it was difficult to separate the Attorney's legal and political functions, and that legal questions in a government context cannot be divorced from wider questions of policy. Ultimately, the Government accepted the submissions that the combination of functions in the office of Attorney-General was its strength, not its weakness.[151]

[145] And see also Jeffrey Jowell QC, 'Politics and the Law: Constitutional Balance or Institutional Confusion', Paper presented at the Justice Tom Sarjant Memorial Annual Lecture, 17 October 2006, making similar arguments.

[146] Ministry of Justice, *The Governance of Britain: Constitutional Renewal* (The Stationary Office, March 2008, CM 7342-I).

[147] Quoting Lord Goldsmith in his evidence to House of Commons Constitutional Affairs Committee, *Constitutional Role of the Attorney General*, Fifth Report of Session 2006–07 (HC306) 15.

[148] House of Commons Constitutional Affairs Committee, *Constitutional Role of the Attorney General*, Fifth Report of Session 2006–07 (HC306) 52.

[149] Edwards, above n 84, 225.

[150] P Archer, *The Role of the Law Officers* (The Fabian Society, 1978) 6.

[151] UK, 'The Government's Response to the Constitutional Affairs Select Committee Report on the Constitutional Role of the Attorney General' (The Stationary Office Limited, April 2008, CM 7355) 4 and 5.

The Government also rejected the call to focus on the *perception* of the office-holder's capacity to exercise his or her obligations independently. Indeed, the then Attorney-General, Baroness Scotland, stated that if the public was under a misapprehension that the Attorney was biased, the appropriate response to this was not structural reform of the office but to address the misconceptions.[152] Lord Goldsmith stated that as the issue was not 'with the role itself but with its perception'. The solution was 'not to change the role but to provide more information as to its boundaries and scope'.[153]

Ultimately, and despite releasing a draft Bill that would have gone some way towards curtailing the Attorney-General's role in prosecutions,[154] the Government made very little change to the role. A reference to the rule of law was added to the oath, a requirement for the Attorney-General to report annually to Parliament was introduced,[155] and a protocol between the prosecuting authorities and the Attorney-General was created to govern the question of how the Attorney would superintend these agencies.[156] The Government initially announced that the Attorney would only attend Cabinet when necessary, but it appears that this has reverted back to the former practice of regular attendance.[157]

Why did this attempt at constitutional reform fail when so many other important constitutional reforms, including to the role of the Lord Chancellor and judicial appointments, had succeeded? The Prime Minister had initially exhibited a large amount of enthusiasm for reform, but yet still it faltered. The answer that the Government provided was that, having undertaken substantial public

[152] House of Lords Constitution Committee, *Reform of the Office of Attorney General* (HL 2007–08, 93), available at <http://www.publications.parliament.uk/pa/ld200708/ldselect/ldconst/93/93.pdf> 33–34).

[153] House of Commons Constitutional Affairs Committee, *Constitutional Role of the Attorney General*, Fifth Report of Session 2006–07 (HC306) i.

[154] See Ministry of Justice, *The Governance of Britain: Constitutional Renewal* (The Stationary Office Limited, March 2008) 27 and Draft Constitutional Renewal Bill.

[155] See, eg: HM Procurator General and Treasury Solicitor, *Annual Report and Accounts 2012–2013* (2013), available at <https://www.gov.uk/government/uploads/system/uploads/attachment_data/file/256102/Departmental_Report_and_Accounts_2012_13.pdf>; HM Procurator General and Treasury Solicitor, *Annual Report and Accounts 2013–2014* (2014), available at <https://www.gov.uk/government/uploads/system/uploads/attachment_data/file/311595/2013-14_DRA.pdf>; <https://www.gov.uk/government/uploads/system/uploads/attachment_data/file/435603/2014-15_HM_Procurator_General_and_Treasury_Solicitor_Annual_Report__Accounts_18.pdf>. The Attorney-General has also started to give evidence to the House of Commons Justice Select Committee on an ad hoc basis: see, eg, session held on 15 September 2015, available at <http://www.parliament.uk/business/committees/committees-a-z/commons-select/justice-committee/news-parliament-20151/work-of-the-attorney-general-ev-session/>.

[156] Protocol between the Attorney-General and the Prosecuting Departments (July 2009), available at <https://www.gov.uk/government/uploads/system/uploads/attachmentdata/file/15197/ProtocolbetweentheAttorneyGeneralandtheProsecutingDepartments.pdf>.

[157] House of Lords Select Committee on the Constitution, *The Office of Lord Chancellor* (HL 2014–15, 75); Evidence to the House of Commons Justice Select Committee, 15 September 2015 (Jeremy Wright), available at <http://www.parliament.uk/business/committees/committees-a-z/commons-select/justice-committee/news-parliament-20151/work-of-the-attorney-general-ev-session/>.

consultation on the question, there was little appetite for reform.[158] The lack of impetus to implement significant structural changes to the office is less surprising when viewed against the existing studies on the English Law Officers. After considering different approaches to the office, Edwards' enduring conclusion was that the key to the independence of the Attorney-General did not lie in the adoption of formal constitutional structures, or even informal conventions, but ultimately rested upon 'the strength of character, personal integrity and depth of commitment to the principles of independence and the impartial representation of the public interest, on the part of holders of the office'.[159]

In his study in 1999, Neil Walker, like Edwards, denied that there was any easy answer to resolving the tensions in the Law Officers' role through institutional design. The Attorney-General's different roles fail one-dimensional classification as political or non-political, and therefore many reform models were inadequate in so far as they sought to isolate political from non-political functions.[160] However, in their respective positions, the Government, Edwards and Walker all failed to address the importance of maintaining *public confidence*, that is, the importance of the *perception* that the role is being exercised independently.

The failure of reform may be explained politically: the Government may have simply lost the appetite, and political capital, required to implement this further reform. The *Guardian*'s Clare Dyer also suggested that, in a political power struggle between the Secretary of State for Justice, Jack Straw, and the Attorney-General, Baroness Scotland, Scotland won.[161]

The limited and informal reforms did little to address the concerns raised by the recent controversies.[162] The arguments by which the Government said it was persuaded against a non-political model were not supported by evidence of how the alternative proposal might operate. In contrast, the practice of non-political Law Officers in other common law countries was subject to little serious investigation and consideration. For example, in its consultation paper, the Government included an appendix containing details of the approaches of foreign jurisdictions to structuring their Law Officers. In relation to Australia, it provides no explanation of the pivotal role played by the Solicitor-General in Australia's constitutional arrangements. It is difficult to avoid the conclusion that a more sustained analysis of the framework and practice in former colonial common law

158 This can be contrasted with the announcement of the reform of the Lord Chancellor *prior* to public consultation.

159 Edwards, above n 84, 67.

160 N Walker, 'The Antinomies of the Law Officers' in M Sunkin and S Payne (eds), *The Nature of the Crown: A Legal and Political Analysis* (Oxford University Press, 1999) 135, 162–65. See also See also CW Clayton, 'Introduction: Politics and the Legal Bureaucracy' in CW Clayton (ed), *Government Lawyers: The Federal Legal Bureaucracy and Presidential Politics* (University Press of Kansas, 1995) 1, 18.

161 C Dyer, 'Straw Insists on Case for Election Change' *Guardian* (26 March 2008), available at <http://www.theguardian.com/politics/2008/mar/26/constitution.law>.

162 See also KA Kyriakides, 'The Law Officers of the Crown and the Rule of Law in the United Kingdom', above n 134, 203.

jurisdictions—including Australia—may have combatted the concerns that were raised, and ultimately accepted by the Government, about the introduction of a non-political Law Officer.

III. Comparative Colonial Experience and Analysis

Before turning to the detailed consideration of the historical development of the Australian office offered in chapter three, it is necessary to outline briefly the evolution and operation of the equivalent offices to the Solicitor-General in the other two former UK colonies that are drawn upon as further comparators in the explanations and analysis of this book: the US and New Zealand. The structural features of the office of Solicitor-General in both of these jurisdictions differ from those of the modern English Law Officers and also those in Australia. Nonetheless, the 'core functions' across the jurisdictions have remained remarkably constant,[163] and they thus present as informative comparators.

A. The United States: Separating Advocacy and Advising

The office of US Attorney-General was largely modelled on the equivalent office in Britain.[164] The American colonies created Attorneys-General who were described as acting as 'delegate[s] of the Attorney-General of England',[165] fulfilling the varied responsibilities that were bestowed on the English office.[166] Some differences emerged. The American Officer did not sit in the legislature[167] and would often perform a much larger administrative function.[168] Colonial Attorneys-General were often assisted by a Solicitor-General.[169] The Law Officers' roles were largely undefined in the State Constitutions, and they operated by reference to common

[163] M Palmer, 'The Law Officers and Departmental Lawyers' (November 2011) *New Zealand Law Journal* 333, 333.

[164] JW Norton-Kyshe, *The Law and Privileges Relating to Colonial Attorneys-General: And to the Officer Corresponding to the Attorney-General of England in the United States of America* (Stevens and Haynes, 1900) 75; R Kramer and N Siegal, 'The Attorney-General of England and the Attorney-General of the United States' (1960) *Duke Law Journal* 524; C Fahy, 'The Office of the Solicitor General' (1942) 28 *American Bar Association Journal* 20, 20; RE Lee, 'Lawyering in the Supreme Court: The Role of the Solicitor General' (1988) 21 *Loyola of Los Angeles Law Review* 1059, 1064; contra EN Griswold, *Ould Fields, New Corne: The Personal Memoirs of a Twentieth Century Lawyer* (West Publishing Co, 1992) 258.

[165] OW Hammonds, 'The Attorney-General in the American Colonies' *Anglo-American Legal History Series*, Series 1 (New York 1939) 3.

[166] Kramer and Siegal, above n 164, 525.

[167] ibid.

[168] Cooley, above n 4, 310.

[169] ibid, 311.

law, custom and statute, much like the offices in England.[170] The federal office of Attorney-General was created by the *Judiciary Act* in 1789, drawing on this experience and practice.[171]

Today the US Attorney-General performs a highly political role with large administrative responsibilities, and is assisted in the legal functions by the more independent Office of Solicitor-General (OSG) and Office of Legal Counsel (OLC).[172] In the US, as in Australia, the offices are governed by statute, but unique to the US context is the division of functions between the OSG and the OLC. The OSG performs the primary function of prosecuting and conducting all suits in the Supreme Court on behalf of the Government.[173] The advisory function of the Solicitor-General is now performed by the OLC.[174] The OLC assists the Attorney-General by providing advice on the constitutionality of proposed legislation, advising on the legality of executive actions, reviewing executive orders and settling disputes among executive agencies.[175]

In the US, as in the UK, much of the scholarly debate around the Attorney-General, the OSG and the OLC has been driven by the search for a model, or as Edwards termed it, a 'philosophic approach', to explain and analyse the offices in light of allegations of inappropriate behaviour on the part of officeholders.[176] In 1987, the publication of Lincoln Caplan's *The Tenth Justice: The Solicitor General and the Rule of Law* generated substantial legal and political interest in the

[170] ibid, 312.

[171] ibid.

[172] CW Clayton, *The Politics of Justice: The Attorney General and the Making of Legal Policy* (ME Sharpe, Inc, 1992) 52–53.

[173] US Code, Title 28, Part II, Chapter 31, § 518(a). See further description of the general functions of the office in US Code of Federal Regulations, Title 28, § 0.20.

[174] Clayton, above n 172, 33–34; CTL Pillard, 'The Unfulfilled Promise of the Constitution in Executive Hands' (2005) 103 *Michigan Law Review* 676, 710.

[175] US Code of Federal Regulations, Title 28, § 0.25.

[176] For example, DJ Meador, *The President, The Attorney General and the Department of Justice* (White Burkett Miller Center of Public Affairs, 1980) followed the Watergate affair; Clayton, above n 172, N Baker, *Conflicting Loyalties: Law and Politics in the Attorney General's Office, 1789–1990* (University Press of Kansas, 1992), D Kmiec, *The Attorney General's Lawyer: Inside the Meese Justice Department* (Praeger Publishers, 1992) were published about the Reagan Administration. A large number of publications also followed the revelations of the Torture Memos, see, eg, J Goldsmith, *The Terror Presidency: Law and Judgment Inside the Bush Administration* (WW Norton & Company, 2009); D Cole, *The Torture Memos: Rationalizing the Unthinkable* (New Press, 2009); D Cole, *Justice at War: The Men and Ideas that Shaped America's War on Terror* (New York Review of Books, 2008); Pillard, above n 174; DE Johnsen, 'Faithfully Executing the Laws: Internal Legal Constraints on Executive Power' (2007) 54 *UCLA Law Review* 1559; DE Johnsen, 'Functional Departmentalism and Nonjudicial Interpretation: Who Determines Constitutional Meaning?' (2004) 67(2) *Law and Contemporary Problems* 105; DE Johnsen, 'What's a President to do? Interpreting the Constitution in the Wake of Bush Administration Abuses' (2008) 88 *Boston University Law Review* 395; B Ackerman, 'Abolish the White House Counsel: And the Office of Legal Counsel, too, while we're at it', *Slate*, 22 April 2009. Although note earlier studies of the office prior to this event: eg, RD Moss, 'Executive Branch Legal Interpretation: A Perspective from the Office of Legal Counsel' (2000) 52 *Administrative Law Review* 1303; FM Wozencraft, 'OLC: The Unfamiliar Acronym' (1971) 57 *American Bar Association Journal* 33.

office.[177] It alleged that Solicitors-General for President Reagan abused the position, and critiqued their conduct against a normative model of the office, emphasising independence from the Administration and commitment to the coherence of Supreme Court jurisprudence (giving rise to the idea of the 'Tenth Justice').[178]

The US does not operate under a Westminster system of responsible government, emphasising, rather, a stricter separation of institutional functions that, some argue, has served to inflate tensions between the Judiciary and the Executive. The US also has a history of comparatively highly politicised judicial decision-making, at least partly referable to the inclusion of the Bill of Rights in the US constitutional text. As in Australia, the US Attorney-General has tended to play a far more overtly political role than the English Law Officers. Despite these many differences in constitutional structure and history, the approaches that have dominated the US literature continue to divide over the same questions seen in the Australian and English literature about the appropriate level of independence of the office from politics and the role of the office in protecting the public interest and the rule of law.

The voluminous US literature on the office continues to struggle with the question of how individuals ought to negotiate tensions between the law, politics and the public interest in the Law Officers' traditional roles. Some have argued that these tensions are even more pronounced in the US context because the Attorney-General's role has been increasingly politicised.[179] Much of the disagreement and obvious tension arises between whether an officeholder should play a narrow role, loyal to the Executive's political interests and therefore prioritising the democratic mandate and responsibility of the President, or should act in the broader public interest (this may be framed in terms of justice, or a morally focused ideal).

[177] L Caplan, *The Tenth Justice: The Solicitor General and the Rule of Law* (Vintage Books, 1987). Subsequent studies have included political science treatises: eg, RM Salokar, *The Solicitor General: The Politics of Law* (Temple University Press, 1992); RL Pacelle Jr, *Between Law and Politics: The Solicitor General and the Structuring of Race, Gender and Reproductive Rights Litigation* (Texas A&M University Press, 2003); PN Ubertaccio III, *Learned in the Law and Politics* (LFB Scholarly Publishing LLC, 2005); academic symposiums (the first of these was held in 1988, the papers of which were subsequently published in the *Loyola of Los Angeles Law Review*, in 2003 the Rex E Lee Conference on the OSG was held, the proceedings of which were published in the *Brigham Young University Law Review*); PhD theses: eg, JL Cooper, *The Solicitor General and Federal Litigation—Principal-Agent Relationships and the Separation of Powers* (PhD, Indiana University, 1993); CA Ditslear, *Office of the Solicitor General Participation before the United States Supreme Court: Influences on the Decision-Making Process* (PhD, Ohio State University, 2003); quantitative analyses: see, eg, J Segal and C Reedy, 'The Supreme Court and Sex Discrimination: The Role of the Solicitor General' (1988) 41(3) *The Western Political Quarterly* 553; J Segal, 'Amicus Curiae Briefs by the Solicitor General During the Warren and Burger Courts' (1989) 41 *The Western Political Quarterly* 135; autobiographical and biographical accounts: eg, C Fried, *Order and Law: Arguing the Reagan Revolution—A Firsthand Account* (Simon & Schuster, 1991); Griswold, above n 164; K Gormley, *Archibald Cox: Conscience of a Nation* (Da Capo Press, 1997); and other academic literature in the fields of both political science and law, although much of the analysis continues to come from officeholders, and employees within the OSG.

[178] Caplan, above n 177, xiv.

[179] Clayton, above n 172, 13–14.

The development within the US constitutional framework of a division between the advisory and advocacy functions has, at least for some commentators, helped alleviate some of the tensions inherent in the combination of these functions. A government-focused approach has been accepted in the advocacy- and adversarial-focused role of the OSG. In contrast, a more independent, public interest-focused approach has been picked up in the controversies over the advisory function of the OLC after the release of the Torture Memos.[180] It is argued that this more independent approach is preferable for the OLC in its *advisory* function.[181] For example, a 2004 memorandum on the guiding principles of the OLC, drafted by former members of that office directly in response to the release of the Torture Memos,[182] asserted that the office must advise based on its best view of what the law requires, in order to assist the President to fulfil his constitutional duty to uphold the laws.[183] The memorandum emphasised the distinction between the ethical framework governing an adviser as against that of an advocate.

B. New Zealand: A Non-political, All-in-One Office

Like Australia and the US, New Zealand inherited the concept of the Law Officers from Britain.[184] As has already been discussed, New Zealand was an early experimenter with the constitutional structure of its colonial Law Officers. In 1866 it enacted legislation to make the offices non-political, permanent appointments outside of the Executive Council (the precursor to Cabinet). Rather oddly, in 1867 the junior Law Officer, the Solicitor-General, was made the political officer. This inverse arrangement was abandoned in 1876, when new legislation was passed allowing the Attorney to be political or non-political, who could be, but was not required to be, a member of the Executive Council.

At about the same time, the Solicitor-General was made a permanent government officer, but without statutory backing. A challenge to the appointment was

[180] Jay S Bybee, Assistant Attorney General, Office of Legal Counsel, to Albert R Gonzales, Counsel to the President, *Re: Standards of Conduct for Interrogation under 18 USC §§ 2340-2340A* (1 August 2002); Jay S Bybee, Assistant Attorney General, Office of Legal Counsel, to John Rizzo, Acting General Counsel, Central Intelligence Agency, *Interrogation of al Qaeda Operative* (1 August 2002); John Yoo to William J Haynes II , General Counsel of the Department of Defense, *Re: Military Interrogation of Alien Unlawful Combatants Held Outside the United States* (13 March 2003).

[181] Moss, above n 176. Contra the analysis of the OLC in SG Calabresi, 'The President, the Supreme Court, and the Constitution: A Brief Positive Account of the Role of Government Lawyers in the Development of Constitutional Law' (1998) 61 *Law and Contemporary Problems* 61, 79.

[182] Office of Legal Counsel, *Principles to Guide the Office of Legal Counsel* (21 December 2004). See also US Department of Justice, Office of Legal Counsel, *Memorandum for Attorneys of the Office Re: Best Practice for OLC Opinions*; and the recommendations to similar effect in HH Koh, 'Protecting the Office of Legal Counsel from Itself' (1993) 15 *Cardozo Law Review* 513, 523.

[183] Office of Legal Counsel, above n 182, 2.

[184] For further history, see D Collins, 'The Role of Solicitor-General in Contemporary New Zealand' in Appleby, Keyzer and Williams (eds), above n 134, 171, 171–74.

brought in the New Zealand Supreme Court, questioning whether it could be made without statutory authority. Williams J stated:

> [U]nless taken away by legislation, the Crown has the power of appointing an Attorney and Solicitor General; and I apprehend that the duties of the persons appointed would be similar to those of persons filling corresponding offices at Home; and that there would be no necessity to specify, by statute or otherwise, the nature and extent of duties already sufficiently defined by long usage.[185]

Today, as in Australia, the modern New Zealand Solicitor-General is contrasted with the Attorney-General because of the non-political and non-responsible nature of the second Law Officer (non-responsible in the sense that the Solicitor-General does not sit in the ministry).[186]

However, the New Zealand arrangements differ from those in Australia in two key respects. First, the office has no statutory basis, and therefore no formal institutional safeguards of independence, for example in the form of statutory security of tenure or remuneration. Secondly, the Solicitor-General's functions are much broader in nature.[187] The New Zealand Solicitor-General is, in effect, Chief Executive of the Crown Law Office, leading counsel for the Crown in both advocacy and advisory roles, and chief Crown prosecutor.[188] Through these broad-ranging obligations, the Solicitor-General is aware of, and responsible for, almost all of the legal work of the Crown.[189] The Solicitor-General's continuing close association with the Crown Law office, and the office's supervision of government litigation, has secured a number of benefits, including consistency in legal advice, the strategic planning of litigation and the ready involvement of the Solicitor-General in important cases.[190]

In 2012 a major review of the role of Solicitor-General was conducted, considering the question of whether one person could continue to discharge so many high-level multiple roles efficiently and effectively.[191] Ultimately, the review did not recommend that the roles of Solicitor-General and Chief Executive of Crown Law Office be split. It warned that 'separation risks weakening the critical role of the Solicitor-General, increasing, rather than decreasing, Crown legal risk'.[192] The review also considered whether to split the advisory and advocacy roles—as occurs in the US—but ultimately recommended against the practice.

[185] *Solicitor-General; ex rel Cargill v Dunedin City Corporation* (1875) 1 NS Jur (NS) 1.

[186] J McGrath, 'Principles for Sharing Law Officer Power—The Role of the New Zealand Solicitor-General' (1998) 18 *New Zealand Universities Law Review* 195, 198.

[187] The Australian Capital Territory Solicitor-General does perform this breadth of functions. This office was only introduced in 2011.

[188] Collins, above n 184, 171.

[189] See further Cabinet Directions for the Conduct of Crown Legal Business 2012, replacing the 1993 rules, available at <https://cabinetmanual.cabinetoffice.govt.nz/appendix-c>.

[190] Collins, above n 184, 180–82.

[191] M Dean and D Cochrane, *A Review of the Role and Functions of the Solicitor-General and the Crown Law Office* (24 February 2012), available at < http://www.crownlaw.govt.nz/assets/Uploads/Reports/review-2012.pdf>.

[192] ibid, v, 17.

As Balfour had argued in 1901 in England, the different legal dimensions of the role can inform and strengthen each other. The 2012 New Zealand report found that 'advice informs advocacy and vice versa',[193] and that the combination of advisory and advocacy expertise gave authority and credibility to the role; it was also thought to make recruitment and retention easier. The review did conclude that the office's key strength was providing consistent and proactive legal *advice*, and that this function should be prioritised over the office's advocacy work.[194]

IV. Conclusion

In 1964 Edwards emphasised the need for a better understanding of the tightrope that Law Officers walk within the British constitutional system.[195] While sharing core functions and dimensions with the comparable offices considered in this chapter, the Australian Solicitor-General is unique in many respects. Its non-political nature distinguishes it from the elected ministerial offices in England. In the US, the OSG is also non-political, in the sense of not being an elected official; but it is unlike the Australian office, because the incumbent is appointed to serve during the tenure of a single Administration, and is therefore expected to be more politically aligned and sensitive. Further, the US Solicitor-General is an advocate only, a function that is statutorily guaranteed. Division of functions between the OSG and OLC in the US has led to the dominance of different normative models for the different offices. While the Australian Solicitor-General shares many similarities with the New Zealand Solicitor-General, as is explained in chapter three, in the twentieth century all of the jurisdictions introduced a statutory basis for the office. Further, Australian Solicitors-General have been largely relieved of administrative responsibilities, and in the 1980s and 1990s responsibility for the administration of criminal justice was also removed. The explanation and analysis of the Australian Solicitor-General provided in this book will therefore not only provide the first detailed explanation of the role in the Australian context, but also provide a further comparator for other jurisdictions examining the institutional arrangements of their own chief government legal officers.

193 ibid, v, 22.

194 ibid, v.

195 Edwards, above n 3, ix.

Part II

The Australian Solicitor-General

3

The Evolution of an Australian Solicitor-General

The British tradition of the Law Officers heavily influenced the early Australian roles of Attorney-General and Solicitor-General. But since the mid-nineteenth century, the evolution of the Australian Law Officers has taken its own path. A very different, non-political role has been forged for the Solicitor-General to complement a now overtly political Attorney-General. No longer is the Solicitor-General simply the deputy of the Attorney, not deserving of dedicated separate study. And yet the office of Australian Solicitor-General and its story remain obscure to legal scholarship.[1] This chapter, which provides an historical study of the Australian Solicitor-General, assists us to understand the underlying objectives behind the modern framework, and therefore better comprehend the features of the office. An historical list of officeholders in each jurisdiction is set out in Appendix C.

The story of the Australian Solicitor-General unfolds in three phases. The first phase, the 'British Colonial Period', commenced in the early nineteenth century. In this phase the Law Officers, as best they could in the colonial conditions, mirrored the British tradition. In the second phase, the 'Public Service Period', the Solicitor-General became a non-political public service position. This period commenced in Tasmania as early as the 1860s and was gradually adopted across the other jurisdictions. During this phase the office closely mirrored the modern New Zealand model, often with heavy responsibilities in administration and criminal law, as well as civil advocacy and advising.

The third phase, the 'Modern Period', started in Victoria in 1951 with the introduction of a quasi-independent statutory office of 'counsel'. In some respects this period represents a regression back to the purely professional role of the very early English Law Officers (see discussion in chapter two, section I.A.). The statutory

[1] The exception being histories available in New South Wales: K Mason, 'The Office of Solicitor General for New South Wales' (Autumn 1988) *Bar News* 22; and in Queensland: Crown Law, *In My Opinion: The History of Crown Law Queensland 1859–2009* (Department of Justice and Attorney General, 2009). A general history is provided in JLJ Edwards, *The Attorney General, Politics and the Public Interest* (Sweet & Maxwell, 1984) 367–88; and more recently see K Mason, 'Aspects of the History of the Solicitor-General in Australia' in G Appleby, P Keyzer and J Williams (eds), *Public Sentinels: A Comparative Study of Australian Solicitors-General* (Ashgate Publishing, 2014) 23. Much of the story told in this chapter is drawn from G Appleby 'The Evolution of a Public Sentinel: Australia's Solicitor-General' (2012) 63(3) *Northern Ireland Legal Quarterly* 397.

office emerged as the preferred model across all of the jurisdictions in the second half of the twentieth century, and in the Australian Capital Territory as late as 2011. Since the stabilisation of this last phase, the Solicitor-General has become a specialist in constitutional and public law advice and litigation of significance. This chapter concludes by explaining the impetus for the creation of the modern office with its distinct features, leaving a full examination of the legislative framework and its practical operation to the following chapters.

I. The 'British Colonial Period'

In the colonies of New South Wales, Van Diemen's Land and, slightly later, Victoria, the roles of the Law Officers were modelled on British historical practice.[2]

As we saw in the previous chapter (chapter two section I.), the modern practice of the English Law Officers was not settled at the time of its reception into the Australian colonies in the early nineteenth century. A number of characteristics were, however, stable. By the nineteenth century both Law Officers sat in Parliament,[3] but it was a generally accepted practice that neither Law Officer sat in Cabinet.[4] Both Law Officers had responsibility for a number of legal and public interest functions, with the Solicitor-General acting as a general deputy to the first Law Officer.[5] The Law Officers were expected to exercise a degree of independent judgement in the fulfilment of these functions, and not to act for the narrow interests of the Monarch but to pursue justice and further the 'public weal' in accordance with the Crown's obligations to the community.[6] There was also a growing recognition of the importance of attracting qualified and capable people because of the positions' importance to the constitutional structure.[7]

[2] In Western Australia and, by and large, in South Australia and Queensland, the position of Solicitor-General did not emerge until the twentieth century (there had been single, brief appointments of Solicitor-General in the 1890s in the last two jurisdictions, but the office was not established permanently). In these colonies other officers, while they lacked the appellation, carried out the functions of Law Officer. For example, in 1836 when the province of South Australia was established it had an Advocate-General: Order-in-Council Establishing Government February 23, 1836 (Imp); GD Combe, *Responsible Government in South Australia* (Government Printer, 1957) 8; *Attorney-General v Adams* [1965] SASR 129, 132 (Napier CJ); HT Burgess, *The Cyclopedia of South Australia* (The Cylopedia Company, 1907–09) 335. Note JW Norton-Kyshe, *The Law and Privileges Relating to Colonial Attorneys-General: And to the Officer Corresponding to the Attorney-General of England in the United States of America* (Stevens and Haynes, 1900) 1.

[3] JLJ Edwards, *The Law Officers of the Crown: A Study of the Offices of the Attorney-General and Solicitor-General of England with an Account of the Office of the Director of Public Prosecutions of England* (Sweet & Maxwell, 1964) ch 3.

[4] ibid, 174–75.

[5] JW Norton-Kyshe, *The Law and Privileges Relating to the Attorney-General and Solicitor-General of England: With a history from the earliest periods, and a series of King's Attorneys and Attorneys and Solicitors-General from the reign of Henry III to the 60th of Queen Victoria* (Stevens and Haynes, 1897) 4.

[6] Edwards, *The Law Officers,* above n 3, ch 4.

[7] ibid, 112.

During the 'British Colonial Period' in Australia, questions arose over how to adjust the British traditions to colonial circumstances. The necessity of having two Law Officers was queried in light of concerns about finances and over-governance. Concerns also appeared about the independence of the Law Officers from politics in their legal and public interest functions, particularly as they became responsible ministers and took up seats in the Executive Council. The Law Officers also bore responsibility for the provision of legal services across the whole of government—a wider mandate than existed in Britain.[8] Government responses to these issues would lead to the evolution of the role of the Australian Solicitor-General towards the non-political.

A. Colonial Beginnings: Adopting and Adapting the British Tradition

The appointment of the first New South Wales Attorney-General, Saxe Bannister, in 1823 was quickly followed by the appointment of John Stephen as Solicitor-General to act as his deputy. From this beginning, the evolution of the two offices was closely related. These first Law Officers were appointed from the English Bar.[9] The appointment of the Attorney-General was made pursuant to the recommendations of the Bigge Report.[10] Prior to that, the colonial Governor would refer important questions of law to the English Law Officers.[11] Prosecutorial functions were performed by the Deputy Judge Advocate, who was also called upon for legal advice.[12] Bigge was critical of the concentration of powers in the Judge Advocate, and recommended the appointment of an Attorney-General to act as grand jury and prosecute criminal matters, as well as to draft legal documents and legislation for the Governor.[13] Once appointed, the Attorney-General's other functions included providing legal advice to the Governor and acting as counsel in civil matters.[14]

[8] A relatively common practice in the colonies: Norton-Kyshe, above n 5, 5.

[9] Edwards, *The Attorney-General*, above n 1, 367; Norton-Kyshe, above n 5, 49, fn 1. As a general rule, the appointment of Law Officers from the English Bar continued during this period. See analysis of appointments in F Hanlon, *An Analysis of the Office of Attorney General in Australia and Directions for the Future* (PhD, University of Melbourne, 2007) 45–46; 73–74.

[10] JT Bigge, *Report of the Commissioner of Inquiry on the Judicial Establishments of New South Wales and Van Diemen's Land (Common's Paper 33, ordered to be printed 21 February 1823, Lords Paper (118) ordered to be printed 4 July 1823) Facsimile* (Libraries Board of South Australia, 1966) 56–57. The appointment was made pursuant to the *New South Wales Act 1823* (Imp).

[11] For example, JM Bennett and AC Castles, *A Source Book of Australian Legal History* (The Law Book Company Ltd, 1979) 263–66. See also HV Evatt, 'The Legal Foundations of New South Wales' (1938) 11 *Australian Law Journal* 409, 416.

[12] Evatt, above n 11, 416; JM Bennett, 'The Status and Authority of the Deputy Judge Advocates of New South Wales' (1956-8) 3 *Sydney Law Review* 501; T Kass, *A Brief History of the Attorney-General's Department* (Attorney General's Department New South Wales, 1996) 5.

[13] Bigge, above n 10, 56–57, 59.

[14] Kass, above n 12, 6.

Stephen was appointed the colony's first Solicitor-General in 1824.[15] The letter to the Governor regarding the appointment read:

> The Solicitor-General will by virtue of his appointment be considered as the legal adviser of Her Majesty's Government in the Colony, either in cases where sickness or absence of the Attorney-General or any other unavoidable cause may render it necessary to employ a substitute for that Office, or in cases which for their peculiar difficulty or importance require that the Attorney-General should have the professional assistance of another Counsel.[16]

Van Diemen's Land was established as a separate colony from New South Wales in 1824, with a Governor advised by a Crown Council. An Attorney-General, Joseph Gellibrand, was appointed in 1824, and a Solicitor-General, Alfred Stephen, in 1825 (Stephen was also shortly thereafter appointed Crown Solicitor, a position that came with a salary of £300).[17]

The appointment of Law Officers early in the history of New South Wales and Van Diemen's Land demonstrates the recognition of the importance of government within the law, even in the context of a penal colony. To be achieved, this required government access to independent legal advisers.

The creation of the colonial Law Officers was considered to have brought with it all the common law duties and powers exercisable by the English Law Officers as were applicable to the circumstances of the colony.[18] These included, for example, the power to initiate and terminate criminal prosecutions, to advise on the grant of pardons, to grant immunities from prosecution, to issue a fiat in relator actions in defence of public rights, to institute proceedings for contempt of court, to intervene in any case where the validity of a colonial law was under challenge, and to provide legal advice to the Executive Council and Governor.[19]

The early appointments of the Law Officers in both colonies mirrored as far as possible those in Britain, despite dramatic differences in constitutional context, namely the absence of representative or responsible institutions and therefore the absence of direct accountability of a Law Officer for the exercise of the public interest functions. Throughout the 1820s and 1830s confrontations arose between

[15] Letter, Earl Bathurst to Sir Thomas Brisbane, 21 January 1824, extracted in The Library Committee of the Commonwealth Parliament, *Historical Records of Australia*, Series I: *Governors' Despatches to and from England*, vol XI: *January 1823–November 1825* (1922) 198–99.

[16] *Historical Records of Australia*, Series I, vol XI, above n 15, 199.

[17] The Library Committee of the Commonwealth Parliament, *Historical records of Australia*, Series 3: *Despatches and Papers Relating to the Settlement of the States*, vol IV: *Tasmania 1821–1825* (1921), 265; see also ibid, 270, and The Library Committee of the Commonwealth Parliament, *Historical records of Australia*, Series 3: *Despatches and Papers Relating to the Settlement of the States*, vol V: *Tasmania* (1921), 61; A Colonist, 'Correspondence: To His Honor Lieutenant Governor Arthur', *Hobart Town Gazette and Van Diemen's Land Advertiser* (Hobart), 10 June 1825, 3; M Rutledge, 'Stephen, Sir Alfred (1802–1894)' in *Australian Dictionary of Biography*, vol 6 (Melbourne University Press, 1976) 180.

[18] *Historical Records of Australia*, Series I, vol XI, above n 15, 883–84; Norton-Kyshe, above n 5, 10; G Griffith, 'The Office of Attorney General in New South Wales' (2007) 11 *Legal History* 79, 95–96.

[19] Griffith, above n 18, 95–96.

the Law Officers over the division of work, and the Colonial Office had to confirm repeatedly that the roles of the Law Officers ought to replicate (as closely as possible) the roles in Britain.[20] Some of the Attorney-General's counsel functions were delegated to the Solicitor-General.[21] As in Britain, the Solicitor-General was the more junior Law Officer appointed to assist the Attorney-General, and a natural stepping-stone to the senior position during this period. The Law Officers were supported by a Crown Solicitor,[22] although at times in Van Diemen's Land, where the profession was fused, the Solicitor-General held this post as well.

As in Britain, officeholders enjoyed the right to private practice until the 1890s.[23] The Bigge Report had recommended that the Attorney-General be given the right to private practice to induce English barristers of appropriate calibre to make the journey to the colonies.[24] In New South Wales the right to private practice was abolished in 1894.[25] As in Britain, this followed public outcry. Attorney-General Edmund Barton and Minister for Justice[26] Richard O'Connor were forced to resign in 1893 after it was revealed they had accepted private briefs against a statutory government authority.[27]

[20] See the correspondence in relation to a number of disputes between the Law Officers in The Library Committee of the Commonwealth Parliament, *Historical Records of Australia*, Series I: *Governors' Despatches to and from England*, vol XIV: *March 1828–May 1829* (1922), 371–73; The Library Committee of the Commonwealth Parliament, *Historical Records of Australia*, Series I: *Governors' Despatches to and from England*, vol XV: *July 1829–December 1830* (1922) 10; The Library Committee of the Commonwealth Parliament, *Historical Records of Australia*, Series I: *Governors' Despatches to and from England*, vol XVII: *1833–June 1835* (1922) 284–94. See also T Chisholme Austey, *A Statement of the case of Herbert George Jones: Serjeant-at-Law, Late Her Majesty's Solicitor-General of Van Diemen's Land, as evidenced by the official correspondence and other documents relating thereto* (T Brettell, 1846).

[21] Kass, above n 12, 6.

[22] In New South Wales, a Crown Solicitor was appointed in 1829 at the request of the Attorney-General Saxe Bannister, who wanted to delegate some of the Attorney-General's more mundane tasks: Kass, above n 12, 7.

[23] ibid, 6; Edwards, *The Law Officers*, above n 3, 98, 100; *The Cyclopedia of Tasmania: An Historical and Commercial Review: Descriptive and Biographical Facts, Figures and Illustrations: An Epitome of Progress: Business Men and Commercial Interests* (Maitland and Krone Publishers, 1900); Letter to Editor from NE Lewis, *The Mercury*, 12 December 1905, extracted in full in Royal Commission on the Proposal to Make the Office of Attorney-General Permanent Non-Political, *Report of the Commission* (Hobart, John Vale, Government Printer of Tasmania, 1908) 39.

[24] Hanlon, above n 9, 50. See also Austey, above n 20.

[25] Edwards, *The Law Officers*, above n 3, 98, 100; K Mason, 'The Office of Solicitor General', above n 1, 22; Griffith, above n 18, 88–89; MG Sexton, 'The Role of the Solicitor General' in G Lindsay (ed), *No Mere Mouthpiece: Servants of All, Yet of None* (LexisNexis Butterworths, 2002) 86, 87.

[26] An office that arose in the ministry during the period of the Solicitor-General's abolition in New South Wales, which is detailed below.

[27] For a full account of the story, see 'Political Crisis in New South Wales—Defeat of the Government—Debate in the Assembly—The Proudfoot Case—Retainer of Legal Ministers—An Unexpected Result—Intentions of the Government', *The Brisbane Courier* (Brisbane) (8 December 1893), 5, available at <http://newspapers.nla.gov.au/ndp/del/article/3570462>; M Rutledge, 'Barton, Sir Edmund (1849–1920)' in *Australian Dictionary of Biography*, vol 7 (Melbourne University Press, 1979) 194; M Rutledge, 'O'Connor, Richard Edward (1851–1912)' in *Australian Dictionary of Biography*, vol 11 (Melbourne University Press, 1988) 56; G Bolton, *Edmund Barton* (Allen & Unwin, 2000) 118–20.

The Law Officers quickly came to be among the appointed advisers to the Governor. In New South Wales, both Law Officers sat on the Executive Council advising the Governor,[28] and in Van Diemen's Land the Attorney-General sat on the Crown Council.[29] At this time the Governor was not bound to follow the Council's advice. The practice of appointing the Law Officers to the Executive Council was a departure from that in Britain,[30] although, unlike the British Cabinet, the Council lacked actual political power at this early stage. However, the practice set a precedent that would continue when responsible government was introduced and substantial public power vested in the Executive Council.

In 1836 the role of New South Wales Solicitor-General was abolished and Attorney-General John Plunkett found himself burdened with the responsibilities of both offices. This was probably caused by bickering between the Law Officers over the appropriate division of responsibilities.[31] In 1840 the Governor petitioned the Colonial Office for the re-establishment of the office to allay concerns about delays in the law business of the Crown, and also to ensure there was a person to perform the Law Officers' duties during the Attorney-General's absence.[32] However, the Colonial Secretary refused the request because of concerns about the finances and over-governance of the colony.[33] Despite this, in 1841 the Governor appointed an Acting Solicitor-General.[34] The Colonial Secretary refused to confirm the appointment,[35] and the position remained filled by an acting appointment until 1843, when the new Colonial Secretary decided to revive the office before the first elections for the newly created Legislative Council.[36]

B. The Colonial Law Officers Take their Seats in the Legislature

In 1842 the creation of a Legislative Council in New South Wales highlighted the increasingly political nature of the role of the Law Officers in the Australian colonies.[37] The new Council was made up of 24 elected members and 12 appointed members. Lord Stanley, the Colonial Secretary, noted that it would be desirable

[28] A Todd, *Parliamentary Government in the British Colonies* (Longmans Green, 2nd edn, 1894) 25–26; Edwards, *The Attorney-General*, above n 1, 367.

[29] Parliament of Tasmania, *Members of the Legislative Council of Van Diemen's Land 1825–1856*, available at <http://www.parliament.tas.gov.au/History/tasparl/mlcs1825to1855.htm>.

[30] Edwards, *The Attorney-General*, above n 1, 367–68; 369; Griffith, above n 18, 85.

[31] *Historical Records of Australia*, Series I, vol XVII, above n 20, 298. See also ibid, 585.

[32] The Library Committee of the Commonwealth Parliament, *Historical Records of Australia*, Series I: *Governors' Despatches to and from England*, vol XX: *February 1838–September 1840* (1922) 524.

[33] ibid, 716.

[34] The Library Committee of the Commonwealth Parliament, *Historical Records of Australia*, Series I: *Governors' Despatches to and from England*, vol XXI: *October 1840–March 1842* (1922) 299.

[35] ibid, 468, 524.

[36] The Library Committee of the Commonwealth Parliament, *Historical Records of Australia*, Series I: *Governors' Despatches to and from England*, vol XXII: *April 1842–June 1843* (1922) 592.

[37] *Australian Constitutions Act (No 1) 1842* (Imp). New South Wales at that time included Victoria and Queensland.

for some of the Governor's executive officers in the Council to be popularly elected, but it would be 'unadvisable' that other officers, including the Attorney-General and the Solicitor-General, 'should be dependent on particular constituencies, and appear to represent particular interests' other than the Governor's.[38]

During this period, Legislative Councils were also created in the other colonies, and the Law Officers took their seats in these bodies. In 1850, a Legislative Council of appointed and elected members was created in Van Diemen's Land. As was the case in New South Wales, the Attorney-General and Solicitor-General were appointed to the Council and expected to act as the 'Governor's men'.[39] Prior to Victoria's separation from New South Wales, the Law Officers of New South Wales were technically also those for the Port Phillip District, although in practice the Superintendent for the District received advice from the local Crown Clerk.[40] After separation in 1851, Victoria appointed its own colonial Law Officers. Both Officers were appointed members of the Victorian Legislative Council (composed of nominated and elected representatives),[41] and the Attorney-General was also a member of the Executive Council, highlighting the more senior and already more politically important nature of this office.[42] Fiona Hanlon's research and analysis of the qualifications of both Law Officers also demonstrates that during this period the Attorney-General was consistently the more politically qualified Law Officer.[43]

C. Responsible Government: Further Breaks with English Tradition

The New South Wales, Victorian and Tasmanian *Constitution Acts* of 1855 brought responsible government to the colonies, and made the Law Officers among the first responsible ministers of the Crown.[44] Under these constitutions, the Governor

[38] Letter Lord Stanley to Governor Gipps, Private, 5 September 1842, CO 202/45, extracted in ACV Melbourne, *Early Constitutional Development in Australia: New South Wales 1788–1856 Queensland 1859–1922* (University of Queensland Press, 1963) 275.

[39] Parliament of Tasmania, above n 29.

[40] Letter, Colonial Secretary to CJ La Trobe, 9 January 1840, extracted in P Jones, *Beginnings of Permanent Government*, Historical Records of Victoria Foundation Series (Victorian Government Printing Office, 1981) 288, referred to in Hanlon, above n 9, 42.

[41] E Sweetman, *Constitutional Development of Victoria 1851–6* (Whitcombe & Tombs Limited, 1920) 28.

[42] ibid, 73; Public Record Office Victoria, *Function VF 169, Solicitor-General*, available at <www.access.prov.vic.gov.au/public/component/daPublicBaseContainer?component=daViewFunction&breadcrumbPath=Home/Access%20the%20Collection/Browse%20The%20Collection/Function%20Details&entityId=169#>.

[43] Hanlon, above n 9, 73–74, 86–87, 91, 96, 99.

[44] *Constitution Act 1855 (New South Wales)* (Imp); *Constitution Act 1855 (Victoria)* (Imp); *Constitution Act 1855* (Tas); H Golder, *Politics, Patronage and Public Works: The Administration of New South Wales*, vol 1: *1842–1900* (UNSW Press, 2005) 108; JM Bennett, *A History of the New South Wales Bar* (Law Book Company Ltd, 1969) 72.

was no longer solely responsible for the government of the colony and had to act on the advice of his elected ministers. In each colony the Law Officers formed part of the Executive Council, the core group of ministers that advised the Governor on the exercise of his power.

In New South Wales the Law Officers were named amongst the five permanent heads of departments who made up the Executive Council.[45] The Solicitor-General shared departmental responsibility with the Attorney-General.[46] While it may appear strange that a small colonial government would need two Law Officers in the Executive Council, this reflected its colonial past, largely defined by legal and convict business.[47] In Victoria the Solicitor-General also joined the Executive Council,[48] although sometimes the Solicitor-General would also be appointed Minister of Justice, or the portfolios would appear in the alternative.[49]

For the first time under these constitutions, the Law Officers were, as in Britain, made responsible and accountable to the Parliament for the exercise of their functions.[50] However, responsible government also saw the introduction of collective accountability, and the inclusion of the Law Officers in the Executive Council brought different challenges to bear on the officeholders' independence.[51] Three episodes from Victoria during this period highlight the tensions between the Law Officers' loyalty to the political Executive as members of the Executive Council on the one hand, and their legal and public interest obligations on the other.

In 1864, the Legislative Council questioned the independence of advice provided by George Higinbotham (the Victorian Attorney-General) and Archibald Michie (the Solicitor-General) that the tacking of a tariff reform Bill onto an appropriation Bill was lawful. Higinbotham had well-known political ambitions and the Legislative Council was wary of the objectivity of the advice.[52] When the Council refused to pass the government's supply Bills, the Law Officers advised the Governor that an arrangement entered into with the London Chartered Bank to obtain money without appropriation from the legislature was legal.[53] When the matter finally came to a head, the Governor refused to accept advice from the English Law Officers, claiming he must accept the opinions of his local Law Officers.[54]

[45] Kass, above n 12, 9.

[46] Golder, above n 44, 121.

[47] A McMartin, *Public Servants and Patronage: The Foundations and Rise of the New South Wales Public Service 1786–1859* (Sydney University Press, 1983) 267.

[48] Sweetman, above n 41, 81, 83.

[49] J Smith, *The Cyclopedia of Victoria: An Historical and Commercial Review: Descriptive and Biographical, Facts, Figures and Illustrations: An Epitome of Progress* (The Cyclopedia Co, 1903) 205.

[50] In the British context, see discussion in ch 2.

[51] Hanlon, above n 9, 91, 127.

[52] C Parkinson, 'George Higinbotham and Responsible Government in Colonial Victoria' (2001) 25 *Melbourne Univesrity Law Review* 181, 187.

[53] ibid, 201.

[54] ibid, 204.

In 1878 the Governor sought advice from the English Law Officers after receiving conflicting advice from his colonial Law Officers over whether approval of the Legislative Council was required in relation to Bills of supply.[55] In a statement that is clearly based on a British assumption that Law Officers operated with a large degree of independence, the Colonial Secretary said that in such cases, the Governor should request the advice of the Law Officers in their capacity as 'the authorised exponents to the law' and not as political advisers.[56] In a debate in the House of Lords over the issue, Lord Carnarvon asserted that in the circumstances he would have preferred for the appointment of 'one permanent and impartial legal advisor, who might be in a position to advise a colonial Governor as emergencies arose'.[57] This suggestion was strongly refuted by Higinbotham as contrary to British tradition, as being 'illegal' and 'absurd'.[58]

Independence from the Cabinet in the exercise of the Law Officers' prosecutorial function emerged as an issue in Victoria in 1893. The Solicitor-General, Isaac Isaacs, was directed by the Attorney-General to drop certain charges that he had brought in a high-profile prosecution. Isaacs refused and ultimately resigned, ostensibly to protect his independence.[59] Isaacs argued that the prosecutorial function of the Solicitor-General had to be exercised independently of the Cabinet, and even of the Attorney-General.

In Queensland, there was no tradition of a Solicitor-General appointed to the Legislative Council. The position was created for only a short period in 1890 due to Premier and Attorney-General Samuel Griffith's immense involvement in the federation movement and the need for him to be relieved of many of the day-to-day obligations of the office of Attorney-General.[60] On his appointment, Solicitor-General Thomas Byrnes was also appointed to the Legislative Council,[61] and retained his right to private practice.[62] Indicating that the position was seen as necessary only for the exigency created by Griffith's workload (rather than broader constitutional need), after Byrnes' elevation to the office of Attorney-General in March 1893 the position disappeared until it was recreated as a public service position in 1922.

[55] Todd, above n 28, 725–26.

[56] ibid, 726–27, see also HV Evatt, *The King and His Dominion Governors: A Study of the Reserve Powers of the Crown in Great Britain and the Dominions* (Frank Cass & Co Ltd, 2nd edn, 1967) 189–90.

[57] Extracted in Evatt, above n 56, 190.

[58] ibid, 190.

[59] Edwards, *The Attorney-General*, above n 1, 374–75; Although it has been surmised that it was also caused by personal machinations between Isaacs and the Attorney-General over priority between them as ministers: Hanlon, above n 9, 93–94.

[60] Crown Law, above n 1, 29. There had been earlier requests for a Solicitor-General to relieve the Crown Solicitor and Attorney-General of work: ibid, 25, 27; Queensland, *Parliamentary Debates*, Legislative Assembly, 19 March 1985, 4096 (NJ Harper, Minister for Justice and Attorney-General).

[61] Crown Law, above n 1, 29.

[62] ibid, 30.

D. Debate Over the Law Officers in Cabinet

The inclusion of the Law Officers in the Executive Council (essentially the precursor to the Cabinet) under a system of responsible government was a major break with British tradition, and likely contributed to increased politicisation of the Australian Law Officers when compared to the position in England. The move was the result of several factors. The colonial practice of including the Law Officers in the Executive Council (before this body wielded any power beyond advising the Governor) set a precedent from which it was difficult to resile. The colonies had also never had an office akin to the Lord Chancellor (who, in Britain, sat in Cabinet and performed legislative, executive and judicial roles), and many of that office's obligations were met by the colonial Law Officers.[63] The inclusion of the Law Officers in the Executive Council did not occur without debate in these early years.

In New South Wales the inclusion of the Law Officers in the Executive Council was particularly controversial in relation to the officeholders' exercise of the prosecutorial function, which led to the drafting of legislation for an independent public prosecutor (although this was never passed).[64] At times during the 1850s and 1860s the New South Wales Attorney-General was not included in the Executive Council, owing to concerns that the officeholder could not properly perform the public interest functions of the office if the role was perceived to be too political.[65] In 1859 the New South Wales Law Officers were relieved of administrative duties in an attempt to remove the incompatibility of these functions with their position as legal advisers, although the strength of vested interests saw the Attorney-General retained in the Executive Council 'for the present'.[66]

In 1873 substantial reform was achieved, albeit fleetingly, when the Attorney-General became a non-Executive Council Minister presiding over the newly created Department of Justice and Public Instruction. The role of Solicitor-General was abolished for a period during this time.[67] The change took place for a number of reasons. Foremost was an attempt to improve efficiency in the colonial administration by removing the necessity of having *two* Law Officers in a ministry that was only composed of between six and eight departments.[68] Another reason was the desire to increase the independence of the Law Officers in advising and prosecuting by bringing the nature of the roles closer to that in England, where they

[63] Mason, 'Aspects of the History of the Solicitor-General in Australia', above n 1, 23.
[64] Golder, above n 44, 121.
[65] Kass, above n 12, 10, referring to P Loveday and AW Martin, *Parliament Factions and Parties: The First Thirty Years of Responsible Government in New South Wales 1856–1889* (Melbourne University Press, 1966) 116.
[66] Golder, above n 44, 133; McMartin, above n 47, 273.
[67] Golder, above n 44, 186.
[68] 'Legislative Assembly: Thursday 27 November 1873', *Sydney Morning Herald* (Sydney) 28 November 1873, available at 2 <http://nla.gov.au/nla.news-article13327384>.

were less overtly political and did not sit as members of Cabinet.[69] In the course of this debate an alternative proposal to have one of the Law Officers appointed outside Parliament was rejected on the same basis that Edwards dismissed it in the 1980s:[70] that the responsibility of the Law Officers to Parliament was a fundamental principle of the operation of British parliamentary government.[71] The 1873 reforms to the Attorney-General's role were short-lived; by 1878 the Attorney-General had returned to the Executive Council.[72]

In the 1850s, the Province of South Australia was debating whether to require both Law Officers to sit in the Executive Council under its new Constitution Bill. Justice Benjamin Boothby was strongly against the move, and warned that the early colonial practice must not be allowed to continue under responsible government:

> The Crown cannot be compelled to seek legal advice from law officers who, after the advice is given, have the power, it may be, by a casting vote to compel that advice to be adopted ... Such a position would unfit the Law Officers of the Crown for the impartial consideration of questions necessarily requiring their decision, and so lessen their power of efficient service to the Crown.[73]

Boothby's warnings drew heavily upon the ideal of having Law Officers within government but aloof from politics: someone who has, as Boothby said, the ability to conduct 'impartial consideration of questions'. It is this ideal that characterised much of the development of the British tradition of the Law Officers, and which would be the driver for continuing reform of the office in Australia into the twentieth century. Ultimately, under the South Australian *Constitution Act 1856* the Attorney-General was included in the Executive Council but the Solicitor-General was not, and the latter was disqualified from sitting in Parliament.[74] This was on the basis of a prohibition on MPs accepting any office of profit from the Crown, during pleasure, excepting those listed.[75] From 1 August to 1 September 1857 John Tuthill Bagot briefly held a ministerial office of Solicitor-General.[76] This appointment, however, was successfully challenged by Richard Hanson on the basis that it was in breach of the prohibition in the *Constitution Act*.[77]

[69] ibid.

[70] Edwards, *The Attorney-General*, above n 1, 66–7. See further discussion of Edwards' critique in Chapter 2.

[71] 'Legislative Assembly: Thursday 27 November 1873', *Sydney Morning Herald* (Sydney) 28 November 1873, available at 2 <http://nla.gov.au/nla.news-article13327384>.

[72] Golder, above n 44, 186.

[73] Benjamin Boothby, 'Memorandum' (1862) 37 *House of Commons Papers*, extracted in Edwards, *The Law Officers*, above n 3, 167–8.

[74] *Constitution Act 1856* (SA), ss 17, 32, 34.

[75] ibid, ss 32; 34; 17 (office of profit under the Crown).

[76] 'The State's First Parliament: A Dip into History', *The Advertiser* (Adelaide) (20 April 1917), 9, available at <http://newspapers.nla.gov.au/ndp/del/article/5579748>.

[77] ibid; 'South Australian Parliament: Legislative Council, Tuesday, April 30', *The South Australian Advertiser* (Adelaide) (1 May 1861), 2, available at <http://newspapers.nla.gov.au/ndp/del/article/24479756>; 'The Parliament: Legislative Council, July 2', *The Advertiser* (Adelaide) (3 July 1889), 6,

E. The Law Officers and an Integrated Government Legal Service

In a further break with British tradition, the move to responsible government also saw the centralisation of legal services in the colonial Law Officers' departments.[78] This was the continuation of a trend that had started when the administration of legal services was a relatively small task overseen by the Law Officers personally. The Law Officers' departments eventually became responsible for providing legal services across the whole of the colonial governments, with relatively few exceptions. Bradley Selway asserts there were probably a number of reasons for this: 'governments were smaller [in the colonies than in England] and centralisation was easier', 'colonial Attorneys-General were adequately paid' and 'usually had the support of competent professional lawyers in the Solicitor-General … and Crown Solicitor'.[79]

The first century of the office of the Solicitor-General in Australia was one heavily influenced by the English model, but colonial administrations struggled to adapt its conventions to the colonial circumstances and the personalities of the appointees. When responsible government was introduced to the colonies, those that had Solicitors-General retained the office in the ministry, as was the convention in Britain, at least initially. However, one major change between the Australian and British practice, evident even at this stage in the colonial history, was the increased politicisation of the Australian Law Officers and particularly the Attorney-General. This would be the impetus for the increased depoliticisation of the office of the Solicitor-General in the late nineteenth and early twentieth centuries.

II. The 'Public Service Period'

The depoliticisation of the Australian Solicitor-General and the creation of a public service office was a major break with the British tradition of the Law Officers. This movement pre-dated Lord Shawcross's call for a similar model in Britain by over a century.[80] As is often the case with constitutional transitions, the

available at <http://newspapers.nla.gov.au/ndp/del/article/24479756>. See also BT Finniss, *The Constitutional History of South Australia: During 21 Years from the Foundation of the Settlement in 1836 to the Inauguration of Responsible Government in 1857* (RVC Rigby, 1886) 470; RM Hague, *Hague's History of the Law in South Australia 1837–1867* (University of Adelaide Barr Smith Press, 2005, first submitted 1936) 721.

[78] For an overview of the English position, see Edwards, *The Attorney-General*, above n 1, ch 7.

[79] B Selway, 'The Different Role of an Australian Attorney-General' (2002) 13 *Public Law Review* 263, 266–67.

[80] See further discussion of Shawcross's proposal in ch 2, section II.D.i.

change was predominantly made to meet the exigencies of a particular situation (namely, to reduce government expenditure) rather than resting on high constitutional principle. But it led to significant, widespread and enduring change. This trend started in Tasmania in the 1860s. It was adopted in Western Australia in 1902.[81] The Commonwealth introduced a similar office in 1916, and New South Wales and Queensland in 1922. While the public service basis for the position was broadly consistent across these jurisdictions, some Solicitors-General performed more administrative functions within the department than others.

A. Tasmania Breaks with British Tradition

In the 1860s the Tasmanian office was the first in Australia to become non-political on a permanent basis.[82] After 1855 there had been occasions where there was no Solicitor-General in the Tasmanian ministry.[83] In 1857, for example, TJ Knight was appointed Solicitor-General and, in accordance with convention, resigned his seat but failed to get re-elected, yet he continued to serve as Solicitor-General from outside Parliament. It was not until 1863 that the 'firm decision' was made to remove the Solicitor-General from a ministerial *and* political post.[84] The development appears to have been advanced at the time as a cost-cutting measure.[85]

The Attorney-General continued the duties of first Law Officer, assisted now by a public service-appointed Solicitor-General. Gradually, the legal duties of the Attorney-General declined, and he became, predominantly, the political and administrative head of the department, although he continued to appear as counsel for Tasmania on occasion in high-profile matters.[86] There was a concomitant rise in the legal duties of the Solicitor-General.[87] These developments, together with

[81] JS Battye, *The Cyclopedia of Western Australia: An Historical and Commercial Review: Descriptive and Biographical Facts, Figures and Illustrations: An Epitome of Progress* (The Cyclopedia Company, 1912) 479. See also 'The Public Service: Classification of Professional Division: The Commissioner's Proposals', *The West Australian* (Perth) 14 September 1907, 5.

[82] RL Wettenhall, *A Guide to Tasmanian Government Administration* (Platypus Publications, 1968) 94; *The Cyclopedia of Tasmania*, above n 23, 61; BE Briggs and CK Murphy, 'Presidents—Speakers—Ministers—Members—Officers' in FC Green (ed), *A Century of Responsible Government 1856–1956* (LG Shea, Government Printer, 1956) 277, 301. Tasmania also led the way for the colony of New Zealand, which experimented with a non-political Attorney-General in 1866, but it was not until 1873 that a non-political Solicitor-General was appointed: J McGrath, 'Principles for Sharing Law Officer Power—The Role of the New Zealand Solicitor-General' (1998) 18 *New Zealand Universities Law Review* 195, 199.

[83] J Fenton, *A History of Tasmania* (Walch & Sons, 1884) 310.

[84] Wettenhall, above n 82; 'Political Changes', *The Mercury* (Hobart), 12 January 1864, 2.

[85] Royal Commission to Inquiry into the Accounts, and the Departments of Government, Southern Side, *Report of the Royal Commission* (Hobart, Government Printer of Tasmania, 1963) 27.

[86] See, eg, *D'Emden v Pedder* (1904) 1 CLR 91, Attorney-General Herbert Nicholls appeared with Solicitor-General Edward Dobbie for Pedder against the Commonwealth Deputy Postmaster-General.

[87] Letter to Editor from NE Lewis, *The Mercury*, 12 December 1905, extracted in full in Royal Commission on the Proposal to Make the Office of Attorney-General Permanent Non-Political, *Report of the Commission* (Hobart, John Vale, Government Printer of Tasmania, 1908) 39.

the centralisation of legal services in the Attorney-General's department meant the Solicitor-General became 'the core of legal administration' in the colony.[88] The office conducted all civil and criminal litigation for the Crown,[89] performing from 1887 the role of Crown Prosecutor.[90] In Tasmania, where there was a fused profession, the Solicitor-General would often appear in a single case as both counsel and instructing solicitor.[91] This continued even after 1983, when Tasmania adopted the modern statutory model and the Solicitor-General was designated 'counsel' for the Crown.[92]

The advantages of the new model for the Solicitor-General were described as bringing continuity of practice and knowledge of government to the role.[93] Depoliticisation meant that the office of Solicitor-General was no longer a stepping-stone to the office of Attorney-General but a professionally focused position.[94]

B. A Commonwealth Office

By Federation, two models for the Solicitor-General had emerged in the colonies: a ministerial officeholder who assisted as a political deputy to the Attorney-General; and a public servant who conducted the majority of legal business to assist an increasingly politicised Attorney-General.

Despite the historical pedigree of the office, a Solicitor-General for the new Commonwealth was not publicly discussed during the constitutional conventions of the 1890s. The framers were aware of the need of the different polities to have authoritative legal advice to ensure the smooth operation of the new federal system. The important role of the Attorney-General in providing legal advice on constitutional questions was referred to on several occasions.[95] The framers also

[88] Wettenhall, above n 82.

[89] *The Cyclopedia of Tasmania*, above n 21, 129.

[90] ibid.

[91] See, eg, *D'Emden v Pedder* (1904) 1 CLR 91, when Solicitor-General Edward Dobbie juniored the Attorney-General, instructed by the Tasmanian Crown Solicitor; *Enever v The King* (1906) 3 CLR 969, when Dobbie appeared both as counsel for the Crown (Tas) and as the instructing solicitor.

[92] During his tenure, William Bale would either act as both counsel and instructing solicitor in a single case under the title Solicitor-General, or, at other times, held joint appointments as Solicitor-General and Crown Solicitor. See, eg, in *Bath v Alston Holdings* (1988) 165 CLR 411; *McGinty v Western Australia* (1996) 186 CLR 140.

[93] Royal Commission, above n 87, 7.

[94] After the adoption of a public service model and into the 'Modern Period', the Solicitor-General was never elevated to the position of Attorney-General directly. Robert Ellicott, former Commonwealth Solicitor-General, was appointed Attorney-General, but this was after he had resigned from office in 1973 and won a seat in the House of Representatives as a member of the then Opposition led by Malcolm Fraser in 1974. When the Opposition came to power in 1975, he was appointed Attorney-General.

[95] See, eg, *Official Record of the Debates of the Australasian Federal Convention*, Sydney, 7 April 1891, 858 (John Cuthbert); *Official Record of the Debates of the Australasian Federal Convention*, Third Session, Melbourne, 8 March 1898, 2008 (Joseph Carruthers); *Official Record of the Debates of the Australasian Federal Convention*, Third Session, Melbourne, 9 March 1898, 2094 (George Reid).

considered the prospect of obtaining advisory opinions from the High Court. The majority of the delegates, however, were wary of an amendment to implement such a measure, fearful that, inter alia, it would compromise the Judiciary and draw it into the political arena.[96]

Why, if the framers were aware of the practical need for a definitive, non-political legal adviser (particularly on constitutional questions), was there no discussion of the role of a Commonwealth Solicitor-General? The likely explanation is two-fold. First, it may have been anticipated that the legal work of the new Government would not be so large as to require the assistance of a second Law Officer. Secondly, the idea that the Attorney-General would continue to operate as an impartial and properly qualified legal adviser was probably still accepted by many of the framers. While this did not reflect the growing trend in the colonies towards an increasingly political Attorney-General, it followed the British tradition of the Law Officers.

After Federation, both of these assumptions proved untrue. The first Attorney-General, Alfred Deakin, appointed Robert Garran as Secretary of his Department.[97] Included in the Department's responsibilities was drafting legislation,[98] advising the Government on legal and constitutional issues and conducting litigation on behalf of the Government.[99] Garran described his functions 'as those of the Chief Permanent Law Officer of the Commonwealth', although he noted he lacked such a title.[100] The position Garran filled was akin to that of the Tasmanian public service-style Solicitor-General. As the Commonwealth grew, so did the work of the Attorney-General's Department, which followed the colonial model of providing legal services across the whole of government. This largely devolved onto Garran, although he rarely appeared as counsel.[101] Instead, Commonwealth appearance work was briefed out to the private Bar[102] or, with increasingly less frequency, the Commonwealth Attorney-General would appear in major cases.[103]

[96] For a historical account of the attempts to include a mechanism that would allow advisory opinions, see H Irving, 'Advisory Opinions, The Rule of Law and the Separation of Powers' (2004) 4 *Macquarie Law Journal* 105; JM Williams, 'Advisory Opinions: "A well-covered harbour"' (2010) 22(3) *Bond Law Review* 169.

[97] RR Garran, *Prosper the Commonwealth* (Angus and Robertson, 1958) 143.

[98] ibid, 143–45.

[99] ibid, 151.

[100] Letter from Robert Garran to CW Harriott, Secretary of the New South Wales Council of the Bar, 5 March 1915, in National Library of Australia, *Family Papers of Sir Robert Garran* (1860–1957).

[101] Exceptions being *Roche v Kronheimer* (1921) 29 CLR 329; *Ex parte Walsh and Johnson; In re Yates* (1925) 37 CLR 36.

[102] In particular, Commonwealth interests were regularly protected by leading counsel of the period, including PD Phillips, EM Mitchell, CI Menhennitt, R Else-Mitchell, W Ham, JD Holmes, EG Coppel, B Macfarlan, AR Taylor, WJV Windeyer, T Bavin, WK Fullaghar, HE Starke, O Dixon, Weston, Dr Cullen, DI Menzies, A Knox, J Latham, AF Mason, JR Kerr, F Gavan Duffy, FW Kitto and KA Aickin. Many of these counsel went on to be appointed to the High Court, or to other superior courts in the State jurisdictions.

[103] See, eg, *D'Emden v Pedder* (1904) 1 CLR 91; *Municipal Council of Sydney v Commonwealth* (1904) 1 CLR 208; *Deakin v Webb* (1904) 1 CLR 585; *Federated Amalgamated Govt Railway and Tramway Service Assoc v NSW Railway Traffic Employes Assoc* (1906) 4 CLR 488; *Baxter v Commissioner of Taxation (NSW)* (1907) 4 CLR 1087; *New South Wales v Commonwealth* (1908) 7 CLR 179

In 1910, William Harrison Moore commented:

> It must be remembered that in Australia, unlike England, the Attorney-General is a member of the Cabinet, so that the office may be filled by reference to political rather than professional qualifications. It is, therefore, the more important that there should be a permanent official of high legal qualification, a necessity which has been recognised in some of the colonies by the appointment of a Solicitor-General as a non-political and permanent officer.[104]

In 1916, during World War I, William (Billy) Hughes, the Prime Minister and also Attorney-General, introduced the Solicitor-General Bill, which contained skeletal provision for a public service office.[105] The purpose of the new office was to provide Hughes with additional support and assistance during the War.[106] Garran was appointed immediately to the position, although he continued in his position as permanent head of the Attorney-General's Department. On its face, little appeared to change. Indeed, it was questioned at the Bill's introduction why the new title was required at all.[107] The major change, according to Hughes, was the ability for the Attorney-General to delegate powers under a wide range of legislation.[108] It is unclear why it would not have been possible to delegate powers to Garran as the Secretary of the Department. While it was more traditional for the Attorney-General to delegate the office's function to the Solicitor-General, it is not constitutionally mandated.

The passage of the Solicitor-General Bill in 1916 engaged Parliament in debate about the accountability of a non-political Solicitor-General. In introducing the legislation, Hughes briefly explained how the new office was intended to operate accountably despite the change from British practice:

> The Minister will declare the policy of the Government in every case, and the Solicitor-General will give effect to it. Thus Ministerial discretion will remain, and Ministerial responsibility will not be lessened. The Government will be as much responsible for every act done by the Solicitor-General as if it had been done by the Attorney-General …[109]

('*Surplus Revenue Case*'); *James v Commonwealth* (1936) 55 CLR 1 (PC); *Bank of New South Wales v Commonwealth* (1948) 76 CLR 1 ('*State Banking Case*'); *Dennis Hotels v Victoria* (1961) 104 CLR 621 (PC); *Airlines of New South Wales v New South Wales (No 2)* (1965) 113 CLR 54 ('*Second Airlines Case*'); *Kotsis v Kotsis* (1970) 122 CLR 69; *Strickland v Rocla Concrete* (1971) 124 CLR 468 ('*Concrete Pipes Case*'); *Bonser v La Macchia* (1969) 122 CLR 177; *Gould v Brown* (1998) 193 CLR 346; *Re Patterson; Ex parte Taylor* (2001) 207 CLR 391. No Commonwealth Attorney-General has appeared since 2001.

104 WH Moore, *The Constitution of the Commonwealth of Australia* (Legal Books, 1910, 2nd edn, 1997 reprint) 179–80.

105 National Archives of Australia, Canberra, A 2863 1916/28.

106 Commonwealth, *Parliamentary Debates*, House of Representatives, 27 September 1916, 8996 (William Hughes, Prime Minister and Attorney-General).

107 ibid, 8998 (James Page, Labor).

108 ibid, 8998 (Hughes); Commonwealth, *Parliamentary Debates*, Senate, 28 September 1916, 9043 (Albert Gardiner, Labor, Vice President of Executive Council). The delegation was included in the Solicitor-General Bill 1916, cl 3.

109 Commonwealth, *Parliamentary Debates*, House of Representatives, 27 September 1916, 8998 (Hughes). See also 8998 (Littleton Groom, Commonwealth Liberal Party) and the debate in the

The debate over ensuring the accountability of a non-ministerial Solicitor-General would continue across the Australian jurisdictions until the 1980s. The point had been used in 1873 to reject a similar move in New South Wales. In Britain, the argument was still persuasive when the Government decided against reforms to the office in 2008 (see chapter two, section II.D.iii.).

C. Other Jurisdictions Move to the Public Service Model

With the exception of Victoria, the other jurisdictions followed Tasmania's move towards a public service Solicitor-General position. In New South Wales the move to a public service model was incremental. After the office of Solicitor-General was abolished in 1873,[110] an 1891 Public Service Inquiry Commission found that the Attorney-General's ability to meet his responsibilities as a Law Officer and political minister had been seriously affected by the removal of the junior Law Officer.[111] The Commission recommended the reintroduction of the office (or the introduction of an equivalent office).[112] It reappeared as a ministerial appointment for brief periods in the 1890s, although these correlate with the absence of the Attorney-General from the jurisdiction rather than as a response to the Commission.[113] The office of Solicitor-General reappeared permanently in 1900. During its period in abeyance, the office was substantially depoliticised.[114] In 1884 it was removed from the responsible ministry.[115] Despite this change, the office was held by both political (in the form of a non-remunerated appointment or an upper-house appointment to avoid the prohibition on a member of the Legislative Assembly's holding an 'office of profit under the Crown') and non-political appointees during the early twentieth century.[116]

Senate: Commonwealth, *Parliamentary Debates*, Senate, 28 September 1916, 9043 (Robert Guthrie, Labor, James Stewart, Labor). See also Garran, above n 97, 221–22.

110 Kass, above n 12, 13.

111 'Report on the Attorney-General's Department' (Public Service Inquiry Commission, 1891) 2–3.

112 ibid, 3.

113 For example, R O'Connor (MLC) was appointed Solicitor-General for a short duration between July and September 1893 to deputise for Attorney-General Edmund Barton who was overseas in Canada: 'The Solicitor-General', *Sydney Morning Herald* (Sydney) (19 July 1893), 4, available at <http://nla.gov.au/nla.news-article13918822>; 'Ministerial Movements', *Sydney Morning Herald* (Sydney) (13 September 1893), 6, available at <http://nla.gov.au/nla.news-article13928783>. During his premiership in the 1890s, George Reid also held the office for brief periods for the same reason. See, eg, New South Wales, *Parliamentary Debates*, Session 1894–5 Volume 75, First Series, 12 December 1894–14 March 1895, 26 February 1895, 3912 (George Reid, Premier).

114 Bennett, above n 44, 72, fn 168.

115 The office was removed as an exception to the disqualification of persons eligible to sit in the House of Assembly on the basis of holding an 'office of profit under the Crown': *Constitution Act 1855* (NSW), s 18 amended by *Constitution Act Amendment Act 1884* (NSW). Sexton, above n 25, 88.

116 Mason, 'The Office of Solicitor General for New South Wales', above n 1, 25.

In 1922 New South Wales permanently adopted a public service model, and the officeholder, Cecil Weigall, performed both administrative and legal functions within the Crown Law Department.[117] In 1953, for the first time, the New South Wales government appointed a well-known Queen's Counsel, Harold Snelling, as Solicitor-General. During Snelling's tenure, the office evolved into a non-political and a non-departmental position. He acted predominantly as counsel and did not have large administrative responsibilities, which devolved instead to the Crown Solicitor.[118] Snelling appeared regularly as counsel in the High Court, although in criminal, property and taxation matters initially.[119] It was only in the late 1960s, when other jurisdictions had moved towards the statutory counsel model of Solicitor-General, that he started to appear regularly in constitutional matters alongside the other Solicitors-General.[120]

In Western Australia, the Solicitor-General emerged for the first time as a public service appointment in 1902 with the appointment of William Sayer.[121] Office-holders tended to serve for long periods, and engaged in administrative duties rather than acting as counsel for Western Australia.[122] During this period, the Solicitor-General did not appear in the High Court to represent Western Australia. Rather, demonstrating the nature of the fused profession in Western Australia, it was the Crown Solicitor who often appeared as instructing solicitor and counsel.[123] The office was abolished when Sayer's appointment finished in 1930, and James Walker was appointed Crown Solicitor.[124] Five years later, in 1935, Walker was appointed to the office of Solicitor-General. The position continued as a public service one until the introduction of the statute to establish a changed form of the office in 1969.

[117] K Mason, 'Weigall, Cecil Edward (1870–1955)' in *Australian Dictionary of Biography*, vol 12 (Melbourne University Press, 1990).

[118] Mason, 'The Office of Solicitor General', above n 1, 25.

[119] See, eg, *Basto v The Queen* (1954) 91 CLR 628; *Australian Provincial Assurance v Roddy* (1956) 95 CLR 478; *Le Brocque v Mason* (1956) 96 CLR 213; *Davis v Commr of Stamp Duties (NSW)* (1958) 100 CLR 392. Weigall, Solicitor-General from 1922 to 1953, had appeared less frequently as counsel for the State, predominantly in criminal matters: see, eg, *Eade v The King* (1924) 34 CLR 154; *Dawson v The King* (1927) 40 CLR 206; *Russell v Bates* (1927) 40 CLR 209; *Whittaker v The King* (1928) 41 CLR 230.

[120] This became regular after *Western Australia v Hammersley Iron Pty Ltd* (1969) 120 CLR 42.

[121] *Wise's Western Australian Directory* (H Wise & Co, 1935–36) 773.

[122] See explanation of the role in A Buti, *Sir Ronald Wilson: A Matter of Conscience* (University of Western Australia Press, 2007) 135, 153.

[123] For example, Dr Stow, Crown Solicitor for Western Australia, often appeared in criminal and tax matters for the State. However, Stow would brief out the important constitutional cases. As Crown Solicitor, JL Walker also appeared for the State as counsel and instructing solicitor. The Crown Solicitor continued to appear regularly for the State as counsel (more often than the Solicitor-General) until the late 1950s. When GJ Ruse was appointed Crown Solicitor, Ronald Wilson, who was Chief Crown Counsel in the Attorney-General's Department, started to appear for Western Australia. In 1969, Wilson was appointed Solicitor-General.

[124] 'Crown Law Officers, Western Australia Appointments', *The Brisbane Courier* (Brisbane) (5 April 1930), 16, available at <http://www.trove.nla.gov.au/ndp/del/article/21505110>.

In Queensland, the Solicitor-General reappeared in 1922 as a non-political public servant within the Crown Law Department.[125] William Flood Webb was appointed Solicitor-General from the position of Crown Solicitor and Secretary of the Attorney-General's Department. As Solicitor-General, Webb started to appear in the High Court for Queensland;[126] however, this was not a trend that continued amongst the public service-appointed Solicitors-General of Queensland.[127] When Webb retired, the Crown Solicitor, HJH Henchman, was not elevated to the position of Solicitor-General. Eventually this occurred in 1937, to give Henchman 'higher status in the courts as representative of the Attorney-General'.[128]

South Australia created a public service office of Solicitor-General in 1969 by simply changing the title of the Crown Solicitor, Andrew Wells, to 'Solicitor-General'.[129] Because of the fused profession in South Australia, prior to this time the Crown Solicitor had often appeared as counsel in important High Court litigation.[130] From the office's establishment, the South Australian Solicitor-General appeared regularly as counsel. In 1970, with a new appointment, Brian Cox, the Solicitor-General was taken outside of Crown Law. The officeholder was still a public servant within the Attorney-General's Department until a statutory basis for the office was introduced in 1972.

In 1978, the year self-government was granted to the Northern Territory, the office of Solicitor-General was also created by the *Law Officers Act 1978* (NT).[131] At that time, it was a public service appointment with the administrative responsibility of a departmental head. The legislation establishing the office was sparse. The Chief Minister, Paul Everingham, said that it was intended that the office would deal with 'more important legal matters', and that the Solicitor-General would be briefed as a barrister.[132]

[125] Crown Law, above n 1, 2, 89.

[126] See, eg, *Public Curator (Qld) v Union Trustee Co of Australia* (1922) 31 CLR 66; *Commr Stamp Duties (Qld) v Lightoller* (1922) 31 CLR 382; *Mount Morgan Gold Mining Co Ltd v Commr Income Tax (Qld)* (1923) 33 CLR 76. See also Crown Law, above n 1.

[127] Webb's public service successors appeared less often in the High Court as counsel for Queensland, and again the Attorney-General would exercise this function on occasion. After the tenure of Neil Macgroarty as Attorney-General in the early 1930s, private counsel were briefed to appear for Queensland until the appointment of the first silk as Solicitor-General in 1989, Geoffrey Davies.

[128] Extract of report from the *Courier Mail* (6 August 1937) in Crown Law, above n 1, 103.

[129] South Australia, *Parliamentary Debates*, House of Assembly, 1 March 1972, 3563 (LJ King, Attorney-General).

[130] From the 1920s, AJ Hannan, the Crown Solicitor, appeared in constitutional cases. When Hannan retired, RR St C Chamberlain was appointed Crown Solicitor, and he often appeared in the High Court as counsel for South Australia. In 1960, on the appointment of a new Crown Solicitor, JR Kearnan, Wells began to appear regularly as primary counsel for South Australia (Kearnan did not appear regularly as counsel, as Hannan and Chamberlain had).

[131] Prior to then, the Northern Territory's legal interests were served by the Commonwealth. See, eg, *McKinnon v The King* (1927) 40 CLR 217; *Tuckiar v The King* (1934) 52 CLR 335; and *Bailey v Kelsey* (1959) 100 CLR 352. The first recorded appearance by the Northern Territory Solicitor-General, Ian Barker, in the High Court was in a criminal matter, *Stephens v The Queen* (1978) 139 CLR 315.

[132] Northern Territory, *Parliamentary Debates*, House of Assembly, 10 May 1978, 948 (Paul Everingham, Chief Minister).

The Tasmanian model of a public service Solicitor-General was influential in many jurisdictions, even into the second half of the twentieth century. It not only offered the advantage of a non-political officer to assist the predominantly political Attorney-General, but it was a relatively cost-effective model. Within the model, however, there was significant variation, with most appointees bearing a heavy administrative burden but some taking on the function of counsel. The counsel function became the fundamental feature of the office during the 'Modern Period', the subject of section III. below.

D. Common Law Powers and Privileges

The adoption of a public service Solicitor-General raised a question about whether the office still exercised the powers and enjoyed the privileges of the office under the common law (or to put it another way, those powers that had been brought across from England).

The Supreme Court of New South Wales confirmed on two occasions that it did. In 1900, the New South Wales Solicitor-General was appointed from the private Bar and held a non-political appointment.[133] He was nonetheless, in accordance with tradition, listed in 1902 next in order of precedence to the Attorney-General in the Bar listing. The Council of the Bar was firmly against such a characterisation, believing that the Solicitor-General did not hold 'the office of Solicitor-General as known to the Constitution; that is, he is not, though called Solicitor-General in the Commission, entitled by virtue of this Commission to any precedence'.[134] The New South Wales government asked the Supreme Court to consider the question. The Court advised that while the non-political nature of the office was a substantial break with Britain, it still received the privileges conferred on the office, including the right of precedence.[135]

In 1945 the matter was considered again in *Solicitor-General v Wylde*.[136] The case concerned the validity of an information laid by the Solicitor-General against the Bishop of Bathurst. The information alleged that the Bishop had acted illegally by administering the Holy Communion other than as required by the *Book of Common Prayer* of 1662. A preliminary issue arose as to whether the Solicitor-General had the necessary standing to lay the information. It was argued unsuccessfully that the Solicitor-General was 'in a radically different position', not comparable to his British counterpart, because the position was only that of a civil servant, and not the agent of the King in the same sense as in Britain.[137] Jordan CJ (with whom

[133] PJ Tyler, *Humble and Obedient Servants: The Administration of New South Wales* (University of New South Wales Press, 2006) 17.

[134] Resolution of the Council of the Bar, extracted in Bennett, above n 44, 147.

[135] Decision extracted, ibid, 147.

[136] *Solicitor-General v Wylde* (1945) 46 SR (NSW) 83.

[137] ibid, 85–86.

Halse Rogers J agreed) said that the change in New South Wales from a responsible minister to a member of the Bar had not removed the Solicitor-General's common law powers and prerogatives.[138] Nicholas CJ (in equity) wrote a strong dissent. He echoed the concerns raised at the introduction of the 1916 Commonwealth legislation,[139] relying heavily upon the ability in Britain to bring the office to account for its decisions and actions before Parliament: 'it is because he is in Parliament that there is a safeguard against the abuse of his power'.[140]

III. The 'Modern Period'

In 1951, Victoria was the last State to remove its Solicitor-General from the ministry.[141] In the years before the move, the Victorian office had often been simultaneously held by the Attorney-General.[142] From 1900 both Law Officers were generally politically qualified and no longer engaged in the day-to-day provision of legal advice and representation, relying instead on their officers in the Law Department.[143] The 1951 legislation created a new office with two functions: representative of, and chief legal adviser to, the Crown. While the Victorian Attorney-General said that the move brought the State into line with the other jurisdictions in Australia, it was actually an innovative step.[144] Other jurisdictions had depoliticised their offices, but Victoria was the first to create a quasi-independent, statutory counsel position without large administrative duties within the Department.

The statutory framework that Victoria adopted for its Solicitor-General was largely based on a formalisation of the non-statutory office of 'Senior Counsel to the Attorney-General' that was established in January 1950 and filled by Henry Winneke.[145] Winneke had a large influence over the features of the legislation, including the requirement to appoint from King's Counsel and to remunerate the appointee appropriately so to compensate him for loss of income at the Bar. Winneke insisted that the office be outside the public service:

> One thing I would insist on, though, is that it should not be a Public Service appointment. He might be required to report on senior officers, including, say, members of the Public Service Board. That would be an embarrassment if he were a public servant himself.[146]

[138] ibid, 93; relying on *Attorney-General v Belson* (1867) 4 WW & a'B (E) 57, 62 (Molesworth J); [1867] VR 57, 62–63; and *Solicitor-General v Dunedin* (1875) 1 NZ Jur R N S 1, 15.

[139] *Solicitor-General v Wylde* (1945) 46 SR (NSW) 83, 108.

[140] ibid, 108.

[141] *Solicitor-General Act 1951* (Vic).

[142] A Dean, *A Multitude of Counsellors: A History of the Bar of Victoria* (FW Cheshire, 1968) 268; Victoria, *Parliamentary Debates*, Legislative Assembly, 27 November 1951, 219 (John Cain, Premier).

[143] Dean, above n 142, 269.

[144] Victoria, *Parliamentary Debates*, Legislative Assembly, 31 October 1951, 5682 (Thomas Mitchell, Attorney-General).

[145] R Coleman, *Above Renown: Biography of Sir Henry Winneke* (Macmillan Company, 1988) 160–62.

[146] ibid, 160.

With only minor changes, the position established in 1951 continues in Victoria to this day.[147] The Victorian paradigm was the main template for the fundamental shift at the Commonwealth level from a public service appointment to the independent counsel model introduced by the *Law Officers Act 1964* (Cth). It also drove change in the other States and the Northern Territory between the 1960s and 1980s.[148] While Victoria had lagged behind in removing the Solicitor-General from the rough and tumble of party politics in the ministry, it was pioneering in adopting the paradigm of a permanent statutory office of Solicitor-General appointed outside of politics and the public service, and relieved from large administrative burdens. The new model recognised the desirability of having a legally qualified officer with some statutory guarantees of tenure, status and remuneration. While not removing the constitutional and statutory links of accountability between the office and the responsible minister (the Attorney-General) it did go some way towards providing formal guarantees of independence from arbitrary interference by the government of the day.

A. The Rise of a Constitutional Specialist

It was not until the 1960s that Solicitors-General started to emerge as leaders of the constitutional Bar, developing in the 1970s and 1980s the stranglehold on this work that now defines the contemporary office. In many of the States the Solicitor-General, in accordance with the traditional Law Officers' responsibilities, also had responsibility for the prosecution of the criminal law until the creation of the Director of Public Prosecution (DPP) in the 1980s and 1990s.[149] For many Solicitors-General, this consumed a large amount of their time, and was often the most contentious work they did. As a throwback to this era, under the Tasmanian statute, whenever a vacancy occurred in the office of the DPP, the Solicitor-General performed that office's functions.[150] After an extended period of the Solicitor-General's acting in the office during 2013, which then Solicitor-General Leigh Sealy described as 'not ideal',[151] this provision was repealed.[152]

[147] The position in Victoria was updated and consolidated in the *Solicitor-General Act 1958* (Vic) and the *Attorney-General and Solicitor-General Act 1972* (Vic).

[148] See, eg, *Solicitor-General v Wylde* (1945) 46 SR (NSW) 83 (Jordan CJ); New South Wales, *Parliamentary Debates*, Legislative Assembly, 17 September 1969, 969 (Kenneth McCaw, Attorney-General).

[149] *Director of Public Prosecutions Act 1982* (Vic); *Director of Public Prosecutions Act 1984* (Qld); *Director of Public Prosecutions Act 1986* (NSW); *Crown Advocate Amendment Act 1986* (Tas) amended the *Crown Advocate Act 1973* (Tas) to become the *Director of Public Prosecutions Act 1973* (Tas); *Director of Public Prosecutions Act 1990* (NT); *Director of Public Prosecutions Act 1991* (SA); *Director of Public Prosecutions Act 1991* (WA).

[150] *Director of Public Prosecutions Act 1973* (Tas), s 12(3).

[151] See C Wahlquist, 'Proposed changes to fill DPP role', *The Examiner* (16 September 2013), available at <http://www.examiner.com.au/story/1780833/proposed-changes-to-fill-dpp-role/>.

[152] *Director of Public Prosecutions Amendment Act 2013* (Tas).

When the Commonwealth adopted the Victorian paradigm in 1964, with its smaller responsibility in the criminal sphere, the intention was to develop an officer who would bring coherency and expertise in the areas of *constitutional and public law*.[153] The States would also move towards this model. While in the first decades of the High Court Solicitors-General played no great part in the constitutional jurisprudence that would define the Australian system,[154] they have subsequently appeared to defend the interests of their polities in the vast majority of constitutional cases.

B. Balancing Responsibility and Independence

The move towards greater independence for the Solicitor-General did not come without consternation from parliaments across the jurisdictions. This was primarily for the same reasons that questions had been raised in 1916 at the Commonwealth level and in 1873 in New South Wales: it was perceived by many parliamentarians that this move was accompanied by less accountability and responsibility. The Victorian government was keen to emphasise that the Solicitor-General had no continuing political role, becoming subject to direction by the Attorney-General, who remained responsible for all actions taken and decisions made by the Solicitor-General.[155] In New South Wales, much was made of ensuring that the Solicitor-General was not a minister of the Crown,[156] so as to make him 'aloof from matters of policy of a political kind'.[157] But it was also emphasised that the New South Wales Attorney-General would remain responsible to parliament for all decisions of the Solicitor-General,[158] and the decisions of the Solicitor-General would be regarded as those of the Attorney-General.[159] The Attorney-General stated that the Solicitor-General would remain 'always under ministerial control'.[160]

When the position of 'Senior Counsel to the Attorney-General' was originally proposed to Winneke in Victoria, he rejected the argument that security of

[153] Interview, Anthony Mason.

[154] In the first decades of federation, the interests of the States and Commonwealth were represented by private counsel in major constitutional litigation or, on rare occasion, the Attorney-General. The States were less involved in constitutional litigation during this period, and there were fewer interventions in constitutional matters. It was only very occasionally that appearances were noted for the Solicitor-General.

[155] Victoria, *Parliamentary Debates*, Legislative Assembly, 31 October 1951, 5684 (Mitchell); Victoria, *Parliamentary Debates*, Legislative Assembly, 27 November 1951, 223 (Cain).

[156] New South Wales, *Parliamentary Debates*, Legislative Assembly, 17 September 1969, 971 (McCaw).

[157] New South Wales, *Parliamentary Debates*, Legislative Assembly, 1 October 1969, 1478 (McCaw).

[158] ibid, 1480 (McCaw).

[159] ibid, 1481 (McCaw).

[160] New South Wales, *Parliamentary Debates*, Legislative Assembly, 17 September 1969, 969 (McCaw).

tenure would be necessary to protect the officeholder's independence. He was said to have asserted that '[t]he right man would need none, if he became dissatisfied, he could always return to the Bar'.[161]

However, many other jurisdictions included guarantees of tenure in the statute establishing the new office of Solicitor-General. This, and other measures in the new model not seen before in the Solicitor-General's office, were lauded for the independence they would foster. At the introduction of the Law Officers Bill 1964 (Cth), federal Attorney-General Billy Sneddon emphasised the importance of retaining a member of the practising Bar to ensure that the officeholder would continue to enjoy the independence of counsel. This would be reinforced by statutory tenure.[162] The intention of the Act was described later, by Justice William Gummow of the High Court, as being to give 'independence (and thus added value) [to] the office'[163]

In the Northern Territory the Attorney-General asserted that the new Solicitor-General was to be considered 'more akin to a judicial or Ombudsman appointment than that of a departmental head'.[164] Therefore, removal was by the Administrator for enumerated reasons only.[165] This, however, caused some debate. The Opposition wanted a less restricted enumeration of the reasons for which the Solicitor-General could be removed by the Administrator, noting that any abuse of the removal power would be closely monitored by the Northern Territory parliament.[166] The amendment was strongly opposed by the government, who argued that it widened the provision to such a degree that the Administrator could be advised to remove the Solicitor-General on purely political grounds: for example if the government did not like the Solicitor-General or, worse, the advice provided in a particular instance.[167] Attorney-General Marshall Perron, said, 'Political removal can only bring into question the Solicitor General's ability to give advice without fear or favour.'[168]

Emphasis was also placed on the provisions relating to the salary, pension and, in the event of a person's not being reappointed so as to qualify for such a pension, a payment to allow them to re-establish themselves at the private Bar.

[161] Coleman, above n 145, 160.

[162] Commonwealth, *Parliamentary Debates*, House of Representatives, 22 October 1964, 2220 (Billy Sneddon, Attorney-General).

[163] WMC Gummow, 'The 2005 Sir Maurice Byers Lecture: Statutes' (Summer 2005/2006) *Bar News* 30, 30.

[164] Northern Territory, *Parliamentary Debates*, Legislative Assembly, 21 November 1985, 2108 (Marshall Perron, Attorney-General).

[165] Law Officers Amendment Bill 1986 (NT), inserting s 15 into the *Law Officers Act 1978* (NT).

[166] Northern Territory, *Parliamentary Debates*, Legislative Assembly, 20 March 1986, 2324–26 (Brian Ede, Labor). See also similar debates in South Australia: South Australia, *Parliamentary Debates*, House of Assembly, 7 March 1972, 3651–52 (Robin Millhouse, Liberal and Country League, Deputy Leader of the Opposition and King).

[167] Northern Territory, *Parliamentary Debates*, Legislative Assembly, 25 March 1986, 2422-8 (Perron).

[168] ibid (Perron).

These provisions, it was thought, would ensure the best legally qualified candidate could be induced to take the position, and guarantee the independence of the office from political considerations.[169]

In the Solicitor-General Bill 1983 (Tas) there was even greater focus on preserving the independence of the office, and a number of new mechanisms were introduced aimed at protecting the officeholder from undue interference from the Executive.[170] This was said to be in recognition of the fact that the office required not only a person of the requisite legal expertise, but also 'the utmost integrity and independence on the part of the incumbent'.[171] The legislation required a resolution of both Houses of Parliament prior to removal on the grounds of misconduct or incapacity, and required the Solicitor-General to tender an annual report to be tabled in Parliament. The provisions were defended on the basis that they would ensure the independence of the office and set it apart from the administration of the department.[172]

The focus of the parliamentarians on the professional qualifications of the officeholder and the independence from the political branch cemented the change in the nature of the position from politician to professional. Reflecting the changed nature of the office, Solicitors-General are no longer elevated to the political position of Attorney-General, but are more likely to receive judicial appointment.[173]

C. Private Practice in the 'Modern Period'

The 1890s saw the revocation of Australian Solicitors-General's right to engage in private practice. But in some jurisdictions, the right was reintroduced in the

[169] New South Wales, *Parliamentary Debates*, Legislative Assembly, 17 September 1969, 969 (McCaw); Commonwealth, *Parliamentary Debates*, Senate, 30 October 1964, 1493 (Samuel Cohen, Labor). See also Coleman, above n 145, 160. When the provisions relating to salary were originally proposed by Winneke, their objective was to offset the disadvantage he might suffer when approached to suggest names for judicial appointments, and he could 'scarcely' suggest his own: at 165.

[170] Tasmania, *Parliamentary Debates*, House of Assembly, 5 May 1983, 825 (Geoffrey Pearsall, Minister for Tourism).

[171] ibid.

[172] ibid.

[173] This is particularly the case in the States, where judicial appointment from the office occurs often, and is reflected in many of the statutes that count tenure served as Solicitor-General towards an individual's entitlement to the judicial pension. See further discussion in ch 4, section II.C. At the Commonwealth level, only one Solicitor-General in the modern period, Stephen Gageler, has been appointed directly from the office to the federal bench (in Gageler's case, the High Court). Anthony Mason was appointed to the New South Wales Court of Appeal from the office of Solicitor-General, and then elevated to the High Court. Maurice Byers was offered an appointment to the High Court during his tenure as Solicitor-General, but this was withdrawn. Similarly, Robert Ellicott was offered appointment to the High Court in 1979, but this was from his position as Attorney-General. He was appointed to the Federal Court in 1981. See further T Simpson, 'Appointments that might have been' in M Coper, T Blackshield and G Williams (eds), *Oxford Companion to the High Court of Australia* (Oxford University Press, 2001, 2007 online edition).

modern statutes.[174] Under the 1951 Victorian legislation, and in accordance with the practice that had arisen since the 1890s across the colonies, the Solicitor-General was in the exclusive employ of the Crown.[175] This was also the case in the New South Wales statute.[176] In the other jurisdictions, however, when the legislation was introduced it included a provision that enabled the Solicitor-General to engage in private practice with the permission of the Governor or the Attorney-General. This has affected the office in different ways.

In Western Australia and South Australia, when concerns were raised over this arrangement, the governments explained that they did *not* intend to allow the Solicitor-General to engage in extensive private practice but small, discrete private employment, such as at a university.[177] Nonetheless, with the appointment of Grant Donaldson as Western Australian Solicitor-General in 2012, consent was granted for him to retain an ongoing right to limited private practice.[178] In the Northern Territory the provision was included to provide flexibility *should* it be required to attract appropriate candidates to the position.[179]

In contrast, in Queensland the government intended *at the time of the legislation's enactment* (1985) to allow the Solicitor-General to engage in private practice in a manner not seen since the nineteenth century. It was thought 'necessary for senior counsel to be permitted to supplement the income which he receives from his statutory duties in order to attract the most capable counsel'.[180]

[174] Although note in the first decades of federation Attorneys-General continued to engage in private practice. The last Attorney-General to engage in extensive private practice was Robert Menzies. When he was appointed Commonwealth Attorney-General he continued to exercise a right of private practice, but this was not without controversy in the political sphere, and no Attorney-General since has engaged in such practice. See the discussion of the controversy that surrounded Menzies' acceptance of a fee in *James v Commonwealth* (1936) 55 CLR 1 (PC) for appearing for Victoria when he was also appearing for the Commonwealth: Commonwealth, *Parliamentary Debates*, House of Representatives, 31 March 1936, 685–702; Commonwealth, *Parliamentary Debates*, House of Representatives, 30 September 1936, 707–08; Commonwealth, *Parliamentary Debates*, House of Representatives, 1 October 1936, 770–71. See full account in AW Martin, *Robert Menzies: A Life* (Melbourne University Press, 1993) 189–90.

[175] *Solicitor-General Act 1951* (Vic) s 3(b).

[176] *Solicitor-General Act 1969* (NSW) s 2(5)(f), although note this prohibits engagement in *remunerated* private practice only.

[177] Western Australia, *Parliamentary Debates*, Legislative Council, 1 May 1969, 3611 (A F Griffith, Minister for Justice); South Australia, *Parliamentary Debates*, Legislative Council, 14 March 1972, 3796 (Sir Arthur Rymill, Liberal and Country League); South Australia, *Parliamentary Debates*, Legislative Council, 16 March 1972, 3963 (Albert Shard, Chief Secretary and Minister for Health). Similar concerns were raised in other jurisdictions, see Northern Territory, *Parliamentary Debates*, Legislative Assembly, 20 March 1986, 2324-6 (Ede); Northern Territory, *Parliamentary Debates*, Legislative Assembly, 25 March 1986, 2422-8 (Terry Smith, Leader of Opposition, Labor and Dan Leo, Labor).

[178] C Porter, Attorney-General, 'New Solicitor General for Western Australia' (Ministerial Media Statement, 23 February 2012).

[179] Northern Territory, *Parliamentary Debates*, Legislative Assembly, 21 November 1985, 2108 (Perron). Michael Grant had considered taking the appointment in 2007 with a right to private practice, but eventually decided against it: Interview, Michael Grant.

[180] Queensland, *Parliamentary Debates*, Legislative Assembly, 19 March 1985, 4098 (NJ Harper, Attorney-General and Minister for Justice). These were also the reasons provided by the Western Australian Attorney-General in 2012 to provide a limited right to private practice in 2012. See C Porter, Attorney-General, 'New Solicitor General for Western Australia' (Ministerial Media Statement, 23 February 2012).

The right to private practice was opposed in Queensland by the Opposition, who argued that the post should be filled on a full-time basis,[181] as this was required by the breadth and difficulty of modern government work.[182] A further concern was raised: it might compromise the independence of an officeholder who did not wish to lose the favour of the government in case it resulted in the loss of the right to continue to engage in private practice.[183] However, one member asserted that the provision in fact supported the independence of the office because of the increased ease of returning to full-time private practice.[184]

D. Reasons for the Move to the 'Modern Period'

Three reasons for the change in Victoria can be distilled. These strands were largely mirrored in the other jurisdictions in the following decades (with the exception of New South Wales, which is considered separately below).

First, the complexity of legal problems faced by government in both advisory and advocacy settings required a dedicated and enduring counsel position: 'a pilot to guide the ship of State through troublous waters'.[185] As the twentieth century progressed, increased constitutional complexities arising from the federal compact had given rise to a concomitant increase in constitutional litigation. This was coupled with the rise of the interventionist state and the increase in legal work associated with it.[186] By the time Western Australia introduced the Solicitor-General Bill 1969, the Attorney-General noted the need and advantages of engaging an enduring, politically astute but non-political legal counsel for the State.[187] In some jurisdictions, the reasons for adopting the office were less focused on the Solicitor-General's legal advisory function and more on the Solicitor-General's increasingly important function as an advocate for government interests before the High Court. Commonwealth Attorney-General, Billy Sneddon, said that the success of the cases in which the Solicitor-General had appeared previously[188]

[181] Queensland, *Parliamentary Debates*, Legislative Assembly, 26 March 1985, 4374–75 (Wayne Goss, Leader of the Opposition, Labor). Although note that as Premier, Goss made Patrick Keane's appointment under the Act with the right to private practice.

[182] ibid, 4389 (Angus Innes, Liberal).

[183] ibid, 4380 (Paul Braddy, Labor).

[184] ibid, 4384 (Douglas Jennings, National).

[185] Victoria, *Parliamentary Debates*, Legislative Assembly, 31 October 1951, 5683 (Mitchell). See also Western Australia, *Parliamentary Debates*, Legislative Council, 30 April 1969, 3524 (Arthur Griffith, Minister for Justice).

[186] Victoria, *Parliamentary Debates*, Legislative Assembly, 31 October 1951, 5682–83 (Mitchell). See similar reasoning given later in Queensland: Crown Law, above n 1, 227, referring to Queensland, *Parliamentary Debates*, Legislative Assembly, 19 March 1985, 4097. See also Queensland, *Parliamentary Debates*, Legislative Assembly, 26 March 1985, 4388 (Innes).

[187] Western Australia, *Parliamentary Debates*, Legislative Assembly, 24 April 1969, 3436 (Charles Court, Minister for Industrial Development).

[188] The Solicitor-General at that time, Kenneth Bailey, had appeared in only a handful of litigious matters as counsel, many of which occurred towards the end of his tenure. Bailey himself described

indicated that 'Crown counsel permanently associated with government legal work can bring special qualifications to the conduct of a case or the furnishing of an opinion at the highest level'.[189]

Secondly, the limits of the Attorney-General's ability to continue personally to play a part in providing legal services to government necessitated an alternative and non-political officer to take over this heavy responsibility. The position of the Attorney-General had developed in Australia to such a degree that it was almost wholly political. Sometimes officeholders had few, or even no, legal qualifications and little experience.[190] In many jurisdictions the office was often held with other important portfolios, leaving the officeholder little time to devote to legal duties.[191]

Finally, in many jurisdictions the post was established to provide an incentive for particularly talented individuals to continue to serve in the Attorney-General's Department.[192]

The change in the position in New South Wales was, unlike the other jurisdictions, not driven by the above reasons. By the time of the introduction of the Solicitor-General Bill 1969 (NSW), the public service appointee had little administrative work and was largely acting as counsel, analogous to the position in the 'Modern Period'. As such, there was no pressing need to introduce new legislation to bring about change in the nature of the position. Rather, codification was introduced to recognise the importance of the position within the government. It also added a number of technical provisions, for example relating to the delegation of powers of the Attorney-General and the appointment of a deputy for the Solicitor-General.[193] It was in fact the need for an express delegation of the Attorney-General's powers that was the catalyst for the introduction of the legislation.[194] During the Attorney-General's absence or illness the common law

his role in the *Victoria v Commonwealth* (1957) 99 CLR 575 ('*Second Uniform Tax Case*') as only the 'nominal leader' of the team: Mel Pratt, Interview with Sir Kenneth Bailey (Mel Pratt Collection, June 1971–March 1972). It was not until Garfield Barwick was appointed Attorney-General in 1958 that Bailey started to appear as leading counsel in a more significant number of high-profile cases for the Commonwealth.

[189] Commonwealth, *Parliamentary Debates*, House of Representatives, 22 October 1964, 2220 (Snedden).

[190] Victoria, *Parliamentary Debates*, Legislative Assembly, 27 November 1951, 222–23 (Cain); Hanlon, above n 9, 154–55; 184–85.

[191] J Hatzistergos, 'The evolving office of the New South Wales Attorney General' (2012) 86 *Australian Law Journal* 197, 199–200.

[192] For example, in Victoria, the move was to retain the services of Winneke: Victoria, *Parliamentary Debates*, Legislative Assembly, 27 November 1951, 224 (Cain). See also Victoria, *Parliamentary Debates*, Legislative Assembly, 31 October 1951, 568 (Mitchell); Coleman, above n 145, 167. This was also behind the move in Western Australia, which wanted to keep Ronald Wilson: Western Australia, *Parliamentary Debates*, Legislative Assembly, 24 April 1969, 3436–37 (Court), then Crown Counsel; and in South Australia, which wanted to keep Brian Cox: South Australia, *Parliamentary Debates*, House of Assembly, 7 March 1972, 3651 (King).

[193] New South Wales, *Parliamentary Debates*, Legislative Assembly, 17 September 1969, 969 (McCaw).

[194] New South Wales, *Parliamentary Debates*, Legislative Assembly, 1 October 1969, 1475 (McCaw).

allowed the Solicitor-General to fulfil the Attorney-General's functions,[195] but not otherwise. Section 36 of the *Constitution Act 1902* (NSW) prohibited the appointment of an Acting Attorney-General or for other ministers to fulfil the role of Attorney in respect of the 'powers, duties, and obligations by law annexed or incident to the office'.[196] The new Act allowed the Attorney-General to delegate the office's powers to the Solicitor-General in the interests of the efficient administration of justice.[197]

E. A Late Addition: The Australian Capital Territory

Upon attaining self-government in 1988,[198] the Australian Capital Territory was serviced by the Government Solicitor, a body corporate that was headed by a public service appointee, the Chief Solicitor.[199] The Chief Solicitor performed the functions of a Crown Solicitor, although he would attend the Special Committee of Solicitors-General (this committee is introduced in section III.G. below). This remained the position until 2011.

In 2011, the Australian Capital Territory introduced a new statutory office of Solicitor-General.[200] The move was driven by two factors. First, there was a perception that the Australian Capital Territory's position in the national arena was being undermined because of the lack of a statutorily appointed Solicitor-General.[201] The second reason was one seen in the other jurisdictions, that the 'increased complexity of the constitutional framework in which the ACT operates' required a Solicitor-General.[202] It seemed to have been assumed that these more complex constitutional questions, and the advocacy function, were more properly performed by 'an independent statutory Solicitor-General'.[203] The comment seems to accept that, in the twenty-first century, the role of the Solicitor-General has stabilised enough so as to prescribe particular functions and a status to the position.

[195] *Solicitor-General v Wylde* (1945) 46 SR (NSW) 83.

[196] See the lengthy discussion in the Second Reading Speech of the inconveniences caused by this, particularly in relation to the commencement of prosecutions: New South Wales, *Parliamentary Debates*, Legislative Assembly, 1 October 1969, 1475 ff (McCaw). For the history of s 36, see M Byers and M Gill, *Review of Legal Services to Government* (New South Wales Attorney General's Department, 1993) [2.12]–[2.14], 5.

[197] New South Wales, *Parliamentary Debates*, Legislative Assembly, 1 October 1969, 1478 (McCaw).

[198] *Australian Capital Territory (Self-Government) Act 1988* (Cth).

[199] *Government Solicitor Act 1989* (ACT).

[200] *Law Officers Act 2011* (ACT), pt 3.

[201] Australian Capital Territory, *Parliamentary Debates*, Legislative Assembly, 23 June 2011, 2353 (Simon Corbell, Attorney-General). See also Australian Capital Territory, *Parliamentary Debates*, Legislative Assembly, 23 August 2011, 3629 (Shane Rattenbury, Greens, supporting the Bill).

[202] Australian Capital Territory, *Parliamentary Debates*, Legislative Assembly, 23 June 2011, 2353 (Corbell).

[203] ibid.

However, while the Australian Capital Territory government wanted a statutory Solicitor-General like the other jurisdictions, it was concerned that there was insufficient work for two separate offices—the Solicitor-General and the Chief Solicitor. The Territory wanted a 'part-time Solicitor-General'. One solution to such a problem would be to appoint a Solicitor-General from the private Bar with a right to continue his or her private practice (as in Queensland).[204] However, the Territory opted for a different system: the Solicitor-General could be directed to exercise the Chief Solicitor's functions by the Attorney-General.[205] In this way, the two offices could be filled by the same person.[206]

By the time the Australian Capital Territory introduced its statutory Solicitor-General, a number of changes in emphasis had occurred. No longer were parliamentarians primarily concerned about maintaining ministerial responsibility for the actions of a non-ministerial Solicitor-General, and questions over whether the officeholder's independence was properly protected had also ceased. It would seem that by this stage, these concerns about establishing a 'statutory' position of Solicitor-General had been settled by the relatively uncontroversial manner in which the officeholders in the other jurisdictions had performed their functions.

F. The Remuneration Dilemma: Judicial Salary or Public Servant's Wage?

An effort to define the historical characteristics of the Solicitor-General is not complete without consideration of the basis for the remuneration of the office. The question of how to remunerate the Solicitor-General highlights the difficulty governments have had in defining exactly what the Solicitor-General is: no longer a politician, not quite a judge, and not just another public servant in the Attorney-General's Department.[207] Indeed, it is the office's remuneration that has been the cause of the greatest number of amendments to the legislation in the jurisdictions. Since the introduction of the model of an independent statutory officer, the jurisdictions have experimented with several models, including models that tie the Solicitor-General's remuneration to that of a public servant, or link the salary and/or pension entitlements to those of the Judiciary (which continues in Victoria, New South Wales, Queensland, South Australia, Tasmania and the Northern Territory). More recently, in the Commonwealth, and in Western Australia, a new model has emerged that sets the wage and/or entitlements and pension of the

[204] Provision was made for this in the ACT legislation. Under the *Law Officers Act 2011* (ACT), s 19, the Solicitor-General may engage in private practice with the consent of the Attorney-General.

[205] ibid, s 17(1)(d).

[206] The first appointment, Peter Garrisson, was already Chief Solicitor, and was appointed to fulfil the functions of both offices: 'ACT Appoints Solicitor-General', *ABC News*, 24 August 2011, available at <http://www.abc.net.au/news/2011-08-23/act-solicitor-general/2852006>.

[207] As ch 2, section I.B. explained, a different, although related, dilemma had arisen in England over the basis on which to pay the Law Officers.

Solicitor-General independently from both the public service and the Judiciary through remuneration tribunals.[208]

The following discussion uses the Commonwealth regime as an example of experimentation with remuneration models. When it was enacted, the *Law Officers Act 1964* (Cth) set the salary of the Solicitor-General at the level of a permanent head of a department (the same as that paid to the public service appointee under the *Solicitor-General Act 1916* (Cth)).[209] However, under the 1964 Act, the officeholder was granted the pension of a High Court judge under the *Judges' Pensions Act 1948* (Cth).[210] Parity with the Judiciary was further cemented in the 1980s with a judicial salary and long-service leave.[211] These moves were explained in 1983 by then Deputy Prime Minister Lionel Bowen as demonstrating 'a clear intention to equate the Solicitor-General with the status of a judge of the Federal Court'.[212] These provisions were also included to attract the most qualified people to the position.

However, this trend ceased in the Commonwealth sphere in 1998, with the retirement of Gavan Griffith as Solicitor-General and the Howard Liberal/National Coalition Government's appointment of David Bennett to the position. Pension and long-leave entitlements of the Solicitor-General were brought into line with those of a public servant.[213] The purpose was to equate the office with a senior member of the Australian Public Service (APS).[214] The Opposition opposed the move, reminding the Government that when the new office was established in 1964, it was expressly intended to be 'outside the public service'.[215] Daryl Melham, Shadow Minister for Aboriginal and Torres Strait Islander Affairs, argued that the Bill 'diminish[ed]' the office, 'strik[ing] at the very heart of the independence of the Solicitor-General' and undermining the Government's ability to attract quality candidates.[216] The Attorney-General defended the Bill, arguing that it was likely the salary and entitlements would be set above the current rate (which was then

[208] In the ACT, the salary of the Solicitor-General is set as a condition agreed between the Executive and the Solicitor-General as stated in the appointment, but may be set by the Remuneration Tribunal It is is currently set by reference to the salary of the DPP (which is set by the Remuneration Tribunal): *Law Officers Act 2011* (ACT), s 16(4).

[209] Commonwealth, *Parliamentary Debates*, House of Representatives, 22 October 1964, 2220 (Sneddon).

[210] *Law Officers Act 1964* (Cth), s 16 (note s 16(4)).

[211] Long leave: *Statute Law (Miscellaneous Provisions) Act (No 2) 1983*; The salary was increased by the Governor-General under s 7 in 1980: Commonwealth, *Parliamentary Debates*, House of Representatives, 21 September 1983, 1046 (Lionel Bowen, Deputy Prime Minister and Minister for Trade).

[212] Commonwealth, *Parliamentary Debates*, House of Representatives, 21 September 1983, 1046 (Bowen).

[213] *Law Officers Amendment Act 1998* (Cth).

[214] Commonwealth, *Parliamentary Debates*, House of Representatives, 3 December 1997, 11925 (Daryl Williams, Attorney-General). See also Commonwealth Parliamentary Library, 'Law Officers Amendment Bill 1997' *Bills Digest No 124 1997–8* (Anne Pyle, 18 December 1997).

[215] Commonwealth, *Parliamentary Debates*, House of Representatives, 10 March 1998, 874 (Daryl Melham, Labor).

[216] ibid.

equivalent to a judicial salary) by the Remuneration Tribunal, and that it removed provisions in the legislation that might provide an incentive to individuals to stay in the job 'simply to get a pension'.[217]

Related to the question of remuneration is that of tenure. In the Commonwealth a limited form of tenure exists in the legislation—the term must not exceed seven years.[218] In some of the State jurisdictions appointment may be for an indefinite period, mirroring judicial tenure,[219] although this appears to be changing. In New South Wales in 2007, in Western Australia in 2006, and in Tasmania in 2015, the position changed from life tenure to an appointment for a limited period.[220] In New South Wales, Attorney-General John Hatzistergos introduced the 2007 amendment as follows:

> Life tenure is an anachronistic concept. … Life tenure fails to provide an incentive for continuous performance improvement. It also fails to acknowledge that turnover can be appropriate, particularly in positions as difficult, demanding and high profile as those covered by this bill.[221]

The move was opposed in the New South Wales parliament. Opposition parties claimed that limited terms and the desire to obtain reappointment would leave officeholders vulnerable. Further, it was argued that life tenure assisted in attracting the highest calibre persons for the positions by providing 'the certainty of independence and non-interference'.[222] Greg James, who had conducted a review for the government that had preceded the amendments, had anticipated these criticisms. He said that other mechanisms sufficiently protected the independence of officeholders, including professional obligations and ethics of independence and detachment, and protection against improper dealings by government through the variety of integrity offices including, for example, the Ombudsman.[223]

James's focus on the professional obligations and ethics of officeholders as legal practitioners guaranteeing independence, rather than statutory guarantees of tenure, to some extent undermines the assertion by politicians that the statutory guarantees of independence in the legislation establishing the Solicitor-General were fundamental.

[217] ibid, 882 (Williams).

[218] *Law Officers Act 1964* (Cth), s 6(1). See also *Solicitor General Act 1985* (Qld), s 5(2); *Solicitor General Act 1969* (NSW), s 2(2); *Solicitor-General Act 1969* (WA), s 3(1a); *Law Officers Act 2011* (ACT), s 16(3).

[219] *Solicitor-General Act 1983* (Tas), s 5(3); *Law Officers Act 1978* (NT), s 13(1); *Solicitor-General Act 1972* (SA), s 5; *Attorney-General and Solicitor-General Act 1972* (Vic), s 4.

[220] *Solicitor General Act 1969* (NSW), s 2(2) inserted by *Crown Law Officers Legislation Amendment (Abolition of Life Tenure) Act 2007* (NSW); *Solicitor-General Act 1969* (WA), s 3(1a), inserted by *Solicitor-General Amendment Act 2006* (WA); *Solicitor-General Act 1983* (Tas) s 4(3A), inserted by *Law Officers (Miscellaneous Amendments) Act 2015* (Tas).

[221] New South Wales, *Parliamentary Debates*, Legislative Council, 17 October 2007, 2671 (John Hatzistergos, Attorney-General).

[222] See, eg, New South Wales, *Parliamentary Debates*, Legislative Council, 23 October 2007, 3030 (John Ajaka, Liberal); ibid (Lee Rhiannon, Greens).

[223] Quoted ibid, 3030 (Fred Nile, Christian Democratic Party); access to the full report was sought through Freedom of Information, but it was denied on the basis of cabinet confidentiality.

G. The Solicitors-General of Australia

The history of the Australian Solicitors-General shows the situation to be different from that in Britain, the US and New Zealand in a very important respect. In the Australian federal system, the modern institutions of Attorney-General and Solicitor-General have developed largely simultaneously across the jurisdictions. In the course of this development, a committee of Solicitors-General has emerged, known formally as the Special Committee of Solicitors-General (SCSG). (Although Anthony Mason has postulated that the correct collective noun is a 'slurry' of Solicitors-General.)[224]

Starting in the 1970s, at around the same time as the statutory counsel model was being adopted across the Australian jurisdictions, regular meetings between Solicitors-General started to occur.[225] This began when the State Solicitors-General were called upon as a collective to assist the Attorneys-General to develop a legal proposal for the severing of constitutional links with Britain.[226] This group came to include the Commonwealth and became more formalised. The SCSG is now a sub-committee of the Law Crime and Community Safety Council (LCCSC, formerly the Standing Committee of Attorneys-General—SCAG—and before then the Standing Council on Law and Justice—SCLJ). Today, the Committee meets regularly (between two and four times a year). The Committee's agenda items include providing advice to the LCCSC on matters referred to the Committee; providing LCCSC with recommendations in relation to possible areas of law reform of its own volition (the Tasmanian Solicitor-General has reported to the Tasmanian parliament that the Committee provides a valuable forum for discussion of law reform and legislative amendment that has occurred in other jurisdictions);[227] and reviewing upcoming constitutional litigation. In this last respect, Solicitors-General may take the opportunity to divide arguments in upcoming cases between themselves, or consider tactics in the presentation of argument.

The SCSG is now a well-established institution within the Australian constitutional order. Since 1996, it has reported annually to the LCCSC (and its predecessors).[228] In addition to its important contribution to drafting the *Australia Acts 1986*, it has also had significant involvement in other nationwide

[224] A Mason, 'Interveners and Amici Curiae in the High Court: A Comment' (1998) 20 *Adelaide Law Review* 173, 175.

[225] This group included Crown Solicitors and the Chief Solicitor of the Australian Capital Territory before the Solicitor-General model was adopted in all of the jurisdictions. It also includes, from time to time, the New Zealand Solicitor-General: Standing Committee of Attorneys-General, *Procedures for the Standing Committee of Attorneys-General* (August 2009) [7.5].

[226] For a full telling of the history of the *Australia Acts*, and the role of the Solicitors-General, see A Twomey, *The Australia Acts 1986: Australia's Statutes of Independence* (Federation Press, 2010).

[227] Solicitor-General, Parliament of Tasmania, *Solicitor-General Report for 2013–2014* (2014) 8.

[228] G Griffith, 'Report: Second Law Officer to the First Law Officer 1 July 1995–31 December 1996' (Solicitor-General of Australia, 1996) (on file with author) [7.2].

constitutional initiatives. Examples include negotiations over the jurisdiction of the seabed off the coast of Australia,[229] the creation of the cross-vesting scheme,[230] the drafting of the crimes at sea legislation and the choice of law scheme.[231] The SCSG has also initiated consideration of potential areas of national policy reform, such as the integration of the Australian courts.[232] Peculiar to the Australian context, the Solicitors-General *as a collective* have evolved into an important institution in the federal constitutional system.

IV. Conclusion

The historical narrative of the Australian Solicitors-General reveals an evolution driven largely by the desire to create a paradigm in which the legal functions of the Law Officers, at least, are freed from many of the controversies that continue to surround the offices in Britain. The contemporary model, with its placement of the Solicitor-General outside politics with a statutory basis, was intended to create an office that provided both the actuality and appearance of independence from politics in the discharge of the Law Officers' legal functions. The non-political nature of the office and its exclusively legal focus has also meant that there has been a shift in its essence: officeholders have moved away from being politicians with some legal qualifications and are now highly qualified legal professionals. This is more akin to the early appearance of the English Law Officers in the thirteenth century as legal counsel for the monarch. The Australian Attorney-General has been, almost since inception of the office, at the core of government as a member of the Executive Council and later Cabinet, heading a large administrative department. This is in direct contrast with Britain. The Australian system secures the benefit of a politically integrated Attorney-General with oversight across all government legal services, but, as this chapter has shown, acknowledges the increased danger of political and administrative pressures in this environment through the

[229] This was necessitated by the High Court's decision in *New South Wales v Commonwealth* (1975) 135 CLR 337 ('*Seas and Submerged Lands Case*'). Buti, above n 122, 173–74.

[230] This was found partly unconstitutional in *Re Wakim; Ex parte McNally* (1999) 198 CLR 511, but in so far as it vested federal jurisdiction in State courts, remains operative.

[231] See 'Report of the Special Committee of Solicitors-General to the Standing Committee of Attorneys General for year ended June 30, 1995' (Secretary, SCSG, 1995) 1 (on file with author). The SCSG was also consulted in 2009 by SCAG regarding the constitutional difficulties of implementing a national mechanism for handling complaints against judicial officers. See Senate Legal and Constitutional Affairs References Committee, 'Australia's Judicial System and the Role of Judges' (2009), 'Additional Information, Attorney-General's Department, 29 September 2009, 1, referred to in the Senate Committee Report at 93.

[232] See 'Report of the Special Committee of Solicitors-General to the Standing Committee of Attorneys General for year ended June 30, 1995' (Secretary, SCSG, 1995) 2. Interview, John Doyle.

development of the independent statutory offices of the Solicitor-General and later the DPP, to complement and assist the Attorney-General.[233]

The codification of the Solicitor-General's role in the second half of the twentieth century acknowledged the growing importance of this Law Officer to government across the Australian jurisdictions. Since its enshrinement in statute, the role has been a stable part of all Australian constitutional orders.

The evolution of the Solicitor-General has allowed it to remain relevant in the Australian constitutional order into the twenty-first century. While this chapter has provided an understanding of the intentions and events that have driven this evolution, to understand the contemporary role of the Solicitor-General also requires a close examination of the statutes, considering the extent to which the traditional Law Officers' functions remain and the impact of the new legislative characteristics of the office. It will also be necessary to examine how the office's functions have been exercised, and to consider the extent to which the goals of the statutes' framers have been realised.

[233] Edwards identified this as a weakness in the overly political Law Officer model: Edwards, *The Attorney-General*, above n 1, 75.

4

Counsel for the Crown

I. Introduction

The evolutionary moment in which the Australian Solicitor-General now rests differs markedly from the British tradition received into the colonies in the nineteenth century, as well as from the modern practice of the English Law Officers. This chapter sketches and analyses the current legal framework within which the Australian Solicitor-General practices.[1] This is a unique interplay of statute, common law, constitutional theory and convention. In exploring the legal framework, the chapter assesses the extent to which the intentions of the framers of the statutes have been realised in the legal sphere. Part III of the book considers the realisation of the historical intentions and legislative framework in practice.

II. Appointment, Tenure, Removal and Remuneration

The manner of appointment and the protections afforded to tenure and remuneration are important dimensions of the independence from government of any statutory office. Amongst the Australian jurisdictions, there is a large degree of variation between the statutory provisions relating to appointment, tenure, removal and remuneration of the Solicitor-General. This section will explain the different statutory provisions before considering the impact they may have on an officeholder's independence.

[1] In this chapter, statutes establishing the Solicitor-General will be referred to by their jurisdiction only, not their full titles. For reference, these statutes are: *Law Officers Act 1964* (Cth); *Solicitor-General Act 1969* (NSW); *Attorney-General and Solicitor-General Act 1972* (Vic); *Solicitor-General Act 1969* (WA); *Solicitor-General Act 1972* (SA); *Solicitor-General Act 1983* (Tas); *Solicitor General Act 1985* (Qld); *Law Officers Act 1978* (NT); *Law Officers Act 2011* (ACT).

A. Appointment

The move from a ministerial position was driven, in part, by the perceived advantages of having an officer who could offer continuity of advice and representation across administrations. In all jurisdictions, appointment of the Solicitor-General is by the Executive. As a matter of practice, the Commonwealth and Victoria have introduced a more formal, application-based appointment process with a selection panel, but this is not mandated by statute. In the other jurisdictions appointment continues to be done through an informal process with little transparency. In many jurisdictions the Solicitor-General's term is temporally limited, ranging from between five and 10 years; although officeholders may be reappointed.[2] In Tasmania, the need to entice practising barristers to give up private practice, and the acknowledgement that finding new officeholders to replace outgoing ones can be difficult in jurisdictions with smaller professions, led the government to adopt a longer, 10-year term, and to keep open the possibility of reappointment.[3] In the other jurisdictions, the term may be unlimited, although in practice the precise terms of appointment may limit it, and in some appointment is made subject to a mandatory retirement age.[4]

Qualification for appointment is similar across jurisdictions and largely mirrors that for appointment to a superior court. In some jurisdictions qualification for appointment as Solicitor-General is less strict than for appointment to the bench,[5] and in others more so, requiring the appointee to be a barrister or Senior Counsel in place of the criterion of being a legal practitioner.[6] The stricter qualifications in Queensland and Victoria emphasise the position of the Solicitor-General as a senior member of the Bar, rather than simply a member of the legal profession.

B. Tenure and Removal

The move from a public service Solicitor-General to a statutory office was explained in many jurisdictions by reference to the increased independence that

2 Cth s 6(1); NSW s 2; Qld s 5(2); WA s 3(1a); ACT s 16(3). Tas s 4(3A).

3 See, eg, discussion of these issues in Tasmania, *Parliamentary Debates*, House of Assembly, 17 September 2015, 63 (Matthew Groom). See also in Committee at 74–75.

4 SA ss 5(1), 8(2); Vic s 4(1); Tas ss 4(1) and 6(1)(a); NT s 13(1).

5 In South Australia the appointee must be a legal practitioner for not less than seven years (as opposed to 10 years for the Supreme Court): SA s 4(1); in Tasmania seven years (as opposed to 10 years): Tas s 4(3); in Northern Territory five years (as opposed to 10 years): NT s 13(1)(a).

6 In Queensland, the appointee must be a barrister: Qld s 5(3) (contra *Constitution of Queensland Act 2001* (Qld), s 59); In Victoria the appointee must be Senior Counsel: Vic s 4(1) (contra *Constitution Act 1975* (Vic), s 75B). The New South Wales legislation initially provided that the Solicitor-General must be one of Her Majesty's Counsel (s 2(1)), but this was removed in 1993 by the *Legal Profession Reform Act 1993* (NSW).

would be guaranteed by statutory tenure.[7] Despite the large degree of symmetry in the underlying purpose of the statutes, the power of removal, and therefore the strength of the security of tenure, differs across the jurisdictions.[8] Four types of removal mechanisms can be identified.

The first is located in the Commonwealth and Northern Territory statutes: the Governor-General or the Administrator '*shall* remove the Solicitor-General from office' in the event of incapacity (except by reason of temporary illness), misbehaviour, or bankruptcy/insolvency.[9]

In contrast, the second type, found in South Australia and Western Australia, provides that the Governor *may* remove the Solicitor-General on similar grounds.[10] The use of the word 'may' implies a discretion as to whether the Governor must actually remove the appointee in event of the listed contingencies.[11]

The statutes in Queensland and the Australian Capital Territory combine these two types of mechanisms.[12] For example, in Queensland the Governor in Council *may* terminate the appointment for misbehaviour or incapacity, but the Governor in Council *shall* terminate the appointment if the Solicitor-General becomes bankrupt, is absent from duty or contravenes the conditions of the office's right to private practice.[13]

Within both of these types, whether the enumerated grounds for removal are the *only* basis on which removal can take place is unclear,[14] although there are strong statutory presumptions, reinforced by the purpose of the provision, that support such a conclusion.[15]

The third type is found in the Tasmanian statute, and most closely resembles the guarantees of judicial tenure. It was described by Tasmanian Minister Matthew Groom as providing a procedure that is 'transparent and at arm's length from the government of the day'.[16] A Solicitor-General's appointment can be revoked only by resolutions passed by both houses of parliament.[17] A revocation must be

[7] See, eg, Commonwealth, *Parliamentary Debates*, House of Representatives, 22 October 1964, 2220 (Billy Snedden, Attorney-General).

[8] The security of tenure afforded to Solicitors-General is in many jurisdictions not replicated in relation to an acting appointment: see Cth s 11(3); Qld s 7(1); Tas s 4(5); WA s 8(1); NT s 13(4).

[9] Emphasis added. Cth s 10; NT s 15.

[10] SA s 7; WA s 7.

[11] See further the explanation of this presumption of statutory interpretation in DC Pearce and RS Geddes, *Statutory Interpretation in Australia* (LexisNexis Australia, 6th edn, 2006) 333; and its expression in *Acts Interpretation Act 1915* (SA), s 34; *Interpretation Act 1984* (WA), s 56.

[12] Qld ss 17(3) and (4); ACT s 21.

[13] Qld s 17(3) and (4).

[14] This ambiguity exists in all jurisdictions other than Northern Territory. Section 15 of the NT Act provides the Administrator shall remove the Solicitor-General from office 'if, and only if,' the grounds exist.

[15] Embodied in the Latin maxin *expressum facit cessare tacitum*. See discussion in Pearce and Geddes, above n 11, 142–44; *R v Wallis; Ex parte Employers Association of Wool Selling Brokers* (1949) 78 CLR 529, 550 (Dixon J).

[16] Tasmanian, *Parliamentary Debates*, House of Assembly (17 September 2015) 64 (Matthew Groom).

[17] Tas s 6F.

preceded by a statement from the Governor laid before both houses requesting them to revoke the appointment of a Solicitor-General on the similar grounds to those that the Governor may suspend an officeholder, including disability, infirmity or incapacity, bankruptcy, conviction of a crime or an offence punishable by imprisonment for 12 months or more, misconduct in office, including by virture of engaging in private practice without the express authorisation of the Attorney-General,[18] or misbehaviour that brings the office into disrepute.[19]

The last type of removal mechanism, found in New South Wales and Victoria, is markedly different, in that the statute provides for apparently discretionary removal, more akin to the notion of appointment at pleasure seen in the early English and colonial appointments.[20]

C. Remuneration

As John Edwards observed in the UK context, studying the changing nature of the remuneration of the Law Officers provides an perceptive insight into the nature of the office at any given time.[21] Since the introduction of the model of an independent statutory officer, the jurisdictions have experimented with several methods of remuneration that reflect different degrees of remunerative independence. Methods have have included the linking of the salary and/or pension entitlements to that of the Judiciary,[22] replicating the public service remuneration packages and, more recently, a new model setting the wage of the Solicitor-General independently from both the public service and the Judiciary through remuneration tribunals.[23]

Throughout most of the nineteenth century in the colonies, Solicitors-General engaged in private practice to supplement their income. This privilege was removed under the public service model, but has re-emerged, in more restricted forms, in a number of the statutes. In Victoria, the incumbent may not engage in any other employment,[24] and in New South Wales the Solicitor-General may not engage in any other remunerated employment.[25] In contrast, in the Commonwealth and the other States and Territories, remunerated employment may be engaged in with the consent of the Attorney-General,[26] the Governor[27] or

[18] And thus in breach of s 10.

[19] Tas s 6A, inserted by the *Law Officers (Miscellaneous Amendments) Act 2015* (Tas).

[20] NSW s 2(5)(a) (note under s 2(5) other grounds on which the Solicitor-General is deemed to have vacated office are enumerated); Vic s 4(1).

[21] See ch 2, section I.B.

[22] Which continues in various guises. See NSW s 6; Qld s 11; SA s 10; Tas s 5(1)(ab) and (b); Vic ss 4(3) and 6; NT s 13(5).

[23] Cth s 7(1); WA s 4; ACT s 16(4).

[24] Vic s 4(3)(b).

[25] NSW s 2(5)(f).

[26] Cth s 9; SA s 6(b); Tas s 10(2)(v); ACT s 19; NT s 14(c).

[27] WA s 6.

the Governor in Council.[28] In Queensland, a general right to engage in private practice has been approved since the first appointment under the Act in 1992,[29] and in Western Australia this was granted in 2012.

D. Impact on Independence

Considerable variation across the jurisdictions exists in terms of the Solicitor-General's tenure, removal, remuneration and pension entitlements. In light of the largely uniform objectives of the legislation and the cross-fertilisation across jurisdictions when the statutes were drafted, this is surprising. The distinctions raise potentially fundamental questions about the level of independence that the office enjoys.

Limited terms with the prospect of reappointment immediately raise questions about the office's independence. Term appointments may contribute to an environment in which officeholders seek to ingratiate themselves, perhaps through the provision of accommodating advice or inappropriately aggressive representation, in the hope of reappointment.

In some jurisdictions, there is the possibility of removal on discretionary grounds which also raises questions around independence. As Geoffrey Hazard and W William Hode postulate in the general lawyering environment, 'the lawyer wishing to maintain employment may be tempted to play sycophant to [the] client'.[30] Even if this does not occur in practice, the possibility of removal or reappointment may create this *perception*, undermining the capacity of an individual to perform the role properly, and the government to receive the full benefits of it.

In some jurisdictions, the pension entitlements create a fiscal incentive for individuals to seek reappointment as Solicitor-General, or to seek judicial appointment. While there is little evidence to support a convention of judicial preferment, Solicitors-General generally possess characteristics that make them well qualified for judicial appointment. The statutes reflect the fact there is a strong likelihood that Solicitors-General will be reappointed to the position or to the bench. Under some of the statutes, depending on their circumstances, appointees may not be entitled to a full pension, or a pension at all, *unless* they either are reappointed as Solicitor-General,[31] or are appointed as a judge.[32]

[28] Qld s 16.

[29] Although note the conditions that attach to this right relating to priority of work and conflicts of interest: Qld s 16(1A).

[30] GC Hazard and WW Hodes, *The Law of Lawyering* (Aspen Publishers, 3rd edn, 2001) § 23.2, 23.3, referred to in KH Michels, 'Lawyer Independence: From Ideal to Viable Legal Standard' (2010) 61(1) *Case Western Reserve Law Review* 85, 112.

[31] See NSW s 2(g). This was also the position in Victoria under s 6(3) prior to amendments in 2006 by the *Justice Legislation (Further Amendment) Act 2006* (Vic).

[32] NSW s 6(3)(a); Qld s 13.

For example, in Victoria prior to 2006, only those officeholders who had served 10 years *and* had attained the age of 65 years received the full pension entitlement.[33] Thus, a Solicitor-General appointed for a 10-year term (the practice in Victoria) at the age of 54 (or younger) would *not* be eligible for the full judicial pension at the end of that term. This created, at least in theory, a financial incentive for that officeholder to seek reappointment. In 2006, legislation was introduced to alleviate this possibility, giving former Solicitors-General full entitlement to a pension upon attaining the age of 65 years if the officeholder had served a 10-year term.[34] In South Australia and the Northern Territory the issue has not arisen because, in practice, appointment is for life. The issue has been highlighted in New South Wales, however, with the introduction of a statutory maximum 10-year term in 2007,[35] with the possibility of reappointment. The full pension entitlement requires an officeholder to have completed a 10-year term *and* attained the age of 60, thus potentially disadvantaging any officeholder appointed younger than 50 years old.[36]

Some statutes provide that the service of an individual as Solicitor-General may be counted as service as a judicial officer if the individual is subsequently appointed to the bench. In those jurisdictions where the Solicitor-General is appointed for an unlimited term and is otherwise entitled to the pension, this gives rise to no independence concerns.[37] In contrast, there are some jurisdictions where this creates an incentive for a Solicitor-General to seek judicial appointment. In Queensland, there is no general entitlement to a judicial pension for the Solicitor-General; however, if the person who holds or has held office as Solicitor-General is appointed to the Supreme or District Courts, then for the purposes of the *Judges (Pensions and Long Leave) Act 1957* (Qld) any period of service as Solicitor-General will be counted as service as a judicial officer.[38] In New South Wales, where, as explained above, the Solicitor-General may not receive the full pension because of the officeholder's age at the time of appointment, the legislation makes similar provision.[39]

The possibility of appointment to the bench in and of itself raises questions as to whether a Solicitor-General, seeking judicial appointment, may have an incentive to act in such a way as to impress the government rather than fulfil their obligations with appropriate professional independence. On the other hand, the possibility of future appointment to the bench, where pension entitlements may

[33] Or have served 20 years; or were appointed prior to the age of 60 years and have been afflicted with a permanent incapacity: *Constitution Act 1975* (Vic), s 83(1).

[34] Vic s 6(3), amended by *Justice Legislation (Further Amendment) Act 2006* (Vic).

[35] This amendment is to commence with the next appointment of Solicitor-General in that State. The terms and conditions of the incumbent, Michael Sexton, have been 'grandfathered' by transitional provisions: *Crown Law Officers Legislation Amendment (Abolition of Life Tenure) Act 2007* (NSW), sch 1, cl 5.

[36] NSW s 2(g).

[37] SA s 10; NT s 13(7); *Constitution Act 1975* (Vic), s 83(6)(a).

[38] Qld s 13.

[39] NSW s 6(3)(a).

be carried across from time served as Solicitor-General, may assist the government in securing lawyers of outstanding merit who might otherwise have aspired to the bench more immediately. Indeed, this was one of the reasons that the idea of 'judicial preferment' was advocated in England (see chapter two, section I.A.). The roll-over of pension entitlements means there is no *disincentive* for these individuals to accept appointment as Solicitor-General rather than the bench.

The divergent protections of tenure and remuneration across the jurisdictions provide *theoretically* differing levels of protection for the independence of the office. However, despite these statutory differences, the following chapters demonstrate that the degree of independence that officeholders exhibit in practice across the jurisdictions differs very little, and that those divergences that do arise are not readily related to the differences in statutory regimes. This raises questions about the effectiveness of 'statutory tenure' in the protection of independence. The operation of the statute in practice and the different ways in which it may contribute to protecting the independence of the office are returned to in chapter seven.

III. 'Counsel' for the Crown: Adviser and Advocate

The statutory functions of the Solicitor-General are substantially uniform across the jurisdictions, and can be broken down into core and peripheral functions. Acting as 'counsel for the Crown' is the core function of the Solicitor-General. However, none of the statutes provides a monopoly to the Solicitor-General over particular types of counsel work, or obliges the government to use the office as counsel. The articulation of the Solicitor-General's core function is sparse in the statutes, perhaps curious given the rich history of the role in England and Australia.

The precise statutory expressions of the office's core function fall into three categories. The statutes in the first category state that the Solicitor-General is to act as counsel for the Crown of the State or 'Her Majesty'.[40] The second category provides that the Solicitor-General acts as counsel for the Crown *at the request of the Attorney-General*.[41] This recognises the Attorney-General's role in representing the Crown and emphasises the relationship between the two Law Officers.

Categories one and two make no distinction between the two main functions of counsel: advocacy and advising. These functions are subsumed in the general function to act as counsel. The dichotomy between the two functions is drawn out in the third category, which exists in the federal statute. In drawing the dichotomy, the *Law Officers Act 1964* (Cth) picks up the different emphases of the first two categories in a unique combination. First, the Solicitor-General is required to act

[40] NSW s 3(1)(a); Tas s 7(a); Vic s 5(a); WA s 9(a); NT s 14(a).

[41] Qld s 8(a); SA s 6(a)(i); ACT s 16(1)(a).

as counsel for the 'Crown in right of the Commonwealth', together with a number of other listed entities. The Solicitor-General is also to furnish his or her opinion *to the Attorney-General* on questions of law referred to him or her by the Attorney-General. The presence of the dichotomy implies that the obligation to act as counsel in the first paragraph includes only the representative functions of counsel. An alternative interpretation would be that the second function—of furnishing opinions on questions of law referred by the Attorney-General—relates to matters of 'pure' law only, as distinct from furnishing opinions that involve questions of both law and fact.[42] This interpretation would, however, require fine distinctions to be made to determine whether a question raises a question of *pure* law or involves questions of law and fact. It is unlikely to be workable in practice. An interpretation that simply draws a distinction between representing the Crown in contentious matters (including by providing advice where required in such matters) and providing legal advice in non-contentious matters thus emerges as the more plausible construction.

The Solicitor-General must perform other acts as counsel as the Attorney-General requests.[43] In some jurisdictions, the Solicitor-General has the express function of performing duties bestowed on the office by other statutes;[44] and in the other jurisdictions, while not express, this occurs. In the Australian Capital Territory, the Solicitor-General may also be directed to exercise the Chief Solicitor's functions.[45]

Other functions have arisen in practice and often differ across the jurisdictions. For example, historically, at the Commonwealth level, the Solicitor-General also represented Australia in a number of international forums, including the United Nations Commission on International Trade Law (UNCITRAL).[46] This involvement ceased in 1998 with the appointment of David Bennett, and the function was absorbed into the Department of Foreign Affairs and Trade.[47] At the State level, Solicitors-General were also previously involved in attending bi-annual meetings in relation to the Law of the Sea Convention[48] and the United Nations

[42] A possibility raised by Justin Gleeson in his interview, although it was not ultimately favoured by him.

[43] Cth s 12(c); NSW s 3(1)(a); Qld s 8(b); SA s 6(a)(ii); Tas s 7(b); Vic s 5(a); WA s 9(a); ACT s 16(1)(b); NT s 14(b). Presumably this includes other roles of counsel that do not fall strictly within the advocate or adviser functions; this may include prosecuting matters on behalf of the DPP (see, eg, *Director of Public Prosecutions Act 1983* (Cth), s 15(e)), or acting to assist executive investigative bodies, such as the Australian Crime Commission (see, eg, *Australian Crime Commission Act 2002* (Cth), s 50).

[44] Tas s 7(c); Vic s 5(b); WA s 9(b); ACT s 16(d); NT s 14(c).

[45] ACT s 16(c). See the explanation of the reasons for this in ch 3, section III.E.

[46] See list of international matters that were within the responsibility of the Attorney-General and Solicitor-General set out in Letter from Prime Minister to Ministers upon the announcement of Mr E Lauterpacht QC as the Legal Adviser to the Department of Foreign Affairs, 21 November 1974, National Archives of Australia, Canberra, M133/25.

[47] Interview, David Bennett; Interview, Robert Ellicott; Interview, Gavan Griffith; Interview, Anthony Mason; G Griffith, 'Report: Second Law Officer to the First Law Officer 1 July 1995–31 December 1996' (Solicitor-General of Australia, 1996) 8.

[48] United Nations Convention on the Law of the Sea III (UNCLOS III).

Working Group drafting the Convention of Rights of Indigenous Peoples as part of the Australian delegation,[49] but these functions have fallen away as they too have been subsumed within other departments.[50] At the Commonwealth level, the Solicitor-General is involved as a committee member overseeing large or important constitutional and non-constitutional litigation involving the Government.[51] In the Northern Territory the Solicitor-General is the legal adviser to the Statehood Steering Committee. In Western Australia, the Solicitor-General performs an extensive role in consulting with the Judiciary and the profession prior to judicial appointments. The Solicitor-General will chair selection panels convened for magistrate appointments and will recommend candidates to the Attorney-General in the higher courts, as well as statutory offices, such as to the Crime and Corruption Commission and the Parliamentary Inspector.[52] The Solicitor-General also has a role in liaising with the Judiciary when there are issues with staffing,[53] or superannuation[54] or allegations of misconduct.[55] In 2012, the Solicitor-General liaised with the Judiciary prior to a murder trial, where the deceased and the accused were prominent members of the Western Australian legal profession. In that instance, an arrangement was made to appoint the former Chief Justice of the Northern Territory as an acting judge of the Western Australian Supreme Court.[56]

A. The Solicitor-General's Independence

Independence as a dimension of the Law Officers' role is prominent in the scholarly debate.[57] In this literature, the Law Officers' independence is thought to be required for two fundamental reasons. The first is to protect officeholders

[49] 'Report of the Special Committee of Solicitors-General to the Standing Committee of Attorneys General for year ended June 30, 1995' (Secretary, SCSG, 1995) 3; J McDonnell, 'Special Committee of Solicitors General Meeting' (Secretary, Special Committee of Solicitors-General, 18 October 1996) (on file with author) 9. See explanation of history behind the State Solicitors-General in these negotiations in RA Herr and BW Davis, 'The Impact of UNCLOS III on Australian Federalism' (1986) 41(3) *International Journal* 674; Legislative and Constitutional Affairs Committee, 'Trick or Treaty: Commonwealth Power to Make and Implement Treaties' (Senate November 1995), available at <http://www.aph.gov.au/senate/committee/legconctte/completedinquiries/pre1996/treaty/report/index.htm>, [13.44]. Note current arrangements: Department of Foreign Affairs and Trade, *Principles and Procedures for Commonwealth-State Consultation on Treaties*, available at <www.austlii.edu.au/au/other/dfat/reports/infokit.html#sect8>, [6.1]–[6.3].

[50] See discussion of involvement of Solicitors-General at overseas meetings in McDonnell, above n 49, 9. See also Interview, Martin Hinton.

[51] Interview, Justin Gleeson.

[52] Interview, Grant Donaldson; Interview, Rob Mitchell; Interview, Michael Mischin; Interview, Jim McGinty. See further discussion in R Sackville, 'Judicial Appointments: A Discussion Paper' (2005) 4 *Journal of Judicial Administration* 117, 127; Judicial Conference of Australia, 'Judicial Appointments: A Comparative Study' (Research Paper, April 2015), available at <http://www.jca.asn.au/wp-content/uploads/2013/10/P170242-RESEARCH-PAPER-final.pdf>, 47–52.

[53] Interview, Rob Mitchell.

[54] Interview, Grant Donaldson.

[55] Interview, Jim McGinty.

[56] Interview, Rob Mitchell.

[57] K Norman-Major, 'The Solicitor General: Executive Policy Agendas and the Court' (1994) 57 *Albany Law Review* 1081, 1084.

from the influence of politics in the exercise of their public interest functions. The second is to ensure that officeholders can discharge their legal functions free from pressures of political agendas.

The statutory functions of the Solicitor-General emphasise the legal nature of the role in the 'Modern Period' (see chapter three, section III.). This emphasises the importance of the legal profession's ethical obligations in maintaining an officeholder's independence. As we have already seen, many of the statutes provide some guarantees of independence through the tenure, removal and remuneration provisions. This section considers the extent to which, by defining the Solicitor-General's role as counsel, the statutes also import professional obligations to retain independence. I return in the section VI. of this chapter to consider the extent to which the Solicitor-General retains any obligations to the public interest and the importance of independence in discharging them.

In the British law tradition 'counsel' refers to practising barristers.[58] The statutes establishing the Solicitor-General dictate, therefore, that the role must be largely informed by that of a barrister,[59] and the independence expected of the office will be predominantly influenced by the professional obligations of barristers. The content of the Solicitor-General's independence will be informed by the formal professional obligations of the Bar (for example, those contained in the Australian Bar Association's Model Rules (ABA Model Rules)). In this section, I explain that the reference to counsel has imported into the statute a minimum level of independence in the office, although this is likely to differ between the advisory and advocacy functions.

To understand the expression of independence caught by the reference to counsel in the statute, this discussion first turns to the meaning of independence and to the three forms of independence that have arisen in relation to legal professionals.

i. *Independence in Theory*

Independence as a conceptual idea implies a level of freedom or autonomy. A distinction is often drawn between the 'freedom *from*' external constraints, an extrinsically focused freedom, and the 'freedom *to*' achieve some objective, which requires an intrinsic capacity to do so.[60] The freedom from external influences

[58] D Greenberg (ed), *Jowitt's Dictionary of English Law* (Sweet & Maxwell Thomson Reuters, 3rd edn, 2010) 569; BA Garner (ed), *Black's Law Dictionary* (Thomson Reuters, 9th edn, 2009), 'counsel'.

[59] In Queensland and Victoria, this relationship between the Solicitor-General and barristers is reinforced by particular qualification requirements: Qld s 5(3); Vic s 4(1). With very few exceptions across the jurisdictions, Solicitor-General appointments after the introduction of the statutory counsel paradigm have been of barristers. The exceptions to this rule have occurred in those jurisdictions operating with a fused profession (for example, Bradley Selway (SA), who was appointed from Crown Solicitor, and Robert Meadows (WA), who was appointed from a partnership at Freehills).

[60] The two definitions of freedom have been closely associated with the work of Isaiah Berlin: I Berlin, 'Two Concepts of Liberty' in I Berlin (ed), *Four Essays on Liberty* (Oxford University Press, 1958) 1, 7, 19. The dichotomy has been applied in the legal context: PS Karlan, 'Two Concepts of Judicial Independence' (1999) 72 *South California Law Review* 535.

requires consideration of the constraints from which an individual is free.[61] Because of its extrinsic nature, this aspect of independence is the most easily identified and assessed. Often, therefore, conceptions of independence within professional regulatory regimes focus only on external influences, for example compromising relationships, or monetary influences. Focus on external constraints will often overlook more subtle pressures that exist and require internal fortitude, that is to say capacity, to overcome.

In the legal context, an intrinsic capacity requirement is closely associated with the characteristic of integrity. Ronald Dworkin describes individual integrity as individuals' capacity to act 'according to convictions that inform and shape their lives as a whole, rather than capriciously or whimsically'.[62] Sharon Dolovich said it

> implies the capacity for and willingness to engage in critical reflection on one's values and principles, a process that involves at the minimum the careful consideration of alternative viewpoints, a logical assessment of relevant evidence, and an openness to the possibility that one could, in the face of sufficiently persuasive arguments, be convinced to re-think one's preferred approach. The engagement in this deliberative process distinguishes the person of integrity.[63]

Integrity as a characteristic of the lawyer is reflected, for example, in the character tests for entrance into the legal profession.[64]

Analysis of the independence of legal professionals is informed by the theoretical discourses on independence. The degree to which the two aspects of independence are required and co-relate will be driven by the underlying objective of independence in a particular context. In *Valiente v The Queen*, the Canadian Supreme Court said, in reference to constitutional guarantees of judicial independence, that independence 'connotes not merely a state of mind or attitude in the actual exercise of judicial functions, but a status or relationship to others, particularly to the executive branch of government, that rests on objective conditions or guarantees'.[65] Similarly, the content of the independence of legal professionals will need to be defined in terms of the freedom from certain defined external constraints, coupled with an internal capacity.

ii. Three Conceptions of Lawyers' Independence

There are three conceptions of lawyers' independence. Each is defined by reference to a different underlying purpose, and incorporates different degrees of the two types of independence—extrinsic and intrinsic—that have been discussed above.

[61] M Cranston, *Freedom: A New Analysis* (Longmans, Green & Co, 1953) ch I.

[62] R Dworkin, *Law's Empire* (Belknap Press, 1986) 166.

[63] S Dolovich, 'Ethical Lawyering and the Possibility of Integrity' (2002) 70 *Fordham Law Review* 1629, 1651.

[64] See, eg, 'fit and proper' person test that the Supreme Courts apply for admission in the Australian jurisdictions.

[65] *Valiente v The Queen* [1985] 2 SCR 673, [15].

The dominant conception of lawyers' independence underpins the dominant conception of lawyers' ethics.[66] This conception is driven by the principle that the client acts as instructor and principal decision-maker. It recognises the inherent legitimacy of the interests of the client.[67] Pursuant to this conception, the lawyer remains independent from the *moral* position of the client, but 'zealously' pursues the client's interests professionally.[68] This moral independence provides the foundation for the 'principle of non-accountability':[69] lawyers are not called to account for their clients' actions, even where those actions are based on legal advice.[70] Deborah Rhode suggested that this type of independence 'serves fundamental interests of individual dignity, privacy and autonomy'.[71] From this underlying liberal objective, independence in this conception is predominantly viewed as independence from the external influence of the *state*—both in terms of its influence on the lawyer–client relationship, and the regulation of the profession—as the legal profession stands between the individual and the state (at least in the criminal context).[72] However, there is a degree of internal capacity involved as well: there must be independence from the subtle pressures of personal interests and other improper motives, to prevent conflicts of interest with the client and abuse of the relationship.[73]

Applying this conception of independence to the government lawyer reveals fundamental difficulties.[74] Primarily, the government lawyer does not stand between the state and the people.[75] Rather, the government lawyer is called upon to assist in achieving and defending the policies and actions of the democratically

[66] Note, 'Rethinking the Professional Responsibilities of Federal Agency Lawyers' (2002) 115 *Harvard Law Review* 1170, 1171. See also Windsor's discussion of the standard conception of legal ethics: M Windsor, 'Government Legal Advisers Through the Ethics Looking Glass' in D Feldman (ed), *Law in Politics, Politics in Law* (Hart Publishing, Oxford) 117, 121–24.

[67] This conception models Neil Walker's explanation of the law as 'an instrument or vessel for the achievement of externally-driven ends': N Walker, 'The Antinomies of the Law Officers' in M Sunkin and S Payne (eds), *The Nature of the Crown: A Legal and Political Analysis* (Oxford University Press, 1999) 135, 145–46.

[68] This model is akin to the 'adversarial advocate' model of lawyers ethics developed in the Australian context by Christine Parker: C Parker, 'A Critical Morality for Lawyers: Four Approaches to Lawyers' Ethics' (2004) 30 *Monash Law Review* 49.

[69] D Luban, 'Twenty Theses on Adversarial Ethics' in H Stacy and M Lavarch (eds), *Beyond the Adversarial System* (Federation Press, 1999) 134, 140.

[70] C Parker, 'Regulation of the Ethics of Australian Legal Practice: Autonomy and Responsiveness' (2002) 25(3) *University of New South Wales Law Journal* 676, 686; for a critique of the position, see L O'Shea, 'Advocacy on trial' (2011) 36(2) *Alternative Law Journal* 87.

[71] DL Rhode, 'Ethical Perspectives on Legal Practice' (1985) 37(2) *Stanford Law Review* 589, 605. See also RW Gordon, 'The Independence of Lawyers' (1988) 68 *Boston University Law Review* 1, 10; D Webb, 'Keeping the Crown's Conscience: A Theory of Lawyering for Public Sector Counsel' (2007) 5 *New Zealand Journal of Public and International Law* 243, 245.

[72] EA Davis, 'The Meaning of Professional Independence' (2003) 103 *Columbia Law Review* 1281, 1281.

[73] Michels, above n 30, 97–98.

[74] Webb, above n 71, 246. See also Windsor, above n 66, 126.

[75] AM Dodek, 'Lawyering at the Intersection of Public Law and Legal Ethics: Government Lawyers as Custodians of the Rule of Law' (2010) 33(1) *Dalhousie Law Journal* 1, 23.

elected government. As such, questions arise as to whether this approach is applicable to the government lawyer.

The dominant model has also been supported on the basis that in the adversarial system, truth and justice are achieved only if the judge is provided with the strongest possible arguments for each side.[76] David Luban warns, however, that this defence of the model can hold true only in an adjudicative context.[77] Given the stronger justifications that exist for this approach in the adversarial advocacy function of the lawyer, in the US it has been adopted most readily in the OSG's advocacy role. While Caplan's book, *The Tenth Justice*, was extremely critical of the approach, it has gained traction as the dominant ethical approach that the Solicitor-General should take.[78]

The second, albeit related, conception of independence is that the lawyer exercises 'independent professional judgement', not for the public interest (which correlates with the third conception) but for the benefit of the client. Independence in this context largely mirrors what is often referred to as 'decisional independence' in the judicial arena. Legal opinions must be formed in accordance with law and not improper considerations: whims, prejudices, fear or other considerations, including the desires of the client.[79] Such a view of independence assumes that clients seek legal advice and representation to be better informed in their own decision-making, rather than to be provided with *any* legally available argument in the blind pursuit of their interests. This conception of independence taps more strongly into the requirement for an internal capacity: a capacity to analyse and evaluate the legal position with integrity; and a capacity to balance the competing interests of justice and the client. In its practical manifestation, it will often look very similar to the third conception of independence.

The third conception is that independence exists to allow the legal practitioner to aid the broader public interest.[80] Acting in the public interest can manifest in two ways. First, simply by providing robust and independent advice, the lawyer encourages the client to act in accordance with the law, not just for the client's

[76] R Wasserstrom, 'Lawyers as Professionals: Some Moral Issues' (1975) 5 *Human Rights* 1, 10; D Luban, *Legal Ethics and Human Dignity* (Cambridge University Press, 2007) 25; KN Llewellyn, *The Theory of Rules* (University of Chicago Press, 2011) 119; Rhode, above n 71, 595; Dolovich, above n 63, 1634.

[77] Luban, above n 76, 28.

[78] See further discussion of the American scholarship and the distinction that has been drawn by some between the independence required of the OSG in its advocacy function and that required by the OLC in its advisory function, in ch 2, section III.A.

[79] See, eg, VR Johnson, 'The Ethical Foundations of American Judicial Independence' (2002) 29 *Fordham Urban Law Journal* 1007, 1012. In the Australian context, see *North Australian Aboriginal Legal Aid Service Inc v Bradley* (2004) 218 CLR 146, 152 (Gleeson CJ); M Kirby, 'Independence of the Legal Profession: Global and Regional Challenges' (2005) 26 *Australian Bar Review* 133, 134.

[80] Note, above n 66, 1171–72. It reflects Walker's explanation of the law as 'an autonomous source of moral and political values': Walker, above n 67, 145–46.

benefit but in the communal interest.[81] The second takes a more proactive form, which finds expression in Anthony Kronman's ideal 'lawyer-statesman'. Such a lawyer requires two traits: 'first, love of the public good, and second, wisdom in deliberating about it'.[82] It requires counsel to operate autonomously from all influences so as to provide the necessary space for that practitioner to determine the best interpretation of the law for the public interest.[83] If the actions of the client do not accord with the lawyer's view of the public interest, there is an obligation to try to change the client's position or refuse to act. It is this model of independence in deliberating about the law and the public interest that has been urged for the OLC's advisory function in the US after the scandals following the release of the Torture Memos (see further chapter two, section III.A.).

This approach has, however, been subjected to heavy criticism. A definitional-based critique asserts that it is impossible to act in accordance with a universal public interest, because the term lacks definition.[84] It can be a cloak for decisions affected by personal biases, and desires to achieve personal, financial and career goals.[85] From a democratic viewpoint, it may undermine public accountability of executive decisions about the public interest.[86] An adversarial critique argues that the adversarial system that underpins the common law legal system *requires* the government's interests to be put forward as forcefully as those of the other side.[87] Lastly, Nancy Baker noted that neutral, robustly independent officeholders may find themselves isolated from important policy areas, including those that have important legal repercussions, because of the perception of aloofness from the political agenda of the President, which can erode trust in the office.[88]

[81] Michels, above n 30, 100.

[82] AT Kronman, *The Lost Lawyer: Failing the Ideals of the Legal Profession* (Harvard University Press, 1993) 54.

[83] This model reflects both the 'Responsible Lawyer' and the 'Moral Activist' put forward by Christine Parker. Parker distinguishes the two on the basis that the Responsible Lawyer will look to advise and encourage action that is most in accordance with the legal system and the spirit of the law, whereas the Moral Activist will pursue substantive moral outcomes: Parker, above n 78, 62–63. See also C Parker and A Evans, *Inside Lawyers' Ethics* (Cambridge University Press, 2007) ch 2.

[84] See, eg, GA Schubert, *The Public Interest: A Critique of the Theory of a Political Concept* (Free Press, 1960); GP Miller, 'Government Lawyers' Ethics in a System of Checks and Balances' (1987) 54 *University of Chicago Law Review* 1293, 1295–96. See also N Lund, 'The President as Client and the Ethics of the President's Lawyers' (1998) 61 *Law and Contemporary Problems* 65, 77; SK Berenson, 'Public Lawyers, Private Values, Can, Should, and Will Government Lawyers Serve the Public Interest?' (2000) 41 *Boston College Law Review* 789, 802–05; J Waldron, 'Gangsters, Statesmen and their Lawyers: The Rule of Law on Matters International' (Paper presented at the ALTA Conference, Auckland, 5 July 2010) 5–6.

[85] Berenson, above n 84, 807–11.

[86] See, eg, ibid, 806; Miller, above n 84, 1295; MW McConnell, 'The Rule of Law and the Role of the Solicitor General' (1988) 21 *Loyola of Los Angeles Law Review* 1105, 1116.

[87] McConnell, above n 86, 1107.

[88] N Baker, *Conflicting Loyalties: Law and Politics in the Attorney General's Office, 1789–1990* (University Press of Kansas, 1992) 145–46; contra the role of the 'Advocate' type at 93, 173–74. See also DJ Meador, *The President, The Attorney General and the Department of Justice* (White Burkett Miller Center of Public Affairs, 1980) 40 (quoting from Antonin Scalia, then assistant Attorney General for the OLC); NW Spaulding, 'Professional Independence in the Office of the Attorney-General' (2008) 60(6) *Stanford Law Review* 1931, 1935.

iii. Advocate and Adviser: A Dichotomy of Independence

The obligations to exercise independence in the context of government lawyers, and more specifically by reference to the statutory functions of the Solicitor-General, are best explained by reference to Luban's dichotomy between the independence of the advocate and that of the adviser.[89]

In examining the obligation to exercise independent professional discretion, Luban draws a distinction between counsel's independence as an advocate and as an adviser. As an advocate, in defending the client's actions from legal challenge, the lawyer can resolve doubts about the law in favour of the client because, at least in orthodox theory, the adversarial system will check against excesses.[90] Joseph Jaconelli said, 'the process of adjudication is fuelled by the presentation of competing arguments from advocates representing opposing perspectives on the legal issue at stake'.[91] Thus, in advocacy, the dominant model of lawyers' independence and ethics is attractive.

In contrast, advisers must provide independent and candid professional opinions as to the law as their arguments are unchallenged by opposing counsel or subject to the overarching decision of the judge.[92] Of course, it remains the client's decision whether he or she chooses to follow the advice. In this function the third view of lawyers' independence must apply. Thus, in so far as the ethical obligations of the lawyer to the client or to the public interest and concomitant obligations of independence are concerned, the functions of adviser and advocate are fundamentally different.

Luban's dichotomy is reflected in the ABA Model Rules, which distinguish between advocacy and opinion work. As an advocate the barrister is a fierce proponent for, but morally independent from, the client's cause.[93] This is subject to the exercise of the barrister's independent forensic judgement in the conduct of a case,[94] and the overarching duty of frankness to the court.[95] In contrast, in opinions, the barrister must step away from the client's interests and 'give the barrister's *truthful opinion* on any matter submitted to the barrister for advice or opinion.'[96]

The attraction of Luban's dichotomy becomes readily apparent when transposed into the setting of the Solicitor-General and the government lawyer. The obligation to exercise independent judgement in advising ensures that the best possible legal advice is provided to government about the exercise of government

[89] Luban, above n 76, 131, 153–54, 201; further developing this dichotomy, see Michels, above n 30. See also Llewellyn, above n 76, 119, ch IV (the dichotomy between judge and advocate).

[90] Luban, above n 76, 153–54, 201; Michels, above n 30, 103.

[91] J Jaconelli, 'Hypothetical Disputes, Moot Points of Law, and Advisory Opinions' (1985) 101 *Law Quarterly Review* 587, 587.

[92] Michels, above n 30, 103.

[93] Australian Bar Association, *Model Rules* (effective 8 December 2002) rule 16.

[94] ibid, rules 18 and 19.

[95] ibid, rules 21–31.

[96] ibid, rule 73, emphasis added.

power. This is congruent with the government lawyer's internally focused position within the machinery of government, acting as a 'check' on government power and ensuring compliance with the rule of law. Edwards said that, as adviser, the Law Officer 'occupies the same degree of constitutional independence as that associated with his position as the State's chief prosecutor'.[97] Of course, the government may always choose not to comply with the government lawyer's advice. This is a necessity in the Australian system to ensure the proper operation of responsible government and the necessary accountability between the ministers and parliament. However, the fact the advice has been given creates a very large incentive to comply with it, and in Australia the accepted practice is that the Solicitor-General's advice is treated as binding. It is in this function that the Solicitor-General is sometimes referred to as the 'conscience of government'.[98] If Solicitors-General remain true to this obligation in the advisory function, they also avoid the risk that their advice may be labelled partisan, creating the potential for distrust upon a change of government.

As an advocate, however, the Solicitor-General has an obligation to defend the actions of the Crown. This is subject to a number of ethical considerations: it must only be done with reasonably available legal argument; it is subject to the forensic decisions of the barrister in court; and, in the government context, it is subject to the model litigant framework within which the Crown has an obligation to act. This paramount duty to the client as advocate exists not, as it may in relation to private clients, to protect their autonomy and liberty from the behemoth of the state, but to ensure against improper external attack on government power and that the democratic mandates of the government are defended in the adversarial context. The Solicitor-General operates as one part of the machinery in the adversarial system of justice. Adopting the zealous advocate conception of independence in the advocacy function, Solicitors-General are again able to avoid allegations of partisanship and ensure they remain above party politics in the event of a change of government. Within this conception, the Solicitor-General remains morally removed from the position taken by the government, whatever its political persuasion.

In Australia, the Solicitor-General as a fierce, but fair, advocate in litigation is reflected in the parallel historical development of the Commonwealth and States' Solicitors-General. Federal issues (which dominate our constitutional text) are now predominantly resolved in an adversarial setting in the High Court between the Commonwealth and States' Solicitors-General. One of the chief drivers behind the adoption of a statutory counsel model across the jurisdictions was to provide the Commonwealth and the States with consistent representation in the High Court, particularly in these cases. Section 78A of the *Judiciary Act 1903* (Cth) now

[97] JLJ Edwards, *The Attorney General, Politics and the Public Interest* (Sweet & Maxwell, 1984) 190.

[98] C Fahy, 'Special Ethical Problems of Counsel for the Government' (1950) 33 *Federal Bar Journal* 331, 335.

grants the Commonwealth and State Attorneys-General the right to intervene in matters arising under the Constitution or involving its interpretation; this ensures that each political unit in the federation has an opportunity to put forward its case whenever a constitutional issue arises that affects its interests.

In furnishing opinions, the Solicitor-General must operate with absolute independence from the direction of the Crown[99] and any other constraints, to ensure that the opinion reached is his or her best opinion on the law. This conclusion raises one further question about the ethical framework that surrounds the Solicitor-General: what normative rules guide the Solicitor-General if there is no clear legal conclusion?

To understand the advisory function of the Solicitor-General more fully it must be placed in the context of an accepted level of indeterminacy in the law. Contemporary legal culture is now generally accepting of subjective influences on legal interpretation, to varying degrees. The focus of this literature and analysis has been on the judicial task. However, it also complicates the approach of the Solicitor-General (and any other government lawyer—and indeed any lawyer) when providing legal advice.[100] How should the Solicitor-General resolve ambiguities within the law 'independently' if the application of traditional legal method yields no objectively 'correct' answer?

Often, the question simply does not arise: there exists a clear legal conclusion to an issue arising on a particular set of facts by the application of traditionally accepted legal-reasoning techniques.[101] In a second set of circumstances there may be legal ambiguity as to the state of legal authority or its application to particular facts, but this can be resolved in favour of a preferable view by the application of the traditional legal method: the view that provides the *most coherent* explanation of the text, previous case authority and the purpose behind the principle. In this case, it is generally accepted to be the role of counsel to present their view as to this best legal position.[102] The advice should also give some indication that the matter lacks the type of clarity seen in the first instance,[103] and good advice should also consider whether the court before which the client may appear is likely to take that view given what is known about how the judges of that court have decided similar decisions.

A third set of circumstances arises less commonly in practice but presents the Solicitor-General with the most difficulty: genuine and deep indeterminacy in the legal position, where the application of legal method reveals no preferable

[99] In some statutes, the Solicitor-General is expressly removed from the public service, taking the office out of the system of public service directions. See NSW s 2(9); Qld s 5(5); SA s 5(4); Tas s 4(4).

[100] Luban, above n 76, 132. Some application of this question to government legal advisers has been attempted in the US, see, eg, WB Wendel, 'Government Lawyers, Democracy and the Rule of Law' (2009) 77(4) *Fordham Law Review* 1333.

[101] Luban, above n 76, 192–93.

[102] RD Moss, 'Executive Branch Legal Interpretation: A Perspective from the Office of Legal Counsel' (2000) 52 *Administrative Law Review* 1303, 1321–22.

[103] Michels, above n 30, 118.

view, a number of views are plausible and there has been no indication about the preferred view of the court. The Solicitor-General's involvement in complex constitutional issues may increase the frequency with which this scenario arises, given the necessarily broad and often ambiguous nature of constitutional provisions. Further, the Solicitor-General is often briefed when an issue raises complex or novel issues, or where there has been disagreement on the legal position between government departments and agencies. It is likely, therefore, that the Solicitor-General confronts these types of issues in the advisory role more often than most barristers, and even most government lawyers.

In such an instance is the Solicitor-General, as he or she would be if appearing for the government in the courts, obliged to resolve legal ambiguity in favour of achieving government objectives?[104] Should the Solicitor-General simply indicate to the government that a particular position is 'arguable', and leave it to the discretion of the government as to whether to pursue it?[105] Should the Solicitor-General adopt the view that is most consistent with what he or she considers to be the ongoing interests of the government?[106] Should the Solicitor-General determine the position based on his or her view of where the public interest lies? Should the Solicitor-General have an obligation to advise the government that it *cannot* avoid the impact of legal constraint where it is A or unclear?

Jeremy Waldron argued for this last position.[107] Waldron based his argument on the fundamental philosophical difference between the position of the private client, with no duty to go out of his or her way to be constrained by the law, and that of the government. The government, Waldron asserted, 'does not have an interest in being unconstrained by law in the way that the individual does. Its freedom of action is in the service of *our* interests and *our* freedom of action; it is not something valued for its own sake.'[108]

Waldron's assertion that, in those hard cases where the legal position is *genuinely indeterminate*, the nature of the government as a client must inform the obligation of the Solicitor-General as an adviser, must be correct.[109] But Waldron's

[104] Luban, above n 76, 163; ibid, 90. See the strong argument made against this position in Wendel, above n 100, 1356–62.

[105] For example, in 1974, the Commonwealth Solicitor-General Maurice Byers, when asked his opinion as to whether the Whitlam Government's loan authorisation for $4 billion fell within a loan for 'temporary purposes' under the Financial Agreement, replied that it was 'arguable' although 'drawing a long bow': see *Sankey versus Whitlam*—Maurice Byers QC regarding involvement in the Loans Affair (April 1976), National Archives of Australia, Canberra, M4081 3/25, 4.

[106] For a description of this theory of interpretation, see M Tushnet, 'Non-Judicial Review' (2003) 40 *Harvard Journal on Legislation* 453, 467.

[107] J Waldron, 'Gangsters, Statesmen and their Lawyers: The Rule of Law on Matters International' (Paper presented at the ALTA Conference, Auckland, 5 July 2010) 11; see also this position as developed in J Waldron, *Torture, Terror and Trade-offs: Philosophy for the White House* (Oxford University Press, 2010).

[108] Waldron, 'Gangsters, Statesmen and their Lawyers', above n 107, 11.

[109] See also Webb, above n 71, 244, 249–50.

conclusion that the government's interests lies in more regulation, not less,[110] overlooks an important part of the role of government and the fundamental duties of the state to the citizen.[111] The government's pursuit of these duties necessarily requires a varied and flexible store of power. Indeed, it is for this very reason that the limits of the 'executive power' of the state are difficult to define.[112] French CJ said of the Executive's power:

> While history and the common law inform its content, it is not a locked display cabinet in a constitutional museum. It is not limited to statutory powers and the prerogative. It has to be capable of serving the proper purposes of a national government.[113]

Government power must be both sufficiently flexible to ensure that the state can respond to its duties on behalf of the community, and confined by appropriate legal constraints, so that it does not intrude, unwarranted, into the private sphere. In pursuit of this ideal equilibrium, it is argued that in instances where legal constraints are genuinely ambiguous, the Solicitor-General has two obligations. The first is to make his or her best assessment of the law. However, in recognition of the impact that legal advice can have on the scope of government power and the lives of citizens, the second is to indicate the indeterminate nature of the legal position.[114] In some ways, this is putting the question back into the government's court. This should not be viewed with cynicism but as consistent with the democratic mandate of the government, and its constitutional duties and responsibilities.[115] It seems far more congruent with the constitutional system that the Solicitor-General, as counsel to the Crown, makes it very clear, where necessary, when the legal position is not clear and must be informed by a *policy* choice about whether to pursue the action or legislation despite this uncertainty, a choice that can then be held accountable through *political* means.

The Solicitor-General's function as 'adviser' must also be understood against the common law functions of the Law Officers to protect the public interest. Section VI. of this chapter explains that this places obligations on the Solicitor-General to

[110] Waldron, 'Gangsters, Statesmen and their Lawyers', above n 107, 10–11.

[111] See, eg, explanation of these duties by Adam Smith, one of the first and most influential writers to question the relationship between sovereignty and the broader polity: A Smith, *An Inquiry into the Nature and the Causes of the Wealth of Nations*, vol II (Oxford University Press, 1776, 1976 reprint) 687. Waldron's comments are made in the US context, where the role of public law in the constraint of government is particularly pronounced.

[112] See, eg, *Davis v Commonwealth* (1988) 166 CLR 79, 92 (Mason CJ, Deane and Gaudron JJ).

[113] *Pape v Commissioner of Taxatio* n (2009) 238 CLR 1, 38 [60].

[114] In the US, for example, the OLC has adopted a practice where conclusions on the constitutionality of proposed Bills are framed as 'litigation risk', 'constitutional concerns' and 'serious constitutional concerns'. This allows the final risk assessment to be made by the Executive, with the benefit of this assessment. See Tushnet, above n 106, 471; Luban, above n 76, 199.

[115] See, in the US context, Moss, above n 102, 1328–29, although note the impact of the *Chevron* doctrine in that context.

furnish advice to the government as to the *appropriate* exercise of government power, informed by what I shall refer to as 'core government principles'.

IV. The 'Crown'

The different statutory frameworks provide, in various forms, that the Solicitor-General acts as counsel for the Crown (although, as is explored below, in some statutes this entity is identified in different guises). It is often said that the Crown is the 'client' of the Solicitor-General. The desire to articulate the client of the Solicitor-General is understandable; lawyers act for clients, and in many respects the professional obligations of the lawyer are informed by reference to the client and the client's interests. However, the characterisation of the Crown as the client of the Solicitor-General carries with it a number of difficulties.

First, the Solicitor-General operates from *within* the client. In this respect it may be correct to view the Solicitor-General as roughly analogous to in-house counsel at a corporation. Adam Dodek, however, argues that this analogy is flawed, because government lawyers are in fact *exercising* public power.[116] There is certainly some attraction to this conclusion. There are even judicial pronouncements to the effect that the executive power of the state includes the functions of the lawyer. The Privy Council, in *Eastern Trust Company v McKenzie, Mann and Co*, said:

> It is the duty of the Crown and of every branch of the Executive to abide by and obey the law … [I]t is the duty of the Executive in cases of doubt to ascertain the law, in order to abide the law, not to disregard it.[117]

In *Dixon v Attorney-General*, Jenkinson J found

> the power to conduct on behalf of the Commonwealth legal proceedings to which the Commonwealth is a party is in my opinion an inherent Executive power and within what is comprehended by the expression, 'The Executive power of the Commonwealth' in s 61 of the *Constitution*.[118]

However, the better conceptualisation of the Solicitor-General is as a statutory officeholder appointed to *assist* the Crown in fulfilling these obligations. The Solicitor-General does not conduct proceedings on behalf of the Commonwealth. Rather, the Solicitor-General *represents* the Attorney-General. It is the latter who brings or defends proceedings on behalf of the Commonwealth.[119] As adviser, it

[116] Dodek, above n 75, 18. See also Interview, Daryl Dawson.

[117] *Eastern Trust Company v McKenzie, Mann and Co* [1915] AC 750, 759. See also B Selway, 'The Duties of Lawyers Acting for Government' (1999) 10 *Public Law Review* 114, 115, fn 7 and reference.

[118] *Dixon v Attorney-General* (1987) 15 FCR 338, 343.

[119] *Kidman v Commonwealth* (1925) 37 CLR 233, 239–40 (Knox CJ). See also ibid, 243 (Isaacs J); and extracted High Court transcript in *Fejo v Northern Territory* (1998) in Selway, above n 117, 115. Note also *Judiciary Act 1903* (Cth), s 61.

is the Solicitor-General's advice that *assists* the Executive to ascertain the law. The explanation of the proper role of the Solicitor-General in determining questions of genuine indeterminacy in the law given above in section III.A. buttresses this conclusion.

There are two statutory exceptions to this statement. In the Commonwealth, New South Wales, Tasmania and Western Australia, the Solicitor-General may exercise powers and perform functions *delegated* by the Attorney-General.[120] In New South Wales, the Solicitor-General assists the Attorney-General in fulfilling his or her public interest functions through a series of delegations relating to charitable trusts, warrants for surveillance devices, criminal contempt proceedings and claims of public interest immunity.[121] In New South Wales there is a unique provision that empowers the Solicitor-General to 'exercise and discharge any powers, authorities, duties and functions conferred or imposed on the Attorney-General by or under any Act or incident by law to the office of the Attorney-General' when the senior Law Officer is absent or ill, or the office is vacant.[122] As delegates, Solicitors-General may not be directed by the Attorney-General. They must exercise the powers at their own discretion,[123] although they will always be subject to any limitations in the delegation instrument.[124] The power of the Attorney to delegate to the Solicitor-General is a throwback to the traditional position of seniority between the Law Officers. In the current statutory context its existence blurs the line between counsel *to the client* and acting *as the client*. The other exception is where legislation bestows functions directly on the Solicitor-General; the extent to which this occurs varies across jurisdictions.

Putting to one side these exceptions, given the role of the Solicitor-General, it is appropriate to speak of, and seek to define, the 'client' of the Solicitor-General. Indeed, this conclusion reflects the historical establishment of the office as the King's Solicitor. In those jurisdictions where the Solicitor-General acts as counsel for the 'Crown' (sometimes expressed as 'Her Majesty'),[125] the 'client' of the Solicitor-General is the 'Crown'.[126] There is a good argument that the description of the Solicitor-General as acting for the Crown is problematic in our modern constitutional order and should be abandoned. It is a highly contested and,

[120] Cth s 17(1); NSW s 4; Tas s 8(1); WA s 13 (note also *Supreme Court Act 1935* (WA), s 154(5a)). In Victoria, other ministers may perform the Attorney-General's functions: Vic s 3.

[121] MG Sexton, 'The Role of the Solicitor General' in G Lindsay (ed), *No Mere Mouthpiece: Servants of All, Yet of None* (LexisNexis Butterworths, 2002) 86, 92; J Hatzistergos, 'The evolving office of the New South Wales Attorney General' (2012) 86 *Australian Law Journal* 197, 206. No other office has such broad-ranging delegations.

[122] NSW s 3(1)(b).

[123] See specifically Tas s 8(7).

[124] Cth s 17(3); NSW s 4(3); Tas s 8(2); WA s 13(2).

[125] This reflects the fact that the Law Officers were originally the monarch's personal lawyers: it was only with the advent of the modern conception of the 'Crown' that the Law Officers came to be the legal advisers to a much larger, and more abstract, entity.

[126] NSW s 3(1)(a); SA s 6(a); Tas s 7(a); Vic s 5(a); WA s 9(a); NT s 14(a).

arguably, even increasing irrelevant concept to public law as the constitutional boundaries of Executive power have developed and evolved.[127] However, the statutes still dictate that the Solicitor-General acts for the Crown or Her Majesty, and the reference occurs in many other statutory contexts in Australia—not least legislation governing Crown proceedings. As such, at least in this legal analysis, we must grapple with the idea of the Crown.

As a concept, the Crown has been described as indeterminate[128] and, famously, as an 'abstraction'.[129] Its lack of definitional rigour has led a number of members of the Australian High Court to criticise the use of the term.[130] Historically, the Crown meant simply the monarch. The term has, however, evolved in its use.

In the context of the legislation establishing the office of the Solicitor-General, two meanings for the Crown can be isolated as relevant.[131] First, it means the body politic.[132] Cobbett points out that the Crown according to British constitutional theory has evolved to mean 'the legal representative of the whole state'.[133] Peter Hogg noted that sometimes the term 'State' or the 'Commonwealth' is used in its place.[134] Thus in British tradition, the Crown represents the state as a juristic person. Australia's High Court has been reluctant to use the terminology of the Crown in relation to the Australian body politic, noting the preference in the Constitution to refer to this body as the 'Commonwealth'.

Australia's federal system complicates the concept of the Crown as representing the body politic of the state. Some statutes expressly provide that the Solicitor-General serves the Crown in right of the State or Territory.[135] This assumes that there are separate Crowns in the federation, and even for the Territories; or at least that the Crown exists in different capacities. This is an accepted assumption in practice and it often appears in statutes—although as a matter of theory it has been contested.[136] Dixon J noted that while the Commonwealth and the

[127] See, eg, C Saunders, 'International Relations and the British Commonwealth: The Concept of the Crown' (2015) 38 *Melbourne University Law Review* 873.

[128] P Johnston, 'Going it Alone—Republican States in a Monarchical Commonwealth' in S Murray (ed), *Constitutional Perspectives on an Australian Republic* (Federation Press, 2010) 82, 91. See also A Twomey, 'Responsible Government and the Divisibility of the Crown' [2008] *Public Law* 742, 747.

[129] *Dixon v London Small Arms Co LR* (1867) 1 App Cas 632, 652 (Lord Penzance).

[130] *Commonwealth v Western Australia* (1999) 196 CLR 392 ('*Mining Act Case*'), 410 [33] (Gleeson CJ and Gaudron J), 429–31 [105]–[109] (Gummow J); *Bass v Permanent Trustee Co Ltd* (1999) 198 CLR 334, 347 (Gleeson CJ, Gaudron, McHugh, Gummow, Hayne and Callinan JJ). Note also the criticism in P Cobbett, 'The Crown as Representing the State' (1903) 1 *Commonwealth Law Review* 23.

[131] For a fuller discussion of meanings, see *Sue v Hill* (1999) 199 CLR 462, 498 ff (Gleeson CJ, Gummow and Hayne JJ).

[132] ibid; *Williams v Commonwealth* (2012) 248 CLR 256 [154] (Gummow and Bell JJ).

[133] Cobbett, above n 130, 25.

[134] P Hogg and PJ Monahan, *Liability of the Crown* (Thomson Professional Publishing, 3rd edn, 2000) 11.

[135] Cth s 12; Qld s 8(a); Tas s 7(a); WA s 9(a); ACT s 17(1)(a)(i); NT s 14(a); contra NSW s 3(1)(a); SA s 6(a); Vic s 5(a).

[136] A Twomey, *The Chameleon Crown: The Queen and Her Australian Governors* (Federation Press, 2006) 271.

States may not be, formally, separate juristic persons, under the Constitution 'they are conceived as politically organized bodies having mutual legal relations and amenable to the jurisdiction of courts upon which the responsibility of enforcing the Constitution rests'.[137]

The passage of the *Australia Acts 1986* left the issue unclear, resulting in two possibilities: there is a single Australian Crown, which includes the Commonwealth and the States in an indivisible sovereign entity; or there are separate Crowns in right of the jurisdictions, which form a single sovereign nation.[138] The possibility that there is only a single Crown would mean that all of the Australian Solicitors-General are serving, ultimately, a single entity. Dixon J pointed out that regardless of whether separate Crowns *actually* exist in the federation, the Commonwealth, States and Territories are separate legal entities, with distinct legal interests, capable of suing, and being sued by, each other.[139] The statutes establishing the Solicitors-General in Australia make it clear that it is these disparate interests that the office represents, not a single, overarching entity.

The next question that becomes relevant is what part of the juristic person of the 'state' does the Solicitor-General represent? The state, in Australia, is a tripartite system of democratic government. The holistic juristic person of the state must be capable of legal representation and the appropriate counsel is, historically, a Law Officer. However, it must be informed by an appreciation that the state, as a juristic person, is represented in our system of government by the Executive arm.[140] As already discussed above, the Attorney-General is the proper person to represent the Crown, in its guise as a juristic entity. It is in the exercise of *Executive power* that litigation is conducted by and on behalf of the Crown. This raises the second relevant definition of the term.

In its second definitional form, the Crown is 'symbolic of the Executive power'.[141] This power, in Australia, is wielded by the Crown's representative (the Governor-General at the Commonwealth level, the Governors in the States and the Northern Territory Administrator) on the advice of the Executive branch of government.[142] The Crown therefore represents this branch of the government polity.[143] As Cheryl Saunders has explained, this is not the government of the day but, rather, 'a more

[137] *Bank of New South Wales v Commonwealth* (1948) 76 CLR 1, 363.

[138] Twomey, above n 136, 271–72.

[139] See provision for this in the *Constitution*, s 75. See also *Sue v Hill* (1999) 199 CLR 462, 525–26 (Gaudron J).

[140] *Williams v Commonwealth* (2012) 248 CLR 256 [21] (French CJ), [217] (Hayne J).

[141] *McArthur v R* [1943] Ex CR 77, 104 Ex Ct (Thorson J). See also *Town Investments v Department of Environment* [1978] AC 359, 397 (Lord Simon of Glaisdale for the House of Lords); Cobbett, above n 130, 26.

[142] Except in exceptional circumstances when the Crown's representative will act alone. The role of the Solicitor-General in acting as a legal adviser in relation to the exercise of these prerogative powers, known as the 'reserve powers', is returned to below at section IV.A.ii.

[143] *Wardle v Management Farm Loan Association* [1956] SCR 3, 10, 18, 23; *Sue v Hill* (1999) 199 CLR 462, 499 (Gleeson CJ, Gummow and Hayne JJ). See also F Hanlon, *An Analysis of the Office of Attorney General in Australia and Directions for the Future* (PhD Thesis, University of Melbourne, 2007) 103.

abstract and continuing understanding of executive government that is distinct from the current administration'.[144]

In this second sense, the Crown includes the Crown's representative and the departments headed by the Crown's ministers.[145] It also includes other bodies under the control of the Crown's Ministers: Crown agents.[146] This interpretation of the Crown is found in the various Crown proceedings statutes that regulate proceedings being brought against the Crown.[147] The Crown in this sense includes executive officers and individuals, agencies and organisations that operate as agents of the Crown in the one, unifying concept: giving rise to the principle of the indivisibility of the Crown.[148] The idea of the Solicitor-General acting as counsel for the Crown in the sense of the whole Executive arm accords with the historical development of the colonial Law Officers as legal advisers to the whole of government.

However, the conclusion that these officers, individuals and other entities form part of the Crown is not the same as concluding that they may all *provide instructions* on behalf of the Crown to the Solicitor-General (or that their interests and instructions will never come into conflict). The proper representative of the Crown, that is, the proper officer to provide legal instructions on behalf of the Crown, is the Attorney-General. Australia's system of responsible government and collective responsibility means that the Attorney-General, when representing the Crown in litigation and providing instructions, will be bound to implement the decisions of Cabinet (perhaps with some continuing exceptions where the Attorney-General has ongoing obligations in public interest litigation that separates the office from the collectivity of Cabinet decisions).[149] The Attorney-General (and often the Solicitor-General) will be advising Cabinet in coming to these decisions.

In practice, the Attorney-General is not always named in litigation as the representative of the Crown. However, the High Court has expressed its concern where other ministers have purported to appear for the body politic (rather than in their official capacity, for example in judicial review proceedings where ministers and other senior government officials are often named as respondents).[150]

[144] Saunders, above n 127, 876.

[145] Hogg and Monahan, above n 134, 11.

[146] ibid, 11, ch 13. See also HE Renfree, *The Executive Power of the Commonwealth of Australia* (Legal Books, 1984) 185; J Clarke, P Keyzer and J Stellios, *Hanks' Australian Constitutional Law: Materials and Commentary* (LexisNexis Butterworths, 8th edn, 2009) 1013.

[147] *Crown Proceedings Act 1998* (NSW), s 3; *Crown Proceedings Act 1992* (SA), s 4(1); *Crown Proceedings Act 1993* (NT), s 4; *Crown Proceedings Act 1980* (Qld), s 7; *Crown Proceedings Act 1993* (Tas), s 4; *Crown Suits Act 1947* (WA), s 3.

[148] At least in respect of the Crown of a particular jurisdiction.

[149] C Jacobi, 'How the ethical duties of the public lawyer are defined by the Constitution and structure of government' (Paper presented at the National Administrative Law Conference: Integrity in Administrative Decision-making, National Wine Centre, Adelaide, 19–20 July 2012) 8.

[150] See extracted High Court transcript in *Fejo v Northern Territory* (1998) in Selway, above n 117, 115. Jacobi equates representation in judicial review with representing the Crown, concluding therefore that ministers often represent the Crown: Jacobi, above n 149, 8, 10. While the ministers are

In areas where other ministers have administrative responsibility, they will often provide instructions, sometimes but not always in consultation with the Attorney-General.[151] If disputes arise between ministers and the Attorney-General, these will be resolved by the Cabinet.[152] While acknowledging this practice, it must be accepted that the Attorney-General has primacy in constitutional theory as the representative of the Crown, and as ultimate instructor for the Solicitor-General.[153]

The statutes generally indicate that there is only one 'client' of the Solicitor-General: the Crown. However, the complexity of the modern Crown threatens the apparent simplicity of this position. Before turning to this, it is necessary to briefly consider those three jurisdictions in which the assumption that the Solicitor-General has only one client, or at least one instructor, is not reflected, at least on the face of the statute: the Commonwealth, Queensland and the Australian Capital Territory.

The *Law Officers Act 1964* (Cth) provides that the Solicitor-General acts as counsel for:

(i) the Crown in right of the Commonwealth;
(ii) the Commonwealth;
(iii) a person suing or being sued on behalf of the Commonwealth;
(iv) a Minister;
(v) an officer of the Commonwealth;
(vi) a person holding office under an Act or a law of a Territory;
(vii) a body established by an Act or a law of a Territory; or
(viii) any other person or body for whom the Attorney-General requests him or her to act.[154]

In the Solicitor-General's function of furnishing opinions, these must be to the Attorney-General only.[155]

The *Solicitor-General Act 1985* (Qld) combines the features of the other State legislation with that of the Commonwealth. Under this statute, the Solicitor-General acts as counsel, upon the request of the Attorney-General, for:

(i) the Crown in right of the State;
(ii) the State;
(iii) a person suing or being sued on behalf of the State;
(iv) a body established by or under an Act; and
(v) any other person or body where it is to the benefit of the State that the Solicitor-General should so act.[156]

undoubtedly *part* of the Crown, it would seem strained to say that the Crown is the respondent in a judicial review proceeding and that anyone other than the decision-maker could defend the proceeding.

[151] Jacobi, above n 149, 8; AS Blunn and S Krieger, *Report of the Review of Commonwealth Legal Services Procurement* (Commonwealth Government, 6 November 2009) 39.

[152] Jacobi, above n 149, 8.

[153] Note the Attorney-General's position is reflected in the Cth, Qld, SA and ACT Acts, to a greater or lesser degree: Cth s 12(b); Qld s 8(a); SA 6(a); ACT s 17(1)(a).

[154] Cth s 12(a).

[155] Cth s 12(b).

[156] Qld s 8(a)

In the Australian Capital Territory, the Solicitor-General is to act, at the request of the Attorney-General, as counsel for:

(i) the Crown in right of the Territory; or
(ii) the Territory; or
(iii) any other entity.[157]

The detailed list of potential 'clients' of the Solicitor-General in these statutes is confusing and appears largely tautological. The above discussion indicates that the Crown as a legal concept in British constitutional theory, and informed by the principle of indivisibility, includes many of the other listed entities,[158] and is viewed as the legal representative of the 'Commonwealth', 'State' or 'Territory'. The terms—Crown and Commonwealth, State or Territory—are, in a legal sense, synonymous.[159]

The most convincing explanation for the inclusion of the listed entities in section 12(a) of the *Law Officers Act 1964* (Cth) comes from a survey of the historical and legal context in which it was drafted. It is likely that the Queensland and Australian Capital Territory legislation was drafted by reference to the Commonwealth Act, so to understand the Commonwealth Act may also be to understand these.

In the Commonwealth legislation, it appears that the term 'Crown' was included to reflect the English history of the Law Officers, and there would have been a general reluctance in 1964, under the Conservative Menzies Liberal/National Coalition Government, to abandon the Crown, given Prime Minister Robert Menzies' avowed loyalty to the Queen. However, the need to include the 'Commonwealth' was driven by the use of the term throughout the Constitution to describe the newly created central body politic.[160] The reference to 'a person suing or being sued on behalf of the Commonwealth' and 'an officer of the Commonwealth' again reflected the constitutional text.[161] When the legislation was drafted, the Territories did not have self-government or their own Solicitors-General, so references

[157] ACT s 16(1)(a). The list of those for whom the Government Solicitor may act is much longer, and reflects largely the equivalent Territory entities of those listed in the federal legislation. See ACT s 26(3).

[158] Selway, above n 117, 116.

[159] See, eg, FW Maitland, 'The Crown as Corporation' (1901) 19(1) *Legal Quarterly Review* 131, 140. Contrast the position taken by the minority in the report on the conduct of the Solicitor-General when called before the Senate in 1975 (this is discussed in further detail below, section V.A.). Dissenting from the majority, Senators Greenwood, Webster and Wright said, 'The distinction between the expression in the Act "second Law Officer of the *Commonwealth*" and Mr Byers' expression, "second Law Officer of the *Crown*", he unfortunately failed to explain. It is, we suggest, most important. As second Law Officer of the Commonwealth surely he has a duty not merely to advise the Executive on proper occasions but also a duty—and maybe a higher duty—to advise the Senate on proper occasions. The Senate is a vital part of the constitutional government of "the Commonwealth".' Senate Standing Committee of Privileges, *Report on Matters Referred by Senate Resolution of 17 July 1975* (7 October 1975) (Minority Report) 55.

[160] See, eg, Constitution, s 75(iii).

[161] Constitution, s 75(iii) and (v).

to 'a person holding office under an Act or a law of a Territory' and 'a body established by an Act or a law of a Territory' were probably included to ensure that representation by the Commonwealth Solicitor-General was available to them.

The reference to 'Minister' may have been included because ministers have increasingly been established as corporations sole, giving them the ability to sue and be sued in their own names. Another overarching reason for the enumeration may have been that, because the Attorney-General is the proper officer to represent the interests of the Crown, and therefore to provide instructions on behalf of the government polity, the inclusion of other entities may have been thought to be necessary to allow the Solicitor-General to accept instructions from government officers *other than* the Attorney-General.

In summary, the Commonwealth, Queensland and Australian Capital Territory statutes appear, on their face, to differ markedly from those statutes that capture the client of the Solicitor-General in the single entity of the Crown. However, it would appear that the inclusion of a list of entities for whom the Solicitor-General may act was not intended to imply a divisibility within the Crown, but reflects the historical, constitutional and practical context in which the statutes were drafted.

A. Conflicts of Interest within the 'Crown'

While it presents itself in many different emanations, the Crown is said to be 'indivisible'. But in practice the manifestations of the Crown may come into conflict with each other, raising the potential for division in the loyalty of the Solicitor-General. One potential source of conflict has arisen from the proliferation of Crown agents enjoying quasi-independence and statutorily directed objectives that may, from time to time, bring them into conflict with the Executive's interest. These agents often have independent authority to sue and be sued. Another difficult question is whether the Solicitor-General can provide legal advice directly to a Vice-regal officer (the Governor-General or Governor, or in the Northern Territory, the Administrator) regarding the exercise of the so-called 'reserve powers'—those powers that are not exercised on the advice of the government of the day. This is particularly difficult in circumstances where the Vice-regal officer may be seeking legal advice in relation to an action that is may be against the interests of the incumbent government, such as the exercise of the reserve power to dismiss a government, or when the Vice-regal officer invites a party or coalition to form a government after an election where there is no party with a clear majority in the lower house.

i. The Solicitor-General and Independent Crown Agencies

The Solicitor-General may act for any number of agencies under the umbrella of the Crown, raising the first situation in which possible conflicts may occur. While some bodies are expressly designated as being part of the Crown,[162] whether an entity falls within the concept of the Crown is otherwise determined based on the specific factual context.[163] There are also instances where an agency has been held to have a separate identity only in the exercise of some of its powers.[164] In some jurisdictions, the statutes provide that the Solicitor-General may act for a person or body not falling within the Crown (with the consent of the Attorney-General), creating a further level of complication.[165]

Even within the Crown, many agencies may sue or be sued in their own capacity, thus having a separate *legal* personality from the Crown.[166] In such cases, Bradley Selway explained:

> [W]here a lawyer acts for a body which is intended by Parliament to have a separate legal existence from the sovereign, it is the body itself which is the relevant client. Assuming that there is a justiciable dispute, that body can sue other government agencies or the sovereign itself and the possibility exists that a government lawyer acting for such a body could have a conflict of interest if that lawyer also acts for the sovereign.[167]

Thus, the theoretical idea that the Solicitor-General's client is the Crown as an indivisible entity belies the complexity that arises, because many emanations of the Crown have been statutorily established to have separate legal personalities and statutory objectives that do not necessarily always correlate with the elected government's interests.

The Solicitor-General may encounter matters in which there are conflicts between the emanations of the Crown: be that because the entity is pursuing a legal position under its own statutory mandate that conflicts with the whole-of-government legal position, or because of a more direct conflict caused by a desire to bring legal proceedings against another emanation of the Crown.[168] *Momcilovic v The Queen* represents an example of the former, where the Queen of Victoria was represented by a Crown Prosecutor, instructed by the Solicitor for Public Prosecutions, the Victorian Attorney-General as second respondent was represented by the Victorian Solicitor General, instructed by the Victorian Government Solicitor's Office (VGSO), and the Victorian Equal Opportunity and Human Rights Commission was represented by private counsel, instructed by the Commission. The nature of the litigation and the arguments brought

[162] Bodies can also be designated as *not* representing the Crown.

[163] Hogg and Monahan, above n 134, ch 12.

[164] *Campbell v Employers Mutual; Yaghoubi v Employers Mutual* (2011) 110 SASR 576. See discussion in Jacobi, above n 149, 5.

[165] Cth s 12(a)(viii); Qld s 8(a)(5); Tas s 7(a); WA s 9(a); ACT s 17(1)(a)(iii); NT s 14(a).

[166] Hogg and Monahan, above n 134, 340–41.

[167] Selway, above n 117, 117–18.

[168] GE Dal Pont, *Lawyers' Professional Responsibility* (Lawbook Co, 4th edn, 2010) 307. Concluding that there are different emanations of the Crown that may have conflicting interests is different from saying that those entities that do not have a separate personality from the Crown can conflict with each other: contra Dal Pont at 300, who notes that different agencies have different objectives and compete for funds. This, *of itself*, is not a legitimate conflict of interest. See a strong riposte to this position in Jacobi, above n 149, 6.

forward by each of these state actors meant that they were not appearing in litigation *against* each other. Nonetheless, French CJ did note that the Queen and the Attorney-General were on opposite sides on at least one contested point,[169] although not the fundamental question of the constitutional validity of the Victorian *Charter of Human Rights and Responsibilities Act 2006* (Vic).[170] It was explained that the two government parties took their respective positions under separate statutory authority.[171]

How should the Solicitor-General resolve a possible conflict between the emanations of the office's client? Maurice Byers and Michael Gill, in their 1993 review of New South Wales government legal services, argued:

> Even where, as is increasingly the case, there is a separate corporate identity we believe it is ludicrous to consider various arms of Government becoming involved in litigation. It is essential that the Government have in place a system to resolve such disputes ...[172]

Any possible conflict ought to be resolved by returning to the theoretical underpinnings of the Solicitor-General's client as the Crown and the proper representative of that sovereign polity. The Attorney-General, as the ultimate representative of the sovereign, must be able to make the determinative call as to the position of the Crown. The Attorney-General must also be able to decide whether the different emanations of the Crown, in accordance with their statutory mandates, could bring actions conflicting with the interests of the Crown proper, and whether the Solicitor-General may act for them in this situation. This is reflected in those statutes that allow the Solicitor-General to act for non-Crown agents *at the request of the Attorney-General.* This conclusion is reinforced by the *Judiciary Act 1903* (Cth). This Act allows a lawyer in the Attorney-General's Department or the Australian Government Solicitor to act for two or more parties, even if they have conflicting interests, if to do so has been approved by the Attorney-General.[173]

How conflicts of interest are resolved in practice is considered in chapter five, section II.B.i. While a *theoretical* possibility, these conflicts occur rarely; and when they have arisen in practice, officeholders have generally been able to manage them appropriately.

ii. The Solicitor-General and Vice-regal Officers

The English Law Officers, as *Her Majesty's* Law Officers, continue to have a separate role in advising the monarch. In Australia, the relationship between

[169] Transcript of Proceedings, *Momcilovic v The Queen* [2010] HCATrans 227 (3 September 2010) 2.

[170] ibid, 13 (Pamela Tate, Victorian Solicitor-General, and French CJ).

[171] Transcript of Proceedings, *Momcilovic v The Queen* [2010] HCATrans 261 (8 October 2010) 7 (GJC Silbert, and French CJ); Transcript of Proceedings, *Momcilovic v The Queen* [2011] HCATrans 16 (9 February 2011), 104 (GJC Silbert and Gummow J).

[172] M Byers and M Gill, 'Review of Legal Services to Government' (New South Wales Attorney-General's Department, 1993) 16 [3.33].

[173] *Judiciary Act 1903* (Cth), ss 55F and 55R.

Vice-regal officers and the Solicitor-General raises three questions.[174] Do Vice-regal officeholders have a role that requires them to make decisions on the boundaries of the law (thus requiring them to seek legal advice)? If so, can a Vice-regal offier seek technical legal advice from persons other than his or her ministerial advisers? These two initial questions are threshold issues to the main question for our purposes, which is whether and in what circumstance the Solicitor-General can provide legal advice to a Vice-regal officer.

At the outset, two types of advice must be distinguished. A Vice-regal officer, with the exception of the reserve powers, acts on the recommendations of the Executive Council. This is referred to as 'advice' in the constitutional sense: it is binding on the Vice-regal officer and has the effect that the responsibility for the officer's actions devolves on the ministers. However, in the course of exercising his or her powers, a Vice-regal officer may also seek technical legal advice. This has sometimes been referred to as the difference between capital 'A' advice or 'formal' advice (in the constitutional sense, which is binding on the Vice-regal officer) and small 'a' advice or 'informal' advice (technical, legal advice or information on how to fulfil the role).[175]

Does a Vice-regal officer have a role that requires the officeholder to make decisions on the boundaries of the law? Generally speaking, the role of the Vice-regal officer is largely symbolic, and he or she acts on the advice of the government of the day (remembering this is capital 'A' or formal advice). Nonetheless, Walter Bagehot famously explained that the Queen (and in Australia, the Vice-regal officer as her representative) retains 'the right to be consulted, the right to encourage, the right to warn'.[176] This is a role that allows the Vice-regal officer to police the legality and regularity of executive conduct.[177] There are also circumstances in which a Vice-regal officer can act independently from the recommendations of the Executive ministry, known as the reserve powers, and these include when the government is acting illegally, or unconstitutionally.[178] As such, a Vice-regal officer has an important role in the overall functioning of the rule of law.[179]

[174] These questions do not arise in the Australian Capital Territory as there is no Administrator. For a recent analysis of the position of the Vice-regal officer in seeking legal advice, see A Twomey, 'Advice to Vice-Regal Officers by Crown Law Officers and Others' (2015) 26 *Public Law Review* 193.

[175] ibid, 194–95.

[176] W Bagehot, *The English Constitution* (Thomas Nelson & Sons, 1867) 150.

[177] See discussion in G Winterton, 'The Evolving Role of the Australian Governor-General' in M Groves (ed), *Law and Government in Australia* (Federation Press, 2005) 51; and further P Hasluck, *The Office of Governor-General* (Melbourne University Press, 1979) 17–20, 29, 38–42. Note also *FAI Insurances Ltd v Winneke* (1982) 151 CLR 342, 365 (Mason J).

[178] The most famous exercise of these reserve powers was the dismissal of the New South Wales Lang government by the Governor Philip Game, see A Twomey, 'The Dismissal of the Lang Government' in George Winterton (ed), *State Constitutional Landmarks* (Federation Press, 2006) 129.

[179] G Green, 'Governors, Democracy and the Rule of Law' (2006) 9(1) *Constitutional Law and Policy Review* 11, 15.

Thus it can be seen that a Vice-regal officer, in the proper fulfilment of his or her functions, may need to seek technical legal advice from time to time.[180]

Can a Vice-regal officer seek technical legal advice from persons other than his or her ministerial advisers (such as the Solicitor-General)? As a legal principle, whether the officeholder can go beyond the ministerial Law Officers (in Australia, this is the Attorney-General only) for technical legal advice has been the subject of differing academic opinion. Alpheus Todd, in his 1894 treatise on colonial government, espouses that Governors must be able to seek legal advice from sources beyond the Law Officers (who at that time sat in the Cabinet), as the Governor may have 'reason to believe that their legal judgment has been unconsciously biased by political considerations, so that he cannot accept their interpretation of the law'.[181] Former Governor-General Paul Hasluck said that the Governor-General, if concerned about the legality of the government's actions, could seek assurances from the Attorney-General, or 'eminent authorities of his choosing'.[182] George Winterton noted that 'strangely' Hasluck omitted to include in this group the Solicitor-General, a source of advice that Winterton referred to as 'the usual source of quasi-independent advice'.[183]

HV Evatt took the opposite position. For Evatt, the Governor ought to avoid seeking advice—even in the sense of technical legal advice—external to the ministry at all costs, limiting the Governor's recourse to responsible ministers and ministerial Law Officers.[184]

In Queensland, the position is somewhat clarified by the inclusion of section 34 in the *Constitution of Queensland 2001* (Qld), which provides that the Governor, in the exercise of the powers of appointment and dismissal of ministers, 'is not limited as to the Governor's sources of advice'.[185]

If the legal position that a Vice-regal officer can request legal advice outside the responsible ministers is accepted, the question arises as to whether, according to the statutory terms of the Solicitor-General's office, the Solicitor-General may so

[180] For a more complete analysis of the circumstances in which independent legal advice might be required in the exercise of the Vice-regal role, see Twomey, above n 174.

[181] A Todd, *Parliamentary Government in the British Colonies* (Longmans Green, 2nd edn, 1894) 59. See also Royal Commission into an Attempt to Bribe a Member of the House of Assembly and other matters, *Report of the Royal Commission* (Hobart, Government Printer, 1991), Exhibit 43 (Proof of Evidence of John Alexander Ramsay, Annexure JAR3, Advice of Bill Bale QC, 'Governors Role in Appointing Administration: Some General Considerations', 4), Exhibit 60 (Memorandum of advice from Professor Colin Howard, *In the Matter of the Tasmanian House of Assembly Election of May 1989 and In the Matter of the Powers and Responsibilities of the Governor or Tasmania*, 23 June 1989, 19–20).

[182] Hasluck, above n 177, 21.

[183] Winterton, above n 177, 51. See also Green, above n 179, 15; A Twomey, 'Advice to the Governor-General on the Appointment of Kevin Rudd as Prime Minister' (2014) 24 *Public Law Review* 289, 290.

[184] HV Evatt, *The King and His Dominion Governors: A Study of the Reserve Powers of the Crown in Great Britain and the Dominions* (Frank Cass & Co Ltd, 2nd edn, 1967) 191.

[185] Note also that the Governor of New South Wales is required in certain instances to act on the advice of people other than the responsible ministers: *Judicial Officers Act 1986* (NSW), s 43. See A Twomey, *The Constitution of New South Wales* (Federation Press, 2004) 633.

advise the officeholder. Anne Twomey has identified a number of issues that may arise if the Solicitor-General is asked to advise a Vice-regal officer:

- Whether the Vice-regal officer may have direct access to the Solicitor-General?
- Whether the Solicitor-General must advise the Attorney-General or Prime Minister/Premier that advice has been sought by the Vice-regal officer?
- Whether the Solicitor-General must provide a copy to the government of any advice provided to the Vice-regal officer?
- And whether the Attorney-General or Prime Minister/Premier must approve of the content of the advice before it is given?[186]

The answer to these questions turn, at least initially, on the construction of the relevant statute. In South Australia and Queensland, the Solicitor-General may act for the Governor *only* at the request of the Attorney-General: this is an express statutory requirement.[187] In the other statutes, excepting the Commonwealth, the stipulation of the Crown as the Solicitor-General's client would appear to include Vice-regal officers. Michael Sexton noted:

> It might be argued that acting as counsel for the Sovereign in these State statutes includes advising the holder of a vice regal office and so does not require the direction of the Attorney-General on the basis that the Governor is the Sovereign's representative in the State in question.[188]

But this must still be subject to the constitutional position of the Attorney-General as the appropriate officer to give instructions on behalf of the Crown. That is, the Attorney-General would have to give instructions for the Solicitor-General to provide advice to the Governor or Administrator, just as he or she would have to do in relation to other emanations of the Crown.

At the Commonwealth level, section 12(a)(i) of the *Law Officers Act 1984* (Cth) makes it clear that the Solicitor-General can act as counsel for the Governor-General in so far as that office is the one of the emanations of the Crown, without the necessity of requiring that office to seek the permission of the Attorney-General. This is in direct contrast to the function of furnishing opinions to the Governor-General on legal questions, which must come through the Attorney-General pursuant to the requirements in section 12(b).

As chapter five, section II.B.c. of the book reveals, in practice the Solicitor-General has been called upon in a number of different situations to advise a Vice-regal officer across the Australian jurisdictions. While governed at one level by the legal position outlined above, in practice a number of different approaches have

[186] Twomey, above n 174, 204.

[187] Qld s 8(a); SA s 6(a).

[188] M Sexton, 'The Role of Solicitors-General in Advising the Holders of Vice Regal Officers' in G Appleby, P Keyzer and J Williams (eds), *Public Sentinels: A Comparative Study of Australian Solicitors-General* (Ashgate, 2014) 91, 93.

been taken across the jurisdictions, and in some ad hoc or ongoing protocols have been developed.[189]

V. The Confidentiality of Counsel's Opinions

Before turning from the Solicitor-General's function as counsel for the Crown, it is necessary to review briefly its impact on the confidentiality of the Solicitor-General's advice. As a general rule, legal advice provided by counsel is afforded confidentiality on the basis that the balance between the social benefit of disclosure and the social benefit of confidentiality tilts towards the latter. Confidentiality encourages people to seek frank and objective legal advice in relation to their activities; this, in turn, fosters a community operating within the bounds of the law.[190] The privilege attaching to legal advice belongs to the 'client' and not the adviser; although the latter has a professional obligation to maintain confidentiality.

The justification for the existence of the duty must apply, *a fortiori*, to the Solicitor-General's advice when acting for the government as a 'client'. Mason and Wilson JJ said in *Waterford v Commonwealth*, '[t]o our minds it is clearly in the public interest that those in government who bear the responsibility of making decisions should have free and ready confidential access to their legal advisers'.[191]

The Solicitor-General is requested by the government to advise on significant legal matters, in the course of which highly sensitive information is provided. A duty of confidentiality encourages recourse to the Solicitor-General by the government in all appropriate circumstances, and the frank disclosure of information by the government to ensure that the most accurate and objective advice is provided.[192] The confidentiality of the Solicitor-General's advice is reinforced in some jurisdictions where the Solicitor-General is made an exempt agency under freedom of information regimes.[193] When speaking of the applicability of the duty of confidentiality to the Crown, one thing must be remembered: the sharing

[189] See similar findings in Twomey, above n 174.

[190] Michels, above n 30, 138.

[191] *Waterford v Commonwealth* (1987) 163 CLR 54, 62.

[192] See Letter from Pamela Tate SC, Solicitor-General, to Mr Richard Willis, Secretary, Select Committee on Gaming, 11 April 2007, extracted in Select Committee of the Legislative Council on Gaming Licensing, '*First Interim Report Upon Gaming Licensing*' (Legislative Council of Victoria, 2007) [3.9]. See also A Mason, 'The Parliament, the Executive and the Solicitor-General' in Appleby, Keyzer and Williams (eds), above n 188, 49.

[193] See, eg, *Freedom of Information Act 1991* (SA), sch 2, item k; *Freedom of Information Regulations 2009* (Vic), reg 6(c), *Freedom of Information Regulation 1991* (ACT), sch 2, item 4. In other regimes, the Solicitor-General's legal advice would be exempt on the basis that it is protected by legal professional privilege: see, eg, *Freedom of Information Act 1982* (Cth), s 42.

of advice among the emanations of the Crown is not in breach of the duty of confidentiality and does not waive the Crown's privilege.[194]

The justification for the existence of the duty of confidentiality is complicated in the parliamentary sphere. To hold the exercise of Executive power to account, parliamentarians require a large volume of information about government processes, including, potentially, advice taken into consideration in the Executive decision-making process. A difficult question therefore arises as to whether the public interest in protecting the confidentiality of legal advice to government is outweighed by the public interest in ensuring that parliamentarians are fully informed of the government's process to scrutinise its actions properly. As is explained in greater detail in chapter two, section II.A., Britain has resolved this tension in practice by what has become known as the 'Law Officer Convention'.[195]

A. The 'Law Officer Convention' in Australia

A practice whereby parliament refrains from requiring the divulgence of confidential Law Officers' opinions has been recognised in Britain since at least the mid-nineteenth century.[196] It has become known as the 'Law Officer Convention'. This is different from the government's voluntarily tabling advice in parliament. In Australia, since the advent of the statutory basis for the Solicitor-General, two incidents have arisen in which the Solicitor-General has been called before parliament to produce documents and give evidence: one in 1975 involving Maurice Byers, Solicitor-General of the Commonwealth; and the second in 2007, involving Pamela Tate, Solicitor-General of Victoria.

In the first instance, Byers was called to the Bar of the Senate to answer questions on the matter commonly referred to as the 'Loans Affair'. This involved attempts by the Whitlam Labor Government in the 1970s to secure significant loans without the consent of the Australian Loan Council, as was required by law. The Senate also asked Byers 'to produce all documents, files or papers in [his] possession, custody or control relevant to these matters'.[197] The Government claimed executive privilege over the material, and issued a direction to a number of public servants (who had also been called) to comply with that claim.[198]

194 New South Wales Law Reform Commission, *Circulation of Legal Advice to Governments* Report No 86 (1998) available at <http://www.lawlink.nsw.gov.au/lrc.nsf/pages/R86TOC>, [3.15]; Tasmania, Attorney-General, *Guidelines for Seeking Advice from the Office of the Solicitor-General* (The Hon Brian Wightman MP, Febraury 2012), [14]; Solicitor General, Parliament of Tasmania, *Solicitor-General Report for 2010–2011* (2011); *Mann v Carnell* (1999) 201 CLR 1 [16] (Gleeson CJ, Gaudron, Gummow and Callinan JJ).

195 JLJ Edwards, *The Law Officers of the Crown: A Study of the Offices of the Attorney-General and Solicitor-General of England with an Account of the Office of the Director of Public Prosecutions of England* (Sweet & Maxwell, 1964) 260; KA Kyriakides, 'The Advisory Functions of the Attorney-General' (2003) 1 *Hertfordshire Law Journal* 73.

196 See further Edwards, *The Law Officers*, above n 195, 256–61; Edwards, *The Attorney-General*, above n 97, 223–27; Kyriakides, above n 195.

197 Commonwealth, *Parliamentary Debates*, Senate, 9 July 1975, 2710.

198 Letter from EG Whitlam to the President of the Senate, 15 July 1975 (extracted in full in Commonwealth, *Parliamentary Debates*, Senate, 15 July 1975, 2729).

The Solicitor-General wrote a letter to the Senate explaining that he could not comply with the summons based on the Executive's claim of privilege. His argument rested on two broad propositions.[199] First, Byers acknowledged that the Crown had made a valid claim of privilege based on the secrecy of Crown deliberations.[200] This privilege, he said, extended to the opinions of the Law Officers as recognised by convention in the House of Commons.[201] Secondly, he argued that the Solicitor-General stood in a particular relationship to the Crown that required him to act consistently with the Government's claim of privilege.[202]

Byers was dismissed by the Senate, but the matter was referred to the Committee of Privileges to report on, inter alia, the claim for privilege by the Solicitor-General. The Majority Report accepted the Solicitor-General's arguments.[203] The Minority Report, (Senators Ivor Greenwood, a former Liberal Attorney-General, James Webster and Reg Wright) found, relevantly,

> [the Solicitor-General] erred in not discharging his higher duty to give evidence before a House of Parliament when lawfully required—subject to all proper privilege in respect of any particular question or class of questions—eg questions which impaired the confidentiality on which his relationship with an Executive was based.[204]

An important caveat that the Minority Report makes is that the Solicitor-General did not explicitly rely upon the confidentiality of the Law Officers' opinions because of the legal professional privilege that attached to them; it seems, therefore, that the minority were willing to entertain the existence of the privilege. The New South Wales Court of Appeal has subsequently held that the Government cannot claim legal professional privilege to resist a call for documents from the Parliament.[205]

In the second incident, the claim for privilege over the Solicitor-General's advice was made more directly. Tate, as Victorian Solicitor-General, was summoned to produce to the Legislative Council Select Committee on Gaming Licensing all documents relating to advice she had given to the Victorian government about a probity investigation conducted in the course of issuing gaming licences.[206] The government claimed privilege over the documents on three bases: first, the confidential nature of legal advice between the Solicitor-General and the Executive; secondly, Cabinet confidentiality; and, thirdly, the confidentiality obligations in the *Gambling Regulation Act 2003* (Vic). In a letter to the Secretary of the Select

[199] See further analysis in Mason, above n 192.

[200] See Letter from Maurice Byers to the President of the Senate, 15 July 1975 (extracted in full in Commonwealth, *Parliamentary Debates*, Senate, 15 July 1975, 2730–31); Commonwealth, *Parliamentary Debates*, Senate, 16 July 1975, 2781, 2787–88 (Maurice Byers).

[201] Letter from Maurice Byers to the President of the Senate, 15 July 1975.

[202] Commonwealth, *Parliamentary Debates*, Senate, 16 July 1975, 2782–83 (Byers).

[203] Senate Standing Committee of Privileges, above n 159, 13.

[204] ibid (Minority Report), 56.

[205] *Egan v Chadwick* (1999) 46 NSWLR 563, discussed below.

[206] Select Committee of the Legislative Council on Gaming Licensing, above n 192, 7, 15.

Committee, Tate claimed that she must decline to produce the documents in the summons on the basis that she could not act contrary to the privilege asserted by the Executive.[207]

As Anthony Mason explains, reliance on the Law Officer Convention in Australia must be informed by an understanding of the legal powers of parliament in its function of bringing the Executive to account.[208] The houses of parliament have power to order the attendance of persons or the production of documents.[209] In Australia, the extent to which these powers extend to compelling the production of documents that may be legally professionally privileged, such as the advice of the Law Officers, was established in the judgment of the New South Wales Court of Appeal in *Egan v Chadwick*.[210] That case considered the refusal by the Treasurer and member of the Legislative Council of New South Wales, Michael Egan, to table documents called for in a Council resolution on the basis of legal professional privilege and public interest immunity. Two questions arose for determination. First, whether the Council had power to order the production of documents protected by reason of legal professional privilege or public interest immunity? Secondly, if it did not, who was to decide the veracity of such a claim? All of the judges found that the Council had power to require production in relation to documents that fell might otherwise fall within a claim for legal professional privilege.[211]

The Court of Appeal had to reconcile the principle of legal professional privilege with the fundamental nature of the Legislative Council's accountability function within the constitutional system of government. Ultimately the judges held that the latter prevailed.[212] Spigelman CJ contrasted the position of a litigant in legal proceedings with the special relationship of accountability that existed between the government and parliament; and found that to scrutinise the conduct of the Executive adequately, parliament may need recourse to the legal advice on which the Executive acted.[213]

All of the judgments emphasised that, despite their conclusions as to the legal existence of the power to order the production of documents, even those subject to legal professional privilege, the *exercise* of that power was governed by practical and political pressures. Spigelman CJ said, 'What, if any, access should occur is a

[207] Letter from Pamela Tate SC, Solicitor-General, to Mr Richard Willis, Secretary, Select Committee on Gaming, 11 April 2007.

[208] Mason, above n 192, 49.

[209] See, eg, Constitution, s 49, *Parliament of Queensland Act 2001* (Qld), s 9; *Constitution Act 1934* (SA), s 38; *Constitution Act 1975* (Vic), s 19; *Parliamentary Privileges Act 1891* (WA), s 4; *Parliamentary Privileges Act 1858* (Tas), s 1; in New South Wales, this rests on the common law: *Egan v Willis* (1998) 195 CLR 224.

[210] *Egan v Chadwick* (1999) 46 NSWLR 563.

[211] A full account and critique of the Court's reasoning in relation to the public interest immunity, which is not relevant to the current discussion, can be found elsewhere: Mason, above n 192.

[212] *Egan v Chadwick* (1999) 46 NSWLR 563, 578 (Spigelman CJ, with whom Meagher J agreed), 593 (Priestley JA).

[213] ibid, 578 (Spigelman CJ, with whom Meagher J agreed).

matter "of the occasion and of the manner" of the exercise of a power, not of its existence. If the public interest is thereby harmed, the sanctions are political, not legal.'[214] This principle is an important acknowledgement of the role of the courts and Parliament in these situations, where competing appeals to the public interest are made. The practical exercise of the power ought to be, and is, governed by political convention and custom.

Parliament has, as confirmed in *Egan v Chadwick*, the power to order the production of documents even if they are subject to a valid claim of legal professional privilege. This would, of course, include the opinions of the Law Officers. However, as a matter of political practice that has probably developed to the status of convention in Australia, the opinions of the Law Officers will be kept confidential, and parliament will not insist that they be produced.[215] A responsible parliament, in flexing its powers, will keep the underlying reasons for the existence of the convention firmly in mind, exercising them only in exceptional circumstances.[216]

As counsel for the Crown, the Solicitor-General has a professional duty to maintain confidentiality in the office's legal opinions. Like all legal advice, there are heavy justifications weighing in favour of ensuring that the Solicitor-General's opinions remain confidential. However, as counsel for the *Crown*, the social benefit that is achieved by retaining the confidentiality of these opinions must be weighed against the public interest in seeing parliament scrutinise Executive conduct and decision-making. The Solicitor-General's advice will often be an integral part of understanding what informed particular decisions and conduct. There are other cases where parliament might wish to access the Solicitor-General's advice to assist it in determining constitutional risk associated with passing particular legislative measures proposed by the Government.[217]

VI. The Solicitor-General as Law Officer

While the office of Australian Solicitor-General has changed significantly from its origins in the English Law Officers, it continues to fulfil some of those traditional

[214] ibid, references omitted.

[215] I say the practice has probably developed to the status of convention in Australia because the strength of the convention and the respect of Parliament for its underlying justification in Australia have been reaffirmed by the relinquishment of the claims by the Senate in 1975 and the Victorian Select Committee in 2007, after its assertion. The position accords with explanations of parliamentary practice, see H Evans (ed), *Odgers' Autralian Senate Practice* (CanPrint Communications Pty Limited, 12th edn, 2008) 488.

[216] Mason, above n 192.

[217] See, eg, G Appleby, 'Releasing governent's advice would help parliament better scrutinise laws' on *The Conversation* (15 December 2015), available at <https://theconversation.com/releasing-governments-advice-would-help-parliament-better-scrutinise-laws-50593>.

functions. The office maintains a 'special relationship' with the Attorney-General.[218] This is clear, to differing degrees, from the statutes establishing the office. The Solicitor-General of the Commonwealth is designated the 'second Law Officer of the Commonwealth'.[219] Other statutes emphasise the relationship in other ways.[220] This relationship continues to inform the role of the Solicitor-General, especially in the conduct of litigation and the advisory function, despite the office's position outside the responsible ministry. At the introduction of the Victorian statute in 1951, the Attorney-General said that 'the office, which is ancient in its tradition and establishment, will remain. This Bill merely creates a new class of person who can fill that office.'[221] It is necessary, therefore, to consider the extent of the traditional functions of the Law Officers that still exist in the Australian jurisdictions.

A. The Law Officers

The traditional role of the Law Officers included, in addition to their political functions as members of the ministry and their legal functions, a role in acting for and protecting the public interest. While initially these offices were established to act as representatives of the monarch's interests, they gradually developed duties and obligations to act for, and in protection of, the public interest, the common good or common weal.[222] This development reflected the idea that the Law Officers were taking up the Crown's obligations to act in the public good.[223]

In this sense, the client of the Law Officers greatly influenced the evolution of their functions. In Australia, even with the politicisation of the Attorney-General's position, the office's role in protecting the public interest has been considered broadly the same as that in Britain.[224] The obligation to act in the public interest

[218] South Australia, *Parliamentary Debates*, House of Assembly, 7 March 1972, 3651 (LJ King, Attorney-General).

[219] *Law Officers Act 1964* (Cth), s 5.

[220] In New South Wales, Tasmania and Western Australia, the Attorney-General can delegate functions to the Solicitor-General. In all jurisdictions the Solicitor-General must perform other duties as counsel as the Attorney-General directs. See also NSW s 3(1)(b); Vic s 5(c); Western Australia, *Parliamentary Debates*, Legislative Council, 30 April 1969, 3436 (Charles Court, Minister for Industrial Development); Tasmania, *Parliamentary Debates*, House of Assembly, 5 May 1983, 825 (Geoffrey Pearsall, Minister for Tourism). In the Australian Capital Territory and Northern Territory the Solicitor-General is established under legislation bearing the title the 'Law Officers Act'.

[221] Victoria, *Parliamentary Debates*, Legislative Assembly, 27 November 1951, 231 (Thomas Mitchell, Attorney-General).

[222] Edwards, *The Law Officers*, above n 195, 295.

[223] Hanlon, above n 143, 7–8, 27. This accepts the explanation of the Crown by Walker that the interests of the Crown may transcend individual preferences, pluralism and discord, and there may exist some underlying public good: Walker, above n 67, 146.

[224] Selway, above n 117, 270. See also G Griffith, 'The Office of Attorney General in New South Wales' (2007) 11 *Legal History* 79, 95. Although note the alternative view that received prominence under former Federal Attorney-General Daryl Williams, which was discussed in the introduction to this book (ch 1, section II.). Many authorities confirm that the Attorney-General in the Australian

manifests itself in a number of ways: in bringing litigation 'in the public interest', in the fair and objective conduct of litigation, and in the advisory function.

i. Litigation

The customary role of the Law Officers in representing the 'public interest' manifests itself most prominently in litigation in the protection of the public interest, distinct from government interests.[225] This arises, for example, in the Attorney-General's function in prosecuting crimes, protecting 'public rights', such as in matters relating to charities, and conducting litigation 'in the public interest', such as in actions for injunctions or declarations for public nuisance, where public bodies may have acted in excess of their powers or in breach of statutory provisions enacted for the benefit of the public, in applications for vexatious litigant declarations and in prosecutions for contempt of court.[226] The Attorney-General can grant his or her fiat for a private litigant to use the office's standing to bring proceedings in the public interest through relator actions.[227] In Australia, the Attorney-General's function to bring proceedings in the public interest on behalf of the public, separate from 'the body politic of the government unit in which he holds office',[228] has been widely accepted,[229] although the ability of an officeholder to exercise the function non-politically has been criticised.[230]

ii. Conducting Litigation

According to Edwards, the Attorney-General's role in protecting the public interest in litigation expanded to reflect a philosophical conception as 'guardian of the public interest generally'.[231] One way this has manifested is in an obligation to make submissions to the court in pursuit of the Crown's interest, particularly

context possesses those public interest functions bestowed upon the office at common law. See, eg, Australian Law Reform Commission, 'Standing in Public Interest Litigation (Report 27)' (1985), available at <http://www.alrc.gov.au/report-27>, ch 6; *Attorney-General (NSW); ex rel Tooth & Co Ltd v Brewery Employees Union of New South Wales* (1908) 6 CLR 469 ('*Union Label Case*'), 499 (Griffith CJ); *Williams v Attorney-General (NSW); Ex rel Cocks* (1913) 16 CLR 404, 415 (Barton ACJ); *Kidman v Commonwealth* (1925) 37 CLR 233, 240 (Knox CJ), 243 (Isaacs J); *Tasmania v Victoria* (1935) 52 CLR 157 ('*Potato Case*'), 171 (Rich J), 188 (Dixon J); *Ramsay v Aberfoyle Manufacturing Company (Australia) Pty Ltd* (1935) 54 CLR 230, 256–57 (McTiernan J); *Victoria v Commonwealth* (1975) 134 CLR 338 ('*AAP Case*'); cf *Attorney-General v Adams* [1965] SASR 129, 132 (Napier CJ); *Hubbard Association of Scientologists International v Attorney-General (Victoria)* [1976] VR 119, 125 (Gowans J).

225 Edwards, *The Law Officers*, above n 195, 286.

226 ibid, 295.

227 *Gouriet v Union of Post Office Workers* [1978] AC 435, 477 (Lord Wilberforce). See also ibid, 494 (Viscount Dilhorne), 508–10 (Lord Edmund Davies), 518 (Lord Fraser).

228 *Queensland v Commonwealth* (1977) 139 CLR 585, 615 (Aitkin J); *Australian Conservation Foundation Inc v Commonwealth* (1980) 136 CLR 483, 526 (Gibbs CJ), 537 (Stephen J).

229 These have even been codified in Queensland. See *Attorney-General Act 1999* (Qld), ss 7(1) and 8.

230 See, eg, Patrick Keyzer, *Open Constitutional Courts* (Federation Press, 2010) ch 4.

231 Edwards, *The Law Officers*, above n 195, 286.

in criminal cases, that represent a fair and objective view of the law, and not give legal argument to assist the Crown's case in a misleading or one-sided fashion. As Queen Elizabeth I was quoted to have said, the Law Officers are retained *Pro Domina Vertate*, not simply *Pro Domina Regina*.[232] The Law Officers must make submissions that are 'accurate, objective, and restrained, and founded firmly on a tenable exposition of the applicable legal principles'.[233]

To a large extent, the obligation of the Law Officers is now captured in the Crown's obligation to act as a model litigant.[234] The obligation itself was originally recognised under the common law,[235] and at the federal level in Australia is now embodied in the *Legal Services Directions 2005* (Cth).[236] According to this instrument, the obligation arises from the Attorney-General's responsibility for the maintenance of proper standards in litigation. The older British authorities have referred to the origins of the obligation in the Crown's position as 'the source and fountain of justice',[237] and have equated the obligations with those of probity and fair dealing for judicial officers.[238] In Australia, Finn J explained that the model litigant obligation is based on the notion that public bodies are owned by

[232] JW Norton-Kyshe, *The Law and Privileges Relating to the Attorney-General and Solicitor-General of England: With a history from the earliest periods, and a series of King's Attorneys and Attorneys and Solicitors-General from the reign of Henry III to the 60th of Queen Victoria* (Stevens and Haynes, 1897) 18–19, fn 1.

[233] J McGrath, 'Principles for Sharing Law Officer Power—The Role of the New Zealand Solicitor-General' (1998) 18 *New Zealand Universities Law Review* 195, 206. See also *Berger v United States* 295 US 78 (1935), 88 (Sutherland J).

[234] See more generally G Appleby, 'The Government as Litigant' (2014) 37 *University of New South Wales Law Journal* 94.

[235] See, eg, *Melbourne Steamship Ltd v Moorhead* (1912) 15 CLR 333, 342 (Griffith CJ); *Kenny v South Australia* (1987) 46 SASR 268, 273.

[236] Appendix B. The Directions are issued under *Judiciary Act 1903* (Cth), s 55ZF. See also guidelines in New South Wales, Victoria, Queensland and the Australian Capital Territory: New South Wales LawLink, Legal Services Coordination, 'Model Litigant Policy for Civil Litigation' (8 July 2008), available at <http://www.lsc.lawlink.nsw.gov.au/agdbasev7wr/lsc/documents/pdf/cabinetapp-mlp.pdf>; Appropriate Dispute Resolution Directorate Victorian Department of Justice, 'Victorian Model Litigant Guidelines' (March 2011), available at <http://www.justice.vic.gov.au/resources/3/4/34fd7f00459fb2b0b6a2b6e6d4b02f11/revisedmodellitigantguidelines.pdf>; Queensland Department of Justice, 'Cabinet Direction: Model Litigant Principles' (4 October 2010), available at <http://www.justice.qld.gov.au/data/assets/pdffile/0006/43881/20100505095729872.pdf>; *Law Officers Act 2011* (ACT) Division 2.2 (Legal Services Directions), *Law Officer (Model Litigant) Guidelines 2010 (No 1)* (ACT). Western Australia has refused to issue formal guidelines, relying instead on the common law: Western Australia, *Parliamentary Debates*, Legislative Council, 21 September 2010, 6886 (Giz Watson, (Greens, WA), Michael Mischin (Parliamentary Secretary representing the Attorney-General, Liberal))

[237] *Sebel Products Ltd v Commissioners of Customs and Excise* [1949] 1 Ch 409, 413 (Vaisey J). See also *Pawlett v Attorney-General* (1667) Hardres 465, 145 ER 550, 552; *Dyson v Attorney-General* [1911] 1 KB 410, 421.

[238] See discussion of *Sebel Products Ltd v Commissioners of Customs and Excise* [1949] 1 Ch 409, 413 (Vaisey J) and *R v Tower Hamlets London Borough Council; Ex parte Chetnik Developments Ltd* [1988] 1 AC 858 in C Cameron and M Taylor-Sands, '"Playing Fair": Governments as Litigants' (2007) 26 *Civil Justice Quarterly* 497, 499 and fn 18.

the Australian community, and that any agency of government 'has no private or self-interest of its own separate from the public interest it is constitutionally bound to serve'.[239] Other rationales for the principles rest on the litigation advantage of the Government: as a repeat player with large resources at its disposal and the higher public profile of government lawyers.[240]

The obligation is, generally speaking, to 'act honestly and fairly in handling claims and litigation brought by or against' the Crown. It goes beyond the general ethical obligations of private legal practitioners.[241] The Crown may still act firmly to protect its interests.[242] The duty to ensure that the Crown acts as a model litigant therefore does not negate the Law Officer's obligations to pursue and protect the Crown's interests as an advocate, it only tempers them.

iii. Advisory Function

Lastly, the Law Officers' obligation to the public interest has manifested in the advisory function. In a primary sense, providing objective legal advice itself contributes to the rule of law and the public interest. The Law Officers also have an obligation to ensure government complies with the law, because of the Crown's obligations to the rule of law.[243] In this sense, the Law Officer's duty as a legal adviser to the Crown is distinct from the duty of other lawyers, because private lawyers must not assist the client to commit illegal acts but do not have a positive obligation to prevent them from doing so.[244]

The Law Officers' advisory function can have a further impact on the public interest by fostering government action and policy in accordance with those principles that underpin its existence.[245] It has been said that one of the common law functions of the Attorney-General is to ensure 'that the laws which the State might propose are both constitutional and accord with generally accepted principles of

[239] *Hughes Aircraft Systems International v Airservices Australia* (1997) 76 FCR 151, 196–97. See also *Morley v Australian Securities and Investments Commission* [2010] NSWCA 331 [716]; C Lohe, 'The Model Litigant Principles' (Paper presented at the Legal Managers' Breakfast Briefing, Queensland, 28 June 2007) 1; B Logan, D Wicks and S Skehill, *Report of the Review of the Attorney-General's Legal Practice* (March 1997) 42.

[240] Cameron and Taylor-Sands, above n 238, 499–506; C Cameron and M Taylor-Sands, '"Corporate Governments" as Model Litigants' (2007) 10 *Legal Ethics* 154, 156.

[241] *Legal Services Directions 2005* (Cth), Appendix B, cl 2, which sets out in detail the specifics of the obligation. The other jurisdictions that have formalised these obligations have relied heavily on this formulation.

[242] ibid, note 4.

[243] *Eastern Trust Co v McKenzie, Mann & Co* [1915] AC 750, 759.

[244] Dodek, above n 75, 24.

[245] Some have even argued that lawyers acting for private clients hold an obligation to draw the client's attention to underlying principles within the legal system. See, eg, T Greenwood, 'Ethics and Avoidance Advice' (1991) 65(8) *Law Institute Journal* 724; B Dunphy, 'Being a Government Lawyer: A Practitioner's Observations' (Paper presented at the Queensland Law Society Government Lawyers Conference, Brisbane, 17 April 2008).

natural justice'.[246] Edwards referred to this type of advice as providing opinions on the 'Law Officers' points'.[247] Such advice will look at matters such as the onus of proof, the form and quality of a Bill, the grant of indemnities and the retrospective operation of legislation.[248]

In Britain, Lord Goldsmith, during his time as Attorney-General, said:

> It is very important that new proposals, from early on in the policy making process, are worked up and developed with the aim of ensuring that they achieve proper respect for the rule of law, for human rights and for our domestic and international legal obligations.[249]

Lord Goldsmith also gave evidence to the House of Commons Constititutional Affairs Committee that one element of the office's obligations to the Rule of Law manifested as 'certain basic values which it is important to stand up for'.[250]

There has been some recognition in Australia that the Attorney-General's traditional public interest functions also extend to providing advice to government on the congruency between government action and the principles that underpin the government system.[251]

The goal of achieving legislative and executive action that accords with the principles that underpin our governance system is statutorily recognised in several jurisdictions across Australia. In Queensland, the *Legislative Standards Act 1992* (Qld) aims to achieve legislation that has sufficient regard to the principles 'that underlie a parliamentary democracy based on the rule of law'.[252]

[246] Y Omergee, 'Is there an Independent Government Lawyer in the House?' (September 1997), *International Legal Practitioner* 102, extracted in Selway, above n 117, 121. See also LJ King, 'The Attorney-General, Politics and the Judiciary' (2000) 74 *Australian Law Journal* 444, 453; R La Forgia, 'Attorney General, Chief Law Officer of the Crown: But where is the law?' (2003) 28(4) *Alternative Law Journal* 163, 164.

[247] Edwards, *The Attorney-General*, above n 97, 189.

[248] ibid and note Edwards' discussion of the use of indemnity legislation in the Clay Cross affair at 347. Sam Silkin said 'no Law Officer of the Crown, of any political party, would be likely to advise the Government of which he was a member to initiate such legislation', adding that it would 'contravene all constitutional practice and set a dangerous precedent'. See also ibid, 352.

[249] Lord Goldsmith, 'Politics, Public Interest and Prosecutions—A View by the Attorney General' (Paper presented at the 13th Annual Tom Sargent Memorial Lecture, London, 20 November 2001), extracted in Kyriakides, above n 200, 74. See also Evidence to House of Commons Constitutional Affairs Committee, *Constitutional Role of the Attorney General*, Fifth Report of Session 2006–07 (HC306) (Lord Goldsmith) 11. In 2007, the reforms to the Law Officers saw the introduction of an oath to 'respect the rule of law'. See also comments of Anthony Mason in relation to the Australian Attorney-General's responsibility to the rule of law: A Mason, 'No Place in a Modern Democratic Society for a Supine Judiciary' (1997) 35(11) *Law Society Journal* 51.

[250] Evidence extracted in House of Commons Constitutional Affairs Committee, *Constitutional Role of the Attorney General*, Fifth Report of Session 2006–07 (HC306), 11.

[251] See, eg, Electoral and Administrative Review Commission, *Report on Review of the Independence of the Attorney-General* (1993) 24 (submission of Dennis Rose); J Hatzistergos, 'The evolving office of the New South Wales Attorney General' (2012) 86 *Australian Law Journal* 197, 203.

[252] *Legislative Standards Act 1992* (Qld), s 4(1). Similar regimes exist for delegated legislation, see, eg, *Legislative Instruments Act 2003* (Cth), s 16, which states the Secretary of the Attorney-General's Department 'must cause steps to be taken to promote the legal effectiveness, clarity, and intelligibility to anticipated users, of legislative instruments'.

These include that legislation has sufficient regard to the rights and liberties of individuals[253]—in this respect the legislation lists considerations such as natural justice, onus of proof, retrospectivity, indemnity, clarity and precision[254]—and the institution of parliament.[255] In Victoria, legislative and executive action is assessed against the human rights set out in the *Charter of Human Rights and Responsibilities Act 2006* (Vic). In the Australian Capital Territory, a similar scheme is contained in the *Human Rights Act 2004* (ACT). At the Commonwealth level, the Joint Committee on Human Rights, inter alia, examines proposed legislation and legislative instruments for compatibility with human rights.[256] The Senate Scrutiny of Bills Committee also reports on the extent to which Bills trespass on personal rights and liberties; make rights, liberties or obligations unduly dependent upon insufficiently defined administrative powers or upon non-reviewable decisions; inappropriately delegate legislative powers; or insufficiently subject the exercise of legislative power to parliamentary scrutiny.[257]

This is also reflected in drafting practice. At the Commonwealth level, the Office of Parliamentary Counsel (OPC) Drafting Directions require the referral of draft legislation to various agencies, other than the instructing agency, which have rights and responsibilities in relation to the legislation.[258] The types of provisions that must be referred to the Attorney-General's portfolio are numerous, including legislation that might attempt to oust judicial review of administrative action;[259] discriminate against an individual or raise human rights issues under international instruments, or infringe civil, political or other human rights relating to privacy or freedom of speech;[260] affect social justice for Aboriginals, Torres Strait Islanders or South Sea Islanders;[261] or affect relations between the Commonwealth and the States and Territories.[262]

This aspect of the Law Officers' traditional advisory function, taking the Law Officer beyond the legal, is closely associated with the relatively recent Australian public law concept of 'integrity' in government. In Australia, former New South

[253] *Legislative Standards Act 1992* (Qld), s 4(2)(a).

[254] ibid, s 4(3).

[255] ibid, s 4(2)(b). See also s 4(4) and (5).

[256] *Human Rights (Parliamentary Scrutiny) Act 2011* (Cth), s 7.

[257] Senate, *Standing Orders and other Orders of the Senate* (Senate Printing Unit, Parliament House, June 2009), order 24(1)(a).

[258] Parliamentary Counsel, *Drafting Direction* (June 2015), available at <https://www.opc.gov.au/about/docs/drafting_series/DD4.2.pdf>, pt 2.

[259] ibid, Attachment A, item 4.

[260] ibid, Attachment A, items 5, 6 and 48.

[261] ibid, Attachment A, item 33.

[262] ibid, Attachment A, item 44. See also GC Thornton, *Legislative Drafting* (Butterworths, 4th edn, 1996) 134; DR Miers and AC Page, *Legislation* (Sweet & Maxwell, 2nd edn, 1990) 61.

Wales Chief Justice James Spigelman argued that bodies fill an 'integrity function' (improving integrity in government) when they

> ensure that each government institution exercises the powers conferred on it in the manner in which it is expected and/or required to do so and for the purposes for which those powers were conferred, and for no other purpose.[263]

Edwards' 'Law Officers' points', and the other concepts formulated by officeholders and commentators set out above, are iterations of the generally accepted principles that ensure that government power is exercised in accordance with its overarching purpose: to protect and provide for the citizenry while ensuring regulation is clear for that citizenry. The Law Officers' traditional advisory function can thus be viewed as an important integrity function.

In addition to the public interest at large informing the role of the Attorney-General in his or her advisory capacity in Australia, the office has responsibility for the provision of legal services to the 'whole of government'. Britain lacks a fully integrated legal service under the responsibility of the Law Officers;[264] however, the Attorney-General in the Australian jurisdictions has, since colonial times, had a responsibility for providing legal services not just to the Cabinet, but to the 'whole of government'.[265] The responsibility of an Australian Attorney-General for the provision of legal services to the Government is encapsulated by the responsibility to ensure that 'whole-of-government' issues are taken into account by the emanations of the Crown, rather than the sometimes narrower interests of an individual department or agency, captured, as they may be, by narrow bureaucratic interests.[266] While this is not analogous to the 'public interest', it produces a number

263 J Spigelman, 'The Integrity Branch of Government' (Paper presented at the National Lecture Series for the Australian Institute of Administrative Law, Sydney, 29 April 2004) 2–3. In the US context, the concept of the integrity branch has similarly developed, see particularly B Ackerman, 'The New Separation of Powers' (2000) 113 *Harvard Law Review* 633, 694.

264 See discussion of the traditional legal services arrangements in England in Edwards, *The Attorney-General*, above n 97, 192. For analysis of modern practice, see B Yong, *Risk Management: Government Lawyers and the Provision of Advice within Whitehall* (The Constitution Society and the UCL Constitution Unit, 2013), available at <http://www.consoc.org.uk/wp-content/uploads/2013/11/J1336_Government Lawyers_WEB.pdf>.

265 See further explanation of how the Australian Attorney-General became responsible for providing legal services across the whole of government in ch 3, section I.E.

266 Electoral and Administrative Review Commission, above n 251, [3.79]; Logan, Wicks and Skehill, above n 239, 38. Selway has argued that this function is no longer part of the Commonwealth Attorney-General's role because of amendments to the arrangements of the Australian Government Solicitor. However, this position failed to consider the full extent of the changes and the mechanisms put in place by those amendments to ensure the continued responsibility of the Attorney-General for the oversight of government legal services: *Report of the Review of the Attorney-General's Legal Practice*, 7; see also 15 (recommendation 11). On 1 July 2015, the Australian Government Solicitor was brought back into the Attorney-General's Department: *Judiciary Amendment Act 2015* (Cth). See also similar concerns in Queensland when the move to commercialisation was considered: Parliamentary Committee for Electoral and Administrative Review, *Report 21: Report on Review of Independence of Attorney-General* (Legislative Assembly of Queensland, December 1993) 12 [4.2.16]; Electoral and Administrative Review Commission, above n 251, 42.

of public interest-related benefits. It ensures that the Crown takes a unified legal position in respect of issues, giving consistency to the actions of government across departments and agencies. It ensures government resources are not wasted pursuing litigation between government departments and agencies, and also that the broader impact of government policies is considered by individual departments and agencies.

The traditional functions of the English Law Officers, as were initially adopted in the early Australian colonial system, together with the changes that have developed in Australia in relation to the provision of legal services across government, emphasise the obligations those offices held to the public interest. The next section will overlay these traditional and common law functions against the statutory framework in which the Solicitor-General operates, ultimately concluding that the public interest obligations—although only in so far as they manifest themselves in relation to the conduct of litigation and in the advisory function—remain relevant to the role of the modern Australian Solicitor-General.

B. The Australian Solicitor-General: Reconciling Common Law and Statute

The transposition of the traditional public interest duties of the Law Officers to the Australian Solicitor-General must be approached with caution. When the statutory office of Solicitor-General was introduced, many questions were raised about how it would relate to the traditional functions of the Law Officers.[267] Any obligation to act in the public interest must be reconciled with the professional duties of the Solicitor-General to act as counsel, and with the necessity of maintaining accountability within the government system and, of course, fidelity to the statutory provisions.

It is apparent that while the Australian Solicitor-General may have an obligation to the public interest because of the office's historical and ongoing relationship with the Attorney-General, this must be limited by the strict delineation of the functions of the office. The Solicitor-General cannot continue to have any obligation to act independently—in the sense of bringing proceedings—to further the public interest, except where such a function is bestowed by statute. Nevertheless, in so far as the Solicitor-General represents the Crown in those proceedings, the Solicitor-General must conduct them with fairness and objectivity. In the office's advisory function, the Solicitor-General must be cognisant of the Law Officers' obligation to provide advice that reflects the core principles that underpin our system of government.

[267] See, eg, Victoria, *Parliamentary Debates*, Legislative Assembly, 27 November 1951, 227 (Lieut-Colonel William Leggatt, Liberal), who asked whether the appointment of a non-political Solicitor-General would cut across the whole traditions of the Law Department.

Underlying my argument for ongoing but carefully delimited obligation to the public interest is the effect of the Solicitor-General's removal from the responsible ministry.[268] In the US, the suggestion that the Attorney-General and Solicitor-General possess independent powers to defy the direction of the (elected) Executive in the pursuit of the public interest has been rejected on the basis that 'the Solicitor-General does not have the political legitimacy to advocate on behalf of "the United States" independent of Congress and the President'.[269] Likewise, in Australia, the Solicitor-General is an appointed official with no electoral mandate to 'speak for the public'.[270] Indeed, responsible government and ministerial accountability through the political process for the actions of non-political officers would not be able to operate if the Solicitor-General had an independent obligation to act in the public interest other than that determined by the elected government.

However, dismissing the existence of the Solicitor-General's common law powers to act in the broader public interest because of these conceptual difficulties runs contrary to the only Australian authority directly on point. In *Solicitor-General v Wylde*,[271] the New South Wales Supreme Court held that the removal of the Solicitor-General from the responsible ministry had not removed the common law powers and prerogatives that attached to the office.[272] More recent *obiter* comments from the Full Court of the South Australian Supreme Court suggest that the powers of the Solicitor-General must be determined by reference to the constituting statute.[273] As far as this statement goes, it must be correct, in that now that the functions of the Solicitor-General are set out in statute, the statute governs what functions the Solicitor-General performs. Whether the common law functions continue to inform the Solicitor-General's statutory functions is, however, a different issue.

The best way to reconcile the common law functions of the Law Officers with the statute establishing the Solicitor-General is to start from the proposition that any actions in the public interest must be undertaken through the responsible minister, the Attorney-General. The Attorney-General's public interest functions manifest themselves predominantly in respect of litigation: the prosecutorial function, and the power to otherwise bring actions in defence of public rights and in the public interest. The Australian Solicitor-General is now wholly independent from the political realm; because of this, the Solicitor-General can no longer have an independent function to bring proceedings or take other *actions* in this

[268] Some of the statutes *expressly* remove the Solicitor-General from the responsible ministry. See NSW s 2(6); Qld s 6, referring to *Constitution Act 1867* (Qld), s 14 (now repealed); Vic s 4(2).

[269] Note, 'The Solicitor General and Intragovernmental Conflict' (1977) 78 *Michigan Law Review* 324, 344–45, 356.

[270] ibid, 345. See different views on this issue in the New Zealand context in ch 2, section III.B.

[271] *Solicitor-General v Wylde* (1945) 46 SR (NSW) 83. See further discussion of this case and an earlier NSW Supreme Court decision in 1902 in ch 3, section II.D.

[272] ibid, 93.

[273] *Question of Law Reserved on Acquittal (No 3 of 1995)* (1996) 66 SASR 450, 456.

way. There can be no ability for the Solicitor-General to *act* independently in the public interest because there is no political mechanism to hold those actions to account.[274] This position can, of course, be changed by statute, and as a remnant of the office's common law origins, in many jurisdictions the Solicitor-General has express statutory authority to instigate certain proceedings, many of which have a public interest element.

However, this does not mean that the obligations to the broader public interest fade into irrelevancy. These conclusions about *bringing actions* in the public interest do not prevent Solicitors-General ensuring that in the conduct of Crown litigation, the model litigant principles are followed—this includes ensuring their own conduct, as advocates, meets these standards as well as bringing them to the attention of the client where appropriate. This is an obligation shared by all government legal service providers.

Lastly, and most importantly, the Solicitor-General may also provide *advice* on actions or policies proposed by the government in respect of the congruence between these and the 'core government principles', as well as taking into account the 'whole-of-government' implications of a policy. The Solicitor-General's role is limited to providing advice on these matters: the final decision must be taken by responsible government officers. This accords with much of the US scholarship, which has emphasised that a different and more public-interest focused ethical framework applies to the advisory function of the OLC in contrast to that under which the OSG operates in its advocacy work.[275] This ensures that the Solicitor-General is not substituting his or her opinion on where the public interest lies in a particular case but ensuring the government is well-advised as to the various considerations that ought to be taken into account in making that decision. This view does not deny that the public interest is a contested idea, but gives the Solicitor-General a role in assisting the government to define its position in light of the many overarching principles that inform it.[276]

My conclusions are consistent with a number of other arguments made in relation to government lawyers. Curtis and Kolts, commenting on the ability of government lawyers to influence the formation of government policy, also asserted it is open, and implicitly proper, for a government lawyer to call to the Attorney-General's attention proposed actions that 'would ignore or prejudice rights given to a citizen by the law'.[277] Similarly in Canada, John Tait said that lawyers for the government have a key responsibility 'to discern how [democracy, the rule of law,

[274] For similar conclusions, see Parliamentary Committee for Electoral and Administrative Review, above n 266, (i), 13 [5.2.2].

[275] See further discussion in ch 2, section III.A.

[276] For a similar analysis in relation to government lawyers, see Note, above n 66, 1186.

[277] L Curtis and G Kolts, 'The Role of the Government Lawyer in the Protection of Citizens' Rights' (1975) 49 *Australian Law Journal* 335, 339.

fairness, the rights of citizens] are relevant and to bring them to the attention of ministers and officials'.[278] He went on:

> The importance of such advice applies with its greatest force to the Constitution, including the conventions, such as responsible government. It is crucial for public service lawyers to *remind* officials of the sources of their authority and the democratic context in which it must be exercised; this is why elected officials, either Cabinet for the government as a whole or Ministers within departments, are the authoritative clients. It is they who decide, within the rule of law, on what the public interest is for government officials.[279]

Drawing on Tait's work, Bradley Selway also advocated for government lawyers to become involved in advising upon ethical issues, although they must be careful not to impose their moral perspectives upon the government.[280]

There is some disconnect between the Solicitor-General's statutory function to act as counsel and this principle that the office ought to provide advice beyond the law regarding government's core obligations to the citizenry. Christine Parker observed:

> In practice, lawyers frequently assume that the client's interest requires the lawyer to maximise and exercise all the client's legal rights and financial interests. It is not the lawyer's role to concern himself or herself with preserving relationships, caring about the impact of the client's actions (or the lawyer's actions as the client's agent) on other people or things (such as the environment), or even common human decency.[281]

However, there has also been recognition that legal advice extends beyond simply advising the client on his or her legal rights and liabilities, and that 'it must include advice as to what should prudently and sensibly be done in the relevant legal context'.[282]

How the tension between this traditional position of the lawyer and that of the Solicitor-General as a Law Officer of the Crown is resolved by individual officeholders is explored in Part III of the book.

i. 'Core Government Principles'

If the Solicitor-General has a role in advising government on the congruence of government actions with the core principles that underlie our constitutional system, what are those principles?[283] Officeholders must ensure that they do not

[278] J Tait, 'The Public Service Lawyer, Service to the Client and the Rule of Law' (1997) 23 *Commonwealth Law Bulletin* 542, 547.

[279] ibid, 548 (emphasis added). See also AC Hutchinson, 'In the Public Interest: The Responsibilities and Rights of Government Lawyers' (2008) 46 *Osgoode Hall Law Journal* 105, 118–19.

[280] Selway, above n 117, 121. See also B Selway, 'The Different Role of an Australian Attorney-General' (2002) 13 *Public Law Review* 263, 271.

[281] Parker, above n 68, 679. References omitted.

[282] *Balabel v Air India* [1988] Ch 317, 330 (Taylor LJ), followed more recently by the House of Lords in *Three Rivers District Council v Bank of England* [2004] UKHL 48.

[283] MA Sargent, 'Lawyers in the Perform Storm' in NB Rapoport, JD Van Niel and BG Dharan (eds), *Enron and Other Corporate Fiascos: The Corporate Scandal Reader* (Thomson Reuters, 2nd edn, 2009) 796.

become involved in advising upon substantive policy, substituting their personal views for those of elected officials, but that they remain within the sphere of promoting better governance, that is, of promoting integrity within government.

In legal and political spheres, any attempt to articulate principles that underlie the constitutional system will always be contested, and will always be susceptible to the criticism that a formulation allows for too much subjective discretion on the part of an individual. Majoritarian democrats often argue that because deciding on the content of these principles involves controversial moral and political choices that lack coherency across the community, these decisions ought to be made by those with 'with a superior democratic pedigree', that is, directly elected officials.[284] This criticism, however, overlooks that there is a broad consensus about the nature of government in Australia, and that concepts such as the rule of law and democracy are generally accepted as core assumptions on which the constitutional system operates, even if the precise definition of these principles remains out of reach.

Even to the extent that the principles are objectively incapable of definition, this does not rebut the need for each individual Solicitor-General to attempt to identify and advise on them in relevant contexts. In fact, it is for precisely this reason that the Solicitor-General, or government lawyer, is simply bringing the government's attention to *the officeholder's interpretation* of these principles, informed by their education, professional training and experience, and also their independent judgement. Allan Hutchinson explained:

> [G]overnment lawyers have a significant contribution to make in debates within government about how to determine what the public interest demands; they often have the training, experience, and knowledge to help develop a nuanced and sophisticated approach to identifying the public interest and crafting a range of practical strategies for its realization in practical circumstances. Indeed, being relatively independent of political pressures and partisan agendas, government lawyers are well placed to act as trusted advisors to their political superiors.[285]

The Solicitor-General's expertise in the law and institutional knowledge of the government's broader legal position provides the office with superior qualifications to provide advice to the government on the impact of actions and policies on legal institutions and principles. This is accentuated in the Australian system, where the Attorney-General is almost always a member of Cabinet and has moved away from Rawlinson's ideal of the 'independent aloofness' that developed in the British context.[286] The Solicitor-General's security of tenure and remuneration provide a level of independence not enjoyed by the Attorney-General.

[284] CR Sunstein, 'Review: Justice Scalia's Democratic Formalism' (1997) 107(2) *Yale Law Journal* 529, 530. See also Note, above n 66, 1177.

[285] Hutchinson, above n 279, 120–21.

[286] B Debus, 'Maintaining the Rule of Law: The Role of the Attorney General' (Winter 2006) *Bar News* 5, 5; G Carney, 'Comment—The Role of the Attorney-General' (1997) 9 *Bond Law Review* 1, 3–4; Griffith, above n 223, 80; King, above n 246, 158.

Many scholars have attempted to articulate the amalgam of principles that informs the 'public interest' in a particular constitutional context.[287] To do so first requires an understanding of the assumptions on which a constitutional system is built. In Canada, the Supreme Court has explained that the four 'fundamental and organizing principles of the Constitution' relevant to addressing the particular question of whether Quebec could unilaterally secede from Canada, were 'federalism; democracy; constitutionalism and the rule of law; and respect for minorities'.[288] These were 'vital unstated assumptions upon which the text is based'[289] and, in the Canadian context, inform the interpretation of the text,[290] and may, in some circumstances, give rise to substantive legal obligations.[291]

The Australian constitutional system gives rise to three broad principles, which I refer to as the 'core government principles' in our system of government. These are the rule of law (which includes the prohibition on arbitrary exercise of government power, protections of judicial independence and fair process, and extends at least some way towards protecting individual rights), the democratic principle and the federal principle. There is some degree of interplay between them. The similarity between these and those set out by the Supreme Court in Canada no doubt rests on a shared common law Westminster tradition.[292]

Since colonial times, government in Australia has operated on the assumption that the Executive will act under the rule of law and not according to the arbitrary whim of the rulers. The principle is subject to robust academic disagreement over its precise content, but without too much controversy, and by avoiding conceptions emphasising the direct protection of individual human rights that have not gained universal recognition,[293] it can be accepted that the rule of law requires that a system of laws that consist of general, open and relatively stable laws that avoid retrospective operation. They must apply equally—binding the exercise of government power as well as individuals—and must be promulgated according to clear rules. Individuals have the right to be treated according to the rules of natural justice, and with recourse to an independent Judiciary that oversees the implementation of the other principles.[294]

[287] For alternative formulations of similar principles, see Selway, above n 122; P Finn, 'A Sovereign People, A Public Trust' in PD Finn (ed), *Essays on Law and Government*, vol 1: *Principles and Values* (The Law Book Company Limited, 1995) 1, 232–33; D Collins, 'Address by Dr David Collins QC, Solicitor-General of New Zealand to the Australian Law Teachers Assocation 65th Annual Conference' (Paper presented at the ALTA Conference, Auckland, 6 July 2010), 4, fn 10; Tait, above n 278, 65.

[288] *Reference re the Succession of Quebec* [1998] 2 SCR 217 [32].

[289] ibid, [49].

[290] ibid, [52]–[53].

[291] ibid, [54].

[292] Although the principle of 'respect for minority rights' is unique to the Canadian context, informed by its particular federal system and the province of Québec, the protection of religion, education and language, and more recently the protection of minorities in the Canadian Charter of Rights and Freedoms.

[293] For proponents of this view see R Dworkin, *Taking Rights Seriously* (Harvard University Press, 1978); and Lord Bingham of Cornhill, 'The Rule of Law' (2007) 66 *Cambridge Law Journal* 67.

[294] See, eg, AV Dicey, *Introduction to the Study of the Law of the Constitution* (Macmillan & Co Ltd, 10th edn, 1959); J Raz, 'The Rule of Law and its Virtue' in J Raz (ed), *The Authority of Law: Essays on*

In Australia, the rule of law is closely associated with the principle of legality.[295] This doctrine requires the construction of legislation so as not to infringe on rights and interests considered fundamental under the common law in the absence of an express intention to do so, or a necessary implication. This rests on an assumption that parliament does not, generally speaking, intend to transgress these rights.[296]

The rule of law creates a framework of legality in which government operates; but alone this does not provide government power with its legitimacy. It is the second principle of democratic government that, when combined with the rule of law, provides this.

The democratic principle in Australia is informed by the pillars of representative and responsible government and the concept of popular sovereignty. These find expression primarily in sections 7, 24, 64 and 128 of the Commonwealth Constitution. The principle requires, in a procedural sense, the exercise of the right to vote and to participate in government affairs.[297] In this way the citizen is able to hold the government to account. Its operation carries with it implicit requirements of freedom of communication, at least regarding matters pertaining to government,[298] together with openness and transparency within government.[299]

The last of the 'core government principles' is federation. John Quick and Robert Garran famously observed that 'the Federal idea … pervades and largely dominates the structure of the newly-created community, its Parliamentary, executive and judiciary departments'.[300] As the dominant organising feature of our Constitution, federalism is, of course, very relevant in the interpretation of the Constitution, and has given rise to an implied, substantive limitation on State and Commonwealth power.[301] Beyond the legal consequences of federalism, however, the federal *idea* ought to inform the actions of government; and thus impacts the role of the Law Officers.[302]

Law and Morality (Clarendon Press, 1979) 210ff; L Fuller, *The Morality of Law* (Yale University Press, 2nd edn, 1969).

[295] See, eg, *Electrolux Home Products Pty Ltd v Australian Workers' Union* (2004) 221 CLR 309, 329 (Gleeson CJ).

[296] See recent analysis of the principle in D Meagher, 'The Common Law Principle of Legality in the Age of Rights' (2011) 35 *Melbourne University Law Review* 449; D Meagher, 'The Principle of Legality as Clear Statement Rule: Significance and Problems' (2014) 36 *Sydney Law Review* 413; B Lim, 'The Normativity of the Principle of Legality' (2013) 37 *Melbourne University Law Review* 372.

[297] As to the content of this in the Australian constitutional context, see *Roach v Electoral Commissioner* (2007) 233 CLR 162 and *Rowe v Electoral Commissioner* (2010) 243 CLR 1.

[298] As to the content of the implied freedom of communication on government and political matters in Australia, see *Lange v Australian Broadcasting Corporation* (1997) 189 CLR 520.

[299] See eg, comments in *Nationwide News v Wills* (1992) 177 CLR 1, 139 (Mason J); *Commonwealth v John Fairfax* (1980) 147 CLR 39, 52 (Mason J).

[300] J Quick and R Garran, *The Annotated Constitution of the Australian Commonwealth* (Legal Books, 1901, 1976 reprint) 332.

[301] *Melbourne Corporation v Commonwealth* (1947) 74 CLR 31 ('*State Banking Case*'); *Austin v Commonwealth* (2003) 215 CLR 185; *Commonwealth v Cigamatic Pty Ltd (In Liq)* (1966) 108 CLR 372; *Re Residential Tenancies Tribunal (NSW); Ex parte Defence Housing Authority* (1997) 190 CLR 410 ('*Henderson's Case*').

[302] HM Seervai, 'The Legal Profession and the State: The Place of Law Officers and Ministers of Justice' (1977) 22 *Journal of the Law Society of Scotland* 265, 266.

In the context of articulating 'core government principles' on which the Law Officers ought to proffer advice, where relevant, to the government, the *proper functioning* of the federal system must be a guiding principle. The federal idea is informed, as it must be, by the judicial interpretations of the constitutional text that have exhibited a clear trend against compartmentalising federal and state jurisdiction, in favour of broad readings of the grants of central power. This, as former Commonwealth Solicitor-General Stephen Gageler has argued, allows flexibility in responding to social, economic and political change within the federal constitutional framework.[303] Within this flexibility, the political actors should nonetheless remain cognisant of the federal principle and strive for those benefits that its *proper* operation promises:[304] that is, federalism as a flexible system capable of uniting diverse populations, increasing local participation in self-government, fostering diversity, creativity, experimentation, competition and increased popular participation in governance. The idea that a Law Officer ought to bring to the attention of the government the impact of policies on this federal idea, is of course ameliorated by acknowledging that if disputes between the States and the centre eventuate, the functioning of the adversarial system requires counsel to put forward the strongest arguments available for the entities they represent.

In summary, the 'core government principles' that inform the advisory role of the Solicitor-General in Australia are taken from the ideas of the rule of law, democracy and federation. These, in turn, emphasise equality, prospectivity, consistency, certainty and publicity of the law, the right to natural justice and an independent Judiciary, the protection of fundamental common law rights and interests, the right to vote and participate in government affairs, accountability, freedom of communication and association, openness and transparency, and the proper functioning of the federal system. What is clear from this articulation of the principles is that in drawing on them, the Solicitor-General will not be dictating to the government a single, substantive policy outcome. Instead, the Solicitor-General will be using them as tools to remind government of its commitment to a fair and open process of governance in pursuit of its policy objectives.[305]

VII. Conclusions on the Legal Position

The legal framework in which the Solicitor-General operates is a unique combination of statute, informed by an understanding of the professional obligations of the legal profession and the common law and constitutional obligations

[303] S Gageler, 'The Federal Balance' in G Appleby, N Aroney and T John (eds), *The Future of Australian Federalism: Comparative and Interdisciplinary Perspectives* (Cambridge University Press, 2012) 27.

[304] See, eg, T Moran, 'The Challenges of Federalism' (Paper presented at the Eidos Institute, Brisbane, 8 June 2011), available at <www.dpmc.gov.au/media/speech20110608.cfm>.

[305] Note, above n 66, 1181.

of the Law Officers inherited from Britain, although evolving to exhibit a number of local features. The role of the Solicitor-General in the Australian system is that of counsel, but counsel of a special kind that exhibits several distinguishing characteristics. As counsel the Solicitor-General is unique among statutory officeholders. As an adviser, the Solicitor-General acts as a check on government power from internal abuse, and in this function must exercise a high degree of independent legal judgement. But the Solicitor-General is also a defender of the exercise of power against external challenge, and in this function acts as a fierce, but fair, advocate for the Crown's interests.

The primary shift between the traditional Law Officer role (that still exists in modern Britain) and that now embodied in the statutory Solicitor-General's office has been its removal from the responsible ministry. This chapter demonstrated that while the statute has in this way effected a large modification of the common law position of the Solicitor-General, crucial aspects of the Law Officers' public interest responsibilities remain. These can be seen in the responsibilities of the Solicitor-General for conduct of Crown litigation and the provision of legal advice to government. The Solicitor-General is consulted not simply to provide the final word on the legal position, but as an adviser that takes into account, first, whole-of-government interests in the matter and, secondly, the congruence between the Crown's proposed actions and 'core government principles'. The Solicitor-General, often setting the outer limits of state power in the advisory function, has enormous potential to influence the relationship between the citizen and the state. It is only appropriate that in this function the Solicitor-General, first and foremost, offers the state the best legal advice possible. But this should be accompanied, where relevant, by his or her opinion, informed by knowledge and experience, as to whether the government's legislative or executive action has met the ideals of good government—informed by the 'core government principles'. While it may be an imperfect obligation,[306] and only one of many important checks and balances within the system of government, its significance should not be overlooked. As a statutory officer removed from the rough and tumble of policy-making, the office is in a unique position to offer a perspective on these principles.

This chapter has presented a theoretical and legal argument for the continuation of the Law Officers' public interest obligations within the modern Australian Solicitor-General's role. Part III of this book tests the positions deduced in this chapter against the experiences and role perceptions of those who have held, or hold, the office of Solicitor-General, and of those closely associated with that office.

[306] G Rainbolt, 'Perfect and Imperfect Obligations' (2000) 98(3) *Philosophical Studies* 233, 233.

Part III

Negotiating the Tensions

5

The Solicitor-General as Adviser

I. Introduction

In Australia, the combination of a non-political Solicitor-General with a highly politicised Attorney-General was introduced with the intention of ensuring independent and impartial legal advice and representation for government through the Solicitor-General, while maintaining a framework of accountability and the benefits of a politically engaged Attorney-General. These historical objectives gave rise to the current status of the office that is now articulated in legislation.[1] Across the Australian jurisdictions, the statutes, supplemented by common law, constitutional theory and convention, provide the normative fabric of the Solicitor-General's role. But the legal picture provides only an outline in which the office's functions must be performed:[2] there is more depth and complexity to the office than this.[3] It is therefore necessary to examine the extent to which the historical objectives are realised, how (if at all) the legal framework has impacted upon the office's functions and the divergences in the practices of individuals to approaching the office's functions.

A common response of participants in this study was that the nature of the Solicitor-General's role was largely dependent on the perspective of the individual who held the office, the attitude of the Attorney-General, and the political circumstances in which the office operated.[4] The role of Solicitor-General has manifested itself differently across jurisdictions and even, within the same jurisdiction, across different periods. This phenomenon has occurred despite the similarities of function that are found in the statutes and their largely shared provenance.

[1] JC Wahlke et al, 'The Roles of Legislators in the Legislative Process from *The Legislative System: Explorations in Legislative Behaviour*' (Wiley, 1962) in BJ Biddle and EJ Thomas (eds), *Role Theory: Concepts and Research* (John Wiley & Sons Inc, 1966) 243, 243.

[2] BJ Biddle and EJ Thomas, 'The Nature and History of Role Theory' in Biddle and Thomas (eds), above n 1, 3, 4.

[3] MM Siems, 'The Taxonomy of Interdisciplinary Legal Research: Finding the Way out of the Desert' (2009) 7 *Journal of Commonwealth Law and Legal Education* 5, 9.

[4] See, eg, Interview, Daryl Dawson; Interview, Trevor Griffin; Interview, Martin Hinton; Interview, Pamela Tate. In the US context, see N Baker, 'The Attorney General as a Legal Policy-Maker' in CW Clayton (ed), *Government Lawyers: The Federal Legal Bureaucracy and Presidential Politics* (University Press of Kansas, 1995) 31.

The generational changes and the distinct versions of the offices that have materialised across the jurisdictions do not readily correlate to changes or differences in the legislative framework; rather, they relate to the role perceptions of individual officeholders and others in contact with the office, together with the political and other practical pressures faced by the office. This observation, of course, applies across many other public (and private) offices and institutions. As Iain McGilchrist explained, 'things only are what they are because they find themselves in the surroundings in which they find themselves, and are connected to whatever it is that they are connected to'.[5]

Little is known of the workings of the office of the Solicitor-General and the views of officeholders concerning the role. Many of those who have taken up the office have admitted to knowing little to nothing about it.[6] Most participants in this study explained there was no formal induction or introduction to the position.[7] The lack of induction and of a more detailed and formalised description of the role means that an individual's background and perceptions of the role are likely to have even more influence than in a situation where the role is largely formalised.

The research presented in this part draws upon a series of interviews (n = 47) that I conducted with current and former officeholders across Australian jurisdictions, as well as with persons having a close relationship to the office: Attorneys-General, government legal officers and members of the Judiciary. I conducted interviews only with those who held office during the 'Modern Period' of the role (the 'Modern Period' is introduced in chapter three, section III.). A full list of interview participants, together with the date and place of the interview, is provided in Appendix B to this book. I shall refer to interviews I have conducted by reference to the participant only, except where the participant has requested anonymity. In addition to interview data, this Part draws upon documentary sources: biographies and biographic dictionaries, memoirs, oral histories, manuscript collections, newspaper reports, government reports and other documents (such as Cabinet documents), and the writings of officeholders.[8] Where possible, the views

[5] I McGilchrist, *The Master and his Emissary: The Divided Brain and the Making of the Western World* (Yale University Press, 2009) 144.

[6] Eg, Interview, Chris Kourakis; Interview, Keith Mason; Interview, Leigh Sealy. Contra Interview, William Bale; Interview, John Doyle; Interview, Robert Ellicott; Interview, Michael Grant; Interview, Tom Pauling; Interview, Michael Sexton; Interview, Walter Sofronoff.

[7] Interview, William Bale; Interview, John Doyle; Interview, Martin Hinton; Interview, Patrick Keane; Interview, Chris Kourakis; Interview, Michael Sexton; Interview, Pamela Tate. In their interviews, William Bale and Patrick Keane referred to the assistance in understanding the scope of the role provided by other officers, particularly in Crown Law, when they first took office.

[8] Including, eg, National Library of Australia, 'Papers of Sir Maurice Byers' (1975–99); Daniel Connell, Interview with Maurice Byers (Law in Australian Society Oral History Project, 10 January 1997); P Burton, *From Moree to Mabo: The Mary Gaudron Story* (UWA Publishing, 2010); R Coleman, *Above Renown: Biography of Sir Henry Winneke* (Macmillan Company, 1988); B Selway, 'The Duties of Lawyers Acting for Government' (1999) 10 *Public Law Review* 114; A Buti, *Sir Ronald Wilson: A Matter of Conscience* (University of Western Australia Press, 2007).

of participants are illustrated, and the recollections and examples of participants are substantiated by examples from case law, written opinions and other sources.[9]

This chapter explores participants' perceptions about the advisory function of the Solicitor-General. The importance and nature of the adviser and advocate functions were perceived differently. The importance of the office to the government system and the overarching concept of the rule of law was generally defined through the advisory aspect of the role. It was this function that gave the office its constitutional significance. This was despite the emphasis upon the benefits of having a permanent advocate available to government when the position was introduced, and the amount of the Solicitor-General's time that the advocacy role consumes.[10]

For a Solicitor-General to fulfil the advisory aspect of the role in a manner that assists in achieving governance under the rule of law, my data demonstrate that four assumptions must be met: the Solicitor-General must be acting for the Executive; the Solicitor-General's advice must be treated as final within government; the government must seek the advice of the Solicitor-General when appropriate circumstances arise; and the office must enjoy a level of independence. This chapter explores the first three assumptions. 'Independence' is returned to separately in chapter seven, as it transcends all aspects of the Solicitor-General's role.

II. Advisory Function and the Rule of Law

The advisory function was described by the English Attorney-General Sam Silkin in 1978 as 'little known and rarely visible to the public', but as 'certainly the most time-consuming, probably the most important, and possibly the most interesting' of the Attorney's responsibilities.[11] In the 2007 House of Commons investigation into the constitutional role of the English Attorney-General, Lord Goldsmith asserted that he had an important function in 'upholding the rule of law'. This he identified 'most obviously' in the Attorney-General's 'role as the Government's chief legal adviser', although, he said, 'it goes wider'.[12] Overwhelmingly, participants in my Australian study also emphasised the importance of the Solicitor-General within the government system by reference to the office's advisory function. A number of Australian participants specifically stressed the importance of the

[9] The support of many of the interview findings by independent measures in this way operates as a form of triangulation: MB Miles and AM Huberman, *Qualitative Data Analysis: An Expanded Sourcebook* (Sage Publications, 3rd edn, 1994) 266.

[10] Interview, Justin Gleeson.

[11] SC Silkin, 'The Functions and Position of the Attorney-General in the United Kingdom' (1978) 59 *The Parliamentarian* 149, 153.

[12] Evidence extracted in House of Commons Constitutional Affairs Committee, *Constitutional Role of the Attorney General*, Fifth Report of Session 2006–07 (HC306). 11.

advisory function over the advocacy work.[13] Former Tasmanian Solicitor-General William Bale explained the increased importance of the Solicitor-General's advisory function by reference to the rise of the modern administrative state and the expansion of the government and government activity into many spheres of private and commercial life.

In the office's advisory function, the Solicitor-General is policing the legal boundaries of government power, filling the role of a 'judge' before a matter reaches the judicial branch (if it ever does). Former Queensland Crown Solicitor and Acting Solicitor-General Barry Dunphy explained that, because in Australia the High Court has no jurisdiction to issue advisory opinions,[14] this role of the Solicitor-General is particularly important.

The Solicitor-General's opinions on the outer limits of government power are generally subject to the courts' view on the position. However, often *in practice* the Solicitor-General's advice establishes these limits, or at least influences them. Often government actions are not challenged: they may remain unknown to those they affect; or if they are known, people may not be inclined or in a position to challenge them. In other cases the government may abstain from acting on the basis of the Solicitor-General's advice, giving rise to no challengeable action or policy. In a small number of cases, the Solicitor-General will be advising on non-justiciable issues. In these cases, in the absence of a 'forensic context', former South Australian Solicitor-General Chris Kourakis explained he believed the Executive's obligation to act lawfully becomes more pronounced, and the work of the Solicitor-General more fundamental.[15]

Even where government actions are challenged in the courts, the Solicitor-General's advice may still be influential in the development of the legal position. Some members of the High Court have recognised the advantages of maintaining stability in the law, and have allowed their decisions to be informed by longstanding government practice.[16] In so far as the Solicitor-General's opinions are relied upon in the creation of such practice, the office's advisory function can be viewed as contributing directly to the development of the government's legal paradigm. For example, when Gavan Griffith was Commonwealth Solicitor-General, he advised the Government that it was constitutional to create posts for 'junior Ministers'.[17] When the matter was challenged in the High Court in 2001, the majority accepted the practice as constitutional, relying partly on the long-standing practice that had been informed by Griffith's advice. Gleeson CJ commented, 'The practice

[13] Interview, William Bale; Interview, Catherine Branson; Interview, Stephen Gageler; Interview, Leigh Sealy; Interview, Christian Porter.

[14] *Re Judiciary and Navigation Acts* (1921) 29 CLR 257.

[15] See also R Posner, *Frontiers of Legal Theory* (Harvard University Press, 2001) 16.

[16] See, eg, comments in *Victoria v Commonwealth* (1975) 134 CLR 338 ('*AAP Case*'), 417–19 (Murphy J); *Re Patterson; Ex parte Taylor* (2001) 207 CLR 391, 403 (Gleeson CJ). Although note that recent High Court decisions in another context—on the scope of the Commonwealth's Executive power—have rejected longstanding practice as relevant to determining and enforcing constitutional meaning: *Williams v Commonwealth* (2012) 248 CLR 256.

[17] Interview, Gavan Griffith.

of appointing Ministers, and Assistant Ministers, is well established.'[18] The High Court has also recently held that the words of a constitutional amendment may be interpreted by reference to a Solicitor-General's opinion where such an opinion was provided to voters during a referendum (at least in so far as the opinion discloses what the contemporary and intended meaning of the text may have been).[19]

A. Rule of Law: Three Perspectives

The Solicitor-General's advisory function assists in policing the boundaries of government power and ensuring the integrity of government action. But to what end? Participants justified the function in three different ways. According to each of these justifications, the function existed for overarching 'rule of law' objectives but each emphasised a different ideal encompassed within its parameters. First, some participants believed the function existed to 'check' government from over-extending its powers into the individual sphere. Secondly, the function existed to assist the democratically elected government achieve its policy agenda with certainty and security. Thirdly, it facilitated the smooth operation of the separation of powers in times of conflict between institutions or of uncertainty over their respective roles and powers.

i. Checking Power and Protecting the Public

Some participants saw the Solicitor-General's advisory function as operating for the benefit of the public *directly* by preventing the government from acting illegally.[20] Professor Itzhak Zamir, public law professor and later Justice of the Supreme Court of Israel, once said, 'The real client of the Attorney General is not the government but the public. He owes it to the public, on trust, to see to it that the law is observed by the government.'[21] Commonwealth Solicitor-General Justin Gleeson said he took Gough Whitlam's statement to Parliament during the second reading speech of the *Law Officers Act 1964* (Cth) as 'an eloquent statement of ideal':[22]

> It is often thought that whoever appears for the government must be the Devil's Advocate. Governments, however, are not only oppressors; they are liberators; and the Solicitor-General will be rather the voice of the people in most of the cases in which he appears.[23]

[18] *Re Patterson; Ex parte Taylor* (2001) 207 CLR 391, 403.

[19] *Wong v Commonwealth* (2009) 236 CLR 573, 591 [52] (French CJ and Gummow J), 625 [185] (Hayne, Crennan and Kiefel JJ), 657 [277] (Heydon J).

[20] Interview, Catherine Branson.

[21] I Zamir, 'The Role of the Attorney-General in Times of Crisis: The Israeli Shin Bet Affair' in S Shetreet (ed), *The Role of Courts in Society* (Brill Archive, 1988) 271, 273.

[22] J Gleeson, *The Role of the Solicitor-General* (Speech to Seven Wentworth Chambers, 27 February 2014) 8.

[23] Commonwealth, *Parliamentary Debates*, House of Representatives, 28 October 1964, 2445, Gough Whitlam.

Former Queensland Solicitor-General Walter Sofronoff commented that the office's advice protects the public by placing government in a position so that,

> if it were tempted to do something that crossed the line, or came close to the line, it has to deal with the fact that there is a piece of written advice that is there that one day might be uncovered by somebody in the course of time, and it makes it harder.[24]

However, the view that the Solicitor-General acted as a check on government power for the benefit of the public and community was less prevalent in the interview responses than the second perspective.

ii. Certainty and Security for Government

The second perspective was that the Solicitor-General's advice gives confidence to government to pursue policies that are legally sound, and gives government security if its actions are called into question in the future.[25] In a society that is underpinned by the rule of law, and where legislative and executive action is subject to challenge in the courts for its constitutional validity, it is imperative for the government to be able to act with some degree of constitutional certainty.

Former Commonwealth Solicitor-General and Attorney-General Robert Ellicott referred to this type of function as a 'protective role'. The Law Officers have a duty *to the government* to speak out if it is doing something beyond its legal boundaries. To illustrate this perspective, Ellicott used the advice that the then Commonwealth Solicitor-General, Maurice Byers, tendered on what eventually became known as the 'Loans Affair' and led to the dismissal of the Government in 1975.

The Whitlam Labor Government had attempted to secure a substantial loan without the consent of the Australian Loan Council. Loan Council consent was required by law except where the loan was 'for temporary purposes'. On the question as to whether the proposed loan was a 'loan for temporary purposes', and therefore did not need the permission of the Loan Council, the Whitlam Government sought Byers' oral view. The Solicitor-General indicated that it might be 'arguable'.[26] Ellicott surmised whether Byers could have prevented the entire affair by putting forward his legal view more forcefully. In Ellicott's opinion, Byers' responsibility to do so would have been for the objective of protecting the Government from harm.

The idea that the Solicitor-General provides security and certainty to government on legal issues—particularly controversial ones—was common in the views of Solicitors-General, and held even more strongly by Attorneys-General.

[24] Interview, Walter Sofronoff. See also Interview, Pamela Tate.

[25] Interview, Peter Garrisson; Interview, Patrick Keane; Interview, Chris Kourakis; Interview, Leigh Sealy; Interview, Walter Sofronoff.

[26] *Sankey versus Whitlam*—Maurice Byers QC regarding involvement in the Loans Affair (April 1976), National Archives of Australia, Canberra, M4081 3/25, 3–4; See also Daniel Connell, Interview with Maurice Byers (Law in Australian Society Oral History Project, 10 January 1997) 52.

Rodney Welford, former Queensland Attorney-General, said that in relation to controversial issues or issues that may adversely affect the interests of different stakeholders, the government 'want[s] the Solicitor-General to be fiercely independent because the last thing you need is gratuitous advice that gets you … hosed out in court'.

The government often publicly relies upon, and occasionally even releases, the Solicitor-General's advice. Former Northern Territory Solicitor-General Thomas Pauling said that Solicitor-General advice is sometimes used as a political counter-attack to any doubts as to the constitutionality or general legality of government actions. In the US context, Trevor Morrison has argued that the Executive's 'self-binding' approach to OLC opinions enhances the Executive's claims of respect for the law, which can be used to generate credibility and public support.[27] Gareth Evans, former Commonwealth Attorney-General, explained that sometimes to relieve political pressure, the Solicitor-General's advice was sought '*for the record*'. He saw 'the label of Solicitor-General' as being important. He explained:

> [T]hese were people of real stature, and it meant something having the Solicitor-General signing off on something. … A bit like [British Prime Minister Tony] Blair and the business with the Iraq war[28] … I mean Blair was desperate to have the advice that he wanted … not just from any old character at the Bar, he wanted it from his own Law Officers. That's the way in which you think about these things when you're in government.

The use of the Attorney-General's opinion by the British Government to give credibility to arguments about the legality of the invasion of Iraq relies on the stature, reputation and authority of the Law Officers' position. However, Pauling explained that government attempts to gain public support, relieve political pressure and cloak government actions with the legitimacy of a Law Officers' opinion, can introduce the potential for political abuse of the Solicitor-General's position.

The Solicitor-General does not always provide the government with a guaranteed 'stamp' of validity to show the public, its political opponents and the media.[29] If this were so, the Solicitor-General's opinion would lose its status and respectability, and therefore its worth to the government. Evans explained that a 'Solicitor-General who was prepared to do something that was intellectually indefensible, or intellectually disreputable', would 'diminish the credibility of that person, the office, and your capacity to rely on him, and your *own* capacity to avoid criticism from the public, from the press, and so on'.[30]

[27] TW Morrison, 'Libya "Hostilities," the Office of Legal Counsel, and the Process of Executive Branch Legal Interpretation' (2011) 124 *Harvard Law Review Forum* 62, 64.

[28] See further discussion of the role of the Attorney-General in providing advice to the Blair Government on the question of the legality of the war in Iraq in ch 2, section II D ii.

[29] A good example of this was referred to in Interview, David Bennett. In 2000 the Howard Government had to retreat from its policy on using the electoral roll to mail out information on the incoming Goods and Services Tax because of Solicitor-General advice on the issue. See Commonwealth, *Parliamentary Debates*, House of Representatives, 8 June 2000, 17442 (Daryl Williams, Attorney-General).

[30] For a similar view about the OLC's value to government in the US context, see Morrison, above n 27, 67.

The Solicitor-General's advice has, on occasion, been used as 'cover' during the introduction of controversial reforms. For example, in 2011 in Queensland, political and public concern erupted over the Bligh Labor government's proposed reform of the parliamentary committee system that reduced many of the traditional roles of the Speaker.[31] A letter was written to the editor of the *Courier Mail*, authored by a number of distinguished jurists, academics, practitioners and politicians, amongst others, alleging that the reforms were 'an insult to the doctrine of the separation of powers' and undermined the independence of the Parliament from the Executive by undermining the position of the Speaker.[32] The government responded by seeking the Solicitor-General's opinion on, inter alia, whether the proposed committee structure would be 'a breach of the doctrine of the separation of powers'. While the government sought the Solicitor-General's advice on the matter, this was not a legal question, as the doctrine of the separation of powers is not a binding constitutional principle in the state constitutional systems in Australia.[33] The Solicitor-General and Crown Counsel concluded that the proposal did not breach the doctrine of the separation of powers, and '[e]ven if the proposal did amount to a breach, there are no legal consequences'.[34] This advice was tabled in Parliament by the government,[35] and relied on extensively in debate as a political shield.[36]

More recently in 2014, the former Queensland Solicitor-General, Walter Sofronoff, was used to defend government policy, but this time in more controversial circumstances following which Sofronoff resigned. After taking power in 2012, Liberal-National Premier Campbell Newman and his Attorney-General, Jarrod Bleijie, pursued an aggressive agenda against organised criminal gangs, and more particularly against outlaw motorcycle gangs: 'bikies'. The Newman government introduced a suite of controversial laws targeting the bikies. It came under heavy criticism for the laws and their incursions into fundamental civil liberties, particularly from members of the legal profession. Following these

[31] Parliament of Queensland (Reform and Modernisation) Amendment Bill 2011 (Qld) (particularly cl 7) and Parliamentary Service and Other Acts Amendment Bill 2011 (Qld).

[32] David Russell QC, the Hon Ian Callinan; Suri Ratnapala; Nicholas Aroney; Dr Michael White QC; Scott Prasser; David Muir; Kevin Rozzoli; Dr Ken Coghill; Jim Fouras; Mike Reynolds; Neil Turner; Lin Powell; Ray Hollis; Rob Borbidge; Terry White; Beryce Nelson; Tom Gilmore; Bill Hewitt; Manfred Cross; David Watson; Judy Gamin; B Cahill, 'Avoid Assault on Democracy', *Courier Mail* (Brisbane), 20 April 2011, 32.

[33] Although the federal separation of powers has some impact at the State level because of the inclusion of the State courts in the federal system: *Kable v Director of Public Prosecutions (NSW)* (1996) 189 CLR 51.

[34] Memorandum of Advice from Walter Sofronoff QC, Solicitor-General and Steve Marton, Crown Counsel, *Re: Draft Parliamentary Service and Other Acts Amendment Bill 2011—Matters relating to the Committee of the Legislative Assembly*, 9 May 2011, 2.

[35] Queensland, *Memorandum of advice, dated 9 May 2011, from the Solicitor-General Queensland regarding the Draft Parliamentary Service and Other Acts Amendment Bill 2011—matters relating to the Committee of the Legislative Assembly*, Parl Paper No 5311T4402 (2011).

[36] See, eg, Queensland, *Parliamentary Debates*, Legislative Assembly, 12 May 2011, 1493 (Anna Bligh, Premier and Minister for Reconstruction).

criticisms, a briefing note from Sofronoff to Bleijie was leaked to the *Courier Mail*. This note suggested that it had been the Solicitor-General who had recommended the introduction of tougher laws based on the US experience, and that he was therefore the true 'architect' of the laws.[37] The leaking of Sofronoff's briefing note countered some of the criticisms of the laws, and particularly the criticism that they were driven by fear-mongering politics and were the result of Bleijie's lack of legal experience. Sofronoff's briefing note provided political cover to the Attorney.

Less than two months later, Sofronoff resigned as Solicitor-General. Bleijie initially claimed that the Solicitor-General had simply been ready to 'move on'. After refusing to comment, a week later Sofronoff wrote a letter to the *Courier Mail* lambasting Bleijie for breaching the confidences of his closest advisers for short-term political objectives.[38] He referred to the Attorney-General's leaking of a conversation between himself and the President of the Court of Appeal regarding future judicial appointments: 'The possibility that such highly confidential conversations could become public would have an instant chilling effect on the willingness of others to participate in an essential process. Mouths would close and tongues would be stilled.' He accused Bleijie of being prepared to 'betray a confidence for momentary personal advantage'. Sofronoff warned that Bleijie's actions had created a situation where the Attorney-General was in danger of being surrounded only by 'the coterie of sycophants who surround every person with power to confer advantages'.[39] While he did not expressly link his resignation to the leaking of his own advice on the anti-bikie laws, with his resignation occurring only weeks after this advice was leaked to the media it can be surmised that at least some of his criticism of Bleijie's breach of confidence was directed at his own experience as Solicitor-General.

In 2011, the Commonwealth Government relied heavily on the then Solicitor-General, Stephen Gageler, to give public credibility to its actions. This led to the office's becoming embroiled in political controversy and subject to public criticism. The incident commenced with a federal Government announcement of a new measure to process those asylum seekers who arrived in Australia by boat offshore.[40] The measure included sending 800 asylum seekers to Malaysia, and came to be known as the 'Malaysia Solution'. The Minister for Immigration issued a declaration under the *Migration Act 1958* (Cth) that Malaysia was a country

[37] D Houghton, 'Revealed: Who was the man who beat Attorney-General Jarrod Bleijie to the punch on bikie laws?', *Courier Mail* (1 February 2014), available at <http://www.couriermail.com.au/news/queensland/revealed-who-was-the-man-who-beat-attorneygeneral-jarrod-bleijie-to-the-punch-on-bikie-laws/story-fnihsrf2-1226815370242>.

[38] W Sofronoff, 'Attorney-General Bleijie's Crisis of Confidence, *Courier Mail* (25 March 2014), available at <http://www.couriermail.com.au/news/opinion/opinion-attorneygeneral-jarrod-bleijies-crisis-of-confidence/story-fnihsr9v-1226863613877>.

[39] See further discussion of this incident in G Appleby, 'Politicising Advice: A Cautionary Tale for All Governments' *The Conversation* (25 March 2014), available at <https://theconversation.com/politicising-advice-a-cautionary-tale-for-all-governments-24773>.

[40] Prime Minister and Minister for Immigration, 'The Regional Cooperation Framework' (Press Release, 7 May 2011).

to which 'offshore entry persons' could be taken.[41] A number of Afghani asylum seekers sought judicial review of that declaration in the High Court.

In response to this legal threat to a politically important policy, the Minister defended the legality of his decision, repeating that 'The Commonwealth Government is on very strong legal grounds.'[42] He also indicated that the Solicitor-General had been involved in ensuring the scheme was strongly defensible in the High Court, although any advice the Solicitor-General provided to the government to this effect was not released. Academic commentators shared the view that the Government would prevail in the challenge.[43] However, the High Court found the Minister's declaration invalid on the basis that it had been affected by jurisdictional error.[44]

A number of journalists drew the conclusion that the Government's legal advice (which, based on the Minister's comments, was assumed to have come from the Solicitor-General) must have been inadequate as it had not predicted the High Court's decision.[45] The legal advice itself was not released. A number of legal professionals came to Gageler's defence.[46] Sydney barrister Darren Ferrari surmised that there was a possibility the Minister had misrepresented the strength of the legal advice.[47] It has subsequently been reported that the Solicitor-General had

[41] *Migration Act 1958* (Cth), s 198A.

[42] C Bowen, Minister for Immigration, 'Malaysia transfer arrangement, High Court case' (Press Conference, 8 August 2011).

[43] See, eg, G Williams, 'Malaysia court case pitches minister against basic refugee rights', *Sydney Morning Herald* (Sydney) (16 August 2011), available at <http://www.smh.com.au/opinion/malaysia-court-case-pitches-minister-against-basic-refugee-rights-20110815-1iuni.html>; P Barry, 'Government power tested in High Court challenge', *The Power Index: Who Really Runs Australia*, 9 August 2011, available at <http://www.thepowerindex.com.au/head-to-head/government-power-tested-in-high-court-challenge/20110809246>; K Parish, 'Legal heaven on a stick', *Club Troppo*, 9 August 2011, available at <http://clubtroppo.com.au/2011/08/09/legal-heaven-on-a-stick/>. See post-case comments by David Bennett, reported in J Kelly, 'Bench ruling on Malaysian Solution slammed as narrow', *The Australian* (Sydney) (2 September 2011), available at <http://www.theaustralian.com.au/national-affairs/bench-ruling-on-malaysian-solution-slammed-as-narrow/story-fn59niix-1226127651701>.

[44] *Plaintiff M70/2011 v Minister for Immigration and Citizenship; Plaintiff M106 of 2011 v Minister for Immigration and Citizenship* (2011) 244 CLR 144 ('*Malaysia Solution Case*').

[45] See, eg, M Grattan, 'Incompetence and disaster: another grim day for Gillard', *The Age* (Melbourne) (1 September 2011), available at <http://www.theage.com.au/opinion/incompetence-and-disaster-another-grim-day-for-gillard-20110831-1jm5a.html?skin=text-only>; M Grattan, 'Gillard needs show of control', *The Age* (Melbourne) (2 September 2011), available at <http://www.theage.com.au/opinion/gillard-needs-show-of-control-20110901-1joau.html>. See also M Gordon, 'The Malaysia solution is shipwrecked', *The Age* (Melbourne) (1 September 2011), available at <http://www.theage.com.au/national/the-malaysia-solution-is-shipwrecked-20110831-1jmfm.html>.

[46] Letter from Ron Merkel QC, Peter Hanks QC, Debbie Mortimer SC, Richard Niall SC, Kristen Walker and Graeme Hill, extracted in M Gordon, 'Support for Top Lawyer', *The Age* (Melbourne) (15 September 2011), available at <http://www.theage.com.au/national/support-for-top-lawyer-20110915-1kbyd.html>. Mortimer, Niall and Walker appeared for the asylum seekers in the *Malaysia Solution Case*.

[47] D Ferrari, 'Political pundits commenting on legal issues, what could go wrong?', *Crikey*, 2 September 2011, available at <http://blogs.crikey.com.au/purepoison/2011/09/02/guest-post-journalists-judging-lawyers/>.

not even been involved in advising the Minister on the matter *prior* to the High Court challenge. Rather, the initial advice on the policy had been provided by lawyers within the Attorney-General's Department.[48] This aspect of the incident demonstrates that the Solicitor-General has no control over how government uses or represents his or her advice (or lack thereof) in the public sphere, and that misrepresentation (intentional or otherwise) is possible, particularly when political stakes are high and the legal issues are complex.

At a press conference a day after the High Court's decision, the Prime Minister, Julia Gillard, made the comment that 'The High Court's decision, basically, turns on its head the understanding of the law in this country prior to yesterday's decision.'[49] The reasons behind the Prime Minister's comments can be postulated. On one level, there must have been a degree of political manoeuvring, an attempt to deflect the fallout of the decision from the Government to the Court. There was also likely an element of the Prime Minister simply giving expression to political frustrations. However, other compelling reasons can also be found. It is important that government be seen to be acting lawfully, with integrity and within the bounds of the legal framework. The Prime Minister's statement could be viewed as a public defence of her government as one that respected the rule of law and believed it was acting within the bounds of what was proper, that is, it had acted according to a general understanding of what the law was, and that the High Court had dramatically changed this.

The Prime Minister may also have been defending the Solicitor-General from an anticipated attack. In the immediate aftermath of the High Court's decision, the Government needed to rely on the reputation of the Solicitor-General's office.[50] In the days following the decision, the Solicitor-General and two private Senior Counsel gave written advice on the implications of the judgment for taking asylum seekers to be processed in the Republic of Nauru (where the Opposition was strongly advocating asylum seekers be sent) or Papua New Guinea (where the Government had also made arrangements to send asylum seekers). The opinion was released by the Government. A summary of its conclusions stated that the authors were not confident a declaration could be made in relation to either country,[51] emphasising that it would depend upon 'complex issues of fact and degree requiring detailed assessment and analysis'.[52]

[48] R Ackland, 'Order in the High Court a cinch as taekwondo judge takes seat', *Sydney Morning Herald* (Sydney) (24 August 2012), available at <http://www.smh.com.au/opinion/order-in-the-high-court-a-cinch-as-taekwondo-judge-takes-seat-20120823-24p2j.html>.

[49] Prime Minister and Minister for Immigration, 'Malaysia Agreement' (Joint Press Conference, 1 September 2011).

[50] ibid.

[51] Opinion of Stephen Gageler, Stephen Lloyd and Geoffrey Kennett, *In the Matter of the Implications of Plaintiff M70/2011 v Minister for Immigration and Citizenship for Offshore Processing of Asylum Seekers under the* Migration Act 1958 *(Cth)*, 2 September 2011, 2 [3].

[52] ibid.

The legal community and political commentators quickly entered a debate around the correctness of the position taken in the Solicitor-General's joint advice.[53] James Allan described the Solicitor-General's position as 'just so risk-averse and so full of giving every single benefit of the doubt to those against the legality of the Nauru solution under the current legislation'.[54] 'Those' to whom Allan referred were the Government's ministers, and implicit in his criticism is the idea that the Solicitor-General was resolving (or perhaps using) legal ambiguity in a manner that assisted the political objectives of the Government. Chris Merritt, Editor of Legal Affairs in *The Australian*, similarly labelled the advice 'an intensely political document', a 'guide to avoiding trouble' and as giving the 'shattered government an out'.[55] The Minister for Immigration described the advice as confirming 'the significant doubts over whether or not the government and Immigration Minister could make a valid declaration for either Papua New Guinea or Nauru'.[56] The Opposition accused the Government of misrepresenting and even 'verballing' the Solicitor-General.[57]

Within the ensuing debate about the need to amend the *Migration Act*, the Opposition was very careful to maintain that it did not disagree with the Solicitor-General's advice, or to avoid any allegations that Gageler's position was itself politically motivated,[58] focusing instead upon the Government's representation of it. The Opposition leader agreed to a briefing by the Solicitor-General and other government officials. A telling exchange occurred between Opposition Leader Tony Abbott and Radio Broadcaster Alan Jones, where Abbott denied that the Solicitor-General may have even been involved in the initial advice.[59]

[53] See, eg, D Bennett, 'Offshore processing still possible despite High Court decision', *Sydney Morning Herald* (Sydney) (12 September 2011), available at <http://www.smh.com.au/opinion/politics/offshore-processing-still-possible-despite-high-court-decision-20110911-1k40s.html#ixzz1xdRigCg6>; J Allan, 'Stephen Gageler too risk-averse in his advice on Nauru option', *The Australian* (Sydney) (16 September 2011), available at <http://www.theaustralian.com.au/business/legal-affairs/stephen-gageler-too-risk-averse-in-his-advice-on-nauru-option/story-e6frg97x-1226138211343>.

[54] Allan, above n 53.

[55] C Merritt, 'Advice gives shattered government an out', *The Australian* (Sydney) (5 September 2011), available at <http://www.theaustralian.com.au/national-affairs/opinion/advice-gives-shattered-government-an-out/story-e6frgd0x-1226129287924>.

[56] C Bowen, Minister for Immigration, 'Government Releases Solicitor-General's Advice On High Court Decision' (Press release, 4 September 2011).

[57] S Benson and G Jones, 'Abbott says no deal on PM's asylum seeker solution', *The Daily Telegraph* (Sydney) (20 September 2011), available at <http://www.dailytelegraph.com.au/news/national/abbott-says-no-deal-on-pms-asylum-seeker-solution/story-e6freuzr-1226141282905>. See also comments by George Brandis, Shadow Attorney-General, that the Immigration Minister had 'misrepresented' the Solicitor-General's advice: AAP, 'Nauru still a possibility: opposition', *Sydney Morning Herald* (Sydney) (4 September 2011), available at <http://www.smh.com.au/national/nauru-still-a-possibility-opposition-20110904-1js2q.html>.

[58] This was later confirmed when Gageler's appointment to the High Court was announced; Brandis welcomed the appointment, indicating that he had recommended Gageler to the Attorney-General. See D Harrison and R Willingham, 'Gageler Appointed to High Court', *Sydney Morning Herald* (Melbourne) (21 August 2012), available at <http://www.smh.com.au/opinion/political-news/gageler-appointed-to-high-court-20120821-24jqb.html>.

[59] Alan Jones, Interview with Tony Abbott (Radio 2GB, Sydney, 20 September 2011, available at http://www.tonyabbott.com.au/News/tabid/94/articleType/ArticleView/articleId/8338/Interview-with-Alan-Jones-Radio-2GB-Sydney.aspx).

A number of conclusions can be drawn from Gageler's involvement in the intensely political 'Malaysia Solution' episode. At least at the federal level, the Solicitor-General's position is respected and defended by the Government and the Opposition (who, of course, might want to rely on the office to maintain the credibility of its own actions if it won government in the future).[60] However, as a pivotal player in the creation of government policy, the office becomes open to criticism, whether that be on the ground of incompetence or of politicisation of the role. While it is understandable why a government may seek to rely on the reputation, independence and integrity of the Solicitor-General to deflect political attacks, this opens the office to criticism that an opinion is politically expedient, and that the functions have not been exercised with the necessary degree of independence and integrity. This is perhaps particularly the case where the Solicitor-General's advice is not released and only representations of the advice are relied upon.

During the entire 'Malaysia Solution' episode, Gageler made no public attempt to defend his advice or the office. This accords with the normal practice for Solicitors-General not to speak directly to the public. However, this has not always been the case. Gageler's reaction may be contrasted with that of former Commonwealth Solicitor-General Maurice Byers in 1975. On 4 November 1975, Byers signed his name to an opinion that stated that the Governor-General was not entitled to dismiss the Prime Minister on the basis that the Government was unable to guarantee the passage of its supply bills through the Senate.[61] The advice was given to the Governor-General by the Attorney-General on 6 November 1975. After the dismissal, the written advice was leaked to the *Australian Financial Review* and extracts of it were published on 17 November 1975. In an unusual and unprecedented turn, on 18 November 1975 the Solicitor-General wrote a letter to the editor of that paper (which was published in full) to remove 'misunderstandings of and misstatements concerning the effect of that opinion'.[62]

The Solicitor-General's advisory function was seen by the majority of participants in this study through the lens of the Executive: providing security, certainty and credibility to government action. While this accords with the role of the Solicitor-General in promoting government under the rule of law, it did raise the very real possibility that the government may use the Solicitor-General's advice in a way that subjects the office to political controversy.

iii. The Separation of Powers

The third view of the Solicitor-General's contribution to the rule of law and the public interest is its role in assisting in the resolution of disputes between branches

[60] See similar conclusions in the US: J Schwartz, 'Two Perspectives on the Solicitor General's Independence' (1988) 21 *Loyola of Los Angeles Law Review* 1119, 1165–66. Although note the exceptional circumstances that occurred in Victoria in the late 1990s, when the Shadow Attorney-General publicly attacked the Solicitor-General. See further explanation of this event below.

[61] Opinion from Kep Enderby and Maurice Byers, 4 November 1975, [39].

[62] Letter from Maurice Byers to the Editor, *Australian Financial Review* (18 November 1975).

of government, particularly the Executive and the legislature. In the US, the OSG is perceived as holding a peculiar place to engage and moderate between the institutions to ensure the appropriate functioning of the system.[63] The relationship between the OSG and the courts is obvious, but it has been observed that Congress also relies upon the OSG to defend the constitutionality of its legislation in the courts.[64] To serve effectively all three branches of government, the office must act with a large degree of independence from each.[65] This view of the OSG as having obligations to serve across the three branches of government has been heavily criticised. The first critique is definitional, targeting the illusory nature of true 'whole of government' interests that can transcend the Executive's interest in times of conflict. The second is more pragmatic, arguing that the theory provides little guidance for how an officeholder should act when conflict occurs between branches. The third critique asserts that there is simply no need for the OSG (or the OLC) to divide their loyalties between the branches: neither the Judiciary nor the legislature requires the assistance of the OSG or OLC to carry out its constitutional functions.[66]

In Australia, similar positions and critiques emerged. Former Queensland Crown Solicitor and Acting Solicitor-General Barry Dunphy explained that the government turns to the Solicitor-General when questions as to the proper functioning of the branches of government arise. This is particularly so when the Executive's actions, policies or legislative agenda are being questioned in so far as they affect the operation of the other branches. Dunphy illustrated his statement by reference to the role the Commonwealth Solicitor-General played in resolving constitutional questions pertaining to an agreement between the major parties and the Independents that was entered into after the 2010 federal election returned a hung Parliament.[67] Part of the agreement was that the Speaker of the House of Representatives would be granted a parliamentary 'pair' from a member of the opposite party to cancel out the loss of the Speaker's vote.[68] There was a

[63] Elena Kagan, Address to the Georgetown University Law Center Conference, 10 May 2009, extracted in Harvard Law School, *Executive Counsel: Meet the President's New Lawyers—And Their New Lawyers*, available at <www.law.harvard.edu/news/spotlight/alumni-pusuits/counsel.html>. See also A Cox, 'The Government in the Supreme Court' (1963) 44 *Chicago Bar Record* 221, 222; comments of Solicitor-General Seth Waxman, extracted in D Marcott, 'The Duty to Defend: What is in the Best Interests of the World's Most Powerful Client?' (2004) 92 *Georgetown Law Journal* 1309, 1311.

[64] See, eg, Schwartz, above n 60, 1123, 1152; Marcott, above n 63, 1318 ff; DW Kmiec, 'OLC's Opinion Writing Function: The Legal Adhesive for a Unitary Executive' (1993) 15 *Cardozo Law Review* 337, 351–52; SP Waxman, 'Defending Congress' (2001) 79 *North Carolina Law Review* 1073, 1084–88. The US Congress also has legal representation that it may call upon in the event that the Solicitor-General refuses to defend its legislation: see The Ethics in Government Act 1978 US Code, Title 2, § 288k(b).

[65] Marcott, above n 63, 1312, 1313–14; Schwartz, above n 60, 1159–60.

[66] GP Miller, 'Government Lawyers' Ethics in a System of Checks and Balances' (1987) 54 *University of Chicago Law Review* 1293, 1296.

[67] See the reporting of the doubts: C Merritt and P Karvelas, '"Pairing" Speaker a Recipe for Chaos, Legal Experts Warn', *The Australian* (Sydney) (18 September 2010).

[68] Agreement between Australian Labor Party and the Independent Members (Mr Tony Windsor and Mr Rob Oakeshott), 7 September 2010, [4], referring to Annex Z, [2.1], 2.

question as to whether this was constitutional. Legal experts and members of the Opposition called for the Solicitor-General's advice to resolve the issue.[69] Ultimately, the Solicitor-General's opinion was sought and the advice made public.[70] This quietened (although did not completely dissipate) the controversy over the issue.[71] Dunphy stressed that the Solicitor-General was able to perform this role in the context of a conflict between the branches because of the respect held across government, politics and the public for the office's independence.

Former Queensland Solicitor-General Patrick Keane also noted that while the office does not often advise parliament directly, parliament benefits from the Solicitor-General's advice to the Executive because it ensures that 'parliament has the certainty it needs to legislate on a firm footing'. Indeed, when parliament is asked to pass legislation the validity of which might be constitutionally uncertain, the government often explicitly refers to the fact that the Solicitor-General has provided advice. This is done to reassure parliament that it has the necessary constitutional powers to enact the legislation. For example, in 2015, when questions were raised about the constitutional validity of a Commonwealth Bill that would extend the circumstances under which Australian dual citizens could lose their citizenship, Parliament's Joint Committee on Intelligence and Security asked the Secretary of the Department of Immigration and Border Protection and the Deputy Secretary of the Attorney-General's Department to ask their ministers to release the Solicitor-General's advice. While the Attorney-General declined to release that advice,[72] he wrote to the Committee in the following terms:

> [T]he Government has received advice from the Solicitor-General, Mr Justin Gleeson SC, that, in his opinion, there is a good prospect that a majority of the High Court would reject a constitutional challenge to the core aspects of the draft Bill.[73]

The majority of the Committee was reassured by the Attorney-General's letter, and the fact that advice had been received from the Solicitor-General.[74]

Participants referred to a number of instances where the Executive used the Solicitor-General to assist in the functioning of government across the three branches. In many of these instances the Solicitor-General provided advice to

[69] See comments of Geoffrey Lindell reported in Merritt and Karvelas, above n 67; and comments of Tony Abbott and Christopher Pyne reported in S Lane, 'Knock Down Advice Amid Speaker Stand-off', *The World Today* (Canberra) (21 September 2010), available at <http://www.abc.net.au/worldtoday/content/2010/s3017687.htm>.

[70] Letter of advice from Stephen Gageler SC, *In the Matter of the Office of the Speaker of the House of Representatives*, 22 September 2010.

[71] K Murphy, 'Legal Advice Clears Path for Speaker Plan', *The Age* (Melbourne) (23 September 2010).

[72] Parliamentary Joint Committee on Intelligence and Security, *Advisory Report on the Australian Citizenship Amendment (Allegiance to Australia) Bill 2015*, 4 September 2015, 33 [3.39].

[73] Letter from the Honourable George Brandis SC to the Honourable Mark Dreyfus QC, 27 August 2015 (Appendix D to the Parliamentary Joint Committee on Intelligence and Security, *Advisory Report on the Australian Citizenship Amendment (Allegiance to Australia) Bill 2015*, 4 September 2015).

[74] Parliamentary Joint Committee on Intelligence and Security, *Advisory Report on the Australian Citizenship Amendment (Allegiance to Australia) Bill 2015*, 4 September 2015, 33 [3.39]. Although not all Committee members in this example were satisfied: 33–34 [3.41]–[3.42].

parliament, through the clerks, the speaker of the lower house, the president of the upper house or committees.[75] One example occurred in 1984, where Attorney-General Senator Gareth Evans tabled the advice of the Solicitor-General in the Senate during the controversy over whether Justice Lionel Murphy of the High Court had engaged in behaviour that would warrant removal under section 72 of the Constitution. The Solicitor-General provided a legal opinion on the construction of term 'misbehaviour' in section 72 to assist Parliament in its deliberations.[76] Two Solicitors-General also recalled advising the Judiciary on administrative matters.[77] In each of the examples offered by participants, advice was provided to the parliament or the Judiciary with the knowledge and consent of the government of the day, through the government, or steps were taken to ensure that no conflict existed with the government. Thus the Solicitor-General remained 'the government's barrister' even when providing inter-branch advice.[78]

A number of participants were skeptical that parliament would seek and rely upon the advice of the Solicitor-General because of the office's association with the Executive.[79] This is exemplified in a disagreement in 1982 between the federal Government and the Senate. The Senate had requested the production of a number of documents that related to what was known as the 'Bottom of the Harbour' tax-avoidance scheme, and other related schemes.[80] Some documents were produced, but executive privilege was claimed over other documents, including legal opinions and investigation reports, on the basis that public disclosure of the contents would be 'harmful to the administration of justice'. The Government relied upon advice from the Solicitor-General in this privilege claim.[81] It challenged the Senate to act contrary to the opinion of the Solicitor-General, 'a person who is politically independent, statutorily independent, [and] has high legal ability'.[82]

[75] For example, Interview, Peter Garrisson (who provided advice to the Clerk of the Parliament); Interview, Chris Kourakis (who provided advice on the definition of a 'money bill' to the Speaker and the President); Interview, Pamela Tate (who advised on the definition of a 'disputed Bill' to the Speaker and the Chief Parliamentary Counsel); see also Victoria, Department of Justice, Protocol for Briefing the Solicitor-General (28 July 2011) ([1]). Note also the advice provided by the Commonwealth Attorney-General and Solicitor-General to the Parliament in 1970s: IJ Greenwood and R Ellicott, 'Parliamentary Committees: Powers over and protection afforded to witnesses' (1973). In 2013 in Western Australia, the Attorney-General sent advice to the Joint Standing Committee on Delegated Legislation regarding whether the proposed Supreme Court Rules were within power: Joint Standing Committee on Delegated Legislation, *Report 66: Supreme Court Amendment Rules 2013* (October 2013), extracted at 9.

[76] Parliamentary Debates, Commonwealth, *Senate*, 28 February 1984, 32–34 (Senator Gareth Evans, tabling advice from Gavan Griffith).

[77] Interview, Keith Mason; Interview, Pamela Tate.

[78] Interview, John Doyle.

[79] Interview, Patrick Keane; Interview, Robert McClelland; Interview, Philip Ruddock. See also Tasmania, *Parliamentary Debates*, House of Assembly, 5 May 1983, 830 (Julian Amos, Labor).

[80] The scheme was so named because it operated by taking a company to the 'bottom of the harbour', that is stripping it of all its assets and profits, prior to its tax falling due.

[81] Commonwealth, *Parliamentary Debates*, Senate, 23 September 1982, 1250 (Fred Chaney).

[82] ibid.

Nonetheless, the Senate resolved to order the production of the documents. Opposition Senator Gareth Evans indicated that the Senate ought to take advice on this matter from an officer outside of the Executive:

> We make it clear, finally, that we make no suggestion whatsoever that the Solicitor-General, Sir Maurice Byers, is in any way politically biased in the judgments that he may have made about the status of these particular documents. I do suggest that he may have erred on the side of caution in protecting information, in protecting documents in the hands of the Executive Government of the day. He may have erred in this respect on the basis of his well-known personal views about the proper extent of Executive privilege, the proper extent to which Executive information should be made available to the public. …
>
> I believe it is appropriate for someone totally outside the apparatus of full time Executive Government, someone who is not an officer in any sense, statutory or otherwise, of this Government, to perform this particular task.[83]

When conflicts of interests arise across the branches of government the Solicitor-General's position is that of counsel for the Executive. This has been particularly evident where parliament is engaged in its function of holding the government to account. For example, in New South Wales, when litigation arose between the State Treasurer and the Legislative Council over whether the Council had power to require the production of documents by the Treasurer, the Solicitor-General was firmly in the corner of the State Executive, acting for the Treasurer in the litigation against the relevant parliamentary officer.[84]

More subtle conflicts can occur where the Solicitor-General has advised government and parliament is reviewing the resulting executive action, for example in a committee inquiry or during Question Time. To ensure the independent exercise of the oversight function in such a situation, parliament cannot be bound to use or follow the Solicitor-General's advice, but must make an independent assessment of the position.[85]

In the Northern Territory the Solicitor-General's advice is regularly sought directly by the Speaker of the Legislative Assembly, even in circumstances where there is, at least potentially, a conflict between the interests of the Territory government and the parliament. Michael Grant, the incumbent Solicitor-General,

[83] ibid, 1238ff (Gareth Evans). The continuing position of the Clerk of the Senate in 2008 that it is for the Senate to review claims of both legal professional privilege and other privilege to determine whether the claims are made out: Letter from Harry Evans, Clerk of the Senate, to Peter Hallahan, *Disclosure of Legal Advice*, 19 February 2008.

[84] *Egan v Willis* (1998) 195 CLR 224, (1996) 40 NSWLR 650 (Court of Appeal); *Egan v Chadwick* (1999) 46 NSWLR 563. Interview, Keith Mason.

[85] See, eg, commentary after a situation like this arose in 2007 in Tasmania: Resources and Development Joint Standing Committee on Environment, 'Joint Venture Log Supply Deal' (Parliament of Tasmania, 2007); M Stokes, 'The Right of a Parliamentary Scrutiny Committee to Seek Independent Legal Advice', *TasmanianTimes.com*, 17 April 2007, available at <http://tasmaniantimes.com/index.php/article/the-right-of-a-parliamentary-scrutiny-committee-to-seek-independent-legal-a>; and note the current position in Tasmania, Attorney-General, *Guidelines for Seeking Advice from the Office of the Solicitor-General* (The Hon Brian Wightman MP, Febraury 2012) [5].

explained this position on the basis that he had a 'standing instruction' from the Attorney-General to provide advice to the Speaker, and that 'the Speaker is effectively the head of the Department of the Legislative Assembly'. He saw no necessary conflict of interest because his principal client, the Northern Territory Executive, and the parliament both served the public interest.

The Solicitor-General's advisory role was perceived by all participants as integral to the proper functioning of the constitutional order. The office's responsibility to provide advice on the limits of government power serves to promote the rule of law in three major ways. Primarily, as an adviser to the Executive, the Solicitor-General's advisory function gives certainty and security to government actions; although this can open the possibility for the government to use the Solicitor-General's advice in political and politicising ways. Not always directly, but more often as a consequence of this first proposition, the office also serves the public interest by protecting the community from arbitrary interference by government. Because each of the three arms of government exists to check and balance the others, keeping one other within the boundaries of these powers, the Solicitor-General has also been recognised as an important actor in ensuring the smooth operation of the three branches of government, assisting to resolve tensions when they arise. Is the Solicitor-General well-suited to fulfilling these important constitutional jobs? The next section of this chapter turns to the assumptions about the Solicitor-General that underpin the office's suitability to meet the objectives of the advisory function, and the extent to which they are met in practice.

B. Assumptions

Four assumptions can be identified as necessary for the Solicitor-General's advisory function to be able to advance the rule of law under any of the three views listed above. First is that the Solicitor-General is operating as an adviser to the Executive—keeping Executive power within its limits. So there is an assumption about the identity of the *client* of the office. The second assumption is that the Solicitor-General's advice is respected as the final word on a legal issue by government, and that a government will follow the office's advice. The third assumption is that the government will seek the advice of the Solicitor-General when appropriate circumstances arise and not seek advice from more friendly quarters, or fail to seek advice at all. Lastly, there is an assumption that the Solicitor-General is providing independent, not accommodating, advice. If these assumptions are not met then the capacity of the office to fulfil the advisory function in a manner that achieves its rule of law objectives is diminished.

i. First Assumption: The Government as Client

The first assumption that underpins the idea of the Solicitor-General's contribution to the rule of law is the identification of the 'Executive' as the office's client. While some benefits were identified to the public and the other branches of government, ultimately participants accepted that the advisory function was primarily intended for the service of the Executive by giving the Executive confidence in its actions and a source of legitimacy for them.

With one exception, all participants accepted the proposition that the Solicitor-General had a 'client'.[86] Further, participants accepted that this client was the 'Executive'. The client was variously described as the Crown, the Commonwealth, the State, the Government or the Executive. South Australian Solicitor-General Martin Hinton said he considered his client 'the people of South Australia', but he accepted that he must act on the instructions of the State Executive.

a. The Government as an Enduring Entity and the Political Executive

The idea that the Solicitor-General's client is represented by the political Executive was recurrent across the interviews, and was generally influenced by a recognition that it was the Attorney-General's responsibility to determine what the Executive's interests were.[87] Commonwealth Solicitor-General Justin Gleeson said the Attorney-General was generally 'the person who is responsible to parliament for what you are doing'. He explained this as an 'important aspect of the client'. Western Australian Solicitor-General Grant Donaldson indicated that this position might change depending on the nature of the matter: that the State as a client is often represented by the Attorney-General, but there will be other circumstances where the State is represented by another office, such as the Premier.

This distinction between the client and the person or officer who has the power to determine the interests of the client was the way in which many participants reconciled the idea that the Executive was both an enduring entity and was represented by a political government.[88] Former Commonwealth Solicitor-General Stephen Gageler said he viewed the Commonwealth as his client; but who was the Commonwealth?

> I've wrestled with this. It is bigger than the government of the day. There is a sense of the polity; there is a sense of a tradition, an ill-defined, tradition; of the common good; the common wealth. All of these things I take quite seriously. I recognise that I cannot easily define them. I also recognise that at the end of the day, I take instructions from the *Attorney-General* … when I'm appearing for the Commonwealth proper.

Some saw the government as an enduring entity as being synonymous with the elected government of the day.[89] Grant Donaldson said that in his experience, particularly on matters of constitutional law, there had never been a misunderstanding or disagreement about what the long-term interests of the State required.

[86] The exception was former Victorian Solicitor-General Daryl Dawson, who questioned the utility of the solicitor-client paradigm (Interview, Daryl Dawson). Commonwealth Solicitor-General Justin Gleeson also indicated that he was not entirely comfortable with the term 'client', but accepted it was used across the Commonwealth Government.

[87] Interview, Thomas Pauling. This reflects the legal position.

[88] Interview, Geoffrey Davies; Interview, Stephen McLeish; Interview, Thomas Pauling.

[89] Interview, Greg Cooper; Interview, Robert Ellicott.

b. The 'Whole of Government'

Many participants held the view that the Solicitor-General serves the broad, overarching executive polity: the 'whole of government'. Therefore, while the government presents as a 'multi-headed beast',[90] the Solicitor-General's client remains the sum of all of its permutations. In Victoria, former Solicitor-General Pamela Tate explained that while many agencies could request her advice directly, she developed a practice where she would always copy advice to the Attorney-General, with the knowledge of the agency concerned, where she believed the advice was relevant and significant to the Attorney-General's role as first Law Officer of the Crown. In this way, she tried to ensure that while she advised many manifestations of the 'client', the Crown retained its status as a single entity and coherency was maintained across its legal position.

A small number of participants indicated that the question of who is the 'client' has become more difficult because of the increase in independent statutory bodies and Government Business Enterprises (GBEs) that may seek advice from the Solicitor-General. Former Commonwealth Solicitor-General Stephen Gageler and former Queensland Crown Solicitor and Acting Solicitor-General Barry Dunphy both said that when acting for an independent statutory body or GBE, the client would be viewed narrowly. Commonwealth Solicitor-General Justin Gleeson said that in these cases the client is 'ostensibly narrower', but was not sure whether this was a difference in 'degree or quality'. Gageler explained that this was because the statute may require the body to act independently and sometimes come into conflict with the government proper. In such situations, participants stressed that they reviewed their instructions carefully for potential conflicts of interest.[91]

During his term Justin Gleeson implemented a formal protocol—particularly around requests for advice—that he explained limited the potential for conflicts of interest. As he viewed his function under section 12(b) of the *Law Officers Act 1964* (Cth) to provide advice only to the Attorney-General,[92] whenever a request for advice in non-contentious matters came to him, he wrote to the Attorney for his or her approval to provide that advice. As in Victoria, a copy of the advice was then provided to the Attorney.[93] In contentious matters, as the statute did not require him to act with the express authority of the Attorney-General, he thought the position was less clear. However, paragraph 10.7 of the Commonwealth Legal Services Directions 2005 provides that the Attorney-General is entitled to obtain access to any legal advice obtained by non-corporate Commonwealth entities (as defined in the *Public Governance, Performance and Accountability Act 2013*), subject to any legislative restriction, and section 55ZH of the *Judiciary Act 1903* ensures that

[90] Interview, Duncan Kerr. See also Interview, Keith Mason.

[91] Interview, Barry Dunphy; Interview, Stephen Gageler; Interview, Peter Garrisson; Interview, Michael Grant; Interview, Patrick Keane; Interview, Stephen McLeish.

[92] See analysis of section 12(b) in ch 4, section III.

[93] Commonwealth, Office of Legal Services Coordination, Guidance Note 11: Briefing the Solicitor-General (Catherine Fitch, 18 February 2014) [13].

this advice-sharing is not taken to waive legal professional privilege. In respect of non-corporate Commonwealth entities, paragraph 4.1 of the Directions requires such entities to comply with any instructions by the Attorney-General about the handling of claims or the conduct of litigation. Against this backdrop, Justin Gleeson took the view that for matters of significance, the Attorney-General should be briefed, and he would work with the agency to ensure that occurred.

Former Tasmanian Solicitor-General Leigh Sealy indicated he advised GBEs and State-owned companies *only if* they were part of the Crown. If not, Sealy believed it inappropriate to advise the body for two reasons: first, it offered the body a commercial advantage if it was operating in a competitive environment; and, secondly, the body would not be bound by a Treasury Instruction that requires all requests for advice from government agencies to be referred to Crown Law, and not to private firms. As such, the body would be free to seek private advice on the same issue, which would undermine the authoritative nature of the Solicitor-General's opinions.[94]

Northern Territory Solicitor-General Michael Grant explained that he advises many independent statutory officers in the Territory, including the Auditor-General, the Electoral Commissioner, the Anti-Discrimination Commissioner and the Children's Commissioner. However, he did not accept instructions from the Ombudsman in situations where there could be a conflict with the government. He explained:

> I don't do [the Ombudsman's] work, because by definition, every matter that she is involved in creates a potential conflict with government. Because that's her whole function: to investigate administrative action by government agencies. So she is *always* potentially in conflict with my primary client body.

Grant only felt comfortable advising the Ombudsman on questions relating to the extent of the office's powers where these arose in the abstract.[95] In Tasmania, Sealy also noted that for many of the statutory officeholders, including the Ombudsman and the Auditor-General, individuals exercise independent statutory discretions, which require officeholders to form their *own* views of their powers; as such, they cannot be *bound* to follow the Solicitor-General's view in the same way the government, by convention, is. The convention exists primarily for the benefit of maintaining a consistent position across the whole of government.[96]

Participants' views in this area demonstrate there exists some desire for the government to speak with one voice, but it also demonstrates an understanding that

[94] Treasury Department, 'Treasurer's Instruction No 1118: Procurement of Legal Services: goods and services (Version 6)' (November 2008). See further discussion of the assumption that the government treats the Solicitor-General's advice as final and authoritative below at section II.B.ii.

[95] See also Interview, Stephen McLeish; and Victoria, Department of Justice, Protocol for Briefing the Solicitor-General (28 July 2011), [1], which sets out the independent agencies of the Auditor-General, Electoral Commissioner, Chief Commissioner of Police and Ombudsman as persons who brief the Solicitor-General.

[96] See further discussion below at section II.B.ii.

there are times when an agency's interests may legitimately conflict with those of the government.[97]

c. Advising Vice-regal officers

The question of whether the Solicitor-General can advise Vice-regal officers is directly relevant to the consideration of the office's role in contributing to the rule of law pursuant to its advisory function. As was explained in chapter four, section IV.A.ii., there will be occasions where a Vice-regal officer requires advice on whether the 'reserve powers' are triggered by illegal actions taken by the Executive. In other circumstances in which the Vice-regal officer may have to exercise his or her powers, just like any other emanation of the Executive, he or she must ascertain the outer limits of those powers to act with certainty. While these occasions may be rare, they often arise in the midst of constitutional crisis and uncertainty.

Where the reserve powers of the Crown are engaged, it falls on the Vice-regal officer to exercise the Crown's powers alone, that is, autonomously from the advice of the government of the day. In such a situation, does the Solicitor-General perform the function of legal adviser to the Vice-regal officer? Chapter four explained that the answer to this is governed, at least initially, by the legislation. The statutes recognise (some expressly and others by implication) the Attorney-General as the appropriate officer to provide instructions to the Solicitor-General on behalf of the Crown. While this may be the formal legal position, there are strong arguments that, just as the rule of law recognises the desirability of the Executive's accessing high quality, independent, legal advice through the Solicitor-General to resolve difficult legal questions with finality, there are advantages in making the Solicitor-General available to advise a Vice-regal officer in his or her constitutional role as head of state.

The desirability of having the Solicitor-General available to Vice-regal officers is reflected in various practices and protocols that have developed across the jurisdictions. Indeed, in the mid-1990s the Special Committee of Solicitors-General attempted to compile a uniform protocol on the role of the Solicitor-General in advising the Governor,[98] although because of the differing detail of these practices across jurisdictions, no single protocol was agreed upon at that time.

At the State and Territory level, a large consensus emerged across participants (at least in those jurisdictions where it had arisen as an issue from time to time) that the Solicitor-General *would* furnish advice to the Governor or Administrator.

[97] For discussion of the US position on this point, see N Devins, 'Unitariness and Independence: Solicitor General Control over Independent Agency Litigation' (1994) 82 *California Law Review* 255; T Lochner, 'The Relationship between the Office of Solicitor General and the Independent Agencies: A Reevaluation' (1993) 79 *Virginia Law Review* 549; RL Stern, '"Inconsistency" in Government Litigation' (1951) 64 *Harvard Law Review* 759, 768–69; RL Stern, 'The Solicitor General's Office and Administrative Agency Litigation' (1988) 21 *Loyola of Los Angeles Law Review* 1073; K Clark, 'Government Lawyers and Confidentiality Norms' (2007) 85 *Washington University Law Review* 1033, 1059.

[98] J McDonnell, 'Special Committee of Solicitors General Meeting' (Secretary, Special Committee of Solicitors-General, 18 October 1996) 5ff.

There was, however, a substantive variation across the jurisdictions as to the exact process: whether the advice would *only* be provided with the permission of the Attorney-General (or Premier) and, once given, whether the advice would also be provided to the Attorney-General (or Premier). In New South Wales,[99] Tasmania,[100] Victoria[101] and the Northern Territory,[102] an accepted practice emerged whereby the Solicitor-General would advise the Vice-regal officer either because of a standing arrangement with the Attorney-General, or under ad hoc arrangements put in place when particular issues arose.[103] In the Northern Territory, Solicitor-General Michael Grant took the view that he could advise the political Executive as well as the Administrator on the same legal question in circumstances where there was no conflict over issues of fact.[104]

No consistent position emerged as to the practice in Western Australia. Attorney-General Michael Mischin was very clear that the Solicitor-General should not advise the Governor, on the basis that the Solicitor-General acts on the instructions of the Attorney-General. His position was that if the Governor wanted advice from the Solicitor-General, he or she must seek it through the Attorney-General. He also explained the undesirability of the Governor's relying on the Solicitor-General for advice, that it might politicise the Solicitor-General's role, it might undermine the status of the Solicitor-General's position if the Solicitor-General's opinion was only one of many sought, and it might compromise the Solicitor-General's position as the final arbiter if a dispute as to the correct legal position were to arise. However, former Acting Solicitor-General Rob Mitchell indicated that in his time as Solicitor-General he had advised the Governor, although on matters that were not politically controversial. On more controversial matters Mitchell was less sure about how the advice would be obtained, and whether it would be done confidentially, but he was certain that 'the appropriate source of advice should be the Solicitor-General in those circumstances'. Current Solicitor-General Grant Donaldson indicated that it was his belief that there was a 'fairly well understood' process, and that he had discussed this protocol with Government House, the Governor's official residence. His understanding of the position was that the Governor could contact the Solicitor-General directly, but this would be done on the basis that the Solicitor-General must seek the consent

[99] Interview, Keith Mason; Interview, Michael Sexton; Interview, Terence Sheahan. See also A Twomey, 'Advice to Vice-Regal Officers by Crown Law Officers and Others' (2015) 26 *Public Law Review* 193.

[100] Interview, William Bale; Interview, Leigh Sealy.

[101] Interview, Pamela Tate. See also Twomey, above n 99.

[102] Interview, Michael Grant; Interview, Thomas Pauling.

[103] In Queensland the issue had not arisen in any contentious setting. In his interview, former Solicitor-General Patrick Keane recalled furnishing advice to the Governor at the request of the Attorney-General on a minor, personal matter. Other Queensland Solicitors-General and Attorneys-General interviewed could not recall the situation arising.

[104] Grant did so in the lead up to, and after, the resignation of a member from the Labor Party in 2009.

of the Attorney-General to provide the advice, and it would be provided to the Attorney-General as well as to the Governor.

At the Commonwealth level there was also diversity as to the accepted practice. An early position emerged in the 1970s under the Whitlam Labor Government. Leading up to the constitutional crisis of 1975, former Prime Minister Gough Whitlam expressed a belief that the Governor-General had recourse to the Solicitor-General only through the Government's Ministers. (Although it appears from other sources that the Governor-General was seeking the Solicitor-General's advice directly during Whitlam's period in government prior to the 1975 crisis.)[105] When John Kerr, the Governor-General, asked for the Law Officers' advice in October 1975, Kerr wrote that he recalled Whitlam's agreeing to get an opinion on Whitlam's own behalf, saying he would 'probably' pass it onto Kerr, but it remained a matter for Whitlam's discretion.[106]

More recently, there seems to be a growing acceptance at the Commonwealth level of the desirability of making the Solicitor-General available to the Governor-General.[107] Current Solicitor-General Justin Gleeson explained that 'at some point between [19]75 and 2010 … the idea was put in place that the Governor-General ought to be able to go to the Solicitor-General for advice in those delicate situations'. In the lead-up to the 2010 election, under the Gillard Labor Government, protocols were put in place that were very close to those used in the States. These would have allowed the Governor-General to access the Solicitor-General in the event of a hung Parliament after the election.[108] Gleeson believed the provision of such advice fell within the Solicitor-General's functions of furnishing opinions on questions of law, which require the consent of the Attorney-General.[109] So, furnishing advice to the Governor-General would ordinarily require the approval of the Attorney-General, and a copy of the advice would ordinarily be provided to the Attorney-General, unless a particular Attorney-General dispensed with that requirement. This understanding or protocol, Gleeson explained, had to be 'renewed' between each Solicitor-General and Attorney-General.

Anne Twomey argues that these practices ought to develop beyond their current level, and, most importantly, should be formalised *before* any future constitutional controversy arises. She argues for the development of a publicly available, written

[105] See, *Sankey versus Whitlam*—Maurice Byers QC regarding involvement in the Loans Affair (April 1976), National Archives of Australia, Canberra, M4081 3/25, 5–6; J Kerr, *Matters for Judgment: An Autobiography* (Macmillan Press Ltd, 1979) 235.

[106] Kerr, above n 105, 271. See also Interview, Michael Lavarch.

[107] Interview, Stephen Gageler; Interview, Robert McClelland; Interview, Philip Ruddock.

[108] This more recent trend in facilitating advice between the Governor-General and the Solicitor-General also reflects earlier practice in the Commonwealth. In 1917, federal Attorney-General William Hughes agreed that the Governor-General was entitled to seek 'independent legal opinion' from a number of legal figures, including, inter alia, Robert Garran, the Solicitor-General. D Markwell, 'Griffith, Barton and the Early Governors-General: Aspects of Australia's Constitutional Development' (1999) 10 *Public Law Review* 280, 288.

[109] *Law Officers Act 1964* (Cth), s 12(b).

procedure to guide Vice-regal officers during times of constitutional crisis. In her opinion, it is preferable that Vice-regal officers be given standing permission to access the Solicitor-General, on a confidential basis:

> On the whole, it would seem preferable if a convention could be established that permitted vice-regal officers to obtain independent legal advice from the Solicitor-General without the necessity for ministerial knowledge or approval. As in the New South Wales example, such advice might satisfy all vice-regal qualms and avoid the perceived need to seek external advice, which might be more erratic in nature.[110]

Twomey's arguments are persuasive, and the development of the practice across the Australian jurisdictions demonstrates that there is a general move in the direction she recommends, at least informally. There is, however, an alternative to the position that Twomey suggests: the appointment of a separate, independent senior legal adviser to the Vice-regal officer. This may take the form of a conferral of such a title on a senior member of the Bar by each Vice-regal officer, or it might amount to the creation of a separate statutory position. This model recognises Twomey's concerns for a clear, written and public process to be put in place to provide Vice-regal officers with a single source of technical legal advice prior to constitutional controversies arising. Its advantage is that it maintains the Solicitor-General as the senior legal adviser to the Executive, as represented by the Attorney-General of the day, should the Attorney require the advice of the Solicitor-General and should there be any conflict of interest that arises.

My interview data demonstrate that participants viewed the primary client of the Solicitor-General as the Executive. The Executive manifested as, and was directed by, the government of the day, usually through the Attorney-General. This meant that the Solicitor-General's ability to advise government agencies and statutory offices was limited, to ensure that no conflict would occur with the primary client. This position also limited the office's ability to advise Vice-regal officers. However, in recognition of the desirability of allowing access to the Solicitor-General by Vice-regal officers, protocols have been developed in many jurisdictions to facilitate this when the need has arisen. While this practice has probably not gone so far as to develop into a constitutional convention, there is increasing uniformity of practice in this area, and there are persuasive reasons for further development and potential reform.

ii. Second Assumption: The Solicitor-General as Trumps

If it is accepted that the Solicitor-General's advisory function assists in the promotion of the rule of law by policing the limits of government power, it is necessary that the Solicitor-General is not merely another legal adviser to government, but the *final* legal adviser to government. Finality is closely associated with the authoritative nature of the Solicitor-General's advice, that is, government will not

110 Twomey, above n 99, 211.

just treat the Solicitor-General as the final adviser, but respect and follow his or her advice. Commonwealth Solicitor-General Justin Gleeson explained that the Solicitor-General's advice has a 'quasi-precedential' effect within government: that it should be followed by everyone within the Commonwealth unless it is

> declared to be wrong by the High Court, or it's departed from by a subsequent Solicitor-General or the Attorney-General disavows it, which the Attorney is entitled to do, because in a sense everything is done by a delegation from the Attorney.

The Victorian Protocol for Briefing the Solicitor-General states that the Solicitor-General should only be briefed either exclusively or for the purpose of finality.[111] Tasmanian Solicitor-General Leigh Sealy also believed that the indivisibility of the Crown underscored the need for it to have a single, authoritative source of legal advice.

Under the rule of law, one facet of the Judiciary's 'independence' from the state is that decisions are respected as final and binding. Independence as the power to influence or achieve a desired outcome has also been developed in political science literature.[112] In the US, Morrison has explained that the significance of the OLC's position rests on the presumption that its advice is final and binding. If this presumption is weakened, the OLC loses its institutional independence to provide advice free from institutional pressure. Loss of its binding status may lead to the OLC starting to tilt its advice in favour of the client's position. If this occurs, the Executive will no longer be able to rely upon the OLC's advice to provide certainty, security and credibility to its actions.[113]

No statutory provisions ground the principle that the Australian Solicitor-General should be the final and authoritative legal adviser to government. According to British practice, the Law Officers' opinions are used to settle disputes within government, and thus settle legal questions with finality.[114] It is this history that grounds the practice in Australia. Michael Sexton, Solicitor-General for New South Wales, explained the reason for such a tradition:

> I've tried to explain to people on occasions that the reason why the Solicitor-General's opinion is or should be final is not because of the person who holds the office, but because you have got to have some notion of finality, in terms of the use of government power.

Similarly, former Victorian Solicitor-General Pamela Tate said that the Solicitor-General was an 'integrity office', because once the Solicitor-General gives advice, it must be final and determinative. The Solicitor-General performs this role not

[111] Victoria, Department of Justice, Protocol for Briefing the Solicitor-General (28 July 2011) [11]. See also ibid, [13] and [14]. Interview, Stephen McLeish.

[112] See, eg, S Lukes, 'Introduction' in S Lukes (ed), *Power* (Basil Blackwell Ltd, 1986) 1, and analysis in the legal context in S Le Mire, 'Testing Times: In-House Counsel and Independence' (2011) 14(1) *Legal Ethics* 21, 34–35.

[113] Morrison, above n 27, 69.

[114] JLJ Edwards, *The Attorney General, Politics and the Public Interest* (Sweet & Maxwell, 1984) 67, 181–82, 185, 190.

because the person is an oracle, or is invariably right, but because there must be finality within government.[115]

The government often finds having a definitive legal view politically expedient. Greg Parker, the former South Australian Crown Solicitor, observed that 'often you'll find in the Parliament that the government likes to say, well, we've checked this with the Solicitor-General and he says it is okay. So they seek a little bit of political justification.'

David Collins, former Solicitor-General for New Zealand, emphasises the importance of a definitive legal position for the government by comparing it to policy advice:

> [T]he Crown can only have one view of the law. Ministers, Chief Executives and others in government who are dependent upon legal advice need to receive just one explanation of the law. That explanation must, of course, be authoritative. It must be right. This contrasts with policy advice. Ministers and other senior decision-makers within government often relish competing policy viewpoints. Competing policy advice assists Ministers and other senior decision-makers in shaping and influencing the ultimate policy outcome. Ministers and senior decision-makers cannot, however, influence and shape explanations as to what the law is, in order to achieve their objectives.[116]

Western Australian Attorney-General Michael Mischin explained that in making policy decisions, he takes into account the legal advice provided by the Solicitor-General, other advice that is available, and political factors that assist him in determining where the interests of the State lies. While the Solicitor-General's advice might be overridden by a policy decision made by the Attorney-General, he emphasised it was nonetheless very important that the Attorney had a single source of final legal advice. In the Australian constitutional system, that source was the Solicitor-General.

Northern Territory Solicitor-General Michael Grant explained why he was always very careful not to provide policy advice to government officers and ministers. He elaborated that this was because of how those in government treated his legal advice:

> I have to be careful because they're not very good at distinguishing between legal advice and policy advice. And because you're in this position where they take everything you say as the final arbitration on the point, rather than seeing policy advice from me as simply just saying this is something you should take into account, they would probably take it as gospel and act on it.

The finality of the Solicitor-General's legal advice is often used to resolve disputes about the correct legal position that arise from time to time across government

[115] Tate's comments are similar to those of Jackson J in *Brown v Allen* 344 US 443 (1953), 540. See also Interview, Catherine Branson; Interview, Daryl Dawson; Interview, Michael Grant; Interview, Stephen McLeish; Interview, Leigh Sealy; Interview, Walter Sofronoff.

[116] D Collins, 'The Role of Solicitor-General in Contemporary New Zealand' in G Appleby, P Keyzer and J Williams (eds), *Public Sentinels: A Comparative Study of Australian Solicitors-General* (Ashgate Publishing, 2014) 171, 180.

(for example between departments or statutory bodies). The Solicitor-General is used in this situation as an 'arbiter' to provide the final and definitive advice that will allow the dispute to be resolved.[117]

The finality of the Solicitor-General's advice within government was generally unquestioned. An exception was former Northern Territory Solicitor-General Thomas Pauling's recollection of the euthanasia debate in the Territory in 1995, where his opinion was sent off to Senior Counsel across the country for comment. Pauling said, 'I was getting bombarded with opinions from Tom Hughes and all sorts of people saying that what we were doing was wrong.' Another Solicitor-General recalled times early in his tenure when the government indicated that it wished to seek a second opinion after receiving his advice. There had not been a Solicitor-General in office in that jurisdiction for some time, and at the political level there was relatively little institutional knowledge about the role or an understanding of the finality of the Solicitor-General's opinion. The public service had a greater understanding of the role and acceptance of the finality of the Solicitor-General's advice, and counselled the government against seeking a further opinion. The result in that instance was that the finality of the Solicitor-General's advice was eventually recognised and accepted by the government.

Some former Attorneys-General indicated that they *were* willing to seek alternative legal opinions where they disagreed with the Solicitor-General's advice. Two of these—Mark Dreyfus and Christian Porter—were experienced lawyers prior to taking office. Christian Porter explained that '*generally speaking*, the advice of the Solicitor-General was accepted as the best advice', but it was not unheard of to seek a view on the Solicitor-General's opinion. He explained, 'if you get three top silks giving advice on an issue, there will sometimes be substantive differences in the nature of that advice. If that weren't the case, there would be no such thing as litigation'.

Similarly, Mark Dreyfus indicated that the Solicitor-General's advice was given a high status within government, higher than advice from the Australian Government Solicitor or from the private Bar. Nonetheless, he would, occasionally, seek another legal opinion. He explained that he might seek another opinion on particularly important political issues:

> Or two. Or three. Perhaps I might feel I needed two to outweigh the Solicitor-General's advice, and I would go and get very senior advice. And I've done that. And I would do it again. Because, despite the fact that I say that the Solicitor-General has got higher status, she or he is still just a barrister. And, most difficult legal problems are capable of another outcome. I mean, if I've learnt [anything] in my legal career, I've learnt that.

As Dreyfus and Porter indicate, at times the Solicitor-General will be asked to advise the government on an issue when the legal position is unclear. In such

[117] In New South Wales, South Australia and Queensland there is a Cabinet directive to this effect: McDonnell, above n 98, 8; Interview, Barry Dunphy. See also *Legal Services Directions 2005* (Cth), cl 10.6.

instances, I have suggested in chapter four, section III.A.iii. that the Solicitor-General should provide not only his or her assessment of the better legal position, but also an indication of the ambiguity of the position. This could be observed, for example, in the way in which the Commonwealth Solicitor-General's advice was framed following the *Malaysia Solution Case* (discussed in section II.A.ii. above).[118] However, the weight given to the Solicitor-General's opinion, and the need for finality in government for it to conduct its business, emphasises the significance of the Solicitor-General's striving to make his or her best assessment of the legal position.

Finality of the Solicitor-General's advice is closely associated with its determinative nature. There is no statutory requirement for the Executive to follow the Solicitor-General's advice.[119] In Britain during the 2007–08 consultations on reforms to the role of the Attorney-General, the view was expressed that the Attorney-General's advice commanded authority because of the Law Officer's position in the ministry.[120] Contrary to this statement, in Australia participants indicated that advice from the non-ministerial Solicitor-General was also invariably followed, and the Solicitor-General's opinion was treated with great weight and respect within government. Former Tasmanian Solicitor-General William Bale indicated that following the Solicitor-General's advice in Australia was a 'constitutional given' or a 'constitutional convention'. Former Queensland Attorney-General Rodney Welford said that the opinions of the Solicitor-General were 'holy writ' and 'utterly unquestioned'. Examples of this expectation include one from as early as 1895 in Tasmania, when Andrew Inglis Clark resigned as Attorney-General because Cabinet failed to follow his legal advice.[121] A more recent example comes from the period after the 1989 election in Tasmania, when a hung Parliament was returned and the government sought opinions from a number of leading barristers and constitutional experts.[122] The Secretary of the Tasmanian Department of Justice expressed concern over the briefing out of constitutional advice, warning the Attorney-General not to undermine the 'strong tradition' that the government takes the Solicitor-General's advice on constitutional issues.[123]

[118] *Plaintiff M70/2011 v Minister for Immigration and Citizenship; Plaintiff M106 of 2011 v Minister for Immigration and Citizenship* (2011) 244 CLR 144.

[119] Interview of Robert Ellicott by Kel Richards, *AM Broadcast*, 17 November 1975.

[120] Evidence to House of Commons Constitutional Affairs Committee, *Constitutional Role of the Attorney General*, Fifth Report of Session 2006–07 (HC306) (Lord Goldsmith) 59–60. See also the report of Professor Anthony Bradley to the House of Lords Committee: House of Lords Constitution Committee, *Reform of the Office of Attorney General* (HL 2007–08, 93), available at <http://www.publications.parliament.uk/pa/ld200708/ldselect/ldconst/93/93.pdf>, as extracted at [37], Appendix 2, page 25 [25] of his report. Contrast this with the position of Professor Jeffrey Jowell QC, extracted at [33], Appendix 3, page 30 [13] of his report. See further discussion in ch 2, section A.D.iii.

[121] F Hanlon, *An Analysis of the Office of Attorney General in Australia and Directions for the Future* (PhD Thesis, University of Melbourne, 2007) 93.

[122] M Sexton, 'The Role of Solicitors-General in Advising the Holders of Vice Regal Officers' in Appleby, Keyzer and Williams (eds), above n 116, 91.

[123] Letter from Mr JA Ramsay (Secretary of the Tasmanian Department of Justice) to Attorney-General JM Bennett, 14 June 1989 (see Annexure 'JAR1' to the Proof of Evidence of John Alexander

Two former Solicitors-General recollected exceptional instances where they *knew* their advice had not been followed by the government. The most significant of these occurred in Tasmania in 2005. The then Solicitor-General, William Bale, had been asked to advise on the legality of a proposed agreement between a government minister and a builder-accreditation firm, which would have created, in effect, a legal monopoly for that firm. This fettered the minister's discretion under the *Building Act 2000* (Tas) to authorise accreditation providers,[124] and a summary of Bale's advice stated that any agreement 'must not give them [the building accreditation firm] "sole" authorised body status'.[125] Despite Bale's advice, the agreement included such a provision. When Bale became aware of it, he recalled 'I was astonished'.[126]

The second instance occurred in the early 1990s in New South Wales, and was less an example of the government wilfully failing to follow the Solicitor-General's advice than demonstrative of the need to disseminate the content of such advice to relevant actors within government that should know of it and be bound by it. The then New South Wales Solicitor-General, Keith Mason, had been asked on a number of occasions to advise upon whether Mr Phillip Smiles had ceased to be a Member of the Parliament. The question involved a legal issue about whether Mr Smiles had been convicted of an 'infamous crime' so as to disqualify him from receiving the non-contributory pension.[127] The Solicitor-General's advice had been requested and provided on the issue to the Clerk of the Legislative Assembly, the Speaker, the Attorney-General, and a number of senior executives in the Cabinet Office and Attorney-General's Department.[128] The series of opinions made it clear that the question as to whether Mr Smiles had been convicted of an infamous crime was difficult, and that the effect of a stay of the court's decision against Mr Smiles pending an appeal further clouded the question. Despite the existence of these opinions, their content was not made known in full to the trustees of the superannuation fund, who resolved that Mr Smiles was entitled to his pension, and payments were made accordingly. The matter was referred to

Ramsay before Royal Commission into an Attempt to Bribe a Member of the House of Assembly and other matters). See also the assertion by the federal Government in 1982, when the Senate questioned the advice of the Solicitor-General supporting the veracity of a privilege claim. Senator Fred Chaney, representing the Acting Attorney-General in the Senate, noted that it was the Government's view was that 'the only appropriate course the Government can take is to accept and act on the views of the Solicitor-General'. Commonwealth, *Parliamentary Debates*, Senate, 14 October 1982, 1487. See further discussion above, section II.A.iii.

124 *Building Act 2000* (Tas), pt 4, s 20.

125 M Denholm, 'Warning on Monopoly', *The Australian* (Sydney) (22 November 2007), available at <http://www.theaustralian.com.au/news/warning-on-monopoly/story-e6frg6ox-1111114933356>.

126 S Cullen, 'Bill Bale', *Stateline Tasmania* (ABC Online), 18 July 2008, available at <http://www.abc.net.au/stateline/tas/content/2006/s2307818.htm>.

127 *Parliamentary Contributory Superannuation Act 1971* (NSW); *Constitution Act 1902* (NSW) s 13A(e).

128 Sole and joint-authored advices were provided.

the Independent Commission Against Corruption (ICAC), which found that the trustees had acted in ignorance of the relevant advice.[129]

The Solicitor-General as trumps is vital to understanding the office's constitutional importance as an adviser. It abates the temptation that will no doubt exist in government to find legal advice to accommodate the government's desires if the Solicitor-General's opinion does not. It is therefore strongly associated with the third assumption.

iii. Third Assumption: The Solicitor-General and Other Sources of Legal Advice

The third assumption is that the government will seek the *Solicitor-General's* advice on appropriate matters; that is, the government will not seek advice from quarters perceived to be more accommodating or fail to seek advice at all. Implicit in this assumption is also the principle that the government will not fragment its work, seeking advice from the Solicitor-General on only part of a larger picture.[130] In the United States, some scholars identify the potential for the Office of Legal Counsel (OLC) to lose work to other institutional actors within the bureaucratic structure. (In the US, the OSG has statutorily guaranteed roles within the administration and therefore is not competing within the larger bureaucracy for work.)[131] James R Harvey III argues that the OLC, upon the creation of the Office of White House Counsel, attempted to maintain its relevance and importance by 'redefin[ing] its role, becoming a more neutral, quasi-judicial decision-maker in order to preserve its position in the bureaucracy'.[132]

In Australia, Solicitors-General have, at times, also been faced with the need to secure the office's position in the wider government setting. Former Commonwealth Solicitor-General Stephen Gageler argues, in the context of government lawyering more generally, that the lack of a guarantee of work is an 'obvious design

[129] B O'Keefe, *Report on Investigation into Circumstances Surrounding the Payment of a Parliamentary Pension to Mr P M Smiles: First Report* (Independent Commission Against Corruption, February 1995). The ICAC Report resulted in an investigation by the New South Wales Law Reform Commission into the dissemination of legal advices among government agencies to try to prevent a similar incident: New South Wales Law Reform Commission, *Circulation of Legal Advice to Government*, Report No 86 (1998), available at <http://www.lawlink.nsw.gov.au/lrc.nsf/pages/R86TOC>.

[130] On fragmentation of work, see, RE Rosen, 'Problem-Setting and Serving the Organizational Client: Legal Diagnosis and Professional Independence' (2001) 56 *University of Miami Law Review* 179, 199–200.

[131] See, eg, JR Harvey III , 'Loyalty of Government Litigation: Department of Justice Representation of Agency Claims' (1996) 37 *William and Mary Law Review* 1569, 1587–91, N Lund, 'Rational Choice at the Office of Legal Counsel' (1993) 15 *Cardozo Law Review* 437, 496–97; JO McGinnis, 'Models of the Opinion Function of the Attorney General: A Normative, Descriptive and Historical Prolegomenon' (1993) 15 *Cardozo Law Review* 375, 423; JM Strine, *The Office of Legal Counsel: Legal Professionals in a Political System* (Phd, Johns Hopkins University, 1992).

[132] Harvey III, above n 131, 1590. See also JK Shapiro and LA Casey, 'Let Lawyers be Lawyers' (2004) 26 *American Lawyer* 73, 73; JO McGinnis, 'Principle Versus Politics: The Solicitor General's Office in Constitutional and Bureaucratic Theory' (1992) 44 *Stanford Law Review* 799, 810–11.

flaw'.[133] Seervai explains that there is an inherent weakness in a non-ministerial Law Officer system because officeholders must generally wait to be consulted by the government rather than actively overseeing the legal position of the government.[134] This weakness in constitutional design has the potential to undermine the important principle that the Law Officers have an obligation to ensure government complies with the law.

The third assumption that underpins the Australian Solicitor-General's advisory function is closely associated with the second assumption (that the Solicitor-General's advice will be treated as final and authoritative within government): if the third assumption is not met and the government simply avoids seeking the Solicitor-General's advice, the government is able to avoid treating the Solicitor-General's advice as final and authoritative.

The extent to which the third assumption was realised differed across jurisdictions. There was some indication that the government would, at times, intentionally *not* seek advice from the Solicitor-General.[135] However this appeared to be the exception rather than the rule. Former Victorian Solicitor-General Pamela Tate explained in response to the 2007 summons for her to appear before a Select Committee of the Victorian Legislative Council, that one of the reasons that legal professional privilege must attach to the Solicitor-General's advice is that it encourages the government to seek the advice of the Law Office in appropriate instances.[136]

Two participants referred to instances in which the Solicitor-General was not briefed and legal advice was sought from other sources in significant matters where they believed the Solicitor-General ought to have been briefed.[137] A prominent example was the advice on the legality of the Iraq War provided to the Government in 2003.[138] Instead of emanating from the Solicitor-General, the advice was authored by the First Assistant Secretary of the Office of International Law (OIL) in the Attorney-General's Department (Bill Campbell) and the senior legal adviser to the Department of Foreign Affairs and Trade (DFAT) (Chris Moraitis). Former

[133] S Gageler, 'Values in Administrative Law and the Role of the Lawyer Acting for an Administrator' (Paper presented at the Australian Government Solicitor Administrative Law Forum, 22 October 2008) 4.

[134] HM Seervai, 'The Legal Profession and the State: The Place of Law Officers and Ministers of Justice' (1977) 22 *Journal of the Law Society of Scotland* 265, 267. See also Interview, John Doyle.

[135] There are not always improper motives behind this. Tasmanian Solicitor-General Leigh Sealy, in his annual report in 2010, explained that 'it is now clear to me that, at least some agencies make conscious decisions to avoid seeking legal advice in order to save money'. See Solicitor-General, Parliament of Tasmania, *Solicitor-General Report for 2009–2010* (2010).

[136] Letter from Pamela Tate SC, Solicitor-General, to Mr Richard Willis, Secretary, Select Committee on Gaming, 11 April 2007. See also Letter from Rob Hulls MP, Attorney-General, to Richard Willis, Secretary, Legislation and Select Committees, Re: Summons to the Solicitor-General, 11 April 2007. Both letters are extracted in full in Select Committee of the Legislative Council on Gaming Licensing, *First Interim Report Upon Gaming Licensing* (Legislative Council of Victoria, 2007) 22.

[137] Interview, Gavan Griffith; Interview, Duncan Kerr.

[138] The Memorandum of Advice on the Use of Force Against Iraq, provided by the Attorney General's Department and the Department of Foreign Affairs and Trade, 12 March, 2003.

Commonwealth Solicitor-General Gavan Griffith publicly questioned the reliance on these relatively junior officers.[139] Several international law experts criticised the legal reasoning in the advice.[140] Questions were raised as to whether the Government believed that advice from these lower-level legal advisers, who were in-house at OIL and DFAT and closely involved in policy-work, would be more accommodating than the Solicitor-General (the potential disadvantages of relying upon in-house legal services are detailed further below). It could be argued that the Solicitor-General was not an expert in international law, and as such the Government went to more junior officers who were more closely involved in the area with greater expertise. Other jurisdictions have, however, dealt with this problem in a way that ensures that the Solicitor-General's seniority, and finality, is respected. For example, former Solicitor-General William Bale said that in Tasmania the Solicitor-General may author joint opinions in areas where the Solicitor-General does not have relevant expertise.

In Tasmania an exceptional position developed during William Bale's tenure: *all* government requests for advice involving the scope and operation of the rights and duties of the Crown came to the Solicitor-General. Bale explained that upon the creation of the statutory office in 1983, the Solicitor-General took on the traditional role of the second Law Officer. But during the term of the first appointment to the office it transpired that the Solicitor-General had become too busy with litigious matters, and the advisory role was performed by many different lawyers, with little supervision for consistency and quality. The government decided to remove the Solicitor-General's responsibility for civil litigation, giving the office sole responsibility for government advice involving the scope and operation of the rights and duties of the Crown. Bale explained the reasons behind the move, 'The responsibility for advising lies with the Law Officers. Otherwise you shop around for advice and you take that which you like; and you become your own judge, because you've determined what legal advice you are willing to accept.'

In 2012,[141] two events changed this state of affairs in Tasmania. First, the Office of the Crown Solicitor became, like the Solicitor-General, fully funded from the Consolidated Revenue Fund, meaning that it no longer had to charge government agencies for advice. This made seeking advice from this office as attractive

[139] G Griffith, 'This War is Illegal: Howard's Last Top Law Man: Notes on the Legal Justification for the Invasion of Iraq and Security Council Resolutions 678 and 1441', *Sydney Morning Herald* (Sydney) (21 March 2003). See also M Kingston, 'The politics of war', *Sydney Morning Herald* (Sydney) (19 March 2003), available at <http://www.smh.com.au/articles/2003/03/20/1047749837969.html>.

[140] See C Banham, 'Experts at odds as PM releases legal advice', *Sydney Morning Herald* (Sydney) (19 March 2003), available at <http://www.smh.com.au/articles/2003/03/18/1047749774530.html>; A Byrnes and H Charlesworth, 'The illegality of the war against Iraq' (2003) 22(1) *Dialogue* 4.

[141] After much campaigning by the then Solicitor-General, Leigh Sealy, to return to the Crown Solicitor responsibility for advising, to allow the Solicitor-General to concentrate more fully on litigation and advice on significant issues. See, eg, his reports on his project in: Solicitor-General, Parliament of Tasmania, *Solicitor-General Report for 2008–2009* (2009); Solicitor-General, Parliament of Tasmania, *Solicitor-General Report for 2009–2010* (2010); and Solicitor-General, Parliament of Tasmania, *Solicitor-General Report for 2010–2011* (2011).

as seeking advice from the Solicitor-General. Secondly, a protocol for briefing the Solicitor-General was issued.[142]

In the Commonwealth, Victoria and Tasmania, there are protocols that set out what matters are to be briefed to the Solicitor-General.[143] The Commonwealth Office of Legal Services Coordination (OLSC) Guidance Note states the Solicitor-General will be briefed for 'very important and legally difficult matters that are of particular significance to the Australian Government'. For advice, a matter will be 'significant' in this respect if it 'raises novel, difficult and important points of legal principle', 'relates to the implementation of Government policy or decisions of the highest importance', 'raises issues of the highest political sensitivity', 'raises legal issues resulting in conflict between agencies' and/or 'has significant financial implications or very important whole-of-Government implications'. The Solicitor-General should be briefed to appear in matters where an agency is a party to an appeal before the High Court, is a party to an application for leave or special leave to appeal to the High Court, or is a party to a proceeding within the original jurisdiction of the High Court, other than proceedings of a kind that are routinely remitted.[144]

The Victorian protocol refers to matters arising from the performance of the functions of the Attorney-General, the Premier, the Governor, the President of the Legislative Council or the Speaker of the Legislative Assembly. Otherwise, it refers to briefs that

> involve a matter arising under the Victorian or Commonwealth Constitution or involving their interpretation; or have whole-of-Government implications; or require a definitive authoritative opinion to resolve a matter about which conflicting legal advice has been obtained from Queen's Counsel or Senior Counsel, or in relation to which legal advice has been obtained from a Queen's Counsel or Senior Counsel which requires confirmation.[145]

The Tasmanian Guidelines refer to 'matters of significance to the Tasmanian Government' and representation in 'cases of constitutional significance and other cases of special government interest'.[146]

[142] Solicitor-General, Parliament of Tasmania, *Solicitor-General Report for 2011–2012* (2012).

[143] Commonwealth, Office of Legal Services Coordination, *Guidance Note 11: Briefing the Solicitor-General* (Catherine Fitch, 18 February 2014); Tasmania, Attorney-General, *Guidelines for Seeking Advice from the Office of the Solicitor-General* (The Hon Brian Wightman MP, Febraury 2012); Victoria, Department of Justice, *Protocol for Briefing the Solicitor-General* (28 July 2011). At the Commonwealth level as well, cl 10A.2 of the *Legal Services Directions 2005* (Cth) states that the Attorney-General's Department or the Australian Government Solicitor (AGS) may consult with the Solicitor-General on whether constitutional advice should be given by the Solicitor-General or the AGS, although this does not *require* consultation.

[144] Commonwealth, Office of Legal Services Coordination, *Guidance Note 11: Briefing the Solicitor-General* (Catherine Fitch, 18 February 2014) 1.

[145] Victoria, Department of Justice, *Protocol for Briefing the Solicitor-General* (28 July 2011) [3]–[4].

[146] Tasmania, Attorney-General, *Guidelines for Seeking Advice from the Office of the Solicitor-General* (The Hon Brian Wightman MP, Febraury 2012) [3].

The existence of a protocol does not guarantee that the Solicitor-General will be briefed in the matters listed. For example, in 2010 it was revealed that the Commonwealth Government had not sought the advice of the Solicitor-General on the constitutionality of its proposed Resources Super-Profits Tax regime;[147] it had instead been relying on advice from the AGS.[148] This was in spite of the tax raising important points of legal principle and relating to the implementation of an important government policy that was of the highest political sensitivity: all factors which should have meant that the Government sought the advice of the *Solicitor-General* under the OLSC Guidance Note. It was not until September 2011, when threats were made by mining companies and Western Australia to challenge the constitutionality of the proposed legislation implementing the Mineral Resource Rent Tax (the renegotiated version of the Resources Super-Profits Tax), that the Treasury sought the Solicitor-General's advice.[149]

A similar point could be made about the Solicitor-General's involvement in the *Malaysia Solution Case*.[150] It was reported that the Solicitor-General was not briefed to advise the Minister at the time of the declaration of Malaysia as a country to which 'offshore entry persons' could be taken. Rather, the Minister relied on departmental advice, and the Solicitor-General became involved only when the matter was challenged in the High Court.[151]

The briefing protocols give an example of the types of issue that ought to be briefed to the Solicitor-General. They identify a similar list of matters to those in previous attempts to list the matters to brief the English Law Officers.[152] They also demonstrate the difficulty of attempting to define these matters. The terms used in the documents are imbued with subjectivity. Further, whether a matter raises the type of issues specified may not be immediately apparent to government officers developing policy. Former Tasmanian Solicitor-General Leigh Sealy also identified a danger with a formal briefing protocol that requires requests to be in writing and in a particular form, or to come through particular officers:

> There is some anecdotal evidence to suggest that some people may regard compliance with the guidelines as being onerous and, for that reason, decide not to obtain advice when they might otherwise do so. That is plainly undesirable. On the other hand ill-considered

[147] G Milne, 'Rudd did not ask Solicitor-General's Advice on Mining Compo', *The Australian* (Sydney) (22 June 2010), available at <http://www.theaustralian.com.au/news/nation/rudd-did-not-ask-solicitor-generals-advice-on-mining-compo/story-e6frg6nf-1225882474994>.

[148] E-mail from Analyst, Resource Taxation Unit to [redacted], Advice on the Constitutionality of the Minerals Resource Rent Tax (MRRT), 23 September 2011 (released by Treasury Department under FOI: http://www.treasury.gov.au/Freedom-of-Information/DisclosureLog/2012/Constitutional-legality-of-the-MRRT-tax-and-the-PRRT).

[149] ibid.

[150] *Plaintiff M70/2011 v Minister for Immigration and Citizenship; Plaintiff M106 of 2011 v Minister for Immigration and Citizenship* (2011) 244 CLR 144. See above at section II.A.ii.

[151] See reporting of R Ackland, 'Order in the High Court a cinch as taekwondo judge takes seat', *Sydney Morning Herald* (Sydney) (24 August 2012), available at <http://www.smh.com.au/opinion/order-in-the-high-court-a-cinch-as-taekwondo-judge-takes-seat-20120823-24p2j.html>.

[152] See, eg, the 1997 Ministerial Code, extracted in ch 2, section II.A.

> and incomplete requests for advice can be both frustrating and unnecessarily time-consuming for those who are required to deal with them. As with so many things, it will be necessary to try to find a suitable point of balance.[153]

The difficulty in defining the types of matters that ought to be briefed to the Solicitor-General raises not only the possibility that these matters will not be identified, but its inverse. In an effort to keep the Solicitor-General updated on the identified matters, departments and agencies may forward matters that are not significant enough to require the Solicitor-General's attention. This is not as harmless as it may appear: it may mean the Solicitor-General spends considerable time reviewing briefs.[154]

Northern Territory Solicitor-General Michael Grant was wary of introducing written directions about the work that ought to come to the Solicitor-General. He believed that directions beget an undesirable level of inflexibility. Instead, he emphasised that in the Northern Territory, it was the Solicitor for the Northern Territory who ensured the proper requests for advice were briefed to the Solicitor-General. However, as is detailed below, relying on individual relations between the Solicitor-General and other government officers is no guarantee that the Solicitor-General will always be briefed in appropriate matters.

In those jurisdictions where the Solicitor-General has no monopoly on the provision of legal advice (that is, all with the exception of the Australian Capital Territory and Tasmania, which are discussed separately below), participants indicated that the Solicitor-General would be involved in constitutional and other public law advice,[155] matters that concerned the government as a constitutional entity,[156] matters with whole-of-government implications[157] and matters that were particularly politically sensitive.[158] Generally speaking, the types of matters in which Solicitors-General were involved did not seem to vary between jurisdictions that had implemented protocols and those that had not. Former Queensland Crown Solicitor and Acting Solicitor-General Barry Dunphy said that in most jurisdictions, the role of the Solicitor-General is to make the 'big calls',[159] to determine the legal position 'for very novel, difficult issues'.[160] In addition to these core matters, a number of participants also indicated that individual Solicitors-General may take on matters in their particular area of expertise.[161] The Solicitor-General was thus

[153] Solicitor-General, Parliament of Tasmania, *Solicitor-General Report for 2011–2012* (2012).

[154] Interview, Patrick Keane; Interview, Stephen Gageler.

[155] Interview, Anthony Mason; Interview, Keith Mason; Interview, Michael Sexton; Interview Christian Porter; Letter from Pamela Tate SC, Solicitor-General, to Mr Richard Willis, Secretary, Select Committee on Gaming, 11 April 2007.

[156] Interview, Geoffrey Davies.

[157] Interview, Stephen Gageler.

[158] Interview, Stephen Gageler.

[159] Interview, Barry Dunphy.

[160] Interview, Barry Dunphy. See also interview, Christian Porter, that the Solicitor-General would be briefed in 'the most important matters and the most complicated matters'.

[161] Grant Donaldson, for example, continued to be involved in native title matters, an area in which he had a large practice prior to his appointment as Solicitor-General.

involved in a wide variety of matters, many of which were not necessarily easily identifiable (even where written protocols attempted to define them).

Two Solicitors-General noted that the commercialisation of government services had affected the role of the Solicitor-General in that it had moved away from the strict constitutional work that may have characterised the role in earlier eras.[162] In South Australia, the Solicitor-General also engaged in a large amount of criminal law work, despite the creation of the DPP to relieve the office of this work.[163]

While there was no guarantee that matters of the type identified would be briefed to the Solicitor-General, most participants across the jurisdictions were comfortable that either the Crown Solicitor (or equivalent) would brief the Solicitor-General, or that government agencies and departments would seek the Solicitor-General's opinion directly when these issues arose. Participants across jurisdictions emphasised that an excellent working relationship between the Solicitor-General and the relevant Crown law office was paramount.[164] Dunphy said there was a 'long history of practice, and I think people understand what work goes to [the Solicitor-General]'. Similarly, Queensland Crown Solicitor Greg Cooper indicated that the 'eminence of the person who occupies the role' ensures that the Solicitor-General is briefed when appropriate. In South Australia, former Crown Solicitor Greg Parker observed that there was an additional guarantee of this:

> [The Solicitor-General]'s totally dependent on me or others to tell him what we're up to. … But at the same time, we're conscious that if something goes wrong, or becomes a big issue, … we get asked the question, why wasn't the Solicitor-General instructed or his opinion sought?

Some Solicitors-General were much more actively involved in overseeing the legal affairs of government, rather than relying upon the Crown Solicitor's office to properly filter work through to them. For example, former New South Wales Solicitor-General Keith Mason explained that during his tenure there was an informal 'mini-committee', composed of the Solicitor-General, Parliamentary Counsel, the Director-General and the Crown Solicitor, that would meet regularly, 'on the basis of keeping each other informed about what was happening in our legal bailiwicks'. Similarly, during his tenure as Victorian Solicitor-General, Daryl Dawson indicated that he had an informal relationship with the various heads of department, which allowed him to be very aware of what was happening throughout government.[165]

Individuals who held office in the early period of the Solicitor-General's statutory creation were more likely to take a proactively involved approach than current

[162] Interview, Martin Hinton; Interview, Patrick Keane.

[163] It may be that this is influenced by the expertise of appointees, with the two most recent (Chris Kourakis and Martin Hinton) having extensive criminal experience.

[164] See, eg, Interview, Geoffrey Davies; Interview, Michael Grant; Interview, Martin Hinton; Interview, Patrick Keane; Interview, Greg Parker.

[165] Ruth Campbell, Interview with Sir Daryl Dawson AC KBE CB (Law in Australian Society Oral History Project, 16, 23 July and 6 August 1998) 25.

officeholders. Dawson offered an explanation for the change: 'things have got more complicated, numbers have got greater'. Former Victorian Solicitor-General Pamela Tate explained why she had taken a somewhat different, more removed view of the role. She saw her role as the 'final adviser' within government for reasons relating to the integrity of the office. As such, she did not think it was appropriate for her to be involved in matters at an early stage, advising informally, for example, on the development of policies. This ensured that when legal issues crystallised in such matters, she would be able to provide an unbiased, determinative opinion, in much the same way as a court would. Tate's position accords with that taken in England by Viscount Simon, former Solicitor-General, Attorney-General and Lord Chancellor, that because of the importance of the impartiality of Law Officer opinions to the Cabinet, it was better that they were not involved in earlier Cabinet deliberations.[166]

In New Zealand, the Solicitor-General performs quite a different role from that in Australia (with the exception of the more recently created Australian Capital Territory position), with the incumbent filling the functions of Chief Executive of the Crown Law Office, principal counsel for the Crown, principal legal adviser to the Crown, supervisor of the prosecution of indictable crime and traditional constitutional/Law Officer functions.[167] David Collins, former New Zealand Solicitor-General, explained that one advantage of having the Solicitor-General actively supervising and overseeing all the advice and representation of the Crown is that the Solicitor-General is able to identify those cases that require his or her immediate attention, minimising the risk that the Solicitor-General will fail to be involved in a matter that has significant consequences for the Crown.[168] This was also identified by Australian Capital Territory Solicitor-General Peter Garrisson as an advantage under the model in that jurisdiction, which performs a similar breadth of functions to that in New Zealand.

This more active involvement reflects the view of some commentators that part of the government lawyers' ethical duties, informed by the idea of government under the rule of law, is to raise matters with their instructors where they believe an incomplete, or wrong, question is being asked.[169] Similarly, my data also revealed instances where a Solicitor-General has 'engineered' requests for advice after becoming aware of legal issues.[170]

[166] Viscount Simon, *Retrospect: the memoirs of Viscount Simon* (Hutchinson, 1952) 89–90. See further discussion in ch 2, section I.B.

[167] Collins, above n 116, 171.

[168] ibid, 181–82.

[169] See, eg, C Jacobi, 'How the ethical duties of the public lawyer are defined by the Constitution and structure of government' (Paper presented at the National Administrative Law Conference: Integrity in Administrative Decision-making, National Wine Centre, Adelaide, 19–20 July 2012) 14.

[170] Interview, Pamela Tate; Interview, Robert Ellicott.

a. Exceptions

Two exceptions to the general rule that the Solicitor-General's advice would be sought on appropriate matters arose in the interviews. These are explained by particular bureaucratic contexts that may lead to the Solicitor-General's being 'frozen out' or 'starved' of work, and the effect of outsourcing of government legal services and the increased use of in-house legal services providers in reducing the intimacy of the Solicitor-General's involvement in government.

b. Exception 1: 'Freezing Out'

From time to time, Solicitors-General have been 'frozen out' or 'starved' of work. This has occurred across a number of different jurisdictions for different reasons. The introduction of the office into the existing bureaucracy proved difficult in some jurisdictions; while in others freezing out was caused by the souring of a relationship between the Solicitor-General and an Attorney-General, the Crown Solicitor or even a senior bureaucrat.

Robert Ellicott was appointed Commonwealth Solicitor-General 1969 after Anthony Mason's initial tenure under the *Law Officers Act 1964* (Cth). Ellicott found that, although, by the time he was appointed Solicitor-General the office's position as second Law Officer had come to be generally accepted within the Attorney-General's Department, there were still occasions when difficulties arose. The most significant difficulties he encountered were when Lionel Murphy became Attorney-General during the Whitlam Labor Government. Ellicott quickly realised that Murphy was ignoring him and the office. Murphy appointed his own constitutional adviser and, without consultation with Ellicott or his knowledge, took a submission to Cabinet to establish a number of Deputy Solicitors-General.[171] Ellicott concluded that, politically, Murphy did not trust him. Ellicott recalled that he thought to himself, 'This is stupid. I'm Solicitor-General but he doesn't want to recognise the fact.'

The teething problems experienced by Ellicott at the Commonwealth level contrasts with the creation of the statutory role of Solicitor-General in Queensland. Former Crown Solicitor and Acting Solicitor-General Barry Dunphy described the new role as being almost immediately accepted and embraced across government, including in Crown Law.

Three other examples of the Solicitor-General's being starved of work emerged from my data.[172] In South Australia in the late 1970s, the poor relationship between Crown Solicitor Graham Prior and Solicitor-General Malcolm Gray, coupled with a level of distrust of the incoming Liberal government towards Gray (who had been appointed by the outgoing Labor government), resulted in the Crown

[171] Submission from Lionel Murphy to Cabinet, *Law Officers Act—Deputy Solicitor-General* (23 February 1973, Submission No 153); MG Sexton, 'The Role of the Solicitor General' in G Lindsay (ed), *No Mere Mouthpiece: Servants of All, Yet of None* (LexisNexis Butterworths, 2002) 86, 104.

[172] There was a period in New South Wales where the Solicitor-General stopped appearing for the government in the High Court, but this appears to be because of illness rather than 'freezing out'.

Solicitor's refusal to brief the Solicitor-General. This extended even to High Court constitutional litigation which, by that time, had become the Solicitor-General's speciality.[173] In the Northern Territory in the late 1990s, a senior bureaucrat 'decided to put on a "freeze"' on Solicitor-General Thomas Pauling, after complaints were made about his handling of an intervention on the part of the Territory.[174]

Also in the late 1990s, this time in Victoria, a vitriolic relationship between Solicitor-General Douglas Graham and incoming Labor Attorney-General Rob Hulls placed the Solicitor-General in a precarious position. When he was Shadow Attorney-General, Hulls had alleged in Parliament that Graham had, unethically, advised the government in proceedings against BHP Billiton at the same time as being a shareholder and director of a family trust that held shares in the company. Hulls made statements to Parliament that Graham was 'absolutely incompetent to be in the position of Solicitor-General of this state, and as a result he must resign immediately, because the longer he stays in that position the longer the position continues to be tainted'.[175] These earlier tensions meant that, upon the election of the Labor government in 1999, Graham was simply not involved with the Attorney-General, and therefore many sensitive government matters that would ordinarily be briefed to the Solicitor-General went elsewhere. While Hulls did not remove Graham, during the rest of his tenure (until December 2002)[176] Graham took his long leave,[177] and otherwise received work from people within government with whom he had established relationships.[178] Graham was still briefed in the constitutional interventions before the High Court after Hulls took over as Attorney-General, although, Tate explained, it appeared that Graham was only used in cases that were not viewed as politically important by the Attorney-General.[179]

[173] Interview, Martin Hinton; Interview Chris Kourakis. When Gray was appointed Solicitor-General in December 1978, the Solicitor-General ceased to appear in cases where the Solicitor-General of South Australia had, until that point, regularly appeared. Of the 16 cases in which South Australia's interests were represented in the High Court between Gray's appointment in December 1978 and Prior's retirement in 1984, the Solicitor-General appeared in just over 10% (one constitutional matter and one criminal appeal, both in 1983, towards the end of Prior's tenure as Crown Solicitor); the Crown Solicitor, in contrast, appeared in over 50% of matters (five constitutional cases and four others, including three criminal appeals).

[174] Interview, Thomas Pauling.

[175] Victoria, *Parliamentary Debates*, Legislative Assembly, 20 November 1996 (Rob Hulls), 1357. See also 1355–56.

[176] Office of Attorney-General, 'Hulls Advertising for New Solicitor-General' (Media release, 11 December 2002).

[177] Graham stopped appearing for Victoria for the final six months of his tenure, presumably as he was on long leave during this period. After May 2002, in the High Court Victoria was represented by Mark Dreyfus, Susan Crennan and Peter Hanks, before Pamela Tate was appointed Solicitor-General on 8 July 2003.

[178] Interview, Pamela Tate.

[179] During this period, the majority of these cases were technical legal questions arising from *Re Wakim; Ex parte McNally* (1999) 198 CLR 511; it is unlikely the Attorney-General would have seen these as politically important. Graham also appeared in some technical cases that concerned private international law questions. He appeared in some other constitutional cases representing the Attorney-General of Victoria, intervening, but he made written submissions only and did not address the Court.

Tate indicated that the relationship between Hulls and Graham had created more general difficulties for the Solicitor-General in that State. It was a period when, in effect, the Solicitor-General had been entirely 'frozen out' of the government machine. Following this period, when Tate accepted her appointment in 2003, there was no recent institutional knowledge within government about the office's role. She had to work to re-establish the authority of the position. In these circumstances, she found it very difficult to ensure that she was briefed in appropriate matters. It was then, in consultation with the Secretary of the Department, Penny Armytage, that she implemented a formal protocol for briefing the Solicitor-General. It was designed to achieve the necessary equilibrium between involving the Solicitor-General in the development of government policy, and ensuring the office was not involved in informal advisings of an insignificant nature. Part of that protocol was that her advice would be provided in writing, to clarify the bounds of her view.[180]

Commonwealth Solicitor-General Justin Gleeson has similarly formalised the office's advisory function. To meet the requirements in the Commonwealth legislation, he formally notifies the Attorney-General of new requests for advice that appear to warrant the attention of an opinion of the Solicitor-General under referral from the Attorney pursuant to section 12(b) of the *Law Officers Act*. Further, he will not provide the advice if the Attorney-General responds that he does not wish to make the referral. The Guidance Note issued by the OLSC states, 'Acceptance of … requests to advise will be confirmed by the Attorney-General, following consideration by the Solicitor-General. The opinion will also be provided to the Attorney-General.'[181] Ideally, advice is provided formally and in writing: the Solicitor-General does not provide oral, e-mail or draft advice. Gleeson introduced these changes, and largely formalised the advisory function, to minimise doubts that had arisen during the *Malaysia Solution Case* (see above at section II.A.ii.) as to whether the Government had acted on the Solicitor-General's advice or on legal advice from some other level of government.

There is thus frailty in the current arrangements. South Australian Solicitor-General Martin Hinton observed that the potential for 'freezing out' to occur 'is by no means ideal'; however, he explained, 'it is not the norm, and it has not been my experience'.[182] It is true that for most participants the possibility of being 'frozen out' of work caused them little concern.[183] The above examples were exceptions rather than the general experience. Nonetheless, the potential for it to occur has ramifications for the office's capacity to fill its advisory function in a manner that

[180] As to the desirability of such a protocol, in the US context see Morrison, above n 27, 68.

[181] Commonwealth, Office of Legal Services Coordination, *Guidance Note 11: Briefing the Solicitor-General* (Catherine Fitch, 18 February 2014) [13].

[182] M Hinton, 'Secundarius Attornatus: The Solicitor-General, the Executive and the Judiciary' (Paper presented at the conference on The Role of the Solicitor-General in the Australasian Legal and Political Landscape, Gold Coast, 15 April 2011) 5.

[183] See particularly Interview, Michael Grant, who knew of Pauling's experience but did not feel his independence was threatened by the possibility.

achieves the desired objectives. The office's lack of monopoly on any legal work in government may also have implications for the independence of the office, a topic to which I return in chapter seven, sections VI. and VII.

c. Exception 2: Outsourcing of Government Legal Services

Most day-to-day government legal advice is not provided by the Solicitor-General. Already we have seen that the Solicitor-General is consulted only on significant legal questions. Traditionally in Australia, government legal services were provided (almost) exclusively by legal practitioners operating within the Attorney-General's Department.[184] This arrangement continues in South Australia, Tasmania, Western Australia and the Australian Capital Territory.[185]

In the other jurisdictions (the Commonwealth, Victoria, New South Wales, Queensland and the Northern Territory), pursuant to reforms implemented throughout the 1990s, government departments are allowed to engage private law firms for advice and representation in certain areas of government legal work. This is referred to as the 'untying' of legal work. The areas of work that remained tied are at the core of the Executive's functions and/or strategically and politically sensitive (these include, for example, constitutional and national security work). In these areas it is perceived to be vital that whole-of-government implications are taken into consideration and consistency in the government's position is maintained.[186] Outsourcing of work has been controversial because of concerns over reduction in the independence of advice and overly client-focused lawyering; reduction in the quality of advice; failures to consider whole-of-government interests; and failures to involve the Solicitor-General in appropriate matters.[187]

[184] Exceptions were made only where there was a conflict of interest, or where the government legal service provider gave permission for a government agency to engage a private firm.

[185] Until 2006, the ACT government allowed government departments to brief private firms, but the growing trend to centralise legal services in the Government Solicitor was formalised as a government policy following a review of government services, and made binding following the introduction of *Law Officers (General) Legal Services Directions 2012* (ACT). Outsourcing may only occur with the Chief Solicitor's approval (that function is performed by the Solicitor-General): Interview, Peter Garrisson.

[186] Note Commonwealth tied work is more narrowly defined than that in New South Wales, Queensland and Victoria. See lists for Commonwealth: *Legal Services Directions 2005* (Cth), Appendix A; New South Wales: Bob Carr, 'M1995-39 Arrangements for Seeking Legal Advice from the Crown Solicitor's Office' (Department of Premier and Cabinet, 12 October 1995), available at <http://www.dpc.nsw.gov.au/announcements/ministerial_memoranda/1995/m1995-39>; and Queensland: Alan Girle, 'Commercialisation of State Government Legal Services' (2004) 63(3) *Australian Journal of Public Administration* 53, 55. In Victoria, the 'core government legal services' appear narrowly defined as well, although the full list is not publicly available. See Victorian Department of Justice, *Government Legal Services: Report to Attorney-General* (1 July 2002–30 June 2003). In the Northern Territory in 2008 the amount of tied work was increased. See Solicitor for Northern Territory, *Agency Legal Services* (20 April 2012) Northern Territory Department of Justice, available at <http://www.nt.gov.au/justice/solicitor/legal/services.shtml>.

[187] See R Beale, *Organisational Audit of the Attorney-General's Department: Final Report* (Allen Consulting Group, January 2009); AS Blunn and S Krieger, *Report of the Review of Commonwealth Legal Services Procurement* (Commonwealth Government, 6 November 2009); Crown Law, *In My Opinion: The History of Crown Law Queensland 1859–2009* (Department of Justice and Attorney General, 2009) 270.

In all jurisdictions, another phenomenon has been an increased use of lawyers working within departments and agencies (in-house). While separate issues, both outsourcing and the increased use of in-house counsel have had a similar impact on the role of the Solicitor-General.

Implications: Intimacy of Solicitor-General's Involvement

In some jurisdictions, the untying of work, together with other factors that have moved the provision of legal services away from the Attorney-General's immediate responsibility, have had significant impacts on the intimacy of the involvement of the Solicitor-General in government activities. Participants agreed that in tied areas of work, the Solicitor-General continued to receive appropriate work and was adequately supported by the government legal services provider.[188]

However, in untied areas, because of the decentralisation of legal advising, the Solicitor-General is often no longer as aware of the legal issues facing government as in the past. In some jurisdictions, the outsourcing of work has led to some work going elsewhere when ordinarily it would have been briefed to the Solicitor-General. The loss of briefing to the Solicitor-General was sometimes exacerbated by the preferences of private law firms for particular counsel other than the Solicitor-General.[189]

In New South Wales, Victoria and Queensland the outsourcing of work was not perceived to have affected the work of the Solicitor-General, although it increased the instances in which the Solicitor-General would be asked to provide a definitive opinion where individual agencies or departments had obtained differing opinions.[190]

Former Commonwealth Solicitor-General Stephen Gageler expressed his concern over the effect of the outsourcing arrangements, together with the increase use of in-house legal services.[191] When he started in the position in 2008, Gageler found he was not being briefed regularly to provide written opinions to the Government. As to why, he explained it was predominantly caused by the structure of government legal services:

> [T]he sort of marginalisation and isolation that I sensed in my role fitted into a broader problem I think around the procurement of government legal services, and with the Attorney-General's Department, and with the spinning off of the Australian Government Solicitor's Office, with the growth of in-house legal services in Commonwealth Government departments.

[188] Interview, Stephen Gageler; Interview, Philip Ruddock.

[189] Interview, Thomas Pauling.

[190] Interview, Patrick Keane; Interview, Keith Mason; Interview Pamela Tate; and see also Victoria, Department of Justice, *Protocol for Briefing the Solicitor-General* (28 July 2011) [4].

[191] See also Interview, Duncan Kerr; Interview, Leigh Sealy. See also investigation of current trends in the provision of government legal services, particularly at the Commonwealth level, in G Appleby, 'The Challenges of Providing Legal Services to Government' in Appleby, Keyzer and Williams (eds), above n 116, 141; G Appleby, 'Reshaping government legal services in the public interest', *The Mandarin* (6 July 2015), available at <http://www.themandarin.com.au/42222-legal-services-review-public-interest/>.

The effect of these factors was investigated in two federal Government-commissioned reviews into the structuring of legal services. In January 2009, the Allen Consulting Group found outsourcing created a decentralisation of legal services, reducing the Attorney-General's Department's former 'intimate advisory relationship with departments as they develop proposals'.[192] This meant the Department no longer received 'early warnings' as issues arose in policy development. These disadvantages were most critically reflected in the weakening of the Attorney-General's capacity to fulfil the first Law Officer's legal services functions and the Solicitor-General's primary responsibilities in this area. This caused deterioration in the intimacy of the Solicitor-General's relationship with government. The report concluded that 'support for the Solicitor-General, and the intimacy and flexibility of his engagement in the Commonwealth's advice and litigation, has deteriorated'.[193]

In November 2009, the Report of the Review of Commonwealth Legal Services Procurement echoed many of the concerns of the earlier report, also noting the impact of increased use of in-house counsel on the role of the Law Officers.[194] One of this Report's recommendations was to introduce measures to reinforce and assist agencies to ensure that the Solicitor-General and/or the Attorney-General are informed of potentially significant emerging issues.[195] The Government has responded to this Report, but only with respect to its recommendations on the most efficient and effective means of delivering legal services.[196] The concerns regarding the involvement of the Law Officers and the Attorney-General's Department in the development of government policy have not been addressed.[197]

The Australian experience contrasts starkly with that of New Zealand. When outsourcing was introduced in that jurisdiction, the Solicitor-General maintained responsibility for the supervision of work that was undertaken by non-government legal service providers, and the right to intervene in matters if he or she considered it appropriate.[198]

The Importance of Individual Role Perception

Some participants identified the rearrangement of government legal services as a significant factor in the perceived change in the role of the Solicitor-General,

[192] Beale, above n 187, ix and 2.

[193] ibid.

[194] Blunn and Krieger, above n 187, recommendations 1 and 3, at 12, and recommendation 10, at 13.

[195] ibid, recommendation 12, at 13.

[196] See Attorney-General Robert McClelland, *Address to the National Legal Officers' Forum 2011*, 9 March 2011, Canberra.

[197] Although note the Commonwealth is currently undertaking a review of Commonwealth legal services, to be completed by 30 June 2016, which is intended to include a review of the scope and effectiveness of mechanisms in support of the Attorney-General's role: Attorney-General's Department, *AGD Secretary's Review of Commonwealth Services: Issues Paper One* (10 November 2015) 6 [17].

[198] See discussion in ch 2, section III.B.

particularly at the Commonwealth level.[199] But the effect of the individual officeholder's perception of the role was also instrumental. For example, many officeholders saw their role as waiting for legal work to be briefed to them, acting as a private barrister would, and not to be intimately engaged with the business of government.[200] Others, however, focused upon being involved in appropriate legal issues to ensure that they were able to provide definitive legal advice, and that other issues were canvassed where necessary.[201]

Former Commonwealth Attorney-General and Minister for Justice Duncan Kerr drew a distinction between 'policy-sensitive' Solicitors-General and non-policy-sensitive Solicitors-General. By 'policy-sensitive', he was not referring to overtly party-political incumbents but to those who actively sought to be the 'dominant legal influence for the Commonwealth', inserting their office into the development of policy and across all legal areas. Non-policy-sensitive Solicitors-General, in contrast, were 'hired guns' in any given matter, 'rather than working through the strategy of how the Commonwealth advances its broader legal interests'.

When Stephen Gageler became Commonwealth Solicitor-General in 2008, he explained that he was well-serviced and the office was integrated in constitutional litigation (an area of tied work), but he was not engaged as broadly across government as he thought necessary for the role. However, Gageler would find re-establishing a more integrated role for the Solicitor-General challenging. Kerr noted that changing entrenched bureaucratic culture is difficult. The temptation to use in-house and private lawyers because of their client focus and more accommodating advice (or at least the perception of more accommodating advice) must be overcome.

In his attempts to change the role, Gageler had the support of then Attorney-General Robert McClelland and the Secretary of the Attorney-General's Department, Roger Wilkins. McClelland said, 'Stephen is a new creature in the sense that he actually likes being involved in a range of matters'. McClelland's view was that Gageler viewed the role as

> not only giving constitutional advice and appearing in cases, constitutional and otherwise. But he thought that given that he may well be asked to appear in a matter of significance, he wanted to be on the ground floor of giving advice as to how those matters would be structured.

McClelland gave a number of examples of the types of questions in which Gageler had been constructively involved, including the establishment of the national emergency warning system and the national health reforms. Demonstrative of Gageler's increased involvement across government, following his appointment,

[199] Interview, Stephen Gageler; Interview, Duncan Kerr.

[200] See, eg, Interview, John Doyle; Interview, Martin Hinton.

[201] Interview, Trevor Griffin; Interview, Keith Mason.

he regularly appeared in the High Court in administrative law appeals,[202] and also for non-constitutional matters for the Australian Crime Commission,[203] the Australian Competition and Consumer Commission,[204] the Australian Securities and Investments Commission,[205] and the Federal Commissioner of Taxation.[206] This breadth of practice has been continued by the current Commonwealth Solicitor-General Justin Gleeson.

The assumption that the Solicitor-General will be briefed by the government to advise in matters of constitutional and other significance is fundamental to the office's capacity to contribute to the promotion of the rule of law. However, the data demonstrate that while this is predominantly the position, there are no safeguards to ensure that the office is not 'starved' of work from within the bureaucracy, or because of a sour relationship with the Attorney-General, or because possibly more accommodating advice is available elsewhere. Ultimately, the extent to which these factors affect the role of the Solicitor-General will depend on the desire of the individual officeholder to ensure that his or her office is consulted in appropriate matters and the attitude of others in government. However, not all officeholders believe that it is appropriate for the Solicitor-General to become intimately involved in policy development; rather, the officeholder must remain appropriately separate and, through this separation, independent.

iv. Fourth Assumption: Independence

The last assumption that underpins the Solicitor-General's advisory function is that the advice will be provided objectively and independently. Former Queensland Crown Solicitor and Acting Solicitor-General Barry Dunphy explained, 'it is really important that there is someone there who will call it straight down the line; who is accessible; and who is respected'. The finality of the Solicitor-General's opinion underscores the importance of this assumption. John Edwards explains, 'It is by virtue of this unique measure of constitutional independence that the Law Officers are enable to insist on their being the "court of last resort" to which the ranks of departmental legal advisers must defer.'[207]

[202] See, eg, *Osland v Secretary, Department of Justice (No 2)* (2010) 241 CLR 320; *Saeed v Minister for Immigration and Citizenship* (2010) 241 CLR 252; *Minister for Immigration and Citizenship v SSZMDS* (2010) 240 CLR 611; *Minister for Immigration and Citizenship v Kumar* (2009) 238 CLR 448; *Minister for Immigration and Citizenship v SZJGV* (2009) 238 CLR 642.

[203] *Hogan v Australian Crime Commission* (2010) 240 CLR 651.

[204] *ACCC v Channel Seven Brisbane Pty Ltd* (2009) 239 CLR 305.

[205] *Lehman Bros Holdings Inc v City of Swan* (2010) 240 CLR 509.

[206] *Federal Commissioner of Taxation v Anstis* (2010) 241 CLR 443; *Travelex Ltd v Federal Commissioner of Taxation* (2010) 241 CLR 510.

[207] Edwards, *The Attorney-General*, above n 114, 190. For a similar view, see J McGrath, 'Principles for Sharing Law Officer Power—The Role of the New Zealand Solicitor-General' (1998) 18 *New Zealand Universities Law Review* 195, 214.

The Solicitor-General's role in providing certainty and security to government also highlights how instrumental it is that the Solicitor-General's view is arrived at independently. However, because of potential political use that can be made of the Solicitor-General in this role, the office's independence may be called into question. The purpose and type of independence of the office is also instrumental in other functions of the Solicitor-General and will be returned to separately in chapter seven.

v. Assumptions: Summary

Advising on the limits of government power, the Solicitor-General's role has the potential to be an important constitutional mechanism in promoting the rule of law and constitutionalism. To be so, a number of assumptions must be met. Some of these are statutorily mandated, but others rest exclusively on practice and convention. The convention that the Solicitor-General's advice will be final within government and that the Solicitor-General will be briefed in appropriate cases are two of the latter. In the majority of circumstances, these assumptions are met. However, there are instances of government disregard for them that demonstrate the frailty of relying on historical convention and principle, undermining the potential of the Solicitor-General's contribution to the rule of law.

III. Advisory Function: Executive Empowerment

The advisory function was predominantly described in terms of ensuring that government operated within the rule of law; but that function, for many participants, had to be viewed in the context of the Executive's role within government and government's role in society more generally. In this sense, while checking and ensuring integrity of government power is important, the Solicitor-General's role must be seen in the context of the Executive's obligations to implement policies on behalf of the electorate and to govern within a public policy framework that reflects the core values of the government system (introduced in chapter four, section VI.B.i. as 'core government principles').

A. Achieving Executive Policy Outcomes

Many participants discussed the Solicitor-General's role in terms of assisting the government achieve its policy outcomes within the law. So in this respect the Solicitor-General was perceived not as a passive linesperson but *actively* assisting the government. Therefore, to describe the Solicitor-General's advisory function as 'quasi-judicial', as has been done in the US and British context, might be misleading.[208] This dimension of the Solicitor-General's role has a natural relationship with the idea of the Solicitor-General's providing security and certainty to the government in advancing its agenda.

This perspective reflects a majoritarian, democratic view of the mandate of government. It also reflects Helen Irving's position, in the context of the High Court's inability to provide advisory opinions, that it is important for government to implement policies and programs that push the boundaries of government power, not simply to operate safely within known limits. It is in this way that the outer limits of government power may be determined and the law advanced.[209] Under this view, the Solicitor-General ought not to provide conservative advice based on a narrow interpretation of the law but assist a government in achieving its policy objectives, alive to the possible development of the law.[210]

The belief that the Solicitor-General ought to assist in achieving government policy was particularly evident in the views of Attorneys-General. Michael Lavarch, former Commonwealth Labor Attorney-General, said:

> You expect [Solicitors-General] to be understanding of the government's policy position and, properly within the bounds of their office, to give proper and full advice: what they call fearless advice. … But they are not there to be obstructionist and hostile, they try to implement and help implement the government's policy position, but ensuring that it was done *always* constitutionally and *always* lawfully.

Lavarch illustrated his point by reference to the Commonwealth's response to the High Court's *Mabo* decision in 1992.[211] Crafting an appropriate statutory response, he explained, was complex, and involved stakeholders from the Aboriginal and non-Aboriginal communities and various economic interests. It was 'a nice little mix of legal, political, moral, economic interests, all coming into the one frame'. The then Solicitor-General, Gavan Griffith, provided the solution to one of the issues by framing the legislation as a 'Special Measure' under the *Racial Discrimination Act 1975* (Cth). This allowed the Government to argue 'with some credible legal force', that it was not suspending that Act. Lavarch explained, 'But I don't think that it would be fair to say that [the Solicitor-General] was contributing to the policy position per se.' Rather, within a policy dilemma, the Solicitor-General assisted in finding a mechanism to achieve an outcome.[212] Other Attorneys-General held similar views.[213]

[208] N Baker, *Conflicting Loyalties: Law and Politics in the Attorney General's Office, 1789–1990* (University Press of Kansas, 1992) Preface; JLJ Edwards, *The Law Officers of the Crown: A Study of the Offices of the Attorney-General and Solicitor-General of England with an Account of the Office of the Director of Public Prosecutions of England* (Sweet & Maxwell, 1964) 1.

[209] H Irving, 'Advisory Opinions, The Rule of Law and the Separation of Powers' (2004) 4 *Macquarie Law Journal* 105, 106–07, 132.

[210] See also WB Wendel, 'Government Lawyers, Democracy and the Rule of Law' (2009) 77(4) *Fordham Law Review* 1333, 1340.

[211] *Mabo v Queensland (No 2)* (1992) 175 CLR 1. See also Interview, Gavan Griffith.

[212] See also Interview, Gavan Griffith.

[213] Interview, Robert McClelland; Interview, Philip Ruddock.

Former Commonwealth Attorney-General Gareth Evans explained that he expected that the duty of the Solicitor-General to assist the Executive implement its agenda would affect the legal method employed by the Solicitor-General. He said that in the 'many twilight areas where you could go one way or the other in terms of the advice', it was the role of the Solicitor-General to 'do what they possibly could to accommodate the wishes of their client, short of putting themselves in a position of saying something that was totally intellectually disreputable'. Evans was not looking for the Solicitor-General's opinion on the 'best' legal position. However, he was very clear that he would not place undue pressure on the Solicitor-General to provide accommodating and 'manifestly' indefensible advice. The Solicitor-General needed to avoid intellectual disreputable positions, to maintain the 'overall credibility of the office, and by extension the government of the day'.

One Attorney-General also indicated he would, on rare occasions, speak to the Solicitor-General as an opinion was being generated, and emphasise the government's objectives to the officeholder to ensure they were adequately considered. The Attorney-General described it as 'a degree of mediation'. As a result of these discussions, the final advice might be 'strengthened a bit from what it originally was', so that the government 'may have been buttressed by a more strongly worded opinion'. The Attorney-General emphasised that this would never amount to a change in the outcome of the advice. Rather, the Attorney-General would indicate to the Solicitor-General the issues the government saw as important, and these 'may have been reflected more starkly in the depth of the advice, or illustrations contained in the advice'.

Current and former Solicitors-General shared, to an extent, the view of their role as assisting in the achievement of executive policy. In the Northern Territory, Thomas Pauling indicated that there were a small number of occasions during which he was called upon to assist the government achieve a particular policy objective in legally challenging circumstances. One such occasion was in 2007, when Xstrata sought to convert its operations at the McArthur River Mine to open-cut mining. The Minister had purportedly approved this conversion, which involved the re-routing of the McArthur River but the Supreme Court of the Northern Territory found the Minister's approval ineffective.[214] Pauling was instrumental in pushing through legislation to remedy the defect: in four days he briefed the Cabinet, Caucus, the Opposition and the Independents, and oversaw the passage of legislation that retrospectively validated the Minister's approval. Within the government's broad policy objective of keeping the McArthur River Mine running, Pauling viewed the Solicitor-General's role as doing whatever was legally needed to overcome any impediments.

Former South Australian Solicitor-General Chris Kourakis also saw his role as helping the government achieve overarching policy aims by considering legally available *means* to achieve the government's *ends*:

> The only reason I am going into the policy area is to formulate a policy that does not have a particular legal risk that I have identified. I don't suggest a change in policy because

[214] *Lansen v NT Minister for Mines and Energy* [2007] NTSC 28.

> I don't like it, or because I think a better public policy is this. I take for granted what they want to achieve, and just … modify it to reduce legal risk.[215]

Many officeholders, current and former, agreed that part of the role of the Solicitor-General was to assist the Executive in achieving its policy outcomes. Many Solicitors-General agreed that it was appropriate for them to assist the Executive to find a legally appropriate means to achieve the desired political outcome. However, whether this changed how a Solicitor-General approached the question of whether a particular measure was legally justified differed markedly from the views of some Attorneys-General, as set out above. In chapter four, section III.A.iii., I developed the argument that the appropriate manner for the Solicitor-General to resolve legal ambiguity is not to do so in favour of the political objectives behind a measure; but where there may be genuine indeterminacy in the law and there is no obvious legally preferable answer, the Solicitor-General ought to indicate this. This approach ensures the Solicitor-General provides the government with an accurate description of the legal landscape to determine its policy course. For some Attorneys-General, however, where there was ambiguity in the law, they expected the Solicitor-General to take a position that would buttress Executive policy, with the caveat that they would never want the Solicitor-General to take an 'intellectually indefensible' position.

More consistent with my conclusions in chapter four, many current and former Solicitors-General countered the idea that their legal method should be influenced by the Executive's policy objectives. Anthony Mason, former Commonwealth Solicitor-General, explained that often

> politicians see the law as something that can be, as it were, I won't use the words bent or manipulated, they're too strong, but that can be *influenced* in a way that can advantage their position. And therefore, they want to deal with lawyers who are at least sympathetic to their political position.

However, he went on to say that this was misguided: 'Whatever a government thinks about how a Solicitor-General will act, almost certainly, they will find eventually that he answers legal questions impartially and objectively.'

Former Victorian Solicitor-General Pamela Tate recalled that her Attorney-General, Rob Hulls, had made it very clear that the Solicitor-General was most valued in her office when she provided independent advice on her best view of the law.[216] She explained that trying to 'assist' the government by moulding advice to fit a government's objectives was dangerous: the government does not speak with one voice, it is dynamic. It is therefore inappropriate for the Solicitor-General to try to second guess what the government wants to hear. Western Australian Solicitor-General Grant Donaldson also explained that what was often overlooked in discussions of the Solicitor-General's independence, was that the government

[215] See also Interview, William Bale; Interview, Stephen Gageler, Interview, Michael Sexton.

[216] See also Interview, Greg Cooper; Interview, Grant Donaldson.

itself was *also* highly concerned about maintaining the office's independence and receiving independent advice.[217] He continued:

> I can't conceive of a circumstance if you have a good Attorney-General and a good government, where they want you to be anything other than independent. I think that's the other thing that's often overlooked. … [The] government in Western Australia actually *wants* independent advice. That's what they *want*. …
>
> [Governments] don't want public servants or Solicitors-General to be giving them advice they want to hear. They've got political advisers who can do all of that sort of stuff. They want to know what the answer actually is. When they know what the answer actually is they can then work out how the politics of it all is going to work out.

In the US, it has also been observed that the longer-term interests of the government will be served better by an independent officer. According to this scholarship, in most instances the Executive itself seeks independent analysis of its position, not advice biased towards its interests.[218] Further, perceptions that legal advisers are acting upon the direction of the Executive can undermine the confidence of the public,[219] the Judiciary[220] and of government itself.[221] Even back in the nineteenth century, as the English Law Officers took their first steps towards tempering their previously dogged pursuit of Crown prosecutions, the King acknowledged the benefits of this approach, that it had 'a useful and important effect upon the public mind'.[222]

As explained in sections B.i.b. and B.i.c. above, a number of Solicitors-General recalled when they had faced potential conflicts of interest caused by requests to act for Vice-regal officers and the Executive, or the Legislative and the Executive. However, many believed that, provided there was no conflict over the factual circumstances, there was no conflict in their providing advice, because the

[217] See also Interview, Pamela Tate and Interview, Rod Welford.

[218] JM Harmon, 'Memorandum Opinion for the Attorney General: Role of the Solicitor General' (1988) 21 *Loyola of Los Angeles Law Review* 1089, 1094; BK Landsberg, 'The Tenth Justice (Book Review)' (1989) 6 *Constitutional Commentary* 165, 168; J Schwartz, 'The President's Lawyer as Frie(n)d—A Review of Order and Law: Arguing the Reagan Revolution—A Firsthand Account' (1992) 60 *George Washington Law Review* 1081, 1122; DS Days III , 'The Solicitor General and the American Legal Ideal' (1995) 49 *Southern Methodist University Law Review* 73, 494–95; WP Barr, 'Attorney General's Remarks, Benjamin N Cardozo School of Law, November 15, 1992' (1993) 15 *Cardozo Law Review* 31, 34–35; RD Moss, 'Executive Branch Legal Interpretation: A Perspective from the Office of Legal Counsel' (2000) 52 *Administrative Law Review* 1303, 1308.

[219] Moss, above n 218, 1311.

[220] K Norman-Major, 'The Solicitor General: Executive Policy Agendas and the Court' (1994) 57 *Albany Law Review* 1081, 1109; R Lee, 'Lawyering for the Government: Politics, Polemics & Principle' (1986) 47 *Ohio State Law Journal* 595, 597; R Wilkins, 'An Officer and an Advocate: the Role of the Solicitor General' (1988) 21 *Loyola of Los Angeles Law Review* 1167; Barr, above n 218, 36; L Fisher, 'Is the Solicitor General an Executive or Judicial Agent? Caplan's *Tenth Justice*' (1990) 15 *Law and Social Inquiry* 305, 306–09; DM Rosenzweig, 'Confession of Error in the Supreme Court by the Solicitor General' (1994) 82 *Georgetown Law Journal* 2079, 2084–87; JL Cooper, 'The Solicitor General and the Evolution of Activism' (1990) 65 *Indiana Law Journal* 675, 684 and fn 54.

[221] Wilkins, above n 220, 1171.

[222] Edwards, *The Attorney-General,* above n 114, 61. See further discussion in ch 2, section I.A.

'advice would have been exactly what it was', uninfluenced by the objectives of the party seeking it.[223] Former Commonwealth Solicitor-General Stephen Gageler explained, 'I mean it is perhaps simplistic and naive but my advice doesn't change depending on who asks the question'.[224]

Current Commonwealth Solicitor-General Justin Gleeson also indicated that consistency was an important influence on his advice. He explained:

> If I'm asked to advise on anything, firstly I need to see everything that's been said on that topic, or close to that topic, by previous Solicitors-General, particularly the most recent ones, because they are the most relevant. And then I don't depart from that unless there is a very good reason to do so. So I don't depart from it just because I might have taken a slightly different view. There has got to be something that has changed or I have to be firmly convinced that there was an error in what was said by the previous person. So, the idea of that is that there is a consistency through the office.

A number of officeholders expressly addressed the difficulty that arises for the Solicitor-General where the law is unsettled and ambiguous in a particular area. Former South Australian Solicitor-General Chris Kourakis explained his position, which closely mirrors that which I developed in chapter four:

> If you can form a relatively clear opinion one way or the other, then you say, that's the end of it. But you should be careful and recognise that there might be two sides to it and if there is an argument that both sides are fairly evenly balanced, it is not for the Solicitor-General or any Crown Law officer to pick which one they prefer and say, well, it is not lawful because in my opinion I would go this way on this argument. I think where there are arguments both ways, the proper thing to do is simply to point out the argument both ways, the risks in acting one way or the other, and then it is a matter for the government to decide.[225]

Former Queensland Solicitor-General Walter Sofronoff explained that questions of this nature did not arise very often:

> Sometimes, more rarely than you would think, it is not possible to give definitive advice, it is only possible to give advice, that this would be the more probable outcome … That the legislation, for example, could be read this way or that way, there are factors going each way, but in my view, this particular way is the preferable way of looking at it because the legal logic is more compelling … in that direction.

The division of opinions which emerged between some Solicitors-General and Attorneys-General as to the appropriate manner to resolve legal ambiguity is perhaps unsurprising. Putting this division to one side, both Solicitors-General and Attorneys-General acknowledged the importance of the Solicitor-General's being actively committed to achieving the Executive's policies. In this sense, rather than being a wholly independent, disinterested agent engaged to provide opinions

[223] Interview, William Bale. See also Interview, Michael Grant.

[224] Robert Ellicott had expressed a similar view. See R Schneider, 'Exit the Liberal party's Moralist', *The Australian* (18 February 1981).

[225] This is the same view taken in Interview, Greg Parker.

on the legality of actions of the government, the Solicitor-General works with the government to achieve its agenda. Another way of framing this is that the Solicitor-General must accept the legitimacy of the government's goals in undertaking the role. This does not necessarily sit well with the regulatory, integrity-driven aspect of the role for the benefit of the community and the individuals within the community. It certainly adds a degree of complexity to the conception of the Solicitor-General as an independent oversight mechanism. It brings with it the potential for abuse by unscrupulous officeholders and government officers.

B. Policy Outcomes and the SCSG

Australia's federal system further complicates the position of the Solicitor-General. Nationwide policy objectives often require the cooperation of all the governments of the federation. During the early phase of the development of the modern model for the Solicitor-General, a collective group of Solicitors-General was formed: the Special Committee of Solicitors-General (SCSG).[226] The need to receive the views of all of the States on legal proposals to sever the remaining constitutional links with Britain drove its immediate formation, but there have been a number of subsequent federal legal schemes of note that have involved the Committee, including the SCSG's involvement in the cross-vesting scheme, the crimes at sea legislation and the choice of law scheme. More recently, Northern Territory Solicitor-General Michael Grant noted that the SCSG's function as adviser to the Law, Crime and Community Safety Council (LCCSC) (previously Standing Committee of Attorneys-General (SCAG) and then the Standing Committee on Law and Justice (SCLJ)) has diminished as the LCCSC relies increasingly on its own officers for advice.

One example in which former Queensland Solicitor-General Patrick Keane recalled the SCSG being involved was the negotiations between the Commonwealth and the states after the decision in *Ha v New South Wales*.[227] That case found the New South Wales tobacco-licensing system invalid. It was a decision that had wide ramifications for the states' capacity to raise future revenue under tobacco-licensing schemes (and similar alcohol and petroleum schemes). At the time of the decision, states and territories were raising 16 per cent of their total revenue through these business-franchise fees.[228] The case also gave rise to serious questions about what would happen to the money collected under invalid schemes. The SCSG had anticipated the consequences of a finding of invalidity in

[226] See further discussion of the SCSG in ch 3, section III.G.

[227] *Ha v New South Wales* (1997) 189 CLR 465.

[228] T Blackshield and G Williams, *Australian Constitutional Law and Theory: Commentary and Materials* (Federation Press, 5th edn, 2010) 1060; J Harrison and M Stretton, 'The GST Debate: Chronology 1 1998–1999' (Australian Parliamentary Library, 1999), available at <http://www.aph.gov.au/library/pubs/chron/1998-99/99chr01.htm>.

Ha before it was even argued before the High Court. At a meeting on 18 October 1995, the SCSG discussed the possibility of the Commonwealth's passing legislation to remedy any finding of unconstitutionality to provide a 'safety net' to the States.[229] The New South Wales Solicitor-General, for example, suggested the Commonwealth 'might be able to say it was reluctantly forced to have a [Goods and Services Tax (GST)]'.[230] The states eventually came to an arrangement with the Commonwealth so that, in the event of a finding of invalidity, the Commonwealth would increase the federal excise on tobacco, alcohol and petroleum, and pass this revenue back to the states. These arrangements were quickly enacted after the decision in August 1997;[231] and eventually a GST was introduced to secure the source of revenue.[232]

The SCSG's establishment recognises the desirability of a legal advisory body constituted by representatives of all of the interests of the Commonwealth. Involvement in the SCSG reveals an aspect of the Solicitor-General's role in which tensions may arise between the interests of the federation and the interests of an individual jurisdiction. A Solicitor-General involved in providing joint advice of the SCSG to the LCCSC does so as a representative for his or her individual government, and as such must ensure that the interests of that entity are protected, but is also acting as an adviser to a collective group of Attorneys-General. In recognition of this potential for conflict, former Commonwealth Solicitor-General Stephen Gageler explained that he was requested by the Government to refrain from participating in joint opinions prepared by the SCSG for the LCCSC.[233]

C. Advising Beyond the Law

Some participants accepted that the advisory function was not narrowly confined to developing different ways of achieving a policy objective within the strict letter of the law. These participants felt that it was appropriate for the Solicitor-General to look beyond the law to broader issues, including advising and warning the Crown on political consequences, 'whole-of-government' issues and broader 'legal policy' questions, which would encompass the impact of policies on rule-of-law principles (including, for example, equality and consistency), on individual rights, and on the principles of representative and responsible democracy. The idea of the Solicitor-General's providing advice on these broader issues beyond the

[229] McDonnell, above n 97, 3.

[230] ibid.

[231] Harrison and Stretton, above n 228. *States Grants (General Purposes) Amendment Act (No 2) 1997* (Cth) amending *States Grants (General Purposes) Act 1994* (Cth); and *Excise Tariff Amendment Act (No 5) 1997* (Cth). See discussion of the episode in MM Scollo and MH Winstanley, *Tobacco in Australia: Facts and Issues*, Cancer Council Victoria, available at <http://www.tobaccoinaustralia.org.au>, [13.2.2].

[232] Treasury Department, 'Tax Reform: Not a New Tax; a New Tax System' (13 August 1998). The tax reforms were implemented in 1999.

[233] Interview, Stephen Gageler.

law—particularly in relation to whole-of-government and legal policy questions—reflects the conclusions in chapter 4, section VI.B.i. that the Solicitor-General has a duty to advise on 'core government principles' as a residual aspect of the traditional Law Officers' public interest functions.

i. The Role of Good Counsel: To Advise and Warn

For many participants, the proposition that the Solicitor-General ought to advise the government beyond strictly legal advice was part of the role of any good counsel.[234] Former South Australian Solicitor-General John Doyle said he thought that all good barristers should ask a client in certain circumstances whether they want to exercise a legal right. Former Commonwealth Solicitor-General David Bennett said this would include, for example, advice on how certain legal actions might be reported in the press, or that a certain legal case might set a disadvantageous precedent for future operations.[235] Similarly, Doyle explained that in the role he also learnt to 'keep an eye out for small p political factors'.[236] Doyle observed that the Solicitor-General's ongoing relationship with a single client meant that an officeholder may become aware of aspects of the client's operations or activities that, in the interests of the client, warranted a comment or cautionary note. Because of the ongoing nature of the appointment, the Solicitor-General was in a better position to provide such advice than a lawyer who might be engaged in a one-off relationship with a client.[237]

Beyond warning and advising on potential tactical and publicity questions, some participants also thought the Solicitor-General had a duty to provide advice on whole-of-government issues and legal policy questions.

ii. A Whole-of-Government Perspective

Many participants endorsed the idea that the Solicitor-General's remit included protecting the interests of the 'government as a whole'. The idea that government legal services are provided within a whole-of-government framework comes from the common law duties of the Australian Attorney-General.[238] Anthony Mason, the

[234] Interview, David Bennett; Interview, John Doyle; Interview, Robert Ellicott; Interview, Gareth Evans, Interview, Michael Mischin.

[235] Interview, David Bennett. See also his view in J Eyers, 'Putting Words to Music in the Constitution's Case', *Australian Financial Review* (Sydney), 2008. He said, 'You can't totally divorce yourself from political considerations in advising government … one might warn the government that fighting or not fighting a particular case may result in a measure of unpopularity with a section of the community.'

[236] See also Interview, Keith Mason; Interview, Terence Sheahan; P Burton, *From Moree to Mabo: The Mary Gaudron Story* (UWA Publishing, 2010) 187.

[237] Letter from John Doyle to Gabrielle Appleby, 19 July 2012 (copy on file with author).

[238] See ch 3, section I.E.

first Solicitor-General appointed under the new legislation at the Commonwealth level, said:

> Of course one of the ideas in having … a professional barrister as Solicitor-General under the new legislation was that the Solicitor-General would be able to have … a principled and coherent overview of Commonwealth legal policy, particularly in the area of constitutional and public law.[239]

An example provided by former Queensland Solicitor-General Patrick Keane illustrates the type of advice that is encompassed by this whole-of-government perspective, and the importance of having the final, authoritative adviser to government alive to it. During the 1990s, before the decision in *Ha v New South Wales*, there was increased litigation around section 90 of the Constitution and the question of what constituted an excise (which the States are constitutionally prohibited from levying). Keane recalled that as Solicitor-General he was advising many different government departments against the backdrop of the High Court's growing trajectory towards a broad reading of the term 'excise'. Some departments were unhappy with the perceived pessimism of the advice that the Solicitor-General was providing. Keane explained that his role was to ensure that they operated consistently with the view taken across the whole of the government:

> [W]hile I was necessarily sympathetic to their position and wanted to help them out, at the end of the day, we are the State of Queensland, and this is what we say, this is what we do and this is the State's position. And, they had to operate within that.

From the government's view, many Attorneys-General also stressed it was important to have a whole-of-government perspective taken by the final and authoritative adviser.[240]

iii. *'Core Government Principles'*

Former Commonwealth Attorney-General and Minister for Justice Duncan Kerr believed that the Solicitor-General's role included advising the government on individual rights issues in relation to the constitutional structure; in fact, for Kerr these questions were such that they 'cannot be avoided':

> I do think that it is the job of the Solicitor-General always to at least alert their instructors of the long-term consequences of taking some particular points that might have some short-term advantage but long-term detriments to the kind of constitutional structures that … we would wish to see in place both to ensure that there is effective governance but also that citizens' rights are not ignored.

This idea that the Solicitor-General had a responsibility to advise on principles that underpin the constitutional system arose in a number of interviews. Catherine

[239] See also Interview, Greg Cooper; Interview, Patrick Keane; Interview, Greg Parker; G Griffith, 'Report: Second Law Officer to the First Law Officer 1 July 1995–31 December 1996' (Solicitor-General of Australia, 1996) [2.11], see also [2.2], [4.2], [10.6(2)], [10.8].

[240] See, eg, Interview, Duncan Kerr; Interview, Robert McClelland.

Branson, former South Australian Crown Solicitor, referred to the idea of ensuring that government operated 'with a high level of constitutional propriety as well as legal propriety'. She explained what she meant by 'constitutional propriety' by reference to the authority of government resting on its citizens and the ideals of a well-functioning democracy. In addition to any more general obligation, Solicitors-General from Victoria and the Australian Capital Territory explained that in those jurisdictions the Solicitor-General has an obligation to advise in light of the human rights standards set out in the statutory charters of rights.[241]

All participants rejected the notion that the Solicitor-General was an independent *actor* for the public interest. Three reasons emerged for this. The first was an acceptance that the Solicitor-General had no democratic mandate, in contrast to that of the government. The second was the modern Solicitor-General's lack of accountability and responsibility to parliament. Lastly was a conception of the role of counsel as operating as an agent of the client, and not an independent agent for the public interest.[242]

Former South Australian Solicitor-General Chris Kourakis dismissed an independent role to act in the public interest for the Solicitor-General:

> That is a complete fiction, and that is a fiction that is designed to allow people to implement their personal views, that they say it is not my personal view, it is the public's view, or the public interest. ... But it is often put that we are the custodians of the wider public interest: governments come and go but we will do what the right thing is.

Former New South Wales Solicitor-General Keith Mason outlined why a Solicitor-General might develop a desire to push and pursue actions or policies that accord with what he or she thinks is right and fair. He said it is a tension

> which I think we are all slightly aware of. But ... whether it is a product of the tenure that most [Solicitors-General] enjoy, or the status of the office, or the de facto durability of the office, as is certainly the case in New South Wales, I suppose it has the capacity to make a Solicitor-General think, well I am the real embodiment of what is right, and what is more, I don't have a political axe to grind like those people, so why don't they listen ... to me.

This consensus that the Solicitor-General must not act independently in the public interest is entirely consistent with the intention behind the statute, and with the conclusions in chapter four, section VI.B. about the proper interpretation of the legal position. That is not to say that participants thought that the role of the Solicitor-General did not contribute, in many other ways, to advancing the public interest. What participants refused to accept, however, was that the Solicitor-General might be able to act independently in what are essentially political matters.

[241] Interview, Peter Garrisson; Interview, Stephen McLeish; Interview, Pamela Tate, who explained that in Victoria this involves, on occasion, expressly advising on the compatibility of a draft Bill with the human rights protected under the Victorian *Charter of Human Rights and Responsibilities Act 2006*, in the light of which further policy development may be required.

[242] Interview, William Bale; Interview, Trevor Griffin; Interview, Martin Hinton; Interview, Thomas Hughes; Interview, Patrick Keane; Interview, Philip Ruddock.

Western Australian Attorney-General Michael Mischin explained that, unlike the DPP, who is vested with statutory functions to *act* independently in the public interest, the Solicitor-General is vested with the functions of being an advocate and an adviser. The officeholder must act independently, but is responsible to the state and must *act* only on instructions.

Many participants accepted that the Solicitor-General has an important role in *advising* the government about the appropriate position of the government in relation to the public interest—both in the development of policies and in defence of the government's interests in the courts. But this role is always circumscribed because final responsibility must remain with the Attorney-General (or other relevant minister).

Former Commonwealth Solicitor-General Anthony Mason explained how, within the advisory function, the Solicitor-General could contribute to the achievement of important public law ideals such as respect for fundamental rights:

> Even if the advice that was sought did not seek advice in relation to the impact of policies on the rights of individuals, then if it occurred, that they had not been taken into account, or inadequately taken into account, then I would have felt it necessary to point that out. I just don't see in giving legal advice, how it would be proper not to draw to attention consequences of that kind.

Former Commonwealth Attorney-General Robert McClelland said that he welcomed advice that assisted the government in achieving its policy objectives while maintaining fidelity to broader governance objectives.[243] McClelland's views were largely reflected in the position taken by his Solicitor-General, Stephen Gageler. Congruence between Attorneys-General and Solicitors-General on this issue was also apparent in Queensland. Former Attorney-General Rodney Welford said the Solicitor-General was resorted to

> where you wanted a *legal* view but a legal view that wasn't based on the current law, that was based on what was the appropriate positioning of government in relation to the law. … [I]f you wanted to ask a question, 'would it be *appropriate* for the State to legislate to do X?' the Solicitor-General would be able to give you that bigger picture issue based on a combination of legal philosophy, an understanding of the institutions of the State, and State interests.

His Solicitor-General for a large period of that time, Patrick Keane, echoed those views, saying that the Solicitor-General's office ought to be looking to promote the 'unifying themes of government'.[244]

South Australian Solicitor-General Martin Hinton explained that the 'ethical principles' that guide government lawyers and Solicitors-General are not a 'subjective appraisal of performance or any attempt to impose one's own value system'. The principles that the Solicitor-General should be taking into account are

[243] Similar views were expressed in Interview, Christian Porter.

[244] Greg Cooper, currently Crown Solicitor of Queensland, who held the position as Crown Counsel for a large part of Keane's tenure as Solicitor-General, also echoed these views.

objective criteria discernible from history, convention, the Constitution, notions of representative government and responsible government, the rule of law and the common law. He also indicated that the ethical principles that should guide the Solicitor-General in providing advice apply to all lawyers acting for the government, but with particular force to the Solicitor-General because 'the weight that will attach in government circles to an opinion of the Solicitor-General requires that he or she applies the principles and values that inform how government should be practised'.[245]

Former Northern Territory Solicitor-General Thomas Pauling used prospectivity as an example of when the Solicitor-General ought to provide advice on broader government principles. In relation to the impact of government on individual rights, he also said that while it did not often arise, 'on occasions you would give the "this is using a sledgehammer to crack a nut" sort of advice'. He saw his role as providing alternative legal options to the government that would allow it to achieve its political objectives in a way that did not transgress basic rights.

The principle that the Solicitor-General must, or ought to, advise on underlying constitutional principles has resonance with the perspective, noted above in section II.A.i., that the office has a role in checking power for the benefit of the community and individuals within it. While this was not the dominant view of the role (the role's importance in giving certainty and security to the government was seen as far more vital), the acceptance by a number of participants of a role to advise the government on underlying constitutional principles demonstrates the conceptual difficulties of separating working for the government and working for the public.

Not all participants agreed with the view that the Solicitor-General should provide advice beyond the law on broader government principles. For example, in direct contrast to Pauling's position, his successor, Michael Grant, emphatically took the opposite view.[246] He explained that he was not government's 'moral arbiter': 'So if it is within the ball park of being lawful, that is a matter for them.' He provided a number of reasons why he took this view. He first emphasised that the view was rooted in a trust in government and majoritarian democracy: he trusted that the government, advised by the policy division, would respect the principles of government on which representative democracy in Australia is based.[247] He also believed that, so as to be properly accountable, it was important that politicians took full responsibility for their decisions.[248] If he started to offer advice on

[245] M Hinton, 'The Courts, the Executive and the Solicitor-General' in Appleby, Keyzer and Williams (eds), above n 116, 67, 79. See also Interview, Leigh Sealy.

[246] See also the view of David Bennett in J Eyers, 'Putting Words to Music in the Constitution's Case', *Australian Financial Review* (Sydney), 2008. He said as a barrister, including his time as Solicitor-General, 'I don't form a view on the justice, or correctness, or desirability, or moral worthiness or unworthiness, of my client—that's not my job.'

[247] See also Interview, Stephen McLeish.

[248] See also Interview, Geoffrey Davies.

non-legal governmental principles, he explained, 'there is a tendency for politicians to abrogate their responsibilities in relation to those sorts of things, because that is what they're elected for, and once you start doing that, you're undermining the democratic process'. And lastly, he was concerned that the respect accorded by the government to his legal advice would be similarly accorded to other advice he might proffer on policy questions, an area where opinions are not final and where it is proper to engage in a dialogue about whether circumstances warrant deviations from a general position. To Grant's views could be added the definitional criticism that the public interest lacks definitional rigidity, giving rise to concerns that individuals could use it as a cover to press personal political agendas. Fiona Hanlon has also argued that if the Solicitor-General were to offer advice beyond the strictly legal, it could result in 'the executive government looking elsewhere for legal advice and encourage further the use of private sector lawyers'.[249]

Former South Australian Solicitor-General John Doyle could not see any role for the Solicitor-General to provide advice on the public interest in government policy creation, and nor did he believe the office was well equipped to do so. He said:

> No, not a role, nor is there a mechanism. In other words, government policies, even in the legal area, the loosely legal area, weren't routinely, as far as I'm aware, run past Solicitors-General, so the opportunity to comment didn't arise. In other words, the platform of information wasn't there.[250]

Counter-arguments exist to many of the objections. To avoid any potential confusion, advice on issues relating to the non-legal might be demarcated from any legal advice. Former South Australian Solicitor-General Bradley Selway wrote:

> A government lawyer must always be meticulous to ensure that advice only involves objective standards of behaviour or, at least, that it is clear to the client what parts of the advice relate to matters where the client is bound to comply and what parts relate to matters where the client's policy opinion is the ultimate determinant.[251]

The lack of democratic legitimacy of the statutory office of Solicitor-General reflects that the obligation is simply one of advice: the final decision rests with a democratically elected and responsible officer, usually the Attorney-General.[252] Commonwealth Solicitor-General Justin Gleeson indicated that he would, on occasion, provide advice on matters of legal policy, such as the desirability of retrospective legislation. He certainly considered this function as 'within the penumbra of the role', and particularly where the proposed measure 'may be quite radical in its effect'. But he was careful to make sure that his advice was clear when it

[249] Hanlon, above n 121, 250.

[250] See also Interview, Gavan Griffith.

[251] Selway, above n 8, 121–22, referring to L Curtis and G Kolts, 'The Role of the Government Lawyer in the Protection of Citizens' Rights' (1975) 49 *Australian Law Journal* 335, 338–39, 342.

[252] Interview, Martin Hinton; Interview, Greg Parker; Interview, Michael Mischin.

concerned these areas, and that it could be overridden by the government as a matter of policy:

> I do think it's important where, if I was to say something which I think is not really what the High Court will say tomorrow or in the next couple of years which is foreseeable but is just a warning that this is … bad in terms of the rule of law, please think about that before you do it, you need to be very clear … where the dividing line is, and that I am not trespassing into what is a political judgement.

The exercise of restraint on the part of the Solicitor-General in these matters, for Gleeson, was also part of protecting the independence of the office:

> I think a large amount of reserve is needed in my position to make sure I'm not, and I'm not seen to be, trespassing into what is a political decision, for which there is true accountability to Parliament, and ultimately the electors … Knowing what is no longer your area. … [T]he extent to which things stray into legal policy, I think keeping the divide is incredibly important. And we only need to look at what's happened to other people at the moment in the public sphere—who are statutory officeholders, or who otherwise hold important government positions—to see how easy it is to be criticised for being so called 'political', even though the person is only carrying out the job as they think they should be carrying it out. … [T]here has to be, I think, an acute degree of reserve.

If it is accepted that one dimension of the Solicitor-General's role is to provide advice on questions of broader government policy, a further difficulty arises because of the inherent debate around the idea and content of the 'public interest'. South Australian Solicitor-General Martin Hinton indicated that the Solicitor-General should only advise on procedural, formal issues that relate to good and ethical governance over which partisan division is irrelevant, rather than the public interest at large.[253] He explained that the operation of the rule of law, democracy and federalism are such issues. Further, Hinton explained, as had Hutchinson in his scholarship,[254] that the operation of the these principles is, unlike perhaps other, more substantive public interest questions, an area in which the Solicitor-General has particular acumen.[255]

IV. Discussion: The Solicitor-General as Adviser

The advisory aspect of the Solicitor-General's role is often viewed as its most significant contribution to the constitutional system, and particularly to the promotion of the rule of law. The office can, in this function, contribute to the

[253] Interview, Martin Hinton.

[254] AC Hutchinson, 'In the Public Interest: The Responsibilities and Rights of Government Lawyers' (2008) 46 *Osgoode Hall Law Journal* 105, 120–21.

[255] ibid.

protection of individuals against abuses of power by the government and assist in relations between the three branches of government. However, there was a large consensus among participants that the advisory function's purpose was primarily to assist and protect the Executive as the office's client. The Solicitor-General's advice gave the Executive legal and political confidence in its policies, although this role was open to abuse by governments seeking to gain political security using the Solicitor-General's advice.

Despite the general consensus on this point, there was some evidence of conflict in the perceptions between Attorneys-General and Solicitors-General as to the extent to which the Solicitor-General should be accommodating of Executive policy objectives in advising on areas of law where there was some ambiguity. I argued in chapter four that the Solicitor-General's statutory function as counsel required him or her to provide his or her best possible objective assessment of the law, or, in cases of genuine legal ambiguity where there was no clearly preferable answer, to inform the Executive that the position was genuinely indeterminate, allowing the government to decide the most appropriate path to take. What the interviews revealed was that Attorneys-General were more likely to view the Executive's political objectives as legitimate influences on the Solicitor-General's role than were Solicitors-General themselves, who saw their role in terms of my analysis: to expound the law objectively without reference to political goals. It can thus be seen that political pressures on the legal role that were present in the traditional ministerial model of the Law Officers continue to exist, despite the intention behind the legislation to insulate the Solicitor-General from such politics.

There was also a lack of consensus among participants about the office's role *beyond* advising on the strict legal position. There was a large amount of conformity in responses to the effect that the Solicitor-General has a role in advising and warning the government on strategic points, and also the government-specific concept of advice taking into account whole-of-government issues. However, there was significant division among responses about whether the office had an obligation to provide advice on the impact of Executive policy on 'core government principles', or whether that was even desirable. This schism reflected a division about the extent to which the Solicitor-General could, or should, advise on issues that have no objective legal grounding and are governed by concepts on which politicians often disagree. As such, many thought the Solicitor-General to be unqualified and unaccountable in this domain. Others, however, saw this as part of the office's role in assisting the government to fulfil its underlying duties to the public interest. What was clear from those who accepted some role in advising on the 'core government principles' was that the Solicitor-General was not in this respect advising on the substance of the government's policy. Instead, the Solicitor-General was advising on the congruency between the proposed actions or decisions with underlying constitutional principles, and considering alternative methods to achieve the government's policy that had a greater degree of conformity to these principles.

These divergences among participants is not unexpected. While I concluded that the best interpretation of the statute, in light of its provenance, is that the Solicitor-General has a duty to advise on the 'core government principles', this is the first time this view has been definitively put forward in relation to the Solicitor-General.[256] Further, the relevance of the public interest to the advisory function, while it has been expounded in some British and Australian literature, is not a well-publicised aspect of the Law Officers' traditional public interest role, in contrast, for example, to the historical role in bringing prosecutions or pursuing other public interest litigation.

While the difference of opinion transcended eras, jurisdictions and political parties, there was some congruence between the expectations of Attorneys-General who had appointed their Solicitors-General. Labor Attorneys-General were more likely to look for a Solicitor-General who provides advice across these 'core government principles', and this would often therefore be reflected in the views of officeholders that they had appointed (for example, the congruence between former Commonwealth Attorney-General Robert McClelland and former Commonwealth Solicitor-General Stephen Gageler, and former Queensland Attorney-General Rodney Welford and former Queensland Solicitor-General Patrick Keane).

The importance of the Solicitor-General's advisory function rests upon a number of assumptions: about the status of the Solicitor-General's office, the nature of the client, the finality of the Solicitor-General's advice, the use of the Solicitor-General and the independence of the office. While, by and large, the experience and practice of the study's participants indicated that these assumptions were met, there were a number of exceptions. The several examples that participants provided where the Solicitor-General was 'frozen out' of government work because of conflicts, whether with the Attorney-General or the bureaucracy, highlight a potential frailty in the office's framework and the lack of exclusivity of its functions. As long as these instances represent exceptions to the generally accepted practice, they are not necessarily cause for concern. But those within government should be vigilant to ensure this is the case, otherwise they may lose the relevance of an office that can play an important function in the overarching constitutional order.

There was remarkable variation among the participants' views of the role of the Solicitor-General as properly embedded in the government machine, being consulted on policy as it was developed, or simply being a barrister to be briefed on the occasions where the government decided it required advice. The responses demonstrate two emerging approaches to the role of the Solicitor-General. By identifying these two approaches I do not want to suggest that there are only two possible approaches as within this dichotomy there is a plurality of legal experience, and

[256] Note Selway, above n 8, 8, but Selway did not consider whether this role continued for the statutory Solicitor-General position.

individual approaches existed along a spectrum between them. The first approach mirrored, as closely as possible, a private barrister on permanent retainer for the Crown: I call this approach that of an '*autonomous expert*'. In accordance with this approach, the Crown chooses when to consult the Solicitor-General and on what issues. This raises questions about whether the Solicitor-General is able to fulfil the traditional role of Law Officer, that is, of monitoring the Crown's compliance with the law. The Solicitor-General may be called upon to assist from time to time, but is by no means an integral and essential part of policy development. This approach, for example, was reflected in the Queensland framework, where the Solicitor-General retains private chambers and private practice, and government work is briefed to the Solicitor-General's chambers. In Western Australia, where a similar framework was introduced in 2012 with the appointment of a leading barrister from the private Bar, although government chambers were retained, it was anticipated that the office would operate in a similar way.[257]

The second approach was of the Solicitor-General involved as a vital and proactive part of the policy development process. This approach manifested itself to differing degrees along a spectrum. This is a far more integrated view of the office, and I call it the '*team member*' approach to the role. Under this perception, the office is involved not only in providing constitutional advice when briefed, but in assisting government to achieve the legally most appropriate outcome in a variety of policy areas. These two approaches—'autonomous expert' and 'team member'—will be returned to in chapter seven, in the more detailed discussion of the office's independence.

The nature of the legal framework governing the office of Solicitor-General means that both of these approaches are able to be accommodated within it. From my data, a number of tentative observations can be made about the nature of those who preferred one approach over another. It appears that there has been a generational shift away from the second approach towards the first in the last decade. In the last half of the twentieth century, there were a number of Solicitors-General actively involved in government. Examples of this are former Victorian Solicitor-General Daryl Dawson's regular meetings with the heads of departments, or former New South Wales Solicitor-General Keith Mason's mini-committee comprising the Solicitor-General, Parliamentary Counsel, the Director-General and the Crown Solicitor. More recently, however, this has decreased. In Victoria, former Victorian Solicitor-General Pamela Tate actively attempted to ensure that legal issues crystallised before she was asked to consider them, especially when different government departments or agencies had differing perspectives on those issues, so that she had not tarnished her ability to consider those issues objectively by close involvement early on. Similarly, it appeared that after the commercialisation of legal services at the Commonwealth level, the Solicitor-General operated as a barrister briefed, predominantly, in the government's High Court constitutional

[257] Interview, Christian Porter.

litigation, but not involved in the extensive legal issues that arose in the myriad of other policy areas.

Findings of two recent reviews into government legal services at the federal level also commented on the decreased intimacy of the Commonwealth Solicitor-General's involvement in broader government policy development. The reports not only support the interview data to the effect that during the 1980s and 1990s, the engagement of the Solicitor-General with government became less intimate (resulting in the distance that is characteristic of the 'autonomous expert' approach), but they also introduce another important explanatory factor to the approaches. The institutional structure of government legal services may influence the approach taken. In a system where government legal services are being provided from the government provider (for example, the AGS) in fierce competition with private firms, firms that have their own set of favourite barristers, it seems natural that the Solicitor-General drifts towards an 'autonomous expert'.

'Transition' between the two approaches has at times been difficult to implement. Ralph Turner has described the phenomenon of 'role persistence': role structures, once stabilised, tend to persist despite changes in actors who may be filling the roles.[258] There is some evidence of this phenomenon in the transitions attempted in Victoria and the Commonwealth. Tate explained how she, in consultation with the government, developed a written protocol about how she intended to operate as Solicitor-General to effect changes in the governmental culture. Gageler encountered hurdles when he attempted to place the Solicitor-General back into the development of policy across many areas of government to better accord with his view of the proper role of the Solicitor-General.

[258] RH Turner, 'Role Theory' in JH Turner (ed), *Handbook of Sociological Theory* (Springer, 2001) 233, 241, 251.

6

The Solicitor-General as Advocate

In many Australian jurisdictions, the perceived benefit of permanent counsel appearing with regularity in the highest appellate courts—particularly the High Court—to protect government interests underpinned the Solicitor-General's establishment. The advocacy function is certainly the oldest, and most public, face of the office. The Solicitor-General's advocacy function differs from providing advice on actions not yet taken, or Bills not yet passed. As an advocate, the Solicitor-General is defending government action from external attack; as an adviser, the Solicitor-General has a role within a system operating under the rule of law, in which the office can assist in checking the legality and integrity of future exercises of government power. Apparent from the US studies of the OSG and OLC is the potential for the two functions to attract different dominant normative frameworks introduced in chapter two, section III.A.; this tendency in the Australian context is explored in this chapter.

Generally, Solicitors-General will act as advocates for their respective governments in appellate courts and the High Court. In some jurisdictions, the Solicitor-General does exclusively High Court work. At the Commonwealth level, the Solicitor-General has also been involved as counsel for Australia in international courts, mirroring the continuing position in the UK. While Australia has only infrequently been a party to international proceedings, when it has, it has often been represented by the Solicitor-General, leading a large international team of senior counsel. For example, Robert Ellicott appeared for the Commonwealth in the French *Nuclear Tests Case*;[1] Justin Gleeson appeared for the Commonwealth in the *Whaling in the Antarctic Case*.[2] Gleeson explained that the Commonwealth Solicitor-General's role in these cases depends on a confluence of factors. This will include the political will of the Government to be involved in an international dispute, as well as a decision by the Attorney-General that the Solicitor-General should lead the legal team in any particular case.[3] He explained that it was not 'an inevitable outcome' that the Solicitor-General would do so, and that the Solicitor-General had not been involved, for example, in certain World Trade Organisation proceedings.

[1] *Australia v France ('Nuclear Tests Case')* [1974] ICJ Reports 253.

[2] *Australia v Japan, New Zealand Intervening ('Whaling in the Antarctic')* (31 March 2014).

[3] Confirmed in Interview, Mark Dreyfus.

I. A Hired Gun: Government Advocate

Despite the large volume of time Solicitors-General must devote to the advocacy aspect of the role, participants' perception of its significance to the constitutional system was that it was not as great as that of the advisory function. Rather than operating to ensure the integrity of government action, the protection of the rule of law and the separation of powers, the advocacy function was seen more simply as acting on the instructions of the Executive to defend its actions in the court. As such, the idea that the Solicitor-General must act with 'independence' was less prevalent in relation to this function. South Australian Solicitor-General Martin Hinton explained that 'the relative freedom that the Solicitor-General has in advising government as to the practice of government is constrained when he or she appears in court. In court, the Solicitor-General must act in accordance with instructions'.

Former Commonwealth Attorney-General Robert Menzies said in 1936 (speaking of the role of Attorney-General as advocate, which was more common at that time, but the principle is equally applicable to that of Solicitor-General as advocate):

> When an Attorney-General goes into court to argue on behalf of the Crown, he has exactly the same duty as any other advocate. He owes to his client all the zeal, all the industry, all the honesty, all the skill that he possesses. If he allows his own personal views and prejudices to cloud the submission that he will make, then he fails in his duty as an advocate. If it were not so—if an advocate presenting a case were at liberty to say 'I will not have that because I hold views to the contrary'—he would be acting as a judge rather than an advocate.[4]

When the Opposition responded to Menzies that perhaps there ought to be a distinction between acting for the Crown and appearing for a private client, Menzies asserted that such a proposition would mean 'a government is to go into court crippled'.[5]

But the 'hired gun'[6] or 'warrior'[7] perception was tempered by what all participants accepted were the overarching obligations of the Solicitor-General to the court as a legal professional. Former New South Wales Solicitor-General Keith Mason's summary of the advocacy function captured the interplay between these sentiments. He said, 'I think, by and large, … I felt able to operate the way barristers do. I'm a hired gun. I'll fight as hard as I can—within the limits of what is proper—for you.'

[4] Commonwealth, *Parliamentary Debates*, House of Representatives, 1 October 1936, 770.
[5] ibid.
[6] Interview, Keith Mason.
[7] Interview, Dean Wells.

Many Solicitors-General stressed that as legal practitioners, their obligations to the court meant that they would only act on instructions where the position was 'legally available'[8] or 'arguable'.[9] Former South Australian Solicitor-General Chris Kourakis explained how he grappled with this obligation when asked to bring a controversial appeal in the case of *R v Nemer*.[10] The case was an appeal against a sentence imposed in accordance with a plea bargain that had been made between the DPP and defence counsel.[11] There was a large public outcry at the perceived leniency of the sentence.[12] The DPP advised that he would be reluctant to lodge an appeal, and the Premier announced he would have the matter re-examined by the Solicitor-General, who advised there were good prospects of success. A direction was issued by the Attorney-General to the DPP to lodge the appeal, although it was argued by the Solicitor-General.[13] Kourakis' decision to argue the appeal was very controversial. He recalled:

> [T]he DPP people were literally lobbying me not to bring that appeal, and giving me authority after authority about it, about Crown appeals only being brought when there's something that shocks the public conscience, and the whole double jeopardy thing. They had formed the opinion that because they as DPP officers thought the appeal would be unsuccessful it should not be brought.

Kourakis, however, disagreed. As counsel representing the Crown he acted on the instructions of the Cabinet:

> The Government wanted to appeal. They are the client: the Cabinet. They took the view that the sentence didn't reflect the public conscience as to the sentence that should have been imposed. My opinion was that if they wanted to appeal, then the appeal should be brought as long as I thought it had reasonable prospects.

His conviction that he must act in accordance with the wishes of his client was tempered only by his obligation to the Court:

> As Solicitor-General … I would have thought I had made the wrong call … if the Court were to say that my appeal was completely unarguable. From my point of view provided the appeal was properly and reasonably arguable, then that would have vindicated my decision to appeal.

The State won the appeal, 2:1.

The idea of the Solicitor-General as a hired gun, acting in cases even where he or she may disagree with the cause, or think the government may be unsuccessful, came out in a number of interviews in the context of the State anti-organised

[8] Interview, Patrick Keane.

[9] Interview, Geoffrey Davies; Interview, Patrick Keane.

[10] *R v Nemer* (2003) 87 SASR 168.

[11] *R v Paul Habib Nemer and K* (Sentencing Remarks, Supreme Court of South Australia, Sulan J, 25 July 2003, No 146/2003).

[12] C Hockley, 'Power of the People', *The Advertiser* (Adelaide) (31 July 2003), 1. See further discussion of the case in RN Moles, *A State of Injustice* (Thomas C Lothian, 2004) ch 14.

[13] C Hockley, 'What judge wasn't told', *The Advertiser* (Adelaide) (7 August 2003), 1.

crime legislation. In the last decade, many State jurisdictions introduced control-order regimes, vesting the courts with the power to issue orders against members of criminal organisations that contained a number of limits on their liberties, such as freedom of movement and freedom of speech.[14] South Australia, New South Wales and Queensland had parts of their legislative schemes challenged in the High Court on the basis of a breach of implications arising out of Chapter III of the Constitution.[15] The Solicitors-General of these States were called upon to defend the State legislation's constitutionality and were supported by other Solicitors-General representing their Attorneys-General, intervening. One Solicitor-General said:

> See, I have a personal view about the [Act]. I think it is a stupid law. I think it will not achieve what it is intended to achieve. I think to have control orders as the centre of your approach to dealing with organised crime is … just lax, considering what is organised crime and how it spreads its tentacles. I just think it is ill-conceived. And yet I have to stand up and sound all very convincing, or attempt to sound like I believe what I'm saying before the High Court, when I say there is nothing wrong with this law.

Another took the view:

> The legislation is there. Some jurisdictions have this kind of legislation, some don't: that is a policy question. Once the legislation is in existence then of course we would, or I would, argue for its validity, in the High Court. And while I might have, I'm not saying what it is, while I might have, or I could have, a view on the merits on that kind of that legislation, or whether it is a good policy proposal, that would be completely irrelevant to the function of defending its validity.

In a broader context, former Queensland Solicitor-General Walter Sofronoff said that like any barristers, Solicitors-General must act even when they personally disagree with the government's case, commenting that the 'psychology is no different in the context of defending repellent legislation, as when acting for a repellent client'.

The hired gun perspective demonstrated that an important aspect of the role of Solicitors-General was to remain objective and independent from their own moral views as to the government position, in accordance with the dominant view of legal ethics and independence[16] and the ideals of the Bar, as reflected in professional obligations such as the cab-rank rule.

Many participants saw the advocacy function as mirroring the function performed on behalf of a private client. However, as the *government's* advocate, the function has an additional constitutional significance. It ensures that the powers of the government as a polity are protected so that it can meet its obligations

[14] This has been introduced in a number of jurisdictions, see, eg, the *Serious and Organised Crime (Control) Act 2008* (SA); *Crimes (Criminal Organisations Control) Act 2009* (NSW); *Criminal Organisation Act 2009* (Qld); *Serious Crime Control Act 2009* (NT).

[15] *South Australia v Totani* (2010) 242 CLR 1; *Wainohu v New South Wales* (2011) 243 CLR 181; *Condon v Pompano Pty Ltd* (2013) 252 CLR 38.

[16] See further discussion of these in ch 4, section III.A.ii.

and implement its policies. Further, some participants commented that the Solicitor-General's advocacy function ensured that an officeholder was aware of the current position of the High Court on legal questions and therefore was able to advise the government with far greater accuracy about the strength of a legal argument.[17] Thus, as AJ Balfour had similarly observed in England in 1901[18] and as has been observed of the all-in-one New Zealand model,[19] the Solicitor-General's advocacy function was perceived as significantly strengthening the office's capacity to perform the advisory function, thus giving greater security and certainty to government action.

A. The Government's Interests

If the Australian Solicitor-General is a hired gun for government interests, how are these defined? In Britain, Neil Walker identified the difficulty of differentiating the long-term interests of the Crown from those of the democratically elected government of the day.[20] In his 1999 examination of the tensions in the English Law Officers' roles, Walker explained that the Law Officers' long association with the abstract idea of the 'Crown' underlies and often obscures those tensions. Because of the historical evolution of this term, it is no longer possible to sufficiently distinguish between the enduring 'Executive government' (divorced from the political Executive), and the 'government of the day' and its political objectives.[21] This confusion, Walker argued, allowed unscrupulous officeholders to pursue narrowly political ends in the name of the public interest, and invoke, as an alibi, the gravitas of the position.[22]

Participants in my Australian study saw the Solicitor-General as a hired gun not for the short-term political interests of the government of the day, but for the government's interests as an enduring constitutional polity. As such, the Solicitor-General had a role in advising the government on the most appropriate position to be taken in relation to protecting the long-term interests of the constitutional polity, which from time to time is occupied by different administrations. Former Commonwealth Solicitor-General Stephen Gageler explained that he saw his role as an advocate as putting forward arguments that would protect the polity in a sense of its long-term interests, and not simply for short-term political interests:

> [The Commonwealth] is ill-defined: there are tensions; there are ambiguities. I think that I have not, in my two and a half years in office, encountered circumstances where I felt

[17] Interview, Michael Grant; Interview, Walter Sofronoff; Interview, Justin Gleeson; Interview, Rob Mitchell.

[18] See ch 2, section I.B.

[19] See ch 2, section III.B.

[20] N Walker, 'The Antinomies of the Law Officers' in M Sunkin and S Payne (eds), *The Nature of the Crown: A Legal and Political Analysis* (Oxford University Press, 1999) 135, 147.

[21] ibid, 147.

[22] ibid, 161. See also B Ackerman, 'Abolish the White House Counsel: And the Office of Legal Counsel, too, while we're at it', *Slate*, 22 April 2009.

> that my instructions were inconsistent with what I regarded as the long-term interests of the polity, where I was not able to seek a revision to those instructions, to really fit with my own view as to what is to be done. Minor adjustments.
>
> *Do you think it is part of your role to seek those revisions, and perhaps advise on those broader issues?*
>
> Yes, absolutely. I feel to some extent I'm a custodian of a legal tradition, and a moral tradition.

While ultimately participants who took this position accepted that their advice on what was in the best interests of the polity could be overridden by instructions from the Attorney-General as the elected and responsible member of the government and the representative of the Crown in litigation, there was still an important role in having the Solicitor-General providing a legal perspective on the position that ought to be taken.

Western Australian Solicitor-General Grant Donaldson saw it as part of his role to advise the government where he thought that its actions or instructions came into conflict with the long-term interests of Western Australia. He said:

> [I]f I formed the view that [the government's position or instructions were] contrary to the interests of the state, I would advise on that without batting an eyelid. And I would be very surprised if any Attorney-General or Premier expected otherwise.

He also indicated that if the circumstance should ever arise where he thought the Attorney's instructions were not in the best interests of the state, and that the Attorney was on a 'frolic' and could not be convinced otherwise, he would seek to speak to the Premier, in consultation with the Attorney, to clarify those instructions. However, he would ultimately accept the decision of the government:

> If I thought it was a contention that couldn't be put up [to the Court] consistent with my professional obligations, well I wouldn't put it up. But if, if the view was, look government, in my view this isn't in the best interests of the state for these reasons, (a), (b), (c), and their view was, well we think it is in the best interests of the state … well, they're elected … to make those decisions.

What amounted to the government's best interests differed among participants, and two main positions can be extracted. The first equates the government's best interests with government power and the protection of it. The second defines the government's best interests in a more holistic way, and so protection of government power is only one aspect of it, and must be balanced against other public policy principles, such as democracy or the protection of individual rights. These other principles accord with the 'core government principles' introduced in chapter four, section VI.B. as part of the Solicitor-General's enduring role to protect and promote the public interest in the advisory function.

Under the first view, locating the government's interests is relatively easy. However, under the second view, in balancing the different principles, there is the possibility that legitimate differences in where the government's interests lie may emerge. The Solicitor-General's legal expertise, experience and understanding of the government's position will place the officeholder in a unique position to advise the government on the intersection of these interests and the appropriate position of the government. However, ultimately, the possibility of legitimate divergence of views means that the Solicitor-General must defer to the Attorney-General's instructions to ensure that contentious decisions about the government's interests are made within an accountable framework, even at the expense of consistency in the government's position before the court.

i. First View: Protecting Government Power

At the start of the twentieth century, English Attorney-General Rufus Isaacs defended the taking of a technical legal defence in court. He said that as Attorney-General, unless expressly instructed to do otherwise, he was 'bound … to maintain the Crown prerogative'.[23] Similar views have been expressed by Solicitors-General in Australia. In 1996, then Commonwealth Solicitor-General Gavan Griffith expressed the following view in a report to the Attorney-General, in reference to the case of *Victoria v Commonwealth*:[24]

> [T]his litigation confirms the truism that it is always in the interests of an incumbent Government to argue for the vindication of Commonwealth power. It is a matter of policy rather than power whether constitutional power should be exercised. But all exercise of power must be defended. There is a very limited scope for policy input where the Commonwealth appears to defend the Constitution.[25]

Former Queensland Solicitor-General Geoffrey Davies recollected his role in protecting the Queensland body politic's power in the *Mabo* litigation.[26] The litigation involved claims for legal recognition of indigenous land rights. In 1982, three plaintiffs commenced proceedings against Queensland. The Queensland National Bjelke-Petersen government, which was in power, had initially rigorously defended the action. After the change of government in 1989, Davies advised the Goss Labor Cabinet on the matter. Davies recalled that the Labor government did not want to continue to defend the claims because politically it supported the plaintiffs. Davies, however, counselled against this position:

> I was really telling them I thought they should [defend the claims] because it did involve governmental powers which they would lose, and they did. But they were very keen, for political reasons, to be seen to be not standing in the way of land rights for Aboriginal people. And I remember having to go to Cabinet, and speak to Cabinet about that to tell them why I thought that it should be argued. And my arguments were entirely legal and constitutional arguments. And they kept coming back to me with political things, and I kept telling them, well I'm not going to answer political questions, … these are the

[23] HC Deb 6 April 1911, vol 23, cols 2466–70, see further discussion in ch 2, section I.A.

[24] *Victoria v Commonwealth* (1996) 187 CLR 416 ('*Industrial Relations Act Case*').

[25] G Griffith, 'Report: Second Law Officer to the First Law Officer 1 July 1995–31 December 1996' (Solicitor-General of Australia, 1996) [1.9]. See also Interview, Thomas Hughes.

[26] *Mabo v Queensland (No 1)* (1988) 166 CLR 186; *Mabo v Queensland (No 2)* (1992) 175 CLR 1.

reasons why I say we should. And eventually, because we had a lawyer as Premier I think, they went ahead to argue it.

Another example comes from the constitutional position adopted by former Commonwealth Solicitor-General Maurice Byers throughout his tenure. Byers was appointed by the Whitlam Labor Government. Constitutionally, the Whitlam Government had views that accorded with Byers' own, particularly around federal powers, and that the grants of legislative power to the Commonwealth in section 51 of the Constitution ought to be interpreted broadly.[27] After the dismissal of the Whitlam Government in 1975, Byers served under the Liberal Fraser Government, which was more committed to federalism and the autonomy of the States within the federation. When asked about how the change affected his approach to the role of Solicitor-General, Byers said:

> Well, [the Fraser Government] were no different from the others. They were as much in favour of wide Commonwealth powers as any other government, and all Commonwealth governments will be in favour of wide powers ... When a question comes to the validity of their legislation, you watch, they'll be in favour of it. All governments want to preserve their legislation; it's like their self-respect, because it looks like a slap in the face, and they're always thinking about votes. They think, well, the population will think we've been behaving illegally, if their legislation is held to be invalid, so they behave in the normal way ...[28]

One former High Court Justice, Ian Callinan, thought that in many cases the States and the Commonwealth were *not* acting in accordance with the long-term interests of the government in the sense of protecting government power. In his view, formed from his experience on the bench, both State and Commonwealth Solicitors-General were often arguing robustly for the protection of short-term political interests, at the expense of the longer-term interests of the polity in terms of legislative and executive powers. Callinan pointed to two cases—*Mabo (No 2)* and *Coleman v Power*[29]—to demonstrate his point. In relation to *Mabo (No 2)*, Callinan asserted that the landmark native title case was won against a single, *weak* contradictor. He did not believe the interests of the State (in terms of protecting the State's powers) had been robustly protected. As the discussion of Davies' recollection of *Mabo* above demonstrates, this probably reflects the fact that politically, the Goss Labor government of Queensland politically wanted to support the Indigenous claimants.

Coleman v Power, Callinan said, was a 'clear occasion' when no advocate provided the Court with arguments protecting the powers of the States or the Commonwealth. In that case, Queensland defended a challenge to its legislation prohibiting

[27] Daniel Connell, Interview with Maurice Byers (Law in Australian Society Oral History Project, 10 January 1997) 47.

[28] ibid, 60–61.

[29] *Coleman v Power* (2004) 220 CLR 1.

the use of insulting words in a public place based on the implied freedom of political communication. In its submissions, Queensland, and many of the other States and the Commonwealth (intervening), accepted the correctness of the earlier judicial test expounded in *Lange v Australian Broadcasting Corporation* for when a law will be in breach of the implied freedom.[30] Further, Queensland conceded that the challenged legislation was capable of burdening communication, thus leaving the only question in issue whether the legislation was an appropriate and adapted means of achieving a legitimate government objective. In his judgment, Callinan J strongly criticised Queensland's position, on the basis that the government did not ask the Court to reconsider the *Lange* test, and the government's concession of the first limb, that is, that the legislation was capable of burdening communication.[31]

In a similar vein to Callinan's criticisms, James Allan publicly criticised the Commonwealth Solicitor-General for concessions made in the electoral case of *Rowe v Electoral Commissioner.*[32] The Commonwealth's submissions accepted the plaintiffs' formulation of an implied constitutional test, based substantially on the earlier decision in *Roach v Electoral Commissioner*, that limited the Commonwealth's power to regulate the electoral franchise.[33] Allan's view was that the Commonwealth Solicitor-General ought *never* to concede arguments to the detriment of Commonwealth power. He said, 'the Solicitor-General ought not to have relinquished, permanently, home-field advantage by assuming the correctness of the plaintiff's test, and hence of *Roach* itself'.[34] His comments are consistent with a view of the Solicitor-General as protecting the scope of the government's power, even to the detriment of other constitutional principles or the Solicitor-General's own reputation before the court.

Former Queensland Solicitor-General Patrick Keane responded to the criticism of the position taken by Solicitors-General representing their governments in these cases (he specifically referred to the states' position on the *Mabo* and *Lange* decisions). He explained that, particularly when a government is presented with a judicial test (that is, a test drawn by implication from the text of the Constitution, and subject to judicial formulation), the position can be 'very unstable'. For example, in *Lange*, the High Court had formulated a 'less open-textured' statement of principle than had been given by many of the judges in *Theophanous* and

[30] *Lange v Australian Broadcasting Corporation* (1997) 189 CLR 520 ('*Lange*').

[31] *Coleman v Power* (2004) 220 CLR 1, 109, 112. More recently, see similar comments made by Heydon J in *Wotton v Queensland* (2012) 246 CLR 1, 18 [40]; *Monis v The Queen Monis* (2013) 249 CLR 92, 181–84 [243]–[251].

[32] *Rowe v Electoral Commissioner* (2010) 243 CLR 1.

[33] *Roach v Electoral Commissioner* (2007) 233 CLR 162; J Allan, 'Until the High Court Otherwise Provides' (2011) 55(10) *Quadrant* 35. See also J Allan, 'Stephen Gageler too risk-averse in his advice on Nauru option', *The Australian* (Sydney) (16 September 2011), available at <http://www.theaustralian.com.au/business/legal-affairs/stephen-gageler-too-risk-averse-in-his-advice-on-nauru-option/story-e6frg97x-1226138211343>.

[34] Allan, 'Until the High Court Otherwise Provides', above n 33, 40. See similar criticisms made by Heydon J in *Rowe v Electoral Commissioner* (2010) 243 CLR 1, 94.

Stephens.[35] Once presented with *Lange*, 'the last thing anyone wanted to do was open up the possibility of an even more unstable statement'. Therefore 'dying in a ditch' for an interpretation of the constitutional text in a way that better protected the plenitude of legislative power was strategically ill-advised. Often it was better to accept the current formulation of principle from the Court on the basis that at least this was a known principle, particularly if there was some likelihood that the government could win on the formulation. Keane explained:

> If we fought that formulation, the likelihood that we would win on what may then emerge was something no one could guess. … If you invite further judicial development, that development may not favour the party you are representing.

Another way of thinking of the government's interests as the protection of Executive and legislative power is from a democratic viewpoint. This view is supported by comments of Callinan J in *Re McBain; Ex parte Australian Catholic Bishops Conference*.[36] In that case, the Victorian government had accepted a Federal Court decision that found section 8(1) of the *Infertility Treatment Act 1995* (Vic) to be inoperative because of its inconsistency with the *Sex Discrimination Act 1984* (Cth).[37] The Victorian statute, in effect, prevented single women or same-sex couples from receiving IVF treatment while the federal statute prohibited discrimination in the provision of services on the basis of marital status. The defendants in the Federal Court action included Victoria and the responsible minister. Neither had resisted the application for a declaration by the plaintiff (a doctor). The only 'contradictor' came in the form of the Conference of Catholic Bishops,[38] which made submissions in support of the Victorian law as *amicus curiae*. None of the respondents appealed the decision of the Federal Court, but the Conference sought to attack it collaterally through an action in the High Court's original jurisdiction. It did this both in its own name and in a second application as relator in an action brought by the Commonwealth Attorney-General. The majority of the Court rejected the applications on the basis that the actions gave rise to no 'matter' so as to engage the jurisdiction of the Court, because of the lack of any distinct interest in the question for either the Conference or the Commonwealth Attorney-General. Callinan J, in dissent, expressed his reservations that

> the State of Victoria, which is to say the Executive of that State, may deliberately and selectively abstain from enforcing an enactment, indeed a relatively recent enactment of the legislature of that State, whether it has or has not the capacity to persuade the legislature to change or repeal that enactment by a subsequent enactment: and whether in those circumstances some other person might be entitled to do so.[39]

[35] *Lange* (1997) 189 CLR 520; *Theophanous v Herald & Weekly Times* (1994) 182 CLR 104; *Stephens v West Australian Newspapers* (1994) 182 CLR 211.
[36] *Re McBain; Ex parte Australian Catholic Bishops Conference* (2002) 209 CLR 372 ('*Re McBain*').
[37] *McBain v Victoria* (2000) 99 FCR 116.
[38] And its corporate trustee the Episcopal Conference.
[39] *Re McBain* (2002) 209 CLR 372, 476.

A similar situation arose in 2004 when the Commonwealth failed to defend its legislation before the High Court in the *Nauru Appeals Case*.[40] In this case the validity the *Nauru (High Court Appeals) Act 1976* (Cth) was challenged. Section 5 confers jurisdiction on the High Court to hear appeals from the Supreme Court of Nauru. Mr Ruhani, an asylum seeker transferred to Nauru by Australian authorities and placed in immigration detention, appealed to the High Court from a decision of the Supreme Court of Nauru denying his *habeas corpus* application. An objection was filed by the respondent, the Nauruan Director of Police, against the competency of the High Court on the basis that section 5 of the *Nauru (High Court Appeals) Act* was invalid. Despite section 78B notices being issued to Commonwealth and State Attorneys-General,[41] and a direct challenge to the constitutionality of federal legislation being involved, the Commonwealth Attorney-General did not intervene in the proceedings, and therefore the Commonwealth's view on the legal position was not presented to the High Court. It was revealed in the course of the written submissions around costs that the Nauruan Director of Police's costs were being indemnified by the Commonwealth.[42]

Kirby J inferred from these facts that the Commonwealth had taken its position for short-term, political interests, not to protect the institutional interests of the federal polity, which he saw as defending the constitutionality of its legislation and the breadth of its Parliament's legislative power.[43] The federal government had invested a lot of political capital in the offshore processing of asylum seekers, and Nauru had done Australia a political favour in allowing a processing centre to be built in its jurisdiction.

More recently, it was again apparent that governments were taking short-term political positions in constitutional litigation in the case of *Commonwealth v Australian Capital Territory*.[44] A challenge was brought by the Commonwealth against the Australian Capital Territory's *Marriage Equality (Same Sex) Act 2013*, which purported to legalise same-sex marriage in the Territory. The Commonwealth claimed the ACT legislation was inconsistent with the federal *Marriage Act 1961* (Cth), which defined marriage as a union between a man and a woman and expressly forbade the recognition of same-sex marriages from foreign jurisdictions. In determining the question of inconsistency, the Court considered whether the Commonwealth Parliament had the power to enact laws with respect to same-sex marriage under the 'marriage' power in section 51(xxi) of the Constitution. The Commonwealth claimed a broad view of its legislative power: that it

[40] *Ruhani v Director of Police* (2005) 222 CLR 489 ('*Nauru Appeals Case*').

[41] *Judiciary Act 1903* (Cth), s 78B requires notices to be issued to Commonwealth and State Attorneys-General in relation to any matter arising under the Constitution or involving its interpretation. Each Attorney-General has a right to intervene in such a matter under s 78A.

[42] *Nauru Appeals Case* (2005) 222 CLR 489, 558–59; see also commentary at 557–58 (Kirby J). The costs were paid pursuant to a Memorandum of Understanding between Nauru and Australia, which stated that Australia 'will assume full financial responsibility for the administration of activities related to asylum seekers': ibid, 531 (Gummow and Hayne JJ).

[43] ibid, 558–59.

[44] *Commonwealth v Australian Capital Territory* ('*Same-sex Marriage Case*') (2013) 250 CLR 441.

did extend to same-sex marriage. The Australian Capital Territory conceded this point. This ran counter to the general position of the States and Territories in arguing against broad readings of federal legislative power. This concession also meant that it was more difficult for the ACT to argue that its legislation was not inconsistent with the Commonwealth Act. The Territory's concession was likely to have been politically motivated, in the hope that in the future the Commonwealth would legislate for same-sex marriage nationally. No other states or territories intervened in the case. Western Australian Solicitor-General Grant Donaldson explained that he undertook 'a lot of consultation with the Attorney' in the case, because the case had 'consequences in terms of the extent of Commonwealth power' but also had 'political consequences', in terms of being seen to be intervening either in support of same-sex marriage, and the Labor government of the Australian Capital Territory, or against same-sex marriage, and the conservative federal Liberal-National Government.

There was some support among Solicitors-General, the Judiciary and academics for the notion that the Solicitor-General's role as an advocate is to protect the scope of Executive and legislative power against *any* encroachment, although sometimes this position may be conceded for political reasons. This places government power as the ultimate public policy objective, relegating other constitutional policy objectives, including democratic values, the rule of law and federalism ('core government principles'), as secondary.

ii. Second View: Government Power as One Aspect of Constitutional Policy

The second view of the government's interests sees the protection of government power within a broader set of constitutional policy objectives. Participants who took this view did not always see protecting the government's power or defending the validity of legislation as the paramount interests of the Crown; rather, adherence to the Constitution's integrity must be sought while defending the position of the government. The policy objective of protecting and expanding government power must be coupled with recognition of the foundations and limits of the constitutional system. South Australian Solicitor-General Martin Hinton explained that in advising the government what position should be taken in constitutional litigation, an overall perspective of where the Executive sits within the polity and where the State sits in the federal structure needs to be adopted:

> It is true that the decision to intervene and what to put by way of submissions may be influenced by partisan political considerations. But those considerations must be informed by a contemporary and rational appreciation of the federal structure. In these determinations, a Solicitor-General has a real opportunity to play a leading role in the development of his or her body politic's theory of the Constitution and how it works, and to make submissions consistent with that theory. This requires that a Solicitor-General develop a coherent construct as to the interrelationship of the powers of the

> Legislature, Judiciary and Executive under the Constitution and the respective limits of Commonwealth and State power. That is an evolutionary process.[45]

Having a permanent officer in constitutional litigation means a level of expertise in this area can be built up, and the government's position can be presented with continuity across administrations.

A series of cases in the Northern Territory illustrates Hinton's position. The cases also emphasise why a Solicitor-General may be better placed than private practitioners to represent the government polity in matters where the enduring interests of the government polity are concerned. During their successive terms as Solicitor-General, Thomas Pauling (former Solicitor-General) and Michael Grant (the incumbent Solicitor-General) have pursued a theory of the Constitution in which the territories are treated as part of the federation. Their position can be contrasted with the 'disparate' theory, in which the territories sit somewhat outside the compact and do not enjoy the benefits afforded to, or the restrictions placed on, the states.[46] Pauling recounted that after the decision in *Capital Duplicators Pty Ltd v Australian Capital Territory (No 1)*,[47] where the High Court found that the territories were excluded from imposing excise duties under section 90 of the Constitution in the same manner as the states, he made a *deliberate choice* to pursue equal treatment for the territories under the various parts of the Constitution. Pauling decided to do so consistently, seeking the benefits conferred on the states (such as the right to compensation for any acquisition of property under section 51(xxxi)) but also accepting any *limitations* on state power (such as section 90, or the *Kable* principle,[48] which protects the institutional integrity of state courts through an implication found in Chapter III of the Constitution). In this sense, he took a view that seeking equal status with the states in the federation, was in the long-term interests of the Northern Territory, even if it did not always accord with the protection or expansion of the government's power.

North Australian Aboriginal Legal Aid Service v Bradley, a challenge to the appointment of the Chief Magistrate of the Northern Territory, raised the question of whether the *Kable* principle applied to the courts of the Northern Territory.[49] Precedent suggested that territory courts sat outside Chapter III of the Commonwealth Constitution (reflecting the disparate view) and therefore any restrictions imposed on Chapter III courts.[50] Pauling, as Solicitor-General, was briefed to appear with private Senior Counsel. In conference, that Senior Counsel suggested

[45] M Hinton, 'The Courts, the Executive and the Solicitor-General' in G Appleby, P Keyzer and J Williams (eds), *Public Sentinels: A Comparative Study of Australian Solicitor-General* (Ashgate Publishing, 2014) 67, 88.

[46] T Pauling and S Brownhill, 'The Territories and Constitutional Change' (2007) 28 *Adelaide Law Review* 55, 56–59.

[47] *Capital Duplicators Pty Ltd v Australian Capital Territory (No 1)* (1992) 177 CLR 248.

[48] *Kable v Director of Public Prosecutions (NSW)* (1996) 189 CLR 51.

[49] *North Australian Aboriginal Legal Aid Service v Bradley* (2004) 218 CLR 146.

[50] *R v Bernasconi* (1915) 19 CLR 629; *Porter v The King; Ex Parte Yee* (1926) 37 CLR 432, this view is canvassed in Pauling and Brownhill, above n 46, 56–59.

that the Northern Territory might be able to rely upon the disparate view as part of its defence. Pauling recalled:

> I sat down with [him] and I said I'm not going to do that; I haven't spent 14 years turning the High Court's mind around about where we sit in the federation only to throw it away for short-term gain. I am going to get up there and say *Kable* absolutely does apply; no question about it. But in this case, as [counsel] will explain in his statutory construction point, this legislation doesn't offend any of the principles espoused in *Kable* or in later cases.[51]

Pauling said the case demonstrated the importance of having a permanently appointed barrister available to develop the government's position. He explained, 'if you were just briefing people at the Bar, it would be very, very difficult to get them to resist the short-term kill, in ignorance of what the long-term aim is'.

The government's pursuit of its interests in a broader constitutional context does not entirely discount that it is appropriate for the government to argue for the protection of government power, but it rejects the view that this is a singular objective that a government ought to pursue at the expense of others. This understanding of the government's interests raises real questions about the role of the Solicitor-General in determining those interests, and the extent to which Solicitors-General can shape their own instructions, or ignore the instructions of the government that may not accord with their own view of the position. All participants accepted that the Solicitor-General's understanding and pursuit of the government's interests in litigation will always be subject to the instructions of the Attorney-General. In section II. below, I consider the extent to which the Attorney-General (or others) will instruct the Solicitor-General, and find that the Solicitor-General is often given wide discretion in determining the government's position in constitutional matters and in others cases, with few exceptions, the Solicitor-General's advice on the appropriate position is followed.

B. Unique Obligations of the Solicitor-General to the Court

In addition to the Solicitor-General's professional obligations to the court to present only those arguments with legal merit, some participants considered that there were additional expectations between the Solicitor-General and the court that would moderate the traditional hired-gun persona of the barrister. However, not all participants were of this opinion, and some were notably against the proposition.[52]

[51] See also record of submissions in *North Australian Aboriginal Legal Aid Service Inc v Bradley* (2004) 218 CLR 146, 159–60.

[52] Most notably see Interview, Gerard Brennan, where Brennan said, 'I don't think that the office *as such* contributed to any difference in relationship.'

Many participants associated the higher standards of the government as a litigant with the higher obligations owed by the Solicitor-General, as the representative of the government.[53] Others expressly associated the additional obligations of the Solicitor-General with the Crown's obligations to justice and the model litigant principles that have been developed to reflect this.[54] Western Australian Solicitor-General Grant Donaldson, for example, thought that the (High) Court perceived the Commonwealth and the states as quasi-amicus on constitutional matters.

Some participants believed that the courts had even higher expectations for the Solicitor-General's standards of advocacy.[55] Former South Australian Solicitor-General Chris Kourakis said that '[the judges] plainly expect a higher standard of work'. Kourakis also said he thought there was an expectation that the Solicitor-General would bring 'an understanding of the policy issues behind a lot of the legal questions'. The extent to which the court seeks guidance on the government's policy from the Solicitor-General is returned to in section III.B.i. below.

Former Queensland Solicitor-General Patrick Keane rejected the idea that the judges expected more in the sense of 'even-handedness', because as a judge he expected *all* Senior Counsel to be 'fair and even-handed and not to exaggerate their case one way or the other'.[56] However, he did think the Solicitor-General was in a unique position in terms of resourcing. As such, there was an expectation that the Solicitor-General would ensure that all relevant material and arguments were brought before the court; there was an expectation of 'greater thoroughness'.[57]

There was also a sense that, at least since Solicitors-General have secured a stranglehold on constitutional litigation on behalf of the States and the Commonwealth, officeholders would bring great expertise and a wealth of experience in this area with which to assist the Court.[58] Former Commonwealth Solicitor-General and Chief Justice of the High Court, Anthony Mason, said that in addition to expertise, a Solicitor-General could bring institutional knowledge of the government to assist the High Court.

At least one participant was firmly of the opinion that the High Court had expectations of the Solicitor-General, particularly in relation to constitutional matters, that were difficult, if not impossible, to meet. Kourakis explained:

> [The High Court] plainly had very different expectations not only of me but of most of the states' Solicitors-General, as to what they wanted us to do. And we didn't meet it.

[53] Interview, Geoffrey Davies; Interview, Trevor Griffin; Interview, Martin Hinton; Interview, Patrick Keane; Interview, Greg Parker; Interview, Walter Sofronoff; Interview, Dean Wells; Interview, Grant Donaldson.

[54] Interview, Martin Hinton; Interview Patrick Keane; Interview, Greg Parker.

[55] Interview, Stephen Gageler; Interview, Martin Hinton.

[56] Similar view shared by Grant Donaldson.

[57] See also Interview, Robert Ellicott; Interview, Anthony Mason.

[58] Interview, John Doyle; Interview, Michael Grant. See also S Gageler, 'Counsel, Role of' in M Coper, T Blackshield and G Williams (eds), *Oxford Companion to the High Court of Australia* (Oxford University Press, 2001, 2007 online edition).

> *And what was that?*
>
> Well, I frankly don't know what they expected from us. Probably they expected us to just lay down and accept their increasingly centralised view of the Constitution. I think that is what they expected.
>
> …
>
> *Was there a distinction then between what the states were doing and what the Commonwealth was doing? Were they more receptive to the Commonwealth Solicitor-General?*
>
> Well, not that much more actually. … They had reached the position, when I was there at least, that they had formed some pretty strong views about the cases that were coming before them. … And any sort of states' rights position was not where they wanted to go. So we copped a lot for that reason. And they also wanted to work at a fairly high level of abstraction in the development of those theories. And often it was in the states' interests to try and pull them back to the factual question involved in the particular case, for example, or to put it another way, the factual difficulties that might be occasioned by a development of principle in a certain way.

This view was echoed in an observation of the High Court during Kourakis' tenure by former Commonwealth Solicitor-General Gavan Griffith. He believed that the Solicitor-General's responsibility as an advocate before the High Court had become increasingly difficult. Griffith's view was that some of the High Court judges, in pursuing their own theory of the constitutional system, were simply not interested in submissions that might not advance the jurisprudence in the same direction.

The view of the Solicitor-General operating as a hired gun in the same way as other barristers was tempered for many, though not all, participants because the Solicitor-General had unique obligations to the court, both on the basis of the nature of the government as a client and its obligations to the court and justice; but also in relation to the expected standards of advocacy, availability of resources, expertise and experience.

II. Advocacy in Practice: The Solicitor-General's Instructions

If the perception of the Solicitor-General's advocacy function as a strong government advocate is accepted, one would expect to find the government closely instructing the Solicitor General. Instructions in this context occur in three different instances:

1. where the government is a party to a matter (or potential matter), there will be instructions to either prosecute, defend or appeal;
2. in constitutional cases where the Attorney-General has a right to intervene under section 78A of the *Judiciary Act 1903* (Cth) (and other matters where

the government may intervene),[59] there will be instructions about whether to intervene and in relation to the position taken upon intervention; and
3. where a decision has been made about prosecution, defence, appeal or intervention, there will be instructions about the legal submissions advanced to support that position.

While there was a large consensus among participants that the role of the Solicitor-General in advocacy was as a hired gun, the expected level of contact with the client and the degree to which instructions were sought and received were surprisingly low.[60]

This appears to reflect the general position that has also evolved in New Zealand. There, two major works on the office have presented different views as to whether litigation decisions are properly made by the political Attorney-General, or the non-political Solicitor-General. A 1998 article by then Solicitor-General John McGrath considered the Solicitor-General's functions in practice.[61] As he was writing as an officeholder, it is unsurprising that his analysis is uncritical of the current balance that has been struck between politics, the law and the public interest in the Solicitor-General's role. McGrath started with the axiomatic premise that the Attorney-General is the responsible Minister.[62] However, he argued that the highly political nature of the New Zealand Attorney-General can cloud a clear vision of justice and the public interest. This highlights the importance of the Solicitor-General's role.[63] The officeholder often, in practice,[64] independently exercises those functions that have caused great controversy in Britain, particularly the prosecution of criminal law,[65] the provision of independent advice,[66] the conduct of public interest litigation and the development of legal argument for the Government.[67] In doing so, the Solicitor-General should consider 'public governmental interest rather than the partisan political government interest'.[68]

[59] See, eg, *Crown Proceedings Act 1992* (SA), s 9; *Charter of Human Rights and Responsibilities Act 2006* (Vic), s 34. Attorneys-General can also intervene in any matter when leave is obtained from the court.

[60] In the US, Kathleen Clark has noted that there are some government lawyers (including the Solicitor-General) who serve both as the lawyer and the 'trustee' of the client, entrusted to make decisions that clients ordinarily make: K Clark, 'Government Lawyers and Confidentiality Norms' (2007) 85 *Washington University Law Review* 1033, 1062. This also reflects the view of John McGrath in New Zealand: J McGrath, 'Principles for Sharing Law Officer Power—The Role of the New Zealand Solicitor-General' (1998) 18 *New Zealand Universities Law Review* 195.

[61] McGrath, above n 60.

[62] ibid, 204, 209–10.

[63] ibid, 204, 216.

[64] Duncan Webb has gone so far to say that there exists in New Zealand a constitutional convention of independence: D Webb, 'Keeping the Crown's Conscience: A Theory of Lawyering for Public Sector Counsel' (2007) 5 *New Zealand Journal of Public and International Law* 243, 258; D Webb, *Ethics, Professional Responsibility and the Lawyer* (LexisNexis NZ Limited, 2006) 269.

[65] McGrath, above n 60, 207.

[66] ibid, 206, 215.

[67] ibid, 214.

[68] ibid; see also at 206.

McGrath's appraisal of the modern arrangements governing the functions of, and relationships between, the Law Officers in New Zealand has been adopted by the Government in official documents.[69]

In response to McGrath's article, academic and now Justice of the Ontario Court of Appeal Grant Huscroft argued that the New Zealand Solicitor-General is actually *poorly* suited to conducting public law litigation independently, and that the politically accountable Attorney-General ought to reassert authority in this area.[70] The current arrangements, Huscroft asserted, have been politically expedient for Attorneys-General, eager to avoid politically contentious issues that often surround involvement in the criminal process.[71] Huscroft's final position is that McGrath's analysis fails to take into consideration the inherently political nature of public law litigation and the need for decisions made on questions of public interest to be politically accountable.[72]

A. Determining Whether to Prosecute, Defend, Appeal or Intervene

Decisions regarding the prosecution or defence of a matter, the appeal of a matter to a higher court, or the intervention in non-constitutional matters by the Attorney-General, appeared to be strongly controlled by the government. An example of the breach of this proposition demonstrates its strength. In 1982, Mary Gaudron, Solicitor-General of New South Wales, without instructions to do so, filed an intervention in the Attorney-General's name in support of a State ward's right to an abortion.[73] The action caused outcry in the New South Wales Cabinet, and the Attorney-General said the Solicitor-General had 'pushed a big boundary'.[74]

However, this is not to say that the Attorney-General will not seek and follow the Solicitor-General's advice on whether to bring a case, or refer and delegate the question to the Solicitor-General. For example, in 2015, following a High Court decision that found the New South Wales Independent Commission of Corruption (ICAC) lacked jurisdiction to conduct an investigation into allegations against Crown Prosecutor Margaret Cunneen,[75] the Attorney-General referred

[69] His position is adopted in the briefing note from the Solicitor-General to the incoming Attorney-General: New Zealand Crown Law Office, Briefing for the Incoming Attorney-General (November 2008), 22. (It appears this note was instituted during McGrath's tenure: Letter from JJ McGrath, Solicitor-General to Attorney-General, Role of the Attorney-General, Solicitor-General and Crown Law Office and Issues of Importance (16 December 1996). The substance has changed little.)

[70] G Huscroft, 'Politics and Principle in Public Law Advocacy—The Role of the Solicitor General' (1999) 18 *New Zealand Universities Law Review* 584, 584–85.

[71] ibid, 587–88.

[72] ibid, 592–93.

[73] P Burton, *From Moree to Mabo: The Mary Gaudron Story* (UWA Publishing, 2010) 192.

[74] ibid.

[75] *Independent Commission Against Corruption v Cunneen* [2015] HCA 15.

the question of whether there was sufficient evidence to proceed with an indictment against Ms Cunneen and two others to the Solicitor-General. In New South Wales, the Solicitor-General is authorised to sign an indictment on behalf of the Crown.[76] Seeking expert counsel opinion, the Solicitor-General determined there was insufficient evidence to bring an indictment.[77] What is important to note about this episode was while the Solicitor-General performed a primary role in determining whether the prosecution was to be brought, it was at the request and referral of the Attorney.

In determining whether to intervene in constitutional matters (which each Attorney-General has a right to do under section 78A of the *Judiciary Act*), the data demonstrate that often the Solicitor-General has a great deal of discretion, or at least influence, in determining the position of the government. In most jurisdictions there is a standing delegation or instruction from the Attorney-General allowing the Solicitor-General to make certain decisions about interventions, usually in consultation with the Crown Solicitor or equivalent, in relation to constitutional matters under section 78A of the *Judiciary Act*, although the scope of these varied.[78]

Former Tasmanian Solicitor-General Leigh Sealy attempted to fetter the Solicitor-General's discretion to determine whether to intervene in matters. He was supportive of an increase in the Attorney-General's supervision over this function. During his tenure, he developed a protocol to define the manner and circumstances in which constitutional issues were referred to the Attorney-General.[79] However, he said that he had found that even when he tried to involve the Attorney-General more in the process, 'the reality is … that there is really no one apart from the people in this office who are equipped to make these judgments'. It does not appear that a protocol exists in the other jurisdictions, although informally there have been lists developed that set out the types of factors that

[76] *Criminal Procedure Act 1986* (NSW), s 126.

[77] M Sexton SC, 'Statement from NSW Solicitor General regarding a referral from the Independent Commission Against Corruption' (24 July 2015), released by the Attorney-General and made available at <http://www.justice.nsw.gov.au/Pages/media-news/media-statements/2015/csostatement-referral-from-icac.aspx>.

[78] At the Commonwealth level, see D Bennett, 'Constitutional Litigation and the Commonwealth' in J Wanna (ed), *Critical Reflections on Australian Public Policy: Selected Essays* (ANU Epress, 2009) 101, 104. In New South Wales, see MG Sexton, 'The Role of the Solicitor General' in G Lindsay (ed), *No Mere Mouthpiece: Servants of All, Yet of None* (LexisNexis Butterworths, 2002) 86, 90. In South Australia, there are delegations to the Crown Solicitor and Solicitor-General, with the exception of industrial relations matters: Interview, Greg Parker. In Tasmania, see Solicitor-General, Parliament of Tasmania, *Solicitor-General Report for 2007–2008* (2008). In the Australian Capital Territory there is a standing instruction not to intervene unless the circumstances warrant referring the matter to the Attorney-General; all decisions to intervene are referred to the Attorney-General (Interview, Peter Garrisson). In the Northern Territory, there is an informal delegation (Interview, Michael Grant). In Western Australia, the State Solicitor's Office has no involvement in making decisions in relation to constitutional matters. The decision is made by the Attorney-General in consultation solely with the Solicitor-General: Interview, Grant Donaldson.

[79] Solicitor-General, Parliament of Tasmania, *Solicitor-General Report for 2007–2008* (2008).

should be considered by the Solicitor-General in making a decision not to intervene, or a recommendation to the Attorney-General to intervene.[80]

While, in theory, the recommendation of the Solicitor-General as to whether to intervene can always be overridden by the Attorney-General, New South Wales Solicitor-General Michael Sexton explained that this rarely occurs. This may largely be because the position the government will take is dictated not by political interests but by the interests of the government polity, which are often but not always easily determined. It can be easy to determine where the government's interests lie where it is simply a matter of protecting government power, but when this objective conflicts with other constitutional principles, the position becomes more controversial and the potential for divergent views arises.

Some participants believed that in these cases there was a very important place for policy input from the government. Former Queensland Crown Solicitor and Acting Solicitor-General Barry Dunphy indicated that in most constitutional cases, while in theory the Solicitor-General would seek instructions from the Attorney-General as to whether to intervene, the advice proffered by the Solicitor-General as to intervention and the position to take 'was invariably accepted'. However, he went on to say:

> I think there is a position for government to actually make a call on their instruction on intervention. And that has occurred, we have seen that in the High Court when occasionally the states will split amongst themselves. Now, that is because it may well be in a particular case that a state sees, from their own perspective, a certain line of argument that another state is pushing may not be where they want to go. And that could be driven by a whole range of reasons.

In the implied freedom of political communication cases that gathered momentum throughout the 1990s, Dunphy believed there was no clear state interest to be protected, that is, it was not immediately apparent what position the government ought to take on a principle that would, on the one hand, limit the legislative power of all parliaments across Australia but, on the other, improve the functioning of the representative institutions of government.[81] Therefore, Dunphy explained that there was legitimate scope for the government to be deciding on which side to intervene, influenced by political agendas.[82]

[80] See, eg, Bennett, above n 78, 104; See also Hinton, above n 45, 88.

[81] The cases thus present tensions between the idea of protecting government power and government power's being only one of many constitutional principles to protect.

[82] See also Electoral and Administrative Review Commission, *Report on Review of the Independence of the Attorney-General* (1993), submission of Patrick Keane, Solicitor-General. Note also Interview, Keith Mason, in which he recalled cases—both constitutional and non-constitutional—where for political reasons his overarching instructions would be changed. This occurred, for example, when a change of government might have brought a change of political viewpoint. See also this possibility being raised by Stephen McLeish for the Victorian Attorney-General in Transcript of Proceedings, *Momcilovic v The Queen* [2010] HCATrans 261 (8 October 2010) 3, noting that there was an election scheduled prior to the pending date for trial, and that a change of government might lead to the result where 'a different Attorney may well take a different position, give different instructions on some of those matters'.

Two other examples highlight instances when the government has actively pushed an agenda that does not necessarily accord with the protection of government power because of a policy choice that prioritises other public law principles. In these cases, the government has exercised closer supervision over the Solicitor-General.

The first example comes from a series of cases in the 1980s that concerned the scope of the Commonwealth's legislative power to enact treaties under the external affairs power (section 51(xxix) of the Constitution). The New South Wales government supported the policy objectives of the challenged Commonwealth laws (the protection of minority rights and the environment), but institutionally was worried about the breadth of the external affairs power on the residual legislative powers of the states. In considering whether to intervene in *Koowarta v Bjelke-Petersen*,[83] the New South Wales government was grappling with this 'philosophical dilemma': it supported the enactment of the challenged *Racial Discrimination Act 1975* (Cth) based on section 51(xxix); but supporting a federal power to implement treaty obligations unequivocally could mean a large erosion of state power.[84] Solicitor-General Mary Gaudron advised that New South Wales could try to walk the 'elusive middle ground', although she admitted that 'no ready argument achieving these objectives springs to mind—although I am not yet convinced that none exists'.[85] Daryl Dawson, Gaudron's colleague in Victoria, recalled how controversially this was seen by the other states:

> Mary Gaudron said I ordered her out of one meeting of Solicitors-General, I don't remember it, but she said you did. … New South Wales was contemplating, I've forgotten what it was, it was one of the external affairs cases, she was contemplating supporting the federal government, and I would have said you can get out, we don't want you here.[86]

Ultimately New South Wales did not intervene in *Koowarta*. However, the same issue arose in similarly difficult political circumstances for the New South Wales government in the *Tasmanian Dam Case*,[87] which involved a challenge to the federal *World Heritage Properties Conservation Act 1983* (Cth) and the regulations under it, enacted for the purpose of giving effect to treaty obligations under the *Convention for the Protection of the World Cultural and Natural Heritage*. Again, when New South Wales tackled the question of intervention, it was confronted with the institutional problem of ceding power to the Commonwealth by accepting the Commonwealth's power to enact treaty obligations, against the political desire to support the federal scheme and the protection of the environment.

[83] *Koowarta v Bjelke-Petersen* (1982) 153 CLR 168.

[84] Burton, above n 73, 195.

[85] Solicitor-General Advice (NSW), 9 November 1981, 302, extracted in ibid 196.

[86] Presumably this was in relation to *Koowarta v Bjelke-Petersen* (1982) 153 CLR 168, where Victoria (together with WA) supported Queensland; in *Commonwealth v Tasmania* (1983) 158 CLR 1 ('*Tasmanian Dam Case*'), Victoria supported the Commonwealth legislation on a narrow reading of the external affairs power (not represented by Dawson but P G Nash).

[87] *Tasmanian Dam Case* (1983) 158 CLR 1.

New South Wales intervened in support of the Commonwealth only on the question of whether section 51(xxix) supported the legislation (the Commonwealth was also relying on a number of other heads of power). Gaudron crafted an argument that while the Commonwealth had power to implement treaty obligations under section 51(xxix), the power ought to be limited to cases where the treaty itself is of an international character.[88]

The second example of when the protection of government power was juxtaposed with other public policy interests supported by the government of the day, occurred in Queensland's intervention in the case of *McGinty v Western Australia*.[89] To understand the tensions that arose in this case requires an explanation of its political background, particularly in relation to Queensland's historical context. *McGinty* was a challenge to amendments passed in 1987 that effected an electoral malapportionment in the Western Australian Parliament through the weighting of non-metropolitan areas.[90] The 1987 amendments deepened the historical disparity in voting power among regions of Western Australia that had existed since before federation.[91] A question arose as to whether the inequalities in voting power effected by the amendments meant that the Members of Parliament were no longer 'chosen directly by the people' as required in section 73(2)(c) of the *Constitution Act 1889* (WA). There was also a question as to whether the requirements in sections 7 and 24 of the Commonwealth Constitution that Members of Parliament be 'directly chosen by the people' impliedly limited the state parliaments' power to determining the voting power in state elections.[92] The Attorneys-General of the Commonwealth, New South Wales and Queensland all intervened in support of Jim McGinty, an opposition MP challenging the amendments. The Attorneys-General of Victoria, South Australia and Tasmania intervened in support of the defendant, Western Australia.

There was a common interest among the state governments in protecting the plenary legislative power of the state against implied limitations in either the state or Commonwealth Constitutions. The division between the states instead reflected the political environment of mid-1990s and the emphasis of the Labor governments at that time on a countervailing constitutional principle: the importance of fair electoral systems. The Commonwealth, New South Wales and Queensland

[88] This came from the judgments in *Koowarta v Bjelke-Petersen* (1982) 153 CLR 168: *Tasmanian Dam Case* (1983) 158 CLR 1, 48.

[89] *McGinty v Western Australia* (1996) 186 CLR 140.

[90] See further explanation of the amendments in K Robinson, 'One Vote, One Value: The WA Experience' in G Orr, B Mercurio and G Williams (eds), *Realising Democracy: Electoral Law in Australia* (Federation Press, 2003) 100, 105–06.

[91] *McGinty v Western Australia* (1996) 186 CLR 140, 178 (Brennan CJ).

[92] Constitution, ss 7 and 24. This argument was rejected in *Attorney-General (Cth); Ex rel Mckinlay v Commonwealth* (1975) 135 CLR 1, but in the early 1990s the High Court accepted an implied right to freedom of political communication from these provisions in *Australian Capital Television Pty Ltd v Commonwealth* (1992) 177 CLR 106 and *Nationwide News v Wills* (1992) 177 CLR 1. By parity of reasoning, it was argued in *McGinty* that the provisions would support an implied equality of voting power.

each had incumbent Labor governments. Western Australia, Victoria, South Australia and Tasmania had Liberal governments. In 1988, the federal Hawke Labor Government had sponsored a referendum that would have required the adoption of fair electoral systems around Australia.[93] The amendment was predominantly aimed at the large malapportionment in Queensland.[94] While the referendum was not successful, it raised significant public awareness of the question. After Labor won government in Queensland in 1989, the matter was referred to the Electoral and Administrative Review Committee, and the malapportionment was substantially replaced by a modified 'one vote, one value' system that existed in many of the other Australian jurisdictions.[95]

The Queensland Solicitor-General at the time of the *McGinty* case, Patrick Keane, was ultimately instructed to *support* the limitation on state legislative power, demonstrating a strong commitment by a state government to support a federal Labor policy giving preference to the principle of equal representation, a 'core government principle', regardless of the constitutional implications this might have had for state power.[96]

At the Commonwealth level, in addition to the Solicitor-General's role in determining interventions, current Solicitor-General Justin Gleeson has also developed a 'gatekeeping' role over applications for special leave to the High Court.[97] Gleeson's practice continues and extends that developed by his predecessor, Stephen Gageler. This practice is akin to, and largely modelled on, the role played by the OSG in the United States. The OSG acts as the gatekeeper for all government petitions for certiorari in the Supreme Court. Gleeson explained that under the Guidance Note issued by the OLSC, the Solicitor-General must be notified of all matters in which a Commonwealth entity is contemplating seeking special leave to appeal to the High Court. The Guidance Note provides the Solicitor-General with an opportunity to appear in the matter. Gleeson has also affirmed the requirement that all applications for special leave be supported by written advice from quality counsel that the matter deserves special leave, and that the Solicitor-General be engaged to form an independent view on whether the application should proceed. As Solicitor-General, while he only rarely appears in special leave applications, he reads every application that involves the Commonwealth. If he believes it has insufficient prospects of success, or might harm the Commonwealth's interests on appeal and therefore special leave ought not be sought, he advises the agency not to bring the matter. In consultation with the agency, these applications may then be withdrawn.

[93] *Constitution Alteration (Fair Elections) 1988* (Cth).

[94] See discussion of the Queensland malapportionment during the Bjelke-Petersen period in G Orr and R Levy, 'Electoral malapportionment: partisanship, rhetoric and reform in the shadow of the agrarian strong-man' (2009) 18(3) *Griffith Law Review* 638.

[95] Robinson, above n 90, 104.

[96] Interview, Patrick Keane.

[97] See also Commonwealth, Office of Legal Services Coordination, *Guidance Note 11: Briefing the Solicitor-General* (Catherine Fitch, 18 February 2014) [9]–[12].

B. The Formulation of Submissions

There was a strong consensus that once instructions were received on whether to prosecute, defend, appeal or intervene, the Solicitor-General would be left to develop the 'legal, actual nuts and bolts, argument'.[98] In very few jurisdictions would the Attorney-General (or another minister if another department was instructing) regularly request to see the submissions prior to their being filed.[99] Just as McGrath had observed in New Zealand then, the Solicitor-General as an advocate has a wide, independent discretion to develop argument, perhaps even wider than the traditional forensic judgement enjoyed by the barrister.[100] New South Wales Solicitor-General Michael Sexton identified a disjunction between the theory that the government instructs the Solicitor-General and the practice, particularly in developing submissions. Former New South Wales Solicitor General Keith Mason indicated that particularly in constitutional litigation, there was little instruction from the government, although the overall position would be set in consultation with the Attorney-General. He explained that 'your instructions would be to oppose this, or to argue a 109 inconsistency, and you were given a free rein, basically, as to how you did it. Attorneys generally are far too busy to be involved with legal issues.'[101]

Among Attorneys-General, it was generally accepted that they left the running of litigation to the Solicitor-General, except in relation to 'big ticket' items, that is, items with large governmental or political consequences. There was a consensus that the Solicitors-General possessed a level of expertise in government litigation that meant that governments should not try to direct them closely.[102]

In this environment, former South Australian Solicitor-General John Doyle explained that the question of when to seek instructions was left to him by the Attorneys-General under which he served. So as Solicitor-General he was left with the discretion to determine whether a matter would have implications for the government that would require instruction. In Victoria, former Solicitors-General Pamela Tate and Daryl Dawson indicated that they were fairly free of instruction once a broad position had been set. However, Tate recalled a couple of times when

98 Interview, Dean Wells. This would happen in conjunction with his or her legal team. In this sense, what is meant by 'left to' the Solicitor-General in this sentence is that there will be no input from the client.

99 This would vary depending on the approach of the Attorney-General. For example, in Victoria under Attorney-General Robert Clark, submissions are regularly presented to the Attorney-General. Interview, Stephen McLeish. As Attorney-General for Western Australia, Christian Porter also indicated that he was 'intimately involved' in the High Court litigation because he had an 'intense interest in it'. Rob Mitchell and Grant Donaldson both indicated that the level of involvement would differ between Attorneys-General, although Donaldson explained that he had never been requested to send submissions to the Attorney-General to be settled.

100 McGrath, above n 60, 214.

101 See also Interview, Michael Grant; Interview, Thomas Pauling.

102 Interview, Michael Lavarch; Interview, Robert McClelland; Interview, Philip Ruddock; Interview, Terence Sheahan; Interview, Rodney Welford; Interview, Dean Wells.

she specifically sought instructions on the submissions she was going to make, as she knew the Attorney-General, Rob Hulls, was particularly interested in the case, or the nature of the submissions.[103] Seeking instructions in these instances was at *her* initiative.[104]

Some participants noted that in important political cases, the Attorney-General would become closely involved in developing submissions, particularly when there were policy choices to be made about balancing constitutional principles. Former Queensland Solicitor-General Patrick Keane saw his level of instruction differ between cases. In interventions the government 'basically left the running of it to us'. However, he recalls that in *Fardon v Attorney-General (Qld)*,[105] which concerned preventative detention of persons previously convicted of serious sexual offences after the expiry of their initial period of imprisonment, the Attorney-General, Rodney Welford, was actively instructing. Keane explained why:

> I think he was a very concerned civil libertarian and wanted to ensure that … [the legislation] not be any more stringent than it needed to be. So I think he probably rode closer shotgun on that case than anything else that I experienced.[106]

An illustrative case study of the parameters within which Solicitors-General operate in developing submissions can be taken from the 2011 High Court hearing of *Williams v Commonwealth (No 1)*.[107] The matter involved a challenge to the National School Chaplaincy Program on the basis, inter alia, that the Commonwealth lacked the power to fund the program. The Commonwealth defendants were represented by the Commonwealth Solicitor-General. The Attorneys-General of New South Wales, South Australia, Tasmania, Queensland, Victoria and Western Australia intervened, each represented by their Solicitor-General. In preparing for the oral argument, all of the parties operated under an assumption that the executive power of the Commonwealth described in section 61 of the Constitution included at least the power to spend money in areas that were or *could be* the subject of Commonwealth legislation. All the written submissions proceeded on this basis, focusing therefore on the necessity for some sort of intersection between the particular expenditure and a head of power. However, at the hearing, the Court questioned this assumption, raising the possibility that the Commonwealth's executive power to spend money and enter into contracts only exists if accompanied by legislative authority, with some exceptions.[108]

[103] For example in *APLA v Legal Services Commissioner (NSW)* (2005) 224 CLR 322, she sought instructions from the Attorney-General on the legal argument, as Hulls had close contact with plaintiff lawyers. Other cases in which she did so included matters involving incursions into individual liberties.

[104] See also Interview, Greg Cooper.

[105] *Fardon v Attorney-General (Qld)* (2004) 223 CLR 575.

[106] See also Interview Greg Cooper; Interview, Rodney Welford.

[107] *Williams v Commonwealth (No 1)* (2012) 248 CLR 156.

[108] See, eg, the first exchange between Bret Walker, French CJ and Gummow J on 9 August 2011: Transcript of Proceedings, *Williams v Commonwealth* [2011] HCATrans 198 (9 August 2011) 6–7; the possible interpretations of executive power if the assumption were abandoned are set out by Heydon J in *Williams v Commonwealth* [2011] HCATrans 199 (10 August 2011) 144–45.

The challenge to the assumed position meant that the parties had to reformulate their submissions on the Commonwealth's executive power at the hearing itself. The Solicitor-General of Queensland formulated a new interpretation that embraced the position that some of the members of the Court had suggested.[109] The Solicitors-General of South Australia and Tasmania requested further time from the Court to seek instructions from their Attorneys-General as to the position of their respective states.[110] South Australian Solicitor-General Martin Hinton submitted to the Court:

> The alternative approach raises large questions as to the way in which the States on a daily basis, or agencies or instrumentalities of the States, do business with the Commonwealth. It was first raised yesterday. I do not point the finger or blame anybody for that, but we have been unable to obtain instructions.[111]

Tasmanian Solicitor-General Leigh Sealy similarly submitted that while Tasmania was 'strongly inclined to associate ourselves with the submissions made by the learned Solicitor-General for Queensland this morning in relation to the matter of the scope of the Commonwealth executive power', he was unable to make further oral submissions because he did 'not have instructions on what is a very large question'.[112] Sealy's statements are particularly telling. As a matter of pure government power, the states would have gained the most from submitting that the Commonwealth's spending power was as narrow as possible, meaning that the Commonwealth could not intrude into areas of state competence.[113] This was Sealy's initial reaction to Queensland's submissions. However, the answer to the question had the potential to impact on past and future agreements between the states and the Commonwealth, and the Commonwealth and parties within the states; as such, it might also have impacted on a state government's political agenda (many states, for example, supported the policy behind the Chaplaincy Program, and did not want to see the individual funding agreements invalidated).

[109] Transcript of Proceedings, *Williams v Commonwealth* [2011] HCATrans 199 (10 August 2011) 97–113.

[110] Solicitors-General from New South Wales, Queensland, Victoria and Western Australia (acting) all made submissions without the need to seek further time to seek instructions.

[111] Transcript of Proceedings, *Williams v Commonwealth* [2011] HCATrans 199 (10 August 2011) 115.

[112] ibid, 118.

[113] This seemed to be the position taken by the Queensland Solicitor-General: see above n 109. It was also, ultimately, the position taken by Tasmania. See Attorney-General of Tasmania, 'Further Submissions of Behalf of the Attorney-General of Tasmania, Intervening', Submission in *Williams v Commonwealth*, No S307 of 2010, 19 August 2011. South Australia, in contrast, took the position that the Commonwealth executive power included the capacities of a natural person, but was limited in scope to the ambit of the legislative power, the execution or maintenance of the Constitution, and to the activities that fall within the executive 'nationhood power'. See Attorney-General of South Australia, 'Further Written Submissions of the Attorney-General for the State of South Australia Pursuant to Leave Granted on 10 August 2011', Submission in *Williams v Commonwealth*, No S307 of 2010, 19 August 2011.

It could also have had an impact on the theory of the *state's* executive power. As such, it was a question with large political consequences.

The Solicitor-General as an advocate represents the government's interests. To a large extent, these interests reflect stable positions that protect government policy from successful challenge, and the government's place and powers in the federal system. This has meant that the Solicitor-General is largely trusted to defend these predetermined and stable interests as he or she sees fit. Solicitors-General have a delegation to make decisions on interventions in some circumstances, and in others, the Solicitor-General's recommendation will invariably be followed. The development of the government's position in submissions is also largely left to the Solicitor-General. Many times, the appropriate position for the government to take is determined by an understanding of the constitutional position of the polity, and not the policy objectives of the government of the day.

That is not to say, however, that the government does not, or should not, have a role in instructing the Solicitor-General. There is substantial evidence that particularly in relation to constitutional litigation that raises the proper relationship between the government and the citizen when the government's interests may not be as readily identified, the government has taken a more proactive role in instructing the Solicitor-General. Where there is the potential for underlying constitutional principles to conflict, the Solicitor-General may advise the government on an appropriate position, one that is most consistent with the integrated constitutional order and the government's previous positions, but ultimately the final position ought to be determined in these areas by an accountable minister, and it is entirely appropriate for the Attorney-General to provide close instructions. As former Commonwealth Solicitor-General Stephen Gageler explained, he saw it as his role to help the government understand where its long-term interests lay. This finding is consistent with the argument advanced in chapter four, section VI.B. as to the legal position: while the Solicitor-General has a vital role in advising the government on the congruency of its actions and decisions with 'core government principles', ultimately, as a matter of constitutional principle, the final position must be determined by a politically accountable minister.

III. The Executive and the Judiciary: Conversations and Confrontations

> It has always been a Law Officer's function to be the public messenger between the government and the court, rather like an ambassador from Tudor times … Sometimes the message conveyed to the court is the silent one that the case has wide ramifications; although undue coyness can backfire … Sometimes the Law Officer's role is to put on record a borderline submission close to the client's heart that a less experienced barrister will announce to be 'on instructions'. Sometimes the actual instructions do not bear

> repeating in polite company with the advocate coming under a professional obligation to put it in his or her own words or merely submit to the order of an angry court.
>
> Message-sending can be a two-way street. And sometimes the messenger gets shot at as the only available target.[114]

The Solicitor-General operates as a conduit between the Executive and the Judiciary. The office's continuous involvement with government means that the Solicitor-General is able to assist the courts to understand the government's position in a coherent and consistent manner.

This section considers two aspects of the relationship between the Solicitor-General, as representative of the Executive, and the Judiciary. First, it may be that the Solicitor-General alerts the Judiciary as to the importance to the Executive of a particular principle, or the ramifications for the Executive of the court's development of a principle in a particular direction. Secondly, I consider the role of the Solicitor-General during times of constitutional confrontation between the Judiciary and the Executive. The Solicitor-General may be used not simply to make the government's submissions on the proper operation of the constitutional order, but to remind the court of its constitutional position in that order and warn it against incursions into the Executive domain. It may also be that the Judiciary wishes the Solicitor-General to take a message back to the Executive: to communicate to the Executive that it is acting inappropriately, or in a way that the court perceives is threatening to its independence or the administration of justice.[115] (In Western Australia, as is explained in more detail in chapter four, section III, the Solicitor-General performs a more direct 'liaison' role between the government and the Judiciary; this role is not considered further in this chapter.)

A. The Implications of Judicial Decision-making

Judges are more than mere passive interpreters of the law. At times they are confronted with judicial choices that actively engage them in value judgements. Issues about practical consequences and policy implications are thus relevant to and and often legitimately inform the judicial task. Submissions may be sought by courts, and particularly the High Court as the final appellate jurisdiction, on the parties' views of the law, but also on the practical and policy implications of a decision.[116] The Solicitor-General is in a unique position to inform the Judiciary of the views

[114] K Mason, 'Aspects of the History of the Solicitor-General in Australia' in Appleby, Keyzer and Williams (eds), above n 45, 23, 30, 44 and 45.

[115] The defence of the Judiciary was traditionally seen as part of the common law functions of the Attorney-General. However, in Australia, this convention has been substantially eroded by the actions and publicly expressed views of officeholders, and even their beliefs as to their role.

[116] C Sampford and K Preston, 'Introduction' in C Sampford and K Preston (eds), *Interpreting Constitutions: Theories, Principles and Institutions* (Federation Press, 1996) 1, 5.

of the Executive on the policy behind particular actions and laws, and of the potential implications of particular decisions.[117] A Commonwealth Attorney-General also once explained that another advantage of having a Solicitor-General representing the interests of the government is that the High Court in particular may explore 'peripheral or related matters difficult to foresee and on which it is difficult to brief outside counsel adequately'.[118]

There are some indications that the High Court is open to, and even seeks, submissions on policy and policy implications, particularly from government litigants. In *R v Gee*,[119] the High Court considered the interpretation of section 68 of the *Judiciary Act 1903* (Cth), a provision that was intended to pick up the procedure for pre-trial, trial and appeal procedure from state criminal law and apply it to the federal criminal law, as well as vest federal criminal jurisdiction in state courts. Only the South Australian Attorney-General, represented by Solicitor-General Bradley Selway, intervened. In the course of Selway's submissions, Kirby J expressed disappointment that the Commonwealth Solicitor-General was not there to put forward *the Commonwealth's* view. He explained to Selway in argument:

> [I]t is really quite an important question of policy here as to how the *Judiciary Act* is to operate, and there are those competing approaches which I mentioned earlier to the appellant, and one would have thought that the Commonwealth would have had something to say. It is, after all, its Act. It is not your Act.[120]

Former Queensland Solicitor-General Patrick Keane recounted that many Solicitors-General regarded the High Court case of *Dietrich v The Queen*[121] as a warning to the Attorneys-General (and Solicitors-General) to appear to assist the Court in important constitutional litigation, particularly to provide evidence of the policy consequences of its decisions. The case turned on a question of whether a court's inherent power to stay proceedings to prevent an abuse of process extended to ordering a stay when a defendant in a criminal trial was unrepresented by counsel. Only the Attorneys-General for the Commonwealth and South Australia (represented by their Solicitors-General) intervened. A possible effect of the failure of the Solicitors-General to appear en masse can be gleaned from the joint reasons of Mason CJ and McHugh J. The Court noted that a finding that

[117] Interview, Michael Lavarch.

[118] Letter from Commonwealth Attorney-General to Western Australian Attorney-General, extracted in Western Australia, *Parliamentary Debates*, Legislative Council, 30 April 1969, 3436 (Charles Court, Minister for Industrial Development).

[119] *R v Gee* (2003) 212 CLR 230.

[120] Transcript of Proceedings, *The Queen v Gee* [2002] HCATrans 384 (Kirby J, 13 August 2002) 27. See also Transcript of Proceedings, *The Queen v Gee* [2002] HCATrans 395 (Kirby and McHugh JJ, 14 August 2002) 73, 75; and discussion in B Selway, 'The Different Role of an Australian Attorney-General' (2002) 13 *Public Law Review* 263, 269.

[121] *Dietrich v The Queen* (1992) 177 CLR 292.

a court could stay proceedings was likely to result in the provision of counsel at public expense. In considering this repercussion, Mason CJ and McHugh J said:

> [O]nly the Attorney-General for the Commonwealth and the Attorney-General for the State of South Australia intervened. But no argument was put to the Court that recognition of such a right for the provision of counsel at public expense would impose an unsustainable financial burden on government. In these circumstances, we should proceed on the footing that, if a trial judge were to grant an adjournment to an unrepresented accused on the ground that the accused's trial is likely to be unfair without representation, that approach is not likely to impose a substantial financial burden on government and it may require no more than a re-ordering of the priorities according to which legal aid funds are presently allocated.[122]

Keane recalled after *Dietrich* the response from Dawson J, a former Victorian Solicitor-General who had written a strong dissent in *Dietrich*:

> Dawson buttonholed … one of the SGs, because I mean he is an ex-SG himself, and he got stuck into him. And he said, you know, where were the SGs? Why weren't they there making the argument that you can't just stay these cases? There are Legal Aid regimes where there are merits and means testing. This is a responsible response to having people who can't afford their own defence. It isn't perfect, but it is as good as you're going to get bearing in mind that the High Court can't levy the taxes and decide how they're spent. And Daryl was very upset that the Solicitors-General hadn't turned up, in a phalanx, to say you just can't pick and choose. … So after that we were always very conscious that you should err of the side of intervening, at least to make sure it couldn't be said that these issues had gone by default.

More recently, in the High Court hearing of *RCB as litigation guardian of EKV, CEV, CIV and LRV v Forrest*,[123] the Attorney-General for Western Australia, intervening, raised with the Court similar concerns to those that the Attorneys-General had failed to raise in *Deitrich*. The matter concerned a Family Court order for the return of four children from Australia back to their father in Italy. It was submitted that in making the order, the judge had not afforded the children procedural fairness because, inter alia, the children had not been provided with separate and independent representation. In the particular type of proceedings in issue, the *Family Law Act 1975* (Cth) provides that a judge may only order separate representation for a child's interests where 'exceptional circumstances' exist.[124]

Counsel for Western Australia (led by the Solicitor-General) submitted that the restriction on the circumstances where independent legal representation can be ordered was 'prudent' having regard to the 'reality' that '[t]here are limits to the capacity of government to fund independent legal representation of children'.[125]

[122] ibid, 312.

[123] *RCB as litigation guardian of EKV, CEV, CIV and LRV v Forrest* (High Court of Australia, B28/2012, 7 August 2012), reported decision *RCB as litigation guardian of EKV, CEV, CIV and LRV v Forrest* (2012) 247 CLR 304.

[124] *Family Law Act 1975* (Cth), s 68L(3).

[125] Attorney-General for Western Australia, 'Intervener's Submissions', Submission in *RCB as litigation guardian of EKV, CEV, CIV and LRV v Forrest*, No B28 of 2012, 20 July 2012, 5–6.

Further, the government's financial limitations had legal consequences the Court ought to take into account. The submissions explained:

> Were the Court to order independent legal representation and a legal aid body not have capacity to fund that representation, staying the application [as occurred in *Dietrich*] is not a consequence that could properly be ordered. A stay simply defeats the purpose of the application by ensuring that abducted children are not returned, and is contrary to Australia's international obligations under the *Convention on the Civil Aspects of International Child Abduction*.[126]

Another illustration of the type of interaction between the Court and the Solicitor-General that may prevent the reasons relied on by Mason CJ and McHugh J in *Dietrich* came in the case of *Re The Governor Goulburn Correctional Centre; Ex parte Eastman*.[127] The case concerned a challenge to the appointment of an acting judge of the Supreme Court of the Australian Capital Territory on the basis it did not comply with section 72 of the Commonwealth Constitution. In his submissions, Northern Territory Solicitor-General Thomas Pauling drew the High Court's attention to the potential 'dire consequences' of such a finding.[128] He explained that since self-government in the territories, judges had not been appointed by the Governor-General as required by section 72. Thus, 'the consequence of a decision in this case is not just that decisions made by acting justices might be invalid because of an invalid appointment, it goes to the whole of the judiciary in both territories'.[129] He went on:

> I was asked by one of my learned friends how many people—we only started locking up people in our own gaols after 1978[130]—how many people might be there and I will not give evidence from here, your Honours, but it is a lot.[131]

Kirby J responded to the submissions:

> Can I just raise in respect to that argument, which I really take the force of because it has very serious consequences, but presumably the same things were said from the Bar Table during the *Boilermakers' Case*.[132]

In *Boilermakers'*,[133] the Court had found key provisions of the *Conciliation and Arbitration Act 1904* (Cth) unconstitutional, as well as orders made under it by the

[126] ibid, 6.

[127] *Re The Governor Goulburn Correctional Centre; Ex parte Eastman* (2000) 200 CLR 322 ('*Eastman*').

[128] *Ex parte Eastman; The Governor, Goulburn Correctional Centre* [1999] HCATrans 65 (24 March 1999), available at <http://www.austlii.edu.au/au/cases/cth/HCATrans/1999/65.html>.

[129] ibid.

[130] The date of self-government in the Northern Territory.

[131] *Ex parte Eastman; The Governor, Goulburn Correctional Centre* [1999] HCATrans 65 (24 March 1999).

[132] ibid. Hayne and Gummow JJ also raised the possibility of retrospectively legislating as was done in *Presley v Geraghty* (1921) 29 CLR 154, but this was addressed by Pauling in the same manner.

[133] *R v Kirby; Ex parte Boilermakers' Society of Australia* (1956) 94 CLR 254 ('*Boilermakers' Case*').

Commonwealth Court of Conciliation and Arbitration. Pauling's response to the question was that, unlike the orders in the *Boilermakers' Case* that were able to be remedied by retrospectively validating the various decisions, the retrospective validation of convictions and sentences of imprisonment could not be achieved by the Legislature. He made this submission on the basis that convictions and sentences of imprisonment cannot be imposed by the Legislature because they involve punishment after determination of guilt, which is an *exclusively* judicial power within Australia's constitutional arrangements.[134] Kirby J suggested that Pauling's submissions were, in effect, asking the Court to be bound by an understanding of the Constitution even if it was wrong. Pauling responded:

> No, I do not suggest that, and there may come times when a major shift is dictated, but as my learned friend, the Solicitor-General for the Commonwealth put it, ultimately one has to put 'the dire consequences', to use your Honour's term, in the balance to see whether or not one solution is better than another. There is no doubt that there is no more vexing part of the Constitution than the relationship between section 122 [the Territories power] and Chapter III and the likely reason for that is that it is badly drafted and whichever argument one runs, it comes to an intellectually unsatisfying result.[135]

Ultimately, in *Eastman* the High Court held that the Territory courts were not federal Chapter III courts and therefore not required to comply with section 72 of the Constitution. Gleeson CJ and McHugh and Callinan JJ held that this conclusion was 'open on the language, and produces a sensible result, which pays due regard to the practical considerations arising from the varied nature and circumstances of territories'.[136]

Another example occurred in 2011 during the *Momcilovic* High Court appeal.[137] After the initial hearing, the High Court posed a series of questions to the parties about, inter alia, the operation of section 109 of the Constitution. The Court had indicated in a previous case,[138] and during oral argument in *Momcilovic*, that it was considering reviewing the settled position on the interpretation and operation of section 109. All of the government parties—the Attorneys-General for Victoria, Commonwealth, New South Wales, Western Australia, South Australia, Tasmania, and the Australian Capital Territory—filed a joint submission arguing that the Court retain the settled construction.[139] The joint submission from the

[134] See, eg, *Chu Kheng Lim v Minister for Immigration* (1992) 176 CLR 1, 27 (Brennan, Deane and Dawson JJ).

[135] Transcript of Proceedings, *Ex parte Eastman; The Governor, Goulburn Correctional Centre* [1999] HCATrans 65 (24 March 1999), available at <http://www.austlii.edu.au/au/cases/cth/HCATrans/1999/65.html>.

[136] *Re The Governor Goulburn Correctional Centre; Ex parte Eastman* (2000) 200 CLR 322, 332. See also the approach in *Victoria v Commonwealth and Hayden* (1975) 134 CLR 338 ('*AAP Case*'), 417–19 (Murphy J).

[137] *Momcilovic v The Queen* (2011) 85 ALJR 957.

[138] *Dickson v The Queen* (2010) 241 CLR 491.

[139] Attorneys-General of Victoria, Commonwealth, New South Wales, Western Australia, South Australia, Tasmania and the Australian Capital Territory, 'Submissions of Second Respondent

government parties was unprecedented.[140] It served a very important purpose in demonstrating that *all* of the government parties were concerned by the Court's contemplation of a radical departure from the settled interpretation of section 109. Such a shift had the potential to invalidate many State criminal regimes, including extensive drug regimes, that had operated concurrently with federal schemes, and under which many people had been convicted and penalised.[141] The submission also noted the practical problems that would arise if State law enforcement bodies were unable to investigate conduct in the area of drug offences.[142]

The Court is not, however, always responsive to these submissions. When asked whether he thought it was proper for the Solicitor-General to alert the Court to practical consequences of decisions, former High Court Chief Justice Gerard Brennan said definitely not:

> There is a great difference between being conscious that the legal consequence of a decision is X, and taking X into consideration in order to reach a decision. ... You are just conscious of the way in which the law operates. But seeking advice about what the results would be, and the sort of economic or political fallout would be, as a means of arriving at the decision, no. No, that wasn't on.

Former South Australian Solicitor-General Chris Kourakis also often felt the High Court was not receptive to submissions on the implications of a particular decision, preferring to work at a high level of abstraction.

Australia's constitutional order attempts to separate the Judiciary from the other branches of government. Nonetheless, the judicial task is still undoubtedly political in the sense that it involves the exercise of public power, and the exercise of that power has direct and indirect influence on the Executive's policies; a fact that has only been highlighted by the acceptance of realism in legal reasoning, and therefore of the influence of value and policy judgements. According to this view, the judicial function is properly and necessarily informed by the Executive's views on the impacts of the trajectory of legal principle. Solicitors-General and some members of the Judiciary understand that in this environment, it is important

and Intervening Attorneys-General', Submission in *Momcilovic v The Queen*, No M134 of 2010, 28 March 2011, [6], [7]. All Attorneys-General, with the exception of Victoria and the Australian Capital Territory, were represented by their Solicitors-General. Victoria had no Solicitor-General at the time. Stephen McLeish was counsel for Victoria (he was appointed Solicitor-General after the filing of the joint submission but before the further hearing of the matter). At this stage, the Australian Capital Territory had not created a position of Solicitor-General. Peter Garrisson appeared for the Australian Capital Territory (he was subsequently appointed Solicitor-General when the position was created).

[140] Transcript of Proceedings, *Momcilovic v The Queen* [2011] HCATrans 145 (7 June 2011, Bret Walker).

[141] Attorneys-General of Victoria, Commonwealth, New South Wales, Western Australia, South Australia, Tasmania and the Australian Capital Territory, 'Submissions of Second Respondent and Intervening Attorneys-General', Submission in *Momcilovic v The Queen*, No M134 of 2010, 28 March 2011, [19]. Interview, Leigh Sealy.

[142] ibid [25].

for the Solicitor-General to inform the courts of the possible larger policy implications of particular decisions. Such a role positions the Solicitor-General as a mouthpiece for the Executive's interests before the Judiciary.

B. Confrontations over Institutional Roles

The Solicitor-General appears before the court to *assist* the judges in the manner described above, but also as an *interface* when tensions arise between the two branches. Former High Court Justice Michael McHugh explained that the constitutional power of judicial review that has been vested in the High Court has meant there will be tensions, even animosity, between the Executive and the Judiciary.[143] This section considers the relationship between the Solicitor-General and the Judiciary when there are confrontations and the Solicitor-General is called upon to act as a conduit between the government and the courts.

i. Carrying the Message from the Executive to the Judiciary

The Solicitor-General may be required to put the position of the Executive to the Judiciary when confrontations arise between the two arms of government, particularly when it appears to the Executive that the Judiciary is inappropriately or illegitimately interfering in an Executive issue.

Former New South Wales Solicitor-General Keith Mason recalled two instances of this occurring. The first was when he was counsel for the New South Wales government, defending a case brought by stipendiary magistrates who had not been offered new positions as magistrates when the old Magistrates Court was reorganised. Five of the magistrates initially brought an action against the Attorney-General's recommendation not to appoint them, and were successful on the basis that they had not been accorded natural justice.[144] After this, the government introduced a new policy whereby the five magistrates had to compete against new applicants in a merit-based process, while their former colleagues were reappointed. The magistrates again brought an action against the government, this time claiming they had a legitimate expectation to be treated in the same manner as their former colleagues.[145] Keith Mason recalled, 'I will never forget the instructions I got in the Magistrates case', which, he explained, did not bear repeating 'in polite company'. They were to the effect that Mason must tell the Court, firmly, to keep out of the Executive's affairs. In this instance, the Executive was using the

[143] MH McHugh, 'Tensions Between the Executive and the Judiciary' (2002) 76 *Australian Law Journal* 567, 570.

[144] *Macrae v Attorney-General (NSW)* (1987) 9 NSWLR 268.

[145] The magistrates were successful in the Court of Appeal: *Quin v Attorney-General (NSW)* (1988) 16 ALD 550; but unsuccessful on appeal to the High Court: *Attorney-General (NSW) v Quin* (1990) 170 CLR 1.

Solicitor-General to take messages from the Executive to the Judiciary when it was anticipated by government that the Court had, or would, overstep its constitutional role.

The second instance Mason referred to was the 1960s case of *Tait v The Queen*,[146] where the Victorian government also used the Solicitor-General as a messenger to the courts, warning them to stay out of Executive processes. The case involved an appeal against Robert Tait's death sentence on the basis of a common law rule that he could not be executed as he was insane. There was a question about whether the common law position had been overridden by legislation. The government had won an appeal in the Court of Appeal, and it was announced that the execution would take place two days after the decision. There was then an application to the High Court for special leave to appeal. Three High Court justices, including Dixon CJ, flew to Melbourne to hear the matter.[147] Tait was to be executed the day after the hearing. Then Victorian Solicitor-General Henry Winneke appeared for the government, with instructions to finalise the matter as quickly as possible.

Exchanges between Winneke and Dixon CJ reveal the tensions between the government's position and the Court's desire to deliver justice in the case. Winneke seemed somewhat embarrassed by the government's instructions, but delivered them all the same. Winneke said that in light of the postponement of the execution on a number of previous occasions, 'it is the considered view of those who are responsible for advising his Excellency in this State that it is essential in the public interest that this matter should be finalised'.[148] Dixon CJ responded, 'When you say it to this court, you are saying it to a court which has supreme jurisdiction in Australia, and in effect saying, "Well, even if you want time to consider this case, we will not give it". Is that what it means?'[149] Winneke took a step back, indicating that the Executive would comply with any order made. When the Court did make the order staying the execution of Tait pending the disposal of the court proceedings, and Dixon CJ asked whether the Court had Winneke's undertaking that that would 'be enough' to stop the scheduled execution, Winneke could give no absolute assurance and suggested that the Court make an injunctive order.[150] Eventually the Court made a further order, restraining the Chief Secretary and the Sheriff and his deputy or deputies from carrying out the execution. This, it seemed, would 'be enough'.[151]

In both of these examples, the Solicitor-General was used as a messenger from the Executive to the courts but, as Winneke's position demonstrates, the

[146] *Tait v The Queen* (1962) 108 CLR 620. See also C Burns, *The Tait Case* (Melbourne University Press, 1962), the Appendix to which extracts the full Transcript of Proceedings in *Scott v The Queen; Tait v The Queen* (High Court of Australia, 31 October 1962).

[147] Burns, above n 146, 132.

[148] ibid, Appendix A, Transcript of Proceedings *Scott v The Queen; Tait v The Queen* (High Court of Australia, 31 October 1962), 174.

[149] ibid, 174.

[150] ibid, 180.

[151] ibid, 181.

officeholder still retains his (or her) obligations to the administration of justice and the court itself. It is these dual obligations that make the Solicitor-General well placed to act as a respectable and fair conduit during these encounters.

ii. The Solicitor-General Carries the Message Back

Sometimes, the courts request the Solicitor-General to take a message *back* to the Executive regarding its behavior, particularly when they perceive it as a threat to their obligations to the administration of justice.[152]

In 2001, then Commonwealth Solicitor-General David Bennett found himself in the difficult position of being at the interface between the Judiciary and the Executive in the politically sensitive arena of immigration. After the Howard Liberal/National Coalition Government's strong stance against allowing the rescued asylum seekers onboard the Norwegian tanker, the *MV Tampa*, to disembark on the Australian territory of Christmas Island, Parliament passed significant amendments to the *Migration Act 1958* (Cth). Among these was the insertion of a privative clause that attempted to curtail the availability of judicial review for decisions made under the Act with few exceptions.[153] However, the Federal Court approached the interpretation of the privative clause in a very restrictive manner. Under this interpretative approach, it continued to review and overturn many migration decisions. Then Minister for Immigration, Philip Ruddock, told the media on 30 May 2002:

> What we are finding is that, notwithstanding that legislation, the courts are finding a variety of ways and means of dealing themselves back into the review game. And what I have said to the Parliament is, look, we've passed this legislation, this was a decision of the Parliament. The High Court of Parliament is saying decisions of the Tribunal should be final and conclusive and if we need to give the court some further advice we may need your support again.[154]

On 3 June 2002, the Solicitor-General, representing the Minister, defended a case in which the privative clause was challenged before the Full Federal Court. Black CJ made it clear that the Court was infuriated by what it viewed as impropriety in the Minister's statements:

> Despite these statements I have not previously responded to any of them publicly. The most recent statement however raises a new issue since it would appear that it could only refer to the issues before the Court on these appeals—appeals to which your client is a party. … The statement was made only a matter of days before the date fixed weeks ago for the hearing of the appeals. You would of course know Mr Solicitor that the Court is not amenable to external pressures from Ministers or from anyone else whomsoever,

[152] Interview, Keith Mason.

[153] *Migration Legislation (Judicial Review) Act 2001* (Cth), which inserted s 474 into the *Migration Act 1958* (Cth), which stated a 'privative clause decision' could not be challenged by any means.

[154] Extracted in F Brennan, 'The Law and Politics of Human Rights in an Isolated Country without a Bill of Rights' (Sir Ronald Wilson Lecture delivered at Perth, 12 May 2003).

> but we are concerned that members of the public might see the Minister's statements as an attempt to bring pressure on the Court in relation to these appeals to which he is a party.[155]

Black CJ then called upon the Minister to explain himself, through the Solicitor-General, the next day in court. With the possibility that the Court could find the Minister in contempt of court, the Solicitor-General responded the next day by reading from a statement that expressed the regrets of the Minister, in which the Minister claimed that his comments had been misinterpreted, that they had been directed at the Opposition and not the Judiciary, and there was no intention to place any pressure on the courts.[156] Further, the Minister said that he respected 'the fundamental importance of the independence of the Judiciary and constitutionally entrenched principle of the separation of powers'.[157] The Federal Court chose not to pursue the issue any further.[158]

In the majority of cases, relations between the Executive and the Judiciary are harmonious, and the judges welcome and seek the assistance and submissions of the Solicitor-General as the Executive's representative. However, on occasion, the tensions in the constitutional relationship between these two branches of government are clearly evident. During these periods, it is natural that the Solicitor-General will be the sometimes reluctant interface between the conflicting interests. The office is uniquely positioned: loyal to the government as counsel, with overarching obligations to the court as a legal professional. As each of the examples illustrate, it is through the Solicitor-General, with his or her mutual obligations, that the tensions have been negotiated and resolved in a measured and respectful manner.

C. The Solicitor-General and the High Court's Jurisprudence

Much of the US scholarship has investigated whether the Solicitor-General holds influence over the Supreme Court's jurisprudence.[159] Anecdotally, similar ideas exist in Australia surrounding particular Solicitors-General, most notably in the myth around the success of legendary former Commonwealth Solicitor-General

[155] Transcript of Proceedings, *NAAV v Minister for Immigration and Multicultural and Indigenous Affairs* (Full Court of Federal Court of Australia, (N265 of 2002), (N282 of 2002), (N399 of 2002), (V225 of 2002), (S84 of 2002), Black CJ, Beaumont, Wilcox, French and Von Doussa JJ, 3 June 2002.

[156] Australian Broadcasting Corporation, 'Ruddock expresses "regret" over court comments', *ABC News*, 4 June 2002.

[157] B Haslem, B Crawford and S Morris, 'Ruddock Regrets and Party Applauds', *The Australian* (5 June 2002).

[158] Similar accusations were made in 2013 against the Queensland Premier by Queensland Supreme Court judge, Justice Fryberg, in a bail hearing. He ultimately decided to stay the proceedings: *R v Brown* [2013] QSC 299. The Solicitor-General did not appear in the Supreme Court matter (which is unsurprising given the nature of the matter: a Supreme Court bail application), but did appear for the State in the appeal to the Queensland Court of Appeal, where the stay was overturned: *R v Brown* [2014] 1 Qd R 419.

[159] See, eg, RM Salokar, *The Solicitor General: The Politics of Law* (Temple University Press, 1992).

Maurice Byers.[160] Former Prime Minister Gough Whitlam wrote that Byers' advocacy 'was central to my government's success in the High Court'.[161] However, some participants questioned the myth of Byers' influence.[162] Anthony Mason, who sat on the High Court through much of Byers' tenure, disagreed with the proposition that Solicitors-General had 'influence' over the jurisprudence of the Court. Another participant commented that the proportionate success of Byers had more to do with his 'singing from the same song sheet' as the Mason Court than his particular skills as Solicitor-General.[163]

There is no systematic evidence to suggest that the Solicitor-General operates as a 'cue' to the High Court (or any court), or enjoys any greater success rate than other Senior Counsel before the courts.[164] As former Commonwealth Solicitor-General Gavan Griffith wrote:

> It has been suggested that the American counterpart is the Tenth Justice of the United States Supreme Court. Similar influence cannot be claimed for the office in Australia, although as the senior counsel for each government in the federation, the Solicitors-General enhance the quality of practice in public law, and contribute to the depth and continuity of constitutional arguments presented for governments to the High Court.[165]

While perhaps not translating to 'influence', many participants indicated that there was a high level of respect between the Court and most, although not all, Solicitors-General. Historically, the special status of the Law Officers rested on their unique position in representing the sovereign before his own courts. In Australia today, it appears more likely that any respect afforded the Solicitor-General must be earned by the individual, and lies in his or her experience and skill, rather than being granted automatically because the Solicitor-General appears for the government.

Commonwealth Solicitor-General Justin Gleeson said that while he did not believe that his advocacy as Solicitor-General might change the outcome in particular cases, his presence might act as a cue, or signal, to the Court about the nature of the matter and the quality of the arguments. In special leave applications, for example, where the Solicitor-General appeared in very few cases, when he *did* appear, he did so to 'nudge' a particularly important case across the line. He explained that the Solicitor-General strives to bring excellent advocacy to the case, but also to signal to the Court that in those very selective cases where the

160 M McHugh, 'Speech in Honour of Maurice Byers' (Speech delivered at the Dinner in Honour of Maurice Byers on behalf of the Australian and New South Wales Bar Associations, 8 February 1984), in National Library of Australia, 'Papers of Sir Maurice Byers' (1975–99); Interview, Patrick Keane.

161 G Whitlam, 'Whitlam Era' in Coper, Blackshield and Williams (eds), above n 58.

162 See, eg, Interview, Geoffrey Davies.

163 Interview, Ian Callinan.

164 Although in Western Australia it was perceived that Crown Counsel was not given the same respect and consideration as the Solicitor-General; it was even said the Court would give particular attention to a Solicitor-General's submissions. Western Australia, *Parliamentary Debates*, Legislative Council, 30 April 1969, 3436 (Court). Crown Counsel, Ronald Wilson, was immediately appointed Solicitor-General. Any effect this had on the respect given to him in the Court is doubtful.

165 G Griffith, 'Solicitors-General' in Coper, Blackshield and Williams (eds), above n 58.

Solicitor-General chooses to appear, there is 'an absolutely compelling Commonwealth interest' involved.

Former High Court Chief Justice Anthony Mason believed it advantageous for the Court to have a Solicitor-General appearing before it, because Solicitors-General would bring a broader vision of how the Constitution fits together, and an ability to develop that consistently through cases in the Court. Byers perhaps epitomised this. Similarly, former Commonwealth Attorney-General and Minister for Justice Duncan Kerr believed that a barrister acting simply as a 'hired gun', advancing any argument that might help an individual case, diminished respect for the polity before the courts.[166] Former Victorian Solicitor-General Pamela Tate also said she believed that, as a repeat player, every time she appeared before the Court, 'your integrity is on the line'. The consequences for losing the respect of the Court are enormous: 'they won't trust you, they won't rely on you'.

Former New South Wales Solicitor-General Keith Mason indicated that the SCSG—that is, the Solicitors-General acting *collectively*—would often indirectly influence the direction of the High Court by shaping its constitutional docket. While this is an example of procedural, rather than substantive, influence,[167] it may nonetheless influence the trajectory of the jurisprudence. Mason explained that the SCSG would monitor the constitutional cases coming through the courts:

> And there were discussions about, well, that is not a suitable vehicle, we ought to slow that one down, and speed that one up, so as the right case would present itself and be argued. … From a legal point of view, this case is a better vehicle than that. Or we would discuss sometimes, this case ought to be left where it is, or ought to be lifted into the High Court to become the vehicle for … deciding that point.[168]

There was a broad consensus in the interviews that the idea that Solicitors-General have particular 'influence' over the trajectory of the High Court's jurisprudence through their submissions was simply unproven in Australia. While Solicitors-General were aware that they ought to maintain good relations with the Court, this appeared to rest on the prudence of repeat players before the Court, and not because they thought that if they did so, this might directly result in an increased success rate.

IV. Discussion: The Solicitor-General as Advocate

The first section of this chapter presented participants' perceptions of the Solicitor-General's advocacy function. The Solicitor-General's function as an

[166] See also Interview, Thomas Pauling.

[167] SP Waxman, 'Foreword: Does the Solicitor General Matter?' (2001) 53 *Stanford Law Review* 1115, 117–18.

[168] See also John McDonnell, 'Special Committee of Solicitors General Meeting' (Secretary, Special Committee of Solicitors-General, 18 October 1996) 1, where, for example, the Committee discusses whether to 'defer' the challenge to *Ha v Lim* to enable the case of *Jarpab* to 'catch up'.

advocate is, in many respects, perceived to be the same as an advocate for any client's cause. There was little consensus that the Solicitor-General had significantly greater professional obligations in his or her relationship with the courts, or any greater influence with them, than any other Senior Counsel appearing before it.

From this standard position, subtle distinctions appeared in many participants' views, demonstrating that the true picture is more complex. The Solicitor-General's conduct of litigation, including making determinations and recommendations about interventions in constitutional matters, and the development of submissions, is not closely monitored by government. The discretion afforded to the Solicitor-General appears to be beyond the traditional forensic judgement enjoyed by the barrister. The Solicitor-General advocates for the government's interests, and often these interests equate to the protection of Executive and legislative power. In cases when this is a singular interest to protect, the Solicitor-General is generally trusted by the government to determine how to do so. However, because the protection of government power must be balanced against competing constitutional principles in other cases, the government's interests may be difficult to determine. In such circumstances, the Solicitor-General is relied upon to advise the government on the intersection of constitutional principles, but the final decision ought to be made by the Attorney-General as the accountable minister. Because the Solicitor-General is largely left alone to conduct constitutional litigation for the Crown, it is often incumbent on the officeholder to identify these cases. The findings therefore present a paradox that tests the hired-gun metaphor in its application to the Solicitor-General even as an advocate.

The US institutional arrangements demonstrate that it is not imperative that the functions of adviser and advocate are combined in a single office. In Australia, many functions of the Law Officers have been separated. The ministerial function remains with the Attorney-General, the prosecutorial function now rests almost entirely with the DPP, and the legal advocacy and advisory functions largely fall to the Solicitor-General and other government lawyers. This division of functions has been driven by the identification of the different focus of each: as a minister, the Attorney-General is closely and almost exclusively attuned to politics; the DPP is given autonomy from political influences to make independent determinations about the public interest in the course of prosecutions; and the Solicitor-General is given independence from politics as a pre-eminent legal expert. But within the Solicitor-General's role there is a need to exercise independent judgement as an adviser (independence that John Edwards referred to as being of 'the same degree' as that required in relation to prosecutions)[169] and also to act on the instruction of the political Attorney-General as an advocate. What are the implications of the fusion of the two functions under the Australian model for the office's role?

In the US, the division of the two functions between the Office of Solicitor-General (OSG) and the Office of Legal Counsel (OLC) was driven by practicalities: the OSG simply did not have time to continue attending to advisory matters.

[169] JLJ Edwards, *The Attorney General, Politics and the Public Interest* (Sweet & Maxwell, 1984) 190.

But it has subsequently been justified on the basis of the distinct ethical frameworks relating to the two functions and the different emphasis within each on the importance of independent judgement. The 2004 memorandum drafted by former members of the OLC in response to the controversy over the Torture Memos, emphasised the importance of maintaining the delineation between the functions and not allowing the advocacy framework to infiltrate into the advisory function.[170] Two justifications were advanced for this argument. First, it reduces the potential confusion for the lawyer between the functions, and thus ensures against a lawyer's employing any reasonably available legal argument in the advisory function as opposed to the *best* legal interpretation available. Secondly, and most importantly, it reduces the possibility that those in government will confuse advice provided in the course of advocacy to defend, *post hoc*, government action, with independent advice given on proposed government action.

There have been warnings in the US that certain instances of unethical lawyering (particularly the controversy over the Torture Memos) have been caused by the combination, or even confusion, of the advocacy and advisory functions. This comparative scholarship raises the question for Australia about whether the institutional structure should separate the functions, guarding against the type of confusion and contamination observed in the US.

While participants in this study perceived the two functions differently, there is little evidence that in practice detriment is being caused because of their fusion. For example, there is no evidence that Solicitors-General have inappropriately advised government in an advocacy framework; or that government has interpreted advice provided in an advocacy context as containing not simply a legally available argument, but the best view of the law.

There was disparity between the views of Attorneys-General and Solicitors-General as to whether the Solicitor-General's legal reasoning process ought to take into consideration the political objectives of the government. Many Solicitors-General agreed that part of their job as adviser was to assist the Executive to achieve its policy objectives; but disagreed with the position of some Attorneys-General that this meant they would accommodate these goals in any way into their legal reasoning. However, there was no evidence that this disagreement had led to the contamination of the Solicitor-General's advice by an advocacy-driven model.

One exception to this conclusion may be former Commonwealth Solicitor-General Maurice Byers' advice allegedly provided to a number of ministers in the Whitlam Cabinet (including the Attorney-General). He advised that the proposition that a particular loan fell within the definition of a 'loan for temporary purposes' was 'arguable'. One participant raised a question as to whether this advice misunderstood the Solicitor-General's obligations in the advisory context where

[170] *Principles to Guide the Office of Legal Counsel* (21 December 2004).

the government had not yet taken action, providing instead advice appropriate for an advocacy framework.[171]

While there is evidence that there is currently no detriment being occasioned by the fusion of the two functions, this position remains contingent on those in the office exercising their functions properly. Any advantages sought by the separation of the two functions in Australia must be considered against a weight of evidence as to the advantages of keeping the functions fused. The advocacy work, particularly in the High Court, was considered by many to be higher profile than the advisory work, and thus providing an incentive to potential candidates to take the position. More fundamentally, many participants stressed that a deep knowledge of precedent, together with an understanding of the trajectory of the current High Court, was paramount for the advisory function. That understanding is grown out of regular exposure to the Judiciary and engagement with the judges during advocacy.

Lastly, many participants emphasised that the Solicitor-General as an advocate is not merely akin to a private barrister in that same role. As an advocate the Solicitor-General is expected to provide a coherent, over-arching narrative to the constitutional position of the polity as presented to the court. In many cases, the Solicitor-General is given little guidance and instruction, leaving the actual position of the government to the Solicitor-General's discretion and independent judgement. The Solicitor-General is also involved in the decision-making process in relation to constitutional interventions across many jurisdictions. So the Solicitor-General as an advocate is often not simply advocating on instruction. In this context, there are significant advantages in having the same individual perform both the advisory and advocacy functions. The officeholder must consider the same questions about the intersection of constitutional principles in both functions and form an opinion about the proper place of the government in the constitutional system. In both functions, the Solicitor-General exercises a large amount of de facto independence. Having these functions vested in the same individual increases the likelihood of coherency and consistency in the government's position. Thus, despite what may appear as large theoretical divergences between the advisory and advocacy functions, seen in its extreme in the US scholarship, the Australian Solicitor-General's advocacy and the advisory functions in practice have much in common.

There may be other ways, short of separating the two functions, of guarding against the fears of confusion and contamination between the functions. For example, the 2004 memorandum drafted by former members of the OLC recommended that if the OLC did advise on the availability of legal arguments to defend actions already taken, this must be clearly indicated so that the advice was not mistaken for an authoritative statement of the law.[172]

[171] See further discussion of this incident in ch 4, section II.A.ii.

[172] ibid, 6.

7

Independence

I'm independent but I'm not.[1]

Independence is many things to many people.[2]

Independence is a 'recurring theme' in all analyses of the Law Officers.[3] Participants commented that the relevance of the office rested on its reputation for independence.[4] It is independence that makes all legal advisers relevant; but in the context of the Solicitor-General, as the 'final' legal adviser to government, the office's independence is a dimension of added importance. Further, the 'independence' of the Law Officers has been promoted as the touchstone by which individual officers negotiate the tensions between the law, politics and the public interest. Chapter two canvassed a diversity of opinion in international scholarship as to the best manner by which to facilitate independence in the office. Several scholars concluded that, regardless of the constitutional and legal frameworks put in place to further an officeholder's independence, its protection rested on the internal ethics and fortitude of the individual.[5]

In Australia, the intention behind the establishment and reform of the Solicitor-General's statutory position was to shield the officeholder from political influences by removing the office from the ministry and the public service.[6] In doing so, the objective was largely to remove the tension that exists in the British tradition, whereby individual officeholders are expected to be able to take off their 'political hats' when they provide legal opinions.[7]

[1] Interview, Martin Hinton.

[2] Interview, Peter Garrisson.

[3] JLJ Edwards, *The Law Officers of the Crown: A Study of the Offices of the Attorney-General and Solicitor-General of England with an Account of the Office of the Director of Public Prosecutions of England* (Sweet & Maxwell, 1964) 11.

[4] Interview, Robert Ellicott; Interview, Stephen McLeish. See also WMC Gummow, 'The 2005 Sir Maurice Byers Lecture: Statutes' (Summer 2005/2006) *Bar News* 30, 30.

[5] See, eg, JLJ Edwards, *The Attorney General, Politics and the Public Interest* (Sweet & Maxwell, 1984) 67; N Walker, 'The Antinomies of the Law Officers' in M Sunkin and S Payne (eds), *The Nature of the Crown: A Legal and Political Analysis* (Oxford University Press, 1999) 135, 162–65. See also CW Clayton, 'Introduction: Politics and the Legal Bureaucracy' in CW Clayton (ed), *Government Lawyers: The Federal Legal Bureaucracy and Presidential Politics* (University Press of Kansas, 1995) 1, 18.

[6] See, eg, South Australia, *Parliamentary Debates*, House of Assembly, 1 March 1972, 3563 (LJ King, Attorney-General); Tasmania, *Parliamentary Debates*, House of Assembly, 5 May 1983, 825 (Geoffrey Pearsall, Minister for Tourism); New South Wales, *Parliamentary Debates*, Legislative Assembly, 1 October 1969, 1478 (Kenneth McCaw, Attorney-General); Victoria, *Parliamentary Debates*, Legislative Assembly, 31 October 1951, 5684 (Thomas Mitchell, Attorney-General).

[7] See Lord Dilhorne, extracted in Edwards, *The Attorney-General,* above n 5, 200.

Chapter four, section III.A.iii. explained that the creation of the Solicitor-General as 'counsel for the Crown' impliedly introduced a dichotomy of independence between the pursuit of the Crown's cause as an advocate acting on instruction of a responsible minister of the Crown, and the independence required as an adviser to come to the best legal interpretation. As explained in chapter five, section II.B.iv, participants identified independence as one of the assumptions that underpins the office's capacity to fulfil its advisory function in a manner that progresses the rule of law. However, perhaps unexpectedly, participants also indicated that the government often relies heavily on the Solicitor-General's independence and expertise in the office's advocacy role to develop the government's position before the court in a manner that considers the enduring interests of the Executive and its proper position in the overarching constitutional structure.

In this chapter, I identify the mechanisms that participants perceived as important in protecting the Solicitor-General's independence, and investigate whether independence is, in practice, respected by governments. In doing so, I explore further the two different approaches to independence introduced in chapter five, section IV.: the 'autonomous expert' and the 'team member'.

I. Protecting the Solicitor-General's Independence

The following analysis considers how participants thought the independence of the Solicitor-General was maintained and protected. Participants in the study were predominantly concerned with ensuring that the Solicitor-General was able to operate independently from inappropriate *external* influences, thus emphasising the importance of relational independence. There was particular focus on inappropriate pressure from the client—that is, the government—to achieve short-term political objectives. Because the client takes the form of the political Executive, independence from the client is inherently associated with independence from political pressures. The focus of participants on the absence of external pressures is consistent with the observation that because external pressures are more overt, they are often the focus of regulatory regimes and ethical standards aimed at protecting independence (see further discussion of the different types of independence in chapter four, section II.A.i.).

While concern over an absence of external influence was emphasised, participants were aware of the need to ensure the Solicitor-General had the internal capacity to fulfil the role with integrity and autonomy.[8] This was usually expressed in terms of the 'ability' and 'skill' to make difficult determinations about the law, particularly when the law was not necessarily clear and unequivocal. Also prevalent was an emphasis on personal integrity.

[8] See, eg, Interview, Trevor Griffin.

Judicial pronouncements on how to protect the independence of government lawyers have focused upon structural protections.[9] Protections offered by the statute, and other written or structural protections, were not seen by participants as entirely irrelevant to the protection of their independence but as more *symbolic* of normative ideals than influential in practice. The vast majority of responses focused on an individual's professional competence and commitment to ethical behaviour as the best way to ensure the two facets of independence, that is, to ensure against inappropriate external influences as well as to foster capacity. Indeed, former Victorian Solicitor-General Henry Winneke had said as early as the 1950s, in relation to security of tenure, that '[t]he right man would need none'.[10]

The next section considers participants' perceptions of the protection provided by professional competence and commitment to ethical behaviour, before the chapter turns to the emphasis participants placed on statutory and other structural mechanisms.

II. Professional Competence and Independence

When participants referred to the individual's professional competence and commitment to ethical behaviour, a number of different concepts were incorporated. The individual's experience and expertise at the time of appointment were considered important, as was their commitment to professional independence. Some participants saw the trappings of independence associated with barristers as important devices to assist in retaining professional independence. Some also spoke of the importance of an individual's 'capacity' to see the law in its broader social context.

A. Professional Qualifications, Experience and Expertise

Overwhelmingly, participants believed it was fundamental that an appropriately qualified and experienced person was attracted to the position of Solicitor-General. This was perceived as vital for two reasons. First, professional competence ensured an understanding of professional ethical obligations. Many participants emphasised the importance of the Solicitor-General's membership of the Bar in protecting independence, with the professional training, understanding and commitment to ethical standards that entails.[11]

[9] See Suzanne Le Mire's analysis of a number of Australian and foreign cases in the context of legal professional privilege and in-house counsel that draws the conclusion that the courts rely heavily on the 'relational barriers' aspect of independence, with only occasional recognition of capacity: S Le Mire, 'Testing Times: In-House Counsel and Independence' (2011) 14(1) *Legal Ethics* 21.

[10] R Coleman, *Above Renown: Biography of Sir Henry Winneke* (Macmillan Company, 1988) 160.

[11] Interview, Gavan Griffith; Interview, Robert McClelland; Interview, Anthony Mason; Interview, Michael Mischin; Interview, Grant Donaldson.

Secondly, professional competence also ensured that an individual had confidence in his or her own opinion and was able to resist inappropriate pressures to change it. Keith Mason explained:

> I don't think the tenure idea is a good thing, frankly. I don't think being tenured gives your advice the status of being a judge, or gives you the security to give fearless advice, it is not a consequence of tenure, it is a consequence of your own value system, and your own confidence in your opinion.[12]

Dean Wells, former Queensland Attorney-General, explained that the Solicitor-General's subscription to the ethics of the Bar, meant he was 'a man of the law … in all its majesty and independence of thought'.[13] Former South Australian Solicitor-General John Doyle explained that, for him, the independence of the Solicitor-General did no more than refer to 'the independence that applies to any barrister'.[14] Former Western Australian Attorney-General Christian Porter explained that what protected the Solicitor-General's independence were 'just professional obligations that all lawyers are under: they work equally well for an articled clerk as they do for a Solicitor-General'. Former Acting Solicitor-General for Western Australia Rob Mitchell said that the independence of the office was guaranteed by 'the integrity of the person and the way that they practice'.

Maintaining this same level of independence may, however, be slightly more complicated for the Solicitor-General than for private barristers. As John Doyle explained:

> But the issue comes in a different guise in relation to a Solicitor-General. … [T]hat is because the Solicitor-General has an ongoing relationship with the client, may well have chambers in premises occupied by the client, and by some may be seen as more than a legal advisor, and as someone who helps formulate policy. It is important that a Solicitor-General makes it clear that he or she provides the same independent and objective advice to the Executive Government that any barrister provides to the client.[15]

Commonwealth Solicitor General Justin Gleeson also emphasised the different and slightly more difficult position in which the Solicitor-General finds himself or herself:

> [I]n the end, in most cases at the private bar, you know what the client wants, and it can be reduced to money, or it can be reduced to liberty, or it can be reduced to avoiding bankruptcy, or it can be reduced to establishing a point of principle before a court. Now, at the government level, and more particularly the Commonwealth level, where it's all just a bit more complicated than at State level or Territory level, there are just so many different things that are being put by people who are, in a sense, all under the one … client umbrella. So … then the challenge for independence is … applying the same standards, or even higher standards, but to a very slippery beast that is underneath.

[12] See also Interview, Catherine Branson; Interview, Walter Sofronoff.
[13] See also Interview, Stephen Gageler; Interview, Pamela Tate.
[14] Letter from John Doyle to Gabrielle Appleby, 19 July 2012 (copy on file with author).
[15] ibid.

Former New South Wales Solicitor-General Keith Mason explained that when he was appointed, he had to fight to gain recognition within the profession that the Solicitor-General enjoyed the same level of independence as those at the private Bar. At that time, the Bar Association did not recognise public barristers, including the Solicitor-General, as *independent* professionals. During his tenure he struggled hard to gain acceptance by the Bar Association that public barristers *did* exhibit the same independence as private barristers. It was a fight he eventually won, and the Solicitor-General and Crown Advocate are now members of the Bar Association.

As we saw in chapter four, section II., the statutory qualifications for appointment emphasise that the government is looking for a highly competent legal professional. They ensure the government is assisted by a qualified legal mind; but they also speak to a candidate's capacities. In New South Wales, when the Solicitor-General Bill was introduced in 1969, the Attorney-General indicated that the qualifications were that the appointee be one of Her Majesty's counsel, 'who has established his eminence and integrity'.[16]

Despite this focus, many participants noted that governments had often found attracting a qualified appointee of appropriate status and integrity challenging. The difficulty in enticing excellent candidates to take up the position has been an historical concern: in the UK back at the turn of the twentieth century, First Lord of the Treasury AJ Balfour had noted the delicacies in setting remuneration because of the need to entice top candidates to the position.[17] When the Commonwealth statutory position was established in 1964, the Government encountered difficulties in attracting established Senior Counsel to the position. In finalising the pension entitlements for the position, the Cabinet 'recognised that the views of prospective appointees might also need to be taken into account'.[18] The first two appointments offered were rejected.[19] Eventually, Anthony Mason, an established junior, was approached and accepted the appointment; he took silk at the request of the Government, at a special ceremony just prior to his appointment.[20]

Upon Mason's retirement in 1969, the Government again encountered difficulties attracting candidates. A Cabinet Submission from the Attorney-General dated 19 March 1969 noted:

> It has been suggested to me that the conditions of appointment would be much more attractive and more likely to attract the kind of person we want if the provisions of

[16] New South Wales, *Parliamentary Debates*, Legislative Assembly, 1 October 1969, 1478 (McCaw).

[17] See further discussion in ch 2, section I.B.

[18] Commonwealth, *Cabinet Decision 448* (27 August 1964).

[19] Interview, Robert Ellicott; Interview, Gavan Griffith; Interview, Anthony Mason. One was John Kerr, the other was a silk from Victoria. Ninian Stephen was also listed to be approached in the event that Anthony Mason did not accept the appointment: ibid.

[20] Interview, Anthony Mason.

> sub-section (4.)[21] applied to a Solicitor-General who had served for at least seven years, and who was not prepared to accept a further appointment.[22]

The amendments were proposed 'to attract a particular man'.[23] Before the matter was finalised, the candidate whom the Attorney-General was courting indicated that he did not intend to accept the appointment, even if the amendment could be secured.[24] Within days, another Queen's Counsel, Robert Ellicott, accepted the appointment and the proposed amendments were dropped.[25]

In South Australia, similar problems were encountered. Upon the retirement of Brian Cox, John Doyle, one of the leading Queen's Counsel at the South Australian Bar, was approached to take the position. He recalled that he initially declined, as he did not want to leave his established practice at the Bar. It was not until he was approached a second time that he accepted.

The role of remuneration packages in attracting the best candidates to public positions is an ongoing debate.[26] The continued amendment of the remuneration and pension entitlements of the Solicitor-General reflects an ongoing awareness of the importance of the package to attracting candidates. In Queensland and Western Australia, one of the reasons for the inclusion of the right to private practice was to attract high-quality candidates to the position. Indeed, when asked whether he would have accepted the position without the right, former Queensland Solicitor-General Walter Sofronoff responded, 'No I wouldn't have; not a chance.'

Christian Porter, the former Western Australian Attorney-General who introduced the arrangements allowing for private practice in that State, explained that the changes were contemplated because it was thought

> it was a difficult thing to attract someone with absolutely *fresh*, top level experience as a barrister in a range of matters—and for *Western Australia*, in a range of constitutional and commercial matters—without allowing that person to have some limited right of practice.

He also noted that, unlike the prospect of a judicial appointment, in Western Australia there were no other remunerative rewards, notably the pension, to attract a candidate to the role of Solicitor-General.[27]

[21] This subsection provided that if a Solicitor-General was appointed for a seven-year term but not *offered* reappointment and did not qualify for a pension, he was to be paid a lump sum payment of double his annual salary. If the Solicitor-General had been *offered* reappointment for a period of at least five years, or sufficient so that he was eligible for the pension, the eligibility for this lump sum payment was removed.

[22] Commonwealth, *Cabinet Submission, Nigel Bowen, Attorney-General* (19 March 1969).

[23] Commonwealth Cabinet Office, *Note for File: Amendment to the Law Officers Act* (22 April 1969).

[24] ibid.

[25] Commonwealth, *Appointment: Cabinet Minute: Decision No 956* (23 April 1969); Letter from EJ Bunting, Secretary of Attorney-General's Department, to Nigel Bowen, Attorney-General, 16 May 1969; Commonwealth Cabinet Office, *Note for File: The Solicitor-General* (16 May 1969).

[26] See, eg, statement of this dilemma in Remuneration Tribunal (Commonwealth), *Annual Report 2007–2008* (Commonwealth of Australia, 2008) 1.

[27] Unlike other jurisdictions, there are no pension entitlements that attach to the office of Solicitor-General in that State. Porter's views were corroborated by Grant Donaldson in his interview.

B. Barristerial Trappings

Many participants emphasised the desirability of replicating the processes of the private Bar within the office of Solicitor-General so as to create distance between the office and the government, and reinforce their commitment to the officeholder's professional obligations.[28]

Former Victorian Solicitor-General Pamela Tate was very cognisant of ensuring that she operated in a manner analogous to that of a private barrister and kept appropriate distance—professionally and also physically—from the client. Her practice and perspective were informed by the experience of Hartog Berkeley, who had been the Victorian Solicitor-General during the Cain and Kirner Labor governments. She described Berkeley as 'moving to government': he had chambers in the Premier's Department, and the administrative arrangements order showed that the Solicitor-General fell under the responsibility of that department.[29] Responsibility for the office returned to the Attorney-General in 1992 with the election of the Kennett Liberal government.[30]

In contrast to Berkeley's position, Tate emphasised the importance she placed on 'actively protecting' the independence of the office. After a brief period when she had chambers in the Attorney-General's Department, she moved back to private chambers on the other side of the city. This removed her from government, and ensured that she was not privy to the 'gossip, hearsay and innuendo' within government, that she did not get too close to the officers within government or the politicians, and that she did not become part of the 'internal ethos'. She developed a number of protocols that reinforced this: she would require legal issues to be highly formulated—crystallised—before they were brought to her. In many ways it was like preparing a matter for determination by a court. She was also wary of becoming involved too early in legal issues that might arise in the development of policy, because she believed this might compromise her independence in being the final determinant of the legal question.

For some participants, one of the strongest symbols of the Solicitor-General's independence as a professional barrister was the maintenance of separate chambers. This physical separation symbolised the ethical separation between the barrister and the client.[31] Former Commonwealth Solicitor-General Stephen Gageler explained the, at least symbolic, importance of his physical separation from the Executive. He explained that he was not necessarily operating as part of the private Bar but nonetheless operating like a private barrister, separate from the

[28] Interview, Chris Kourakis; Interview, Robert McClelland; Interview, Pamela Tate; Interview, Dean Wells.

[29] *Administrative Arrangements Order (No 38) 1985* (Vic). See also P Tate, 'The Role of the Solicitor-General for Victoria' (Speech Delivered at the University of Melbourne, 12 November 2003).

[30] *Administrative Arrangements Order (No 114) 1992* (Vic).

[31] See also Interview, Geoffrey Davies; Interview, Barry Dunphy.

client: 'I do not see myself as a member of the Executive. I see myself as occupying a separate, statutory, position ... symbolised in a sense by the location of my office in a court building.'[32]

C. Beyond Professional Qualities: Questions of Politics

Many participants who were or had been Attorneys-General went further than simply looking at the professional qualities of candidates. They indicated that they were not seeking a Solicitor-General who was simply the best *technical* legal professional they could find, but a legal professional who had the capacity to situate the law in a wider governance framework that broadly accorded with the viewpoint of their political party.

This was described in detail by former Queensland Attorney-General Rodney Welford, who appointed then Solicitor-General Patrick Keane to the Court of Appeal and Walter Sofronoff as Solicitor-General:

> In selecting a Solicitor-General, and in the appointment of judges, it was important to me, and every Attorney-General might have their own view about what was important, but it was important to me, that you had, one, high quality legal minds, but, two, legal minds that had a willingness to be innovative with the law. That is, they were prepared to see the law as serving a public policy purpose, namely some higher concept of serving the public interest; and that they had an essential sense of the concept of social justice for example, and they saw the law operating as a vehicle for making a better society, rather than just operating in a vacuum.[33]

Former Commonwealth Attorney-General Robert McClelland expressed a similar view, noting the importance, first, of the candidate's competency as an advocate, but in addition:

> [Y]ou want someone ... who has got some view, in the case of a Labor government, a progressive view about how the Constitution should evolve. Now that is from a Labor government's point of view, and a conservative government may well have a different view depending on the person who holds the office.[34]

[32] The Commonwealth Solicitor-General's Sydney residences are in the Supreme Court building; the Canberra office is located in the Attorney-General's Department. Grant Donaldson also commented on the importance of his physical separation from the government in his chambers.

[33] See also Interview, Gareth Evans. When Evans was appointed Attorney-General, he inherited Maurice Byers as Solicitor-General, but Byers resigned soon after. Byers had been appointed by the Whitlam Government. After Byers' first term expired, he was reappointed by the Fraser Government. However, he resigned after three years. Evans postulated that Byers was ready to retire after his first term, but took a second appointment and 'held on' to allow a Labor appointee to replace him. Evans said, 'although he was a good honest slave of the system ... I think his instincts were on our side than the other side'.

[34] Similar sentiments were expressed by former Commonwealth Labor Attorney-General Mark Dreyfus, who indicated that having 'a love for government, having a respect for the processes of government, having a care for government, is really important'.

Three points can be observed about those participants who held this belief. First, the Attorneys-General who held this opinion also encouraged the advice of their Solicitors-General on the congruency between proposed government action and 'core government principles'.[35] Unsurprisingly, then, the government's expectations of the Solicitor-General's role impacted on the type of internal capacities they sought in an appointee. In circumstances where the expectations were that the Solicitor-General continued to have an important role in advising the government on where the public interest lay, capacity to make fine distinctions and weigh potentially conflicting public law principles is pertinent.

Secondly, they were Attorneys-General who were or had been members of a Labor government. In contrast to the position of Labor Attorneys-General, an Attorney-General under the federal Howard Liberal-National Coalition Government, Philip Ruddock, explained that he was particularly concerned that a Solicitor-General would not push a progressive agenda, and instead wanted to ensure that his Solicitor-General remained strictly within the confines of the law.[36]

Any divergence between views of Labor and Coalition Attorneys-General about Solicitor-General appointments is consistent with that in relation to judicial appointments. At its core it reflects a very different conception of the process of legal reasoning, contrasting a realist perspective that now embraces, in some cases, policy as a legitimate guide to judicial reasoning, with a more traditional conservative perspective that continues to accept orthodox reasoning processes focused on objective attainment of legal principle.[37]

Lastly, the trend identifiable among Labor Attorneys-General seems to be a relatively modern development, emerging in the second half of the twentieth century. Former Commonwealth Solicitor-General Anthony Mason believed that the relevance of political persuasion to appointment as Solicitor-General was a recent development, and could be traced to a belief in political circles that political persuasion may influence the legal advice received.

Many participants rejected the idea that the political views of the Solicitor-General, or at least a shared sense of the purpose of the law and government with the Executive's political persuasion, were relevant in appointing a Solicitor-General. Many thought political connections and views might be relevant, but only in a limited way: they might act as a negative factor, in that affiliations with the opposite party might operate to disqualify a candidate;[38] or they might play

[35] See further discussion of their views on this point in ch 5, section III.C.iii.

[36] In the US context, a similar comment was made by former Bush Administration Attorney-General Michael Mukasey, that government lawyers must ensure that they *only* 'do law': M Mukasey, 'The Role of Lawyers in the Global War on Terrorism' (2009) 32 *Boston College International and Comparative Law Review* 179, 181.

[37] In relation to the different approaches to judicial appointment between the major parties, see JL Pierce, *Inside the Mason Court Revolution: The High Court of Australia Transformed* (Carolina Academic Press, 2006) 192–211.

[38] See Interview, David Bennett; Interview, Daryl Dawson; Interview, Grant Donaldson.

a relatively innocuous part in appointment, in that they might make a potential candidate better known to the government.[39]

Some Solicitors-General recounted that when, during their tenure, a new government of a different political persuasion was elected, they spoke to the incoming Attorney-General about continuing in the position or resigning, to ensure that the incoming government had confidence in them as Solicitor-General—and perhaps more importantly, had confidence in their independence as Solicitor-General.[40] Other participants thought that such a practice brought with it perceptions that undermined the distance that was expected between the Solicitor-General and the Executive.[41] For these participants, to consider resignation at a change of government would be to encourage an incorrect perception of the office. The lengths of the terms set by the statutes indicate that it was intended for officeholders to serve governments that often would be of different political persuasions. While the Solicitor-General was no longer a public servant, it was intended that he or she would be a 'non-political officer … serving different governments in succession'.[42]

The delicacy of the situation was highlighted in South Australia in the late 1970s. Malcolm Gray was appointed as Solicitor-General in the final months of the Dunstan/Corcoran Labor government. This was viewed with resentment by the incoming Tonkin Liberal government, and Gray found himself largely starved of work because of political distrust.[43]

In Australia, there are relatively few allegations that Solicitors-General have been appointed on purely political grounds. But there are inevitably dangers inherent in the closed nature of the appointment process in most jurisdictions (excepting the Commonwealth and Victoria).[44] One example serves to highlight these. In 2007, it was alleged that the Tasmanian Police Commissioner had disclosed official secrets to the Premier. One of the secrets related to a police investigation that was to be launched into allegations about an agreement between a private barrister, Stephen Estcourt, and the Premier. The alleged agreement was that if Mr Estcourt acted pro bono for former Deputy-Premier Bryan Green in criminal proceedings, Mr Estcourt would be appointed Solicitor-General (a post that was vacant at that time).[45] The matter was referred to the DPP, but the allegations were ultimately

[39] Interview, John Doyle; Interview, Patrick Keane; Interview, Chris Kourakis.

[40] Interview, Geoffrey Davies; Interview, John Doyle; Interview, Patrick Keane; Interview, Keith Mason.

[41] Interview, John Doyle (although he recalled having a conversation with the incoming Attorney-General, he did not think a practice of resigning upon a change of government should be implemented); Interview, Walter Sofronoff.

[42] Commonwealth, *Parliamentary Debates*, House of Representatives, 22 October 1964, 2220 (Billy Snedden).

[43] Interview, Catherine Branson. See discussion of the practice of 'freezing out' in ch 5, section II.B.iii.b.

[44] See further explanation of the appointment process and the introduction of a merits-based system in the Commonwealth and Victoria in ch 4, section II.A.

[45] See *Tasmania v Johnston* (2009) 18 Tas R 195; M Rae, 'Top Cop Arrested Over Official Secrets', *The Mercury* (Hobart) (13 October 2008).

found to be untrue.[46] Nonetheless, the event illustrates the potential danger in a closed appointment system for political influence to undermine the propriety of the appointment process. Underlining the gravity of the danger is the perception by many that it is the scrupulous ethical practice of appointees that ultimately guarantees the independence of the office.

Despite its potential weaknesses, Northern Territory Solicitor-General Michael Grant defended the closed appointment system. He explained that the system ensures that all eligible candidates are considered and not only those willing to go through the 'cattle call' associated with formal selection panels. It also facilitates informal consultations that may be more likely to reveal an individual's character and ethical soundness than a formal and structuralised process.

In some jurisdictions, political persuasion seemed to play no role at all in the appointment of a Solicitor-General.[47] This appeared to be the case in Victoria, with its more open, merits-based appointment system, including an interview round undertaken by a selection panel. The process was first used with Pamela Tate's appointment in 2003. Former Victorian Solicitor-General Daryl Dawson, who sat on Tate's selection panel, recalled that the Attorney-General at the time 'may have wanted someone else'. However, when he was provided with the recommendation of the panel, 'he had to accept that, and did, and I must say did'.

The emphasis placed by participants on the professional qualities, ethics and experience in protecting the Solicitor-General's independence demonstrates that for the majority of participants, the importance of 'independence' in practice lay in the individual's capacity for independent judgement and his or her professional competence and commitment to ethical behaviour. While, as will be shown in section III. below, the structural barriers against inappropriate external pressures were not necessarily discounted, for many participants they, alone, would be insufficient to ensure that the Solicitor-General had the necessary independence to perform his or her functions.

III. Statutory and Structural Mechanisms that Protect Independence

Less emphasised by participants was the importance of the statutory mechanisms, particularly the protection of tenure that bears some resemblance to the

[46] *Tasmania v Johnston* (2009) 18 Tas R 195, [8] (Evans J). Following the allegations around the promise made to Mr Estcourt regarding his appointment as Solicitor-General, the Legislative Council established the Select Committee on Public Sector Executive Appointments. Mr Estcourt, the Solicitor-General Leigh Sealy and the DPP, Mr Tim Ellis, were all summonsed to appear. Their evidence is available on the Committee's webpage at <http://www.parliament.tas.gov.au/ctee/Council/psea.htm>.

[47] See Interview, Michael Grant; Interview, Thomas Pauling.

protections afforded to judicial independence in Chapter III of the Constitution. So little weight was placed on these mechanisms by some that a few participants indicated that they believed the statute contained no formal mechanisms to protect the independence of the office.[48] For others, however, the statute was important.

The structural guarantees of tenure, remuneration and pension were seen by some as keeping at bay unwanted external influences—most particularly from the pressures that might be brought to bear by the client. Former Commonwealth Solicitor-General Stephen Gageler, for example, believed that what protected his independence was 'partly structural' in the sense of his fixed term and statutory office.[49] For Northern Territory Solicitor-General Michael Grant, the importance of the statutory tenure was instrumental in his accepting the appointment. When Grant was offered the position, he said he would only be prepared to accept the appointment without term (under the Northern Territory legislation the Solicitor-General can be appointed with or without term):[50]

> [B]ecause I don't want to be put in a position where I am appointed for five years, and reliant on the good will of government for any sort of reappointment. I think that is entirely unsatisfactory. I think you need to be appointed, in these sorts of jobs, and the DPP's job, you need to be appointed either until the statutory retirement age, so without term, or appointed for a fixed period with no possibility of reappointment, to stop any sort of subconscious desire to please government in your advising.

It was the appointment without term, together with the security of tenure (as he could not be removed except on similar grounds as applied to a judge),[51] that meant Grant felt 'entirely unconstrained by any sort of political influence'. These statutory protections ensured that government understood the Solicitor-General was independent, 'and they know that if they heavy you, there is nothing stopping you from making an issue of it'. It was, for Grant, the statutory structure that meant 'it is almost impossible either theoretically or in practice for you to be suborned in this job'.

Similar concerns about a term appointment were expressed by former Acting Solicitor-General of Western Australia, Rob Mitchell. In that jurisdiction, a change had been implemented to move the appointment from an appointment with a mandatory retirement age, to a fixed-term appointment. Mitchell explained that this change raised, at the least, the perception that independence might be compromised. He said that in a constitutional crisis—for example where the Solicitor-General might be called upon to provide independent advice to the Governor—while the individual officeholders might act in a fiercely independent

[48] Interview, David Bennett; Interview, Michael Lavarch.

[49] See also Interview, Catherine Branson; Interview, Michael Grant; Interview, Stephen McLeish; Interview, Michael Sexton.

[50] *Law Officers Act 1978* (NT), s 13(1).

[51] ibid, s 15.

manner, 'the protection that is offered to the Solicitor-General in that sort of extreme situation is less obvious if he is on contract perhaps with a term coming up, than if he had a security of tenure to retirement'. The current Western Australian Solicitor-General, Grant Donaldson acknowledged the concerns, particularly around the *perception* of independence, that had been expressed over the move from essentially a judicial term of appointment to a limited-term appointment. Nonetheless, he saw advantages to the new model:

> I think changeover in all government positions over a period of time is not such a bad idea. I don't think there is only one person who can do this job. … I suspect people get stale in jobs after 20 years.

Former South Australian Solicitor-General Chris Kourakis emphasised the importance of the Solicitor-General's tenure by reference to the Crown Solicitor's lack of similar statutory protections. For Kourakis, other government legal advisers without statutory tenure, such as the Crown Solicitor, could seek protection under the Solicitor-General's statutory tenure guarantees. He explained:

> So a terrific safeguard for them in terms of independence, when they've got a tricky problem, when they're not sure whether they should just say outright don't do it, or to say look it is balanced, you can go ahead, but these are the risks, is that they come to me. … [A]n advice which the government seeks from the Crown Solicitor can be referred by the Crown Solicitor to the Solicitor-General. Then you've immediately got that independence in terms of tenure, and that helps protect them.

In Victoria, the statute provides for a discretionary removal mechanism, so that the Solicitor-General's security of tenure rests on convention, if it exists at all. Former Victorian Solicitor-General Stephen McLeish referred to the position as a 'weakness in the Victorian legislation'.[52]

Former Commonwealth Solicitor-General Anthony Mason believed the statute not only guaranteed independence, but also assisted in promoting the *perception* of that independence: 'I think it provides more independence. Certainly *outwardly* there is a greater appearance of independence. But I think in truth, it also provides independence.' Former Victorian Solicitor-General Pamela Tate said that the statute played a significant role in terms of understanding the position within government: she believed the statutory entitlements of the office gave the Solicitor-General a status and independence analogous to those of a Supreme Court judge.[53]

[52] See also discussion of this point in G Taylor, *The Constitution of Victoria* (Federation Press, 2006) 187–89.

[53] See also Interview, Stephen McLeish.

IV. Other Structural Mechanisms

In addition to professional obligations and commitment to ethical standards, and the more tangible (although less important for some) statutory protections, participants drew attention to a number of other mechanisms that protect the office's independence.

A. Acting Beyond Counsel

Many participants were alive to the fact that the independence of the office might be undermined by the engagement of an officeholder in activities—sometimes politically charged—that would go beyond the statutory functions of adviser and advocate. This might include, for example, the engagement of the Solicitor-General to conduct inquiries on behalf of the government, or sit on government committees. For example, Michael Grant, the Northern Territory Solicitor-General, was recently appointed by the government to sit as a member of a panel conducting an inquiry into the appointment of judges.[54] Commonwealth Solicitor-General Justin Gleeson sits as a committee member overseeing important constitutional and non-constitutional litigation across the whole of government. This role is discrete from the actual provision of legal advice in any matter, and he takes steps to keep the two distinct.

A significant example of the Solicitor-General's engagement in politically charged functions was the office's earlier involvement in decisions around prosecutions. Prior to the statutory creation of a DPP in the different Australian jurisdictions, the Solicitor-General was also responsible for the Attorney-General's prosecutorial functions. These mainly involved making recommendations as to decisions on whether to bring a prosecution and whether to file a *nolle prosequoi*. They have a strong public interest-orientated focus. The function requires the weighing up of various factors, including political questions and direct evaluations of the public interest before decisions are made. The inclusion of these types of responsibilities led, on some occasions, to public political controversy over the office's independence.[55] Former New South Wales Solicitor-General Keith Mason

[54] John Doyle, Julie-Ann Schafer and Michael Grant, *Review of the Processes for the Appointment of Judicial Officers in The Northern Territory*, December 2014.

[55] See, eg, the controversy around the exercise of these functions by Mary Gaudron, and accusations of political bias and protecting political bosses in regard to recommendations for prosecutions: P Burton, *From Moree to Mabo: The Mary Gaudron Story* (UWA Publishing, 2010) chs 11 and 12. In relation to the prosecutorial role more generally, see the controversies around the exercise of this function by the British Law Officers that were considered in the recent reforms. The House of Commons Constitutional Affairs Select Committee said, 'The Attorney General's responsibility for prosecutions has emerged as one of the most problematic aspects of his or her role.' House of Commons Constitutional Affairs Committee, *Constitutional Role of the Attorney General*, Fifth Report of Session

explained that in New South Wales, with the transfer of these duties to the DPP went the political issues that were associated with them. The statutory removal of a very politically charged aspect of the office protected the independence of the office in its other functions. Indeed, in Tasmania, former Solicitor-General Leigh Sealy worked hard to remove the provision in the Tasmanian legislation requiring the Solicitor-General to fulfil the DPP's functions when the office was vacant. These amendments were passed in 2013.[56]

Northern Territory Solicitor-General Michael Grant reflected on the remaining residual function in the New South Wales statute that provides that the Solicitor-General may act for the Attorney-General if that office is vacant or the officer is absent. He thought it was problematic, because it moved the Solicitor-General into the political and administrative processes of government, undermining the independence of the office. This very issue was raised at the introduction of the Solicitor-General Bill of 1969 in the New South Wales Legislative Assembly. Jack Mannix, for example, argued that any delegations ought to be in the area of the Attorney-General's legal rather than political responsibility.[57] Attorney-General Kenneth McCaw explained that the wide delegation was needed because of difficulties in definitions, but that it was not intended that the Solicitor-General would accept any policy-making responsibility.[58] When interviewed, former Solicitor-General Keith Mason believed this section must *only* relate to the Attorney-General's legal services and public interest functions, and not the political functions of the office.

In relation to these roles that take the Solicitor-General beyond the traditional function of counsel, former Commonwealth Attorney-General Michael Lavarch said:

> [I]f you could not do it you would be better off. It is just a bit messy. And … those things invariably still [provoke] all sorts of interests and things. In my view it is better off to keep your Solicitor-General away from it so he doesn't attract slings and arrows.

To a large extent Lavarch's position reflects that of the High Court regarding the involvement of the Judiciary in political questions. The Court has held that such involvement is unconstitutional if it is such as to undermine the courts' independence from the political branches, and therefore the public's perception of judges as

2006–07 (HC306) [56]; see also *The Governance of Britain: A Consultation on the Role of the Attorney General* (The Stationery Office Limited, 2007) 13; House of Lords Constitution Committee, *Reform of the Office of Attorney General* (HL 2007–08, 93), available at <http://www.publications.parliament.uk/pa/ld200708/ldselect/ldconst/93/93.pdf>, 14 [40] ff.

56 *Director of Public Prosecutions Amendment Act 2013* (Tas).

57 New South Wales, *Parliamentary Debates*, Legislative Assembly, 17 September 1969, 970.

58 ibid, 971.

impartial arbiters.[59] By engaging in politically associated activities, the Solicitor-General may inadvertently reintroduce the overt tensions that historically existed in the English model of the Law Officers. In Australia, removing the Solicitor-General from the political realm of the ministry was intended to remove these tensions and the inevitable controversies that resulted from relying on the office-holder's personal integrity alone to separate the office's political duties from the professionally focused legal functions.

In many instances, the Solicitor-General will be asked to engage in non-legal activities precisely *because* of the independence of the office.[60] A number of examples of this arose in the interviews. In the Northern Territory, under the *Legal Profession Act 2006* (NT), the Solicitor-General was appointed as the 'Statutory Supervisor'[61] to oversee the regulation of the legal profession in the Territory. Solicitor-General Michael Grant explained that when negotiations were occurring around the establishment of the position, it had originally been proposed that the Statutory Supervisor would be a government officer from within the Department of Justice.[62] However, the Bar Association had perceived that such an officer would not be sufficiently independent from government. The Solicitor-General was settled upon as a satisfactory compromise.

Many Solicitors-General indicated they would *only* become involved in non-legal activities if they did not conflict with the primary functions of the role or undermine its independence and status.[63]

Former Victorian Solicitor-General Pamela Tate acted as Special Counsel to the Human Rights Consultation Committee (an independent body established by the government to consult within the community on the question of whether Victoria should adopt a Charter of Rights).[64] She was asked to participate in this Committee by the Attorney-General, but, she explained, she was very careful to limit her involvement to technical advice on the legal features of the project, keeping her office removed from political considerations that might have undermined her independence. As the Charter of Rights was a major policy initiative of the State government of considerable legal complexity, she played a significant role in advising on the operation of the Charter throughout her tenure, with respect

[59] See, eg, the discussion of the involvement of Justice Jane Mathews as a reporter under the *Aboriginal and Torres Strait Islander Heritage Protection Act 1984* (Cth) in *Wilson v Minister for Aboriginal & Torres Strait Islander Affairs* (1996) 189 CLR 1, which required her to consider matters of policy. See also D Webb, 'Keeping the Crown's Conscience: A Theory of Lawyering for Public Sector Counsel' (2007) 5 *New Zealand Journal of Public and International Law* 243, 250–51; GP Miller, 'Government Lawyers' Ethics in a System of Checks and Balances' (1987) 54 *University of Chicago Law Review* 1293.

[60] Interview, Michael Grant; Interview, Martin Hinton; Interview, Chris Kourakis; Interview, Greg Parker.

[61] Section 678(2).

[62] Incidentally, he was involved in these negotiations prior to his appointment as Solicitor-General, as the representative of the Bar Association.

[63] Interview, Geoffrey Davies; Interview, Martin Hinton; Interview, Anthony Mason; Interview, Greg Parker.

[64] Similarly, Michael Grant is Special Counsel to the Statehood Committee in the Northern Territory.

to litigation, draft legislation and Executive action. She also appeared in Charter cases in a variety of courts within the Victorian hierarchy. This involved her in close and consistent contact with many government officers to facilitate the implementation of government policy within a legal framework.

For similar reasons related to the protection of the non-partisan perceptions of the office, participants generally accepted that the Solicitor-General should avoid the media where possible.[65] So, for example, former Queensland Attorney-General Dean Wells said:

> Engaging with the media can lead to all sorts … of trouble. The mere … appearance in the public eye is sufficient to provoke a frenzy of character assassination. It is probably best to stay out of the public eye if you are trying to pursue a job that requires a degree of gravitas that the role of the Solicitor-General does.[66]

The statutory removal of the Solicitor-General from the political realm was a substantial and innovative step by the Australian jurisdictions. While only a few participants saw the statutory safeguards as vital in protecting the office's independence, there was a high degree of caution among participants about involving the Solicitor-General in activities that might undermine the perception of the Solicitor-General as being separated from politics. It was generally perceived that involving the Solicitor-General in functions not traditionally associated with counsel would largely undermine the advantages sought to be gained by introducing a non-political, legal professional model.

B. Relationship with the First Law Officer and Traditional Role of the Law Officers

> The protection of the respective Attorneys-General, as the first Law Officers of the Crown, should extend to all of these officers, so that none of them will be affected in the performance of their professional duty by any sense of loyalty or duty to, or hope of reward from, the government of the day.[67]

Many participants commented on the importance of the relationship between the two Law Officers as protecting the independence of the Solicitor-General.[68] For example, former Commonwealth Solicitor-General Gavan Griffith wrote in 1996, '[t]he First [Law Officer] provides an insulation from the political process so

[65] Interview, Greg Parker.

[66] See also Interview, Chris Kourakis.

[67] *Waterford v Commonwealth* (1987) 163 CLR 54, 73 (Brennan J). See also *Attorney-General (NT) v Kearney* (1985) 158 CLR 500, 517 (Mason and Brennan JJ).

[68] Interview, Greg Cooper; Interview, Stephen Gageler; Interview, Michael Lavarch; Interview, Robert McClelland; Interview, Pamela Tate. In the US context, see EN Griswold, *Ould Fields, New Corne: The Personal Memoirs of a Twentieth Century Lawyer* (West Publishing Co, 1992), 271, 325–26.

that the Second is able to practise as counsel in an apolitical mode'.[69] In Western Australia, Attorney-General Michael Mischin noted that one of the important dimensions of requiring all advice sought from the Solicitor-General to come through the Attorney-General was that it ensured the Attorney was able to protect the Solicitor-General from inappropriate political pressures.

Former Victorian Solicitor-General Stephen McLeish commented that he believed the respect within government of the finality of his advice as a 'Law Officer' was also part of maintaining his independence.

C. 'So Long, Thanks for All the Fish': Financial Security

Queensland and Western Australia are currently the only jurisdictions to have reintroduced a general right to private practice. For some participants, this was an important facet of the protection of their independence, as well as being a drawcard for highly experienced senior barristers. In the Second Reading Debates in Queensland, Douglas Jennings indicated that the right to private practice in the Solicitor-General Bill 1985 (Qld) gave the Solicitor-General 'independence that is not available in other States'.[70] Former Queensland Solicitor-General Patrick Keane said that the right of private practice allowed him to leave the position if his independence was challenged. It

> made things a lot easier, at a practical level because you just say, so long, thanks for all the fish. You go your way, I'll go mine. It would not be the end of 'the career', whereas for public servants it is. So at a practical level, apart from the theoretical level, there is no doubt that the independence was very real.[71]

Indeed, the only resignation of a Solicitor-General done for reason's explicitly relating to the actions of the government occurred in Queensland in March 2014. It appears that former Solicitor-General Walter Sofronoff resigned because the Attorney-General had breached the confidences of his closest advisers—including judges, and himself—in pursuit of his own personal and political objectives.[72] Sofronoff returned to a full-time practice at the private Bar.

However, while some viewed the Queensland office's right to private practice as protecting the Solicitor-General by ensuring that financial pressures would be

[69] G Griffith, *Report: Second Law Officer to the First Law Officer 1 July 1995–31 December 1996* (Solicitor General of Australia, 1996) [1.10].

[70] Queensland, *Parliamentary Debates*, Legislative Assembly, 26 March 1985, 4384. Other justifications for the right were that it would attract leading members of the Bar, and it would allow the Solicitor-General to retain a breadth of experience while in office: Interview, Greg Cooper; Interview, Geoffrey Davies; Interview, Dean Wells.

[71] See also Interview, Geoffrey Davies; Interview, Dean Wells.

[72] See further discussion of this incident in ch 5, section II.A.ii.

irrelevant (all participants that held this view were from Queensland), others were less sure. Some participants held concerns about potential conflicts of interest and time, reflecting the same concerns that led to the abolition of the right in Australia and the UK at the end of the nineteenth century.

The right to private practice in Queensland was originally inserted by former High Court Justice Ian Callinan, who had been asked to draft the Queensland Bill by the Bjelke-Petersen National Government. He had included the right to private practice in it. He was then approached by the Queensland government to take the first appointment under the Act. He said that after drafting the legislation, he gave the idea of the right to private practice some more thought and decided that it 'really wasn't right'. He explained that he feared that private parties briefing the Solicitor-General in private matters might expect government favour and that the courts would extend additional gravitas to the individual because of the appointment. There would be the possibility, and therefore the perception, of abuse of a public position.

Some participants from other jurisdictions saw no impropriety in allowing private practice, but they thought it might cause conflicts regarding the allocation of time to government work.[73] Others saw immense dangers of legally compromising conflicts of interest arising.[74] In Western Australia, while the right to maintain a private practice was reintroduced in 2012, Grant Donaldson, who has held office under the current arrangements, has exercised only a small private practice. There are a number of reasons for this. Western Australian Attorney-General Michael Mischin explained that the Solicitor-General had to ensure his availability to fulfil the role as it was practised in Western Australia (which had previously been filled by a full-time appointee and therefore the responsibilities had evolved to reflect this).[75] A smaller practice also avoided the potential for actual and perceived conflicts of interest to arise.[76]

The ability of the Attorney-General under the Commonwealth legislation to allow the Solicitor-General to engage in private practice sparked some controversy in 1991 during then Solicitor-General Gavan Griffith's tenure. It was proposed that he would be granted a year's leave, during which time he was given permission by the Attorney-General to engage in private practice pursuant to section 9 of the *Law Officers Act 1964* (Cth). A number of conditions were attached to

[73] Interview, William Bale; Interview, Anthony Mason; note this possibility was raised in the Second Reading Debate: Queensland, *Parliamentary Debates*, Legislative Assembly, 26 March 1985, 4376 (Wayne Goss, Labor, Leader of the Opposition).

[74] See also Interview, William Bale; Interview, John Doyle; Interview, Trevor Griffin; Interview, Michael Sexton; note this possibility was raised in the Second Reading Debate by: Queensland, *Parliamentary Debates*, Legislative Assembly, 26 March 1985, 4378–79 (Paul Braddy, Labor).

[75] The officeholder, Grant Donaldson, also commented that he was unable to maintain a large private practice simply because of time, and the requirement in his contract that he prioritise government work.

[76] Interview, Michael Mischin.

the permission.[77] The matter became controversial when the Attorney-General refused to answer questions from Parliament as to why the deal was put in place, referring only to the fact that the reasons behind the request from the Solicitor-General were 'personal'.[78] Andrew Peacock for the Opposition said the use of the provision in the way proposed had the potential to undermine the Solicitor-General's independence, because there would be at least a perception that the Solicitor-General had received a very generous favour from the Government.[79]

Former Commonwealth Solicitor-General Anthony Mason considered that fundamental to the protection of the office's independence was the ability of the officeholder to resign with no, or few, financial ramifications. When asked about what protected the Solicitor-General's independence, his answer was immediate:

> Resignation. I say that seriously. If you felt that a position was being reached where you were being overborne, or attempts to overbear your independent, impartial judgement, then resignation was obviously the sanction. And in the case of a Solicitor-General, generally speaking … I think universally up to the present point of time, people who have been appointed under the *Law Officers Act* have an established reputation which would enable them to resume practice at the Bar. It is not as if they are in the position of some people, whose whole career and livelihood is at risk if they don't, as it were, toe the line. So resignation is a sanction that the Solicitor-General has.

Former Victorian Solicitor-General Henry Winneke, when involved in the drafting of the 1951 Victorian statute, had expressed similar sentiments. 'The right man,' he had said, needed no tenure, because 'if he became dissatisfied, he could always return to the Bar.'[80]

D. External Institutions: The SCSG and the Courts

Former Queensland Solicitor-General Patrick Keane identified two additional mechanisms that he believed assisted in the protection of the Solicitor-General's independence: the SCSG and the courts. Of the first, he said:

> [W]e met regularly, to talk about matters of mutual interest and I think it was terrific for morale, that there was this little group of people who were in the same club, who had the same problems to a greater or lesser degree. So you had the opportunity for a sounding board, to just make sure that you were never on a limb all by yourself.[81]

[77] See an explanation of the arrangements made between the Attorney-General and the Solicitor-General in Commonwealth, *Parliamentary Debates*, House of Representatives, 12 November 1991, 2842 (Michael Duffy, Attorney-General).

[78] ibid.

[79] ibid, 2835.

[80] Coleman, above n 10, 160. A similar position was expressed in Interview, Rob Mitchell.

[81] See also Interview, Peter Garrisson; Interview, Stephen McLeish; Interview, Leigh Sealy.

He also explained why he believed the courts could assist in protecting the independence of the office:

> [B]eing confident that there were some things that the court would accept and some things they wouldn't, if you can be confident about that it makes you more confident in your own position. … I mean if the courts are blowing in the wind, then it gets really hard. … Certainly in my time … the courts were regular … you know, innovation wasn't happening for innovation's sake. But I think it would be very destabilising for independence's sake, if you did have the courts blowing in the wind. Because then the pressure to just run anything because who can tell; 'run it up the flagpole and see if someone salutes it' would have been a very hard … instruction to resist.

The notion that the predictability of the courts buttresses the independence of the Solicitor-General was illustrated in the reaction to the Solicitor-General's advice after the decision in the *Malaysia Solution Case*, which has been detailed in chapter five, section II.A.ii.[82] A number of aspects of the episode demonstrate the destabilisation that can be caused to the practical independence, the perceived independence and also the integrity of the office where the courts, and particularly the High Court, come to conclusions not predicted by a large part of the legal community. The media attacks on the integrity and competence of the Solicitor-General's original advice to the Government on the Malaysia Solution (which was assumed to exist, but was never released) contained within them implicit attacks on the independence of the Solicitor-General from the Government's policy imperatives in the immigration arena.

The conclusion of the authors of the joint opinion (the Solicitor-General and Stephen Lloyd SC and Geoffrey Kennett SC) was to the effect that they did not have reasonable confidence, on the material provided, that the *Migration Act 1958* (Cth) could be used to transfer asylum seekers from Australia to either Nauru (an option opposed by the Government politically) or Papua New Guinea for processing.[83] The opinion is certainly couched in terms that demonstrate that the Solicitor-General and the other authors were not at all confident as to which way the High Court might decide future cases. The authors expressly say as much, and their identification of a number of significant issues left unresolved by the case heightens this sense that the future direction of the Court in this area remains less than certain.[84] Lawyers are often confronted with difficult situations where *they* may have a firm view of the correct legal position, but must advise their clients on whether a majority of the Court would share that view. After the *Malaysia Solution Case*, there was great uncertainty because the Court had left a number of issues

[82] *Plaintiff M70/2011 v Minister for Immigration and Citizenship; Plaintiff M106 of 2011 v Minister for Immigration and Citizenship* (2011) 244 CLR 144.

[83] Opinion of Stephen Gageler, Stephen Lloyd and Geoffrey Kennett, *In the Matter of the Implications of* Plaintiff M70/2011 v Minister for Immigration and Citizenship *for Offshore Processing of Asylum Seekers under the* Migration Act 1958 *(Cth)*, 2 September 2011, 2 [3].

[84] ibid [12]–[13].

undecided in the decision itself. It is this unpredictability that opens the door for critiques that the advice was political. Each criticism carries with it an undertone that the Solicitor-General's independence was being manipulated to achieve the political objectives of the Gillard Government—to avoid using Nauru as an offshore processing country.

V. Independence in Practice

To what degree is the independence of the Solicitor-General respected in practice? As a whole, participants were of the view that in the vast majority of cases the government and its emanations acted with the greatest respect for the independence of the office.[85] So, for example, former Commonwealth Attorney-General Michael Lavarch said:

> [I]t is convention and custom that does tend to rule here. So in terms of the behaviours and the expectations of Ministers and the government, not to ask or expect things which are improper. And we can be all terribly cynical about the government and government processes, but in my experience, … people overwhelmingly acted properly in understanding the—almost instinctively to some extent—the boundaries of their role. The officeholders themselves obviously needed a bit of understanding as to what is proper and right, to not be moved from that.

Former Commonwealth Attorney-General Robert McClelland indicated that, in practice, there will always be difficulties in ensuring that the appropriate level of respect is provided to the independence of the Solicitor-General from within the Government:

> [N]ow there will be some members of Cabinet who want to get the advice they want to hear. And [the Solicitor-General] won't do that, and nor will I put pressure on him. And he is appointed for that period of time. And he is not the sort of person who would do that. But you will always find in any endeavour someone who wants to pressure the adviser to give the advice they want to hear. [The Solicitor-General] scrupulously resists that. But there is a need for a sense of maturity across Cabinet, to ensure that that doesn't happen, people putting pressure to get the advice they want to here. As best I can, supported by Cabinet colleagues, we emphasise that to other colleagues, but there is, and inevitably will be in the future, tensions about that.

As McClelland noted, there was evidence of instances where some pressure was brought to bear on the Solicitor-General. A Solicitor-General related one incident in which he was involved:

> *Have you ever had any improper pressure placed on you by the department, or perhaps a minister, that threatened that independence?*

[85] See, eg, William Bale, rejecting the idea that his advice had been subject to political interference in an interview on Lateline: S Cullen, 'Bill Bale', *Stateline Tasmania* (ABC Online), 18 July 2008, available at <http://www.abc.net.au/stateline/tas/content/2006/s2307818.htm>.

> Yes, once. Yes.
>
> *Are you able to elaborate on that?*
>
> Probably not, but if the question is, 'Did I succumb to it'? The answer is absolutely not.
>
> *How did you deal with it?*
>
> I did what I was asked to do in the timeframe in which I was asked to do it and I did it in my own terms. I knew what was wanted but I did it in my own terms. When it was done, I spoke to the Attorney-General about it, and I made it clear that I didn't think it was acceptable.

The incident relays an important aspect of the Solicitor-General's independence. Particularly where most participants emphasised that the statutory mechanisms played no role, or were only partially relevant in protecting the office's independence, it is the individual's commitment to professional ethical standards that must resist the pressures that can be brought to bear on the office. As such, former Commonwealth Attorney-General Thomas Hughes described it as a 'duty of imperfect obligation', in the sense that 'it is not capable of being reduced to a duty punishable for non-observance'. It is a moral duty, 'to be performed in the light of the principles that should govern the execution of the office'.

VI. Discussion: Protecting Independence: Comparing Structural and Individual Protections

While the statutory basis for tenure might provide the normative framework in which government and society more generally considers the Solicitor-General, my research reveals that far more important in protecting the independence of the officeholder in practice is ensuring that quality candidates with appropriate integrity and professional experience continue to be attracted to the position.

A prevalent view in the US is that relying on the strength of individuals' commitment to independence in offices such as the Solicitor-General is inadequate. Bruce Ackerman warned that relying on individuals' ethical and professional conduct to ensure the integrity of a public office gives rise to the possibility of abuse by the less scrupulous.[86] Often this is only possible because of a reputation fostered by previous, *ethical* officeholders.[87] Norman Spaulding considered

[86] B Ackerman, 'Abolish the White House Counsel: And the Office of Legal Counsel, too, while we're at it', *Slate*, 22 April 2009. See also Book Note, 'Probing the Role of the Solicitor General' (1992) 106 *Harvard Law Review* 504, 509; CTL Pillard, 'The Unfulfilled Promise of the Constitution in Executive Hands' (2005) 103 *Michigan Law Review* 676, 685.

[87] Ackerman, above n 86.

the independence of government lawyers in the aftermath of the Torture Memos revelations.[88] His firm conclusion was that the individual's commitment to independence was simply insufficient to ensure against abuse: 'genuine independence requires structural support'.[89]

Australia already has some structural support for the independence of the Solicitor-General; this is what the tenure and remuneration provisions of the statute were largely intended to achieve. Tenure and remuneration guarantees have been identified by the High Court as key planks in protecting the decisional independence of the Judiciary.[90] They are, at the least, important signals that articulate a normative proposition to the public about the government's commitment to protecting the independence of the Solicitor-General. However, as discussed in chapter four, section II., a number of deficiencies exist even in these protections of the Solicitor-General's independence. The statute also fails to guarantee that the Solicitor-General will be briefed by the government in relation to particular matters, creating the possibility that a Solicitor-General who falls from government favour may be 'frozen out' of work, a possibility that is canvassed in greater detail in chapter five, section II.B.iii.b. It is within contemplation that providing robust and independent advice could be one reason why an individual may be frozen out.

Even if the deficiencies in the tenure and remuneration guarantees could be sufficiently remedied across the jurisdictions to alleviate these concerns, there are real questions about whether structural guarantees can protect against inappropriate incursions into independent practice by officeholders bent on malfeasance; and also whether rigid frameworks may unnecessarily remove legitimate influences, and maintaining the Attorney-General's ultimate responsibility for the office's conduct. Former South Australian Crown Solicitor Catherine Branson said, 'we have to be realistic about the protection [the statute] provides'. Ackerman agreed that structural support could never be sufficient. He argued, therefore, for the *abolition* of the post of lawyer for the Executive because, conceptualised as the Executive's lawyers, these institutions breed one sided advocacy. Ackerman argued for drastic institutional reform to replace such positions with court-like institutions operating within the Executive.[91]

[88] NW Spaulding, 'Professional Independence in the Office of the Attorney-General' (2008) 60(6) *Stanford Law Review* 1931.

[89] ibid, 1977.

[90] See, eg, *The Waterside Workers' Federation of Australia v JW Alexander Ltd* (1918) 25 CLR 434 ('*Alexander's Case*), 469—70 (Isaacs and Rich JJ); *Harris v Caladine* (1991) 172 CLR 84, 159 (McHugh J). The High Court has found that there is no single model of tenure that will guarantee independence, but that the question will be whether a particular framework ensures the independence and impartiality of the Judiciary: *North Australian Aboriginal Legal Aid Service Inc v Bradley* (2004) 218 CLR 146, 152 (Gleeson CJ). See also G Brennan, 'Independence of the Judiciary: Declaration of Principles on Judicial Independence, Announcement by the Chief Justice of Australia' (1997) 15 *Australian Bar Review* 175, which sets out the *Declaration of Principles on Judicial Independence issued by the Chief Justices of the Australian States and Territories* and the *Beijing Statement of Principles of the Independence of the Judiciary in the LAWASIA Region*. See particularly at 175, 177, 182–83.

[91] Ackerman, above n 86; B Ackerman, *The Decline and Fall of the American Republic* (Belknap Press of Harvard University Press, 2010) 143–45.

Spaulding advocated less drastic structural reform. He acknowledged the difficulties in introducing structural guarantees of independence without creating overly rigid frameworks that compromise the benefits of political accountability and responsiveness.[92] In the Australian context, the Solicitor-General has no claim to an independent mandate to make binding decisions or take autonomous actions in a system where the responsible officer is the Attorney-General. Therefore, as an advocate, the Solicitor-General acts on the Attorney-General's instruction (even if in practice there is a large degree of autonomy of action); and even as an adviser has an obligation to *assist* the government in pursuing its political objectives within a legal framework. Participants emphasised that the Solicitor-General should not be an independent linesperson, performing a function akin to a court, but work constructively with the democratically elected government representatives.

Spaulding argued that flexible structural support could be achieved in a number of ways. These included making enforceable the guidelines drafted by former members of the OLC on the ethical framework in which advice must be drawn. Spaulding also suggested that greater transparency could be introduced to facilitate political accountability, and a first step towards this would be making the OLC's opinions public. Public release of Solicitor-General opinions could promote more ethical practice and avoid the temptation to provide accommodating advice. As Jeremy Bentham said, 'Publicity is the very soul of justice. It is the keenest spur to exertion and the surest of all guards against improbity.'[93] It may also protect the Solicitor-General's independence from attacks, as were evident in 2011 when the government refused to release the Solicitor-General's advice on the legality of the Malaysia Solution.

But the proposal contradicts the justifications proposed for the existence of legal professional privilege and the Law Officers' Convention. Legal professional privilege exists to encourage clients actively to seek legal advice and, when they do so, to provide frank disclosure to obtain complete legal advice. These justifications apply with considerable weight in the government arena.[94] The convention that the Law Officer's advice is not released even to the Parliament continues to be strongly adhered to in Australia. Further, there is a very real possibility that the Solicitor-General's advice may not be sought by government (because either government fails to seek advice at all, or seeks advice from quarters perceived to be more accommodating) because of the lack of any guaranteed work. The Law Officer's Convention, if it does encourage the government to seek the Solicitor-General's advice, is therefore an important part of the proper operating of our constitutional system, and its removal, or even weakening, should be approached with appropriate caution.

[92] Spaulding, above n 88, 1977.

[93] As quoted by Lord Shaw in *Scott v Scott* [1913] AC 417, 477.

[94] *Waterford v Commonwealth* (1987) 163 CLR 54, 62 (Mason and Deane JJ).

The independence of the Solicitor-General in Australia is protected by statute, but officeholders and government officials are keenly aware of the importance of the individual's integrity in ensuring that independence is not undermined by inappropriate pressures. The current model provides normative protection while recognising the limits of statutory guarantees. Following Spaulding's suggestion, this protection may be increased by developing a deeper understanding within government of the role, and the ethical and professional standards that attach to it.

VII. Discussion: 'Autonomous Experts' and 'Team Members'

There were a number of participants in this study who believed that part of maintaining their professional independence from the political Executive was through the maintenance of professional distance—that is, by mirroring the professional distance that exists between a private barrister and a private client. This reflects the view of the role of the Solicitor-General as distinct from the government machine, to be briefed by government on matters of its choosing at points where significant legal issues have arisen. I have called this the 'autonomous expert' approach to the role. This approach emphasises the status of the office as protecting its independence from improper pressures from the Executive.[95]

Former Victorian Solicitor-General Pamela Tate emphasised that, for her, this professional distance took her away from the 'internal ethos' of the government, and was a barrier against any unintended, insidious political influence. Just as with a private barrister, this meant that when the Solicitor-General was briefed, he or she was not influenced by any subliminal pressures that arose because of involvement in the development of a policy, with any resulting vested interests and pre-drawn conclusions. This permitted Tate to assist the government to achieve its policy objectives consistently with the rule of law. This model also combated any tendency by government lawyers to discuss advice with the Solicitor-General casually, and then to claim that the advice had the assent of the Solicitor-General, or had been confirmed by the Solicitor-General.[96]

A similar position was adopted by Commonwealth Solicitor-General Justin Gleeson. He expressly noted, however, the potential compromise involved in a highly formalised position, that there was 'a trade off here between independence on the one hand, and … it's somewhere between pragmatism and usefulness to government on other hand'. Despite his concerns about the potential costs of

[95] For further discussion of independence as 'status' in the context of lawyers, see Le Mire, above n 9, 34.

[96] Interview, Stephen McLeish; Interview, Pamela Tate.

formalising the independence of the advice function, nonetheless he has adopted a formalised system of advice under which he notifies the Attorney-General of all requests for advice in non-contentious matters, provides copies of all advices on those matters to the Attorney-General, and provides all advices in writing. He explained:

> Now that is, in the eyes of some, not being pragmatic, not being responsive, not being sufficiently … accommodating of the objective. Now, … there may be some in government saying, we'd like to know what the Solicitor-General thinks before we ask him or her to put it down on paper.

Gleeson also claimed there were 'dangers' in a system where 'informal advice can lead to people interpreting it as they wish, and claiming they have received more advice than they have received'. He acknowledged, however, the danger of an overly formalised approach:

> And at some point there is a balance. There is no perfect answer to these cases. And if you sit in the ivory tower completely, the end result is that no-one sends any requests to the ivory tower. … It's an important topic… I don't think there is a single right answer.

This first view of the position of the Solicitor-General can be contrasted against the view that the Solicitor-General ought to be more embedded within the government: to be involved during policy development to ensure that the government addresses arising legal issues, and to tackle problems as they materialise in the most legally appropriate manner.[97] I called this the 'team member' approach. At a recent conference on the role of legal advisers in international law, a similar approach was described by reference to the 'aeroplane rule': 'to be in at the landing, you have to be there at the take-off and in the loop throughout the journey'.[98]

This view arose in a number of variations. One of the more extreme examples was the position of former Victorian Solicitor-General Hartog Berkeley *within* the Premier's Department; a less absolute form was taken by former New South Wales Solicitor-General Keith Mason, who met regularly with a number of other statutory officeholders and the department head to ensure he was aware of the issues existing across the government.[99]

In the Australian Capital Territory, legal services directions require all legal services to be provided through the Australian Capital Territory Government Solicitor (ACTGS), unless by agreement with the ACTGS and with the approval

[97] This view largely reflected that of Sam Silkin's 'intimate but independent involvement': SC Silkin, 'The Functions and Position of the Attorney-General in the United Kingdom' (1978) 59 *The Parliamentarian* 149.

[98] Jean-Pierre Gauci, Kate Jones, Chanu Peiris, Joseph Crampin, Conference Report: 'The Role of Legal Advisers in International Law' (Foreign and Commonwealth Office, British Institute of International and Comparative Law, and Brill Nijhoff, 26 February 2015) 4, available at <http://www.biicl.org/documents/570_the_role_of_legal_advisers_in_international_law_-_conference_report_final26_feb.pdf>.

[99] See also Interview, Daryl Dawson and Interview, Stephen McLeish.

of the Solicitor-General.[100] This has meant that the Solicitor-General (who also performs the functions of the Chief Solicitor of the ACTGS) is aware of *all* of the legal issues arising across the government, and can decide whether to involve the office in particular matters.[101] Australian Capital Territory Solicitor-General Peter Garrisson believed that without this overarching, helicopter view of the legal position of government, 'there would be no value for [the Solicitor-General] role in government'.

John Edwards warned that more intimate involvement in government would erode the public's perception of the Law Officer's independence.[102] Any reduction in the independence of an officeholder who adopts a 'team member' approach is subtle. Client capture can occur: a 'team member' may become too closely identified with the government's policy, resulting in legal analysis being subconsciously framed through the client's lens.[103] A 'team member' may be influenced by the development of group norms and social pressures. The more cohesively embedded the Solicitor-General is within a group entrusted with policy implementation, the greater the potential danger that the office will no longer realistically and independently appraise alternative courses of action because of the motivation to achieve the goals of the group.[104]

A 'team member' Solicitor-General, at least in theory, risks losing professional distance from the Executive's policy desires: not necessarily consciously, but simply because of the ongoing exposure to policy development in a team atmosphere of shared goals. This propensity may seem particularly acute against the background of my findings that the Solicitor-General's independence is largely protected by the individual officeholder's personal commitment to independence. Even if these types of incursions into independence do not occur in practice, the closer relationship between the Solicitor-General and the Executive increases the likelihood of such a perception. In many ways, the 'autonomous expert' is actively protecting against any sort of group-cohesiveness that could thwart independence, while also reinforcing the perception of the office's independence.

Neither approach was necessarily more associated with a government–agent perception of the Solicitor-General as opposed to a view that the Solicitor-General should be actively advising the government on the congruence between its actions and the public interest. However, the increased likelihood of a 'team member's' loss of independence because of being embedded more integrally within government processes perhaps meant that even if an individual had hoped to advise on the public interest in the development of government processes, he or she might lose the necessary distance to provide advice of that nature.

[100] *Law Officers (General) Legal Services Directions 2012* (ACT), sch, cl 1; Interview, Peter Garrisson.
[101] Interview, Peter Garrisson.
[102] Edwards, *The Attorney-General*, above n 5, 75.
[103] See analysis of the Torture Memos to this effect in Le Mire, above n 9, 27.
[104] I Janis, *Victims of groupthink* (Houghton Mifflin, 1972); I Janis, 'Groupthink' (1971) 5 *Psychology Today* 43.

An 'autonomous expert' might have adopted an approach that placed his or her independence outside of subtle group-driven influences, but my research demonstrates that such an officeholder was not necessarily more likely to adopt a public-interest driven approach to the role of Solicitor-General. A private barrister is also physically removed from the client, analogous to the 'autonomous expert'. However, often the independence of private barristers is considered to be precisely the reason why they can become 'hired guns' for their clients' causes. *Morally* independent from the interests of their clients, they do not directly further the public interest but, rather, their clients' interests, unencumbered by any personal judgement on its desirability. Such a view can be found in journalist and author David Marr's description of former Commonwealth Solicitor-General David Bennett, 'Perhaps after a hard day in court, David Bennett, QC, goes home and scrubs down with a strong carbolic soap. Lawyers have to do grim things for their clients at times, and Bennett's client is the Commonwealth Government.'[105]

An 'autonomous expert' Solicitor-General may fail to gain the trust of the government: government officers may treat a fiercely independent Solicitor-General with defensiveness and distrust. In the US context, Nancy Baker had observed that neutral, or fiercely independent, officeholders may be isolated from policy development by government because of erosion of trust in the office's commitment to the government's agenda.[106] In the historical development of the UK Law Officers, one factor in the Attorney-General's rise to seniority over the King's Serjeants was not because of their robust independence and fidelity to the law, but because the King wanted their political experience and awareness gained from involvement, at that time, in Parliament. In the corporate context, a similar phenomenon has been observed. Suzanne Le Mire has argued that when a lawyer adopts independent status from the client, it may 'lead to exclusion or marginalisation if managers see the lawyer as someone who is not motivated to achieve organisational goals'.[107]

As there is no statutory requirement to seek the advice of the Solicitor-General, where trust is eroded, the government may simply fail to consult a Solicitor-General because of a perceived distance between the goals of the government and those of the office. This means that the government may go without advice on actions where advice is needed, or may obtain advice from quarters where there is a paucity of understanding of whole-of-government interests. There is also the possibility that the government may, intentionally or not, fragment its legal work, briefing the Solicitor-General on small parts of a larger legal picture. To guard against these potentialities, many participants emphasised the importance of a cultural fit when appointing a Solicitor-General, and the delicate

[105] D Marr, 'Liberty is Left in Shaky Hands when the High Court no Longer Defends It', *Sydney Morning Herald* (Sydney) (31 March 2005).

[106] N Baker, *Conflicting Loyalties: Law and Politics in the Attorney General's Office, 1789–1990* (University Press of Kansas, 1992) 145–46.

[107] Le Mire, above n 9, 34.

positioning that was required when a government of a different political persuasion was elected, to ensure this cultural fit continued. My research has revealed a number of instances of Solicitors-General being 'frozen out' of government legal work, demonstrating the frailties of the current arrangements with their lack of any formal guarantee of work for the Solicitor-General.

An 'autonomous expert' may be consulted later in the continuum of decision-making than a 'team member'. Indeed, former Victorian Solicitor-General Pamela Tate explained that she intentionally waited for legal issues to crystallise before becoming involved. Robert Rosen has argued that the later a lawyer is involved, the more power must be wielded by the lawyer, as organisations are already committed to a particular course of action.[108] So while an 'autonomous expert' may increase confidence in the office's independence from the political, a 'team member' can be the most effective in ensuring the legality and integrity of the government's actions.[109] A 'team member' may also be more engaged in a larger number of issues, thus able to monitor compliance across government departments and agencies.

The advantages and costs associated with adopting a more team-orientated or more distanced approach reflect the debates that have occurred in the UK over the desirability of the Attorney-General's regularly attending Cabinet. In the 2007–08 government and parliamentary consultations, strong views were expressed that the Attorney-General should attend only when legal issues and legal policy arose. This ensured that the Attorney's decisions in relation to public interest discretions were not coloured by the Government's political agenda, and that when the Attorney-General came to give advice, he or she had the necessary distance from the policy itself to do so with integrity. Then Attorney-General Baroness Scotland expressed the counter-argument:

> Another view has been expressed slightly differently, namely that it is far better for people to get legal advice early, particularly when they are debating issues or issues are crystallising, than to get advice after it has crystallised and before you can change things. I think there has been an issue as to whether it is not helpful … to have someone who does have that legal discipline, who can perhaps make a contribution, a judicious contribution, when the need arises.[110]

The 'team member' and 'autonomous expert' approaches are not mutually exclusive. Tate strove throughout her tenure to reinforce the independence and integrity of office, whilst maintaining an appropriate level of involvement with the development of government policy. She was appointed after a period when the office

[108] RE Rosen, 'Problem-Setting and Serving the Organizational Client: Legal Diagnosis and Professional Independence' (2001) 56 *University of Miami Law Review* 179, 205–06.

[109] See similar arguments that have been made in relation to the advantages of in-house counsel over the engagement of external legal providers more generally: Le Mire, above n 9, 24–25; DA De Mott, 'The Discrete Roles of General Counsel' (2005) 74 *Fordham Law Review* 955, 955.

[110] House of Lords Constitution Committee, *Reform of the Office of Attorney General* (HL 2007–08, 93), available at <http://www.publications.parliament.uk/pa/ld200708/ldselect/ldconst/93/93.pdf> 46.

had limited involvement with government, and she worked with senior officers in the Attorney-General's Department to re-establish the authority of the position. However, she also understood the importance of the office's involvement in the development of policies to ensure that government objectives could be met within a legal framework. She observed:

> [T]here are a number of strands to the role of Solicitor-General, some of which are in tension with each other. Part of the difficulty of the job is knowing how to straddle the various demands so that, when necessary, one must assert one's independence, and, at other times, when the boundaries are very clear, one can be more of a 'team member'. It is not a matter of being one extreme or the other.[111]

Similarly, Stephen McLeish, who succeeded Tate as Victorian Solicitor-General, attempted to find his own position along the spectrum between the two approaches, thereby receiving the benefits of a level of autonomy while maintaining involvement with government. He initially chose to continue, by and large, the arrangements that Tate had put in place to keep the office somewhat distinct from government: he maintained private chambers, and continued to operate in accordance with the protocol implemented by Tate, with only minor adjustments. However, he subsequently agreed with the Attorney-General to set up a second set of chambers within the government. McLeish saw a number of advantages in maintaining the two sets of chambers: having private chambers meant that he maintained a level of autonomy and involvement with the private Bar, and was symbolically independent from government; but having chambers with government might combat the sense of isolation from government (felt by him and those in government) and allow him to become better acquainted with those in government with whom he had regular dealings.

[111] Letter from The Hon Justice Tate to Gabrielle Appleby, 12 August 2012, 1 (copy on file with author).

8

Conclusions

The Solicitor-General is next to the High Court and God.[1]

The Law Officers within those common law systems examined in this book are major actors in the constitutional order. Across these systems, debate has arisen around how the Law Officers ought to meet the constitutional expectations of their roles, whether certain cases illustrate a failure of judgement and whether they demonstrate a need to 'reform' the offices. Dominating this debate are competing ideas about whether the public interest, politics or the law have exerted legitimate influence over the exercise of a Law Officer's judgement.

As an historical narrative, the development of the Australian Solicitor-General demonstrates a desire on the part of Australian governments to respond creatively to many of the tensions associated with the traditional Law Officer role. Governments adopted a statutory design intended to remove the office from political pressures, while maintaining the office's accountability through the Attorney-General. The result is a unique statutory paradigm that places the Solicitor-General outside the political ministry and imports professional obligations of independence. In some respects, the design of the Australian Solicitor-General represents a regression to the early model of the English Law Officers as *professionals* on retainer for the Crown.

However, since the thirteenth century, the Crown has become a more complex legal entity. It now comprises three branches with distinct constitutional mandates. It is an enduring entity headed by a representative of the monarch, but occupied at any given time by an elected government with a democratic mandate to implement its political agenda. Its legitimacy rests on grounds that have evolved from the idea of absolute power ordained by God, to restrained power, contingent upon the agreement of individuals within the community, and built upon assumptions about the obligations of the Crown to both the individual and the community. In Australia, complicating this further is the federal structure of government.

Given the complexity of Australian government, unique pressures are placed on the Solicitor-General's role as a legal professional. So, despite the office's withdrawal from the political arena, its close relationship with the Crown continues to pull the officeholder in different, and at times conflicting, directions. The Solicitor-General must strike a delicate balance between independence *from* the political agenda,

[1] Interview, Linda Lavarch.

to ensure fidelity to the law, and constructive engagement *with* that agenda, to assist the Executive in pursuing its objectives.[2] This raises immediate questions about the extent to which the Solicitor-General ought to be, and can be, insulated from political pressures. The legitimacy of the government is not drawn entirely from its democratic mandate but rests also on enduring public policy values that emphasise government under the rule of law. It was the traditional role of the Law Officers to assist the government to adhere to these values, and the struggle to achieve them continues to influence the Solicitor-General's role today.

In this conclusion, I return to evaluate the major research findings of the book. Each of them demonstrates an overarching theme: while the non-political grounding of Australia's Solicitor-General has in some important respects removed the office from the immediate tensions between the public interest, the law and politics, the office's continuing relationship with the democratic government means that these tensions resurface in practice and must be negotiated by individual officeholders.

I. The Crown: A Conflicted Client

Across the Australian jurisdictions, the Solicitor-General acts as 'counsel for the Crown'. The 'Crown' referred to in the statutes means the Executive, distinct from the other branches. Thus, the removal of the office from parliament has removed the potential for conflicts to arise between the interests of the Legislature and the Executive. Yet even within this narrower definition of the Crown there is the potential for conflicts to occur between the political Executive and other emanations of the Crown, often in the form of Vice-regal officers and independent statutory bodies, particularly those statutory agencies tasked with monitoring the exercise of government power.

The propensity for disparate interests to arise within the Crown raises difficult questions for the Solicitor-General, who must determine the primary client and avoid acting for other conflicting interests. It also raises a difficult conundrum for the operation of the constitutional system. In striving towards constitutionalism under the rule of law, it is imperative that *all* of the Crown's emanations have access to high-quality legal advisers who can resolve legal questions with finality and authority. This allows the different emanations of the Crown to act with confidence, and provides confidence to the citizenry. It is in recognition of this ultimate objective that practices and protocols have been developed to facilitate access to the Solicitor-General by as many parts of the Crown as possible, even in instances of possible conflict with the political Executive. For example, there is increasing

[2] See also AC Hutchinson, 'In the Public Interest: The Responsibilities and Rights of Government Lawyers' (2008) 46 *Osgoode Hall Law Journal* 105, 117.

uniformity of practice among the jurisdictions about when and in what circumstances the Solicitor-General can advise Vice-regal officers. The practice may not yet have reached the level of constitutional convention, but Solicitors-General and Attorneys-General have indicated the desirability of introducing uniformity in this area to lessen confusion, and to ensure that the rule of law is maintained in those very rare but important instances where Vice-regal officers are called upon to act independently from the government of the day.

The loyalties of Australian Solicitors-General are further complicated by the federal nature of the Australian Commonwealth. This implies that there is some larger 'common wealth' that transcends the governments of each jurisdictional entity and encompasses the people as a whole, the 'new political community created by the union of the people and of the colonies of Australia'.[3] Solicitors-General have often been involved in nationwide policy initiatives through the collective group, the SCSG, where they must carefully balance the interests of their government and the interests of the federation.

II. The Public Interest and 'Core Government Principles'

In chapter four, section VI.B., I developed an argument that even within the modern statutory framework, the common law obligations of the Law Officers to the public interest continue to inform the role. These original common law duties arose in conjunction with the idea that the Crown had obligations to act in the interests of the citizenry. Most specifically, I develop a position that the Solicitor-General retains a duty to warn and advise the government about 'core government principles'. Unlike the political Law Officers in Britain, in Australia the duty relates only to the Solicitor-General's *advisory* function and the conduct of litigation in the form of ensuring that the Crown adheres to the model litigant principles. This more narrowly drawn duty recognises the legitimacy, and necessity, of the Solicitor-General's acting as the legal agent of the Crown; but also recognises the existence of autonomous moral and political values that the Crown must strive to uphold. The Solicitor-General's duty to warn and advise on the 'core government principles' assists the Crown to ascertain, and act in pursuit of, these values.

Historical convention underpins the duty to act in the public interest. However, there is a lack of public scholarship and debate about how the traditional Law Officers' functions can continue in the Solicitor-General's role under the contemporary statutes and explain the continuing relevance of the public interest to

[3] J Quick and R Garran, *The Annotated Constitution of the Australian Commonwealth* (Legal Books, 1901, 1976 reprint) 312.

the advisory function.[4] Therefore it was unsurprising to find that interview participants were divided over whether the Solicitor-General ought to provide advice of this nature. As a duty resting on tradition and convention, it is only through understanding and diligence on the part of individuals that it can continue.

III. Briefing the Solicitor-General

Governments *choose* to seek the Solicitor-General's advice if and when they like. Governments, like any client, may avoid seeking 'unwelcome' advice either by simply not asking for advice, or by framing questions in a particular manner. This possibility raises serious questions about the legality and quality of government actions taken without appropriate legal scrutiny. A fundamental dimension of constitutionalism is that the Executive has a positive obligation to ascertain the law and comply with it in its actions and decisions. To do so, it requires access to legal experts to guide it in this interpretative exercise.[5]

The ability of governments to avoid legal advice raises concerns beyond the legality of individual actions. It may also threaten the independent resolve of a Solicitor-General. An appropriate level of trust must exist between the government and the Solicitor-General in order to ensure recourse to the Solicitor-General and prevent the relationship from breaking down. Even with a good working relationship, the ability of the government to sideline or 'freeze out' the Solicitor-General raises at least a possibility of the perception of bias, on the ground that an individual may adopt a course of action to remain within the government's trusted circle.

The lack of guaranteed work for the Solicitor-General raises a further concern about the quality of advice received from other quarters if the Solicitor-General is not briefed. One alternative source of advice is that provided by in-house legal services. There are serious concerns that this advice may lack the necessary professional independence from the interests of the client, and may fail to understand the implications of a particular action for the broader legal interests of the whole

[4] Former South Australian Solicitor-General Bradley Selway had written on a similar obligation in the context of government lawyers under the responsibility of the Attorney-General more broadly: B Selway, 'The Duties of Lawyers Acting for Government' (1999) 10 *Public Law Review* 114. Selway based his conclusions on an earlier Canadian piece: J Tait, 'The Public Service Lawyer, Service to the Client and the Rule of Law' (1997) 23 *Commonwealth Law Bulletin* 542. See a more recent airing of Selway's position by the current South Australian Solicitor-General Martin Hinton: M Hinton, 'The Courts, the Executive and the Solicitor-General' in G Appleby, P Keyzer and J Williams (eds), *Public Sentinels: A Comparative Study of Australian Solicitor-General* (Ashgate Publishing, 2014) 67. Beyond this, there is sparse scholarship that explains the function. Although see D Webb, 'Keeping the Crown's Conscience: A Theory of Lawyering for Public Sector Counsel' (2007) 5 *New Zealand Journal of Public and International Law* 243.

[5] See also Interview, Leigh Sealy.

of government. In some jurisdictions another alternative is that advice is sought from a private law firm. This source of advice has been similarly criticised because of its market-driven client focus and lack of institutional knowledge of government to ensure that whole-of-government interests are considered when advising an individual department or agency. The competitive environment has even led to shifts towards client-centred lawyering within government legal services providers, giving rise to similar criticisms of lawyers within the responsibility of the Attorney-General.

The role of government lawyers and other legal service providers to government is a largely unstudied field in Australia. Study of this nature is particularly pertinent at a time when the outsourcing reforms of the 1990s in several jurisdictions are under government review. One possible alternative to the current arrangements is to amend the statutes establishing the Solicitor-General so that matters that raise particular issues *must* be briefed to the Solicitor-General (as exists for the work of the OSG in the US). In some jurisdictions, a protocol or a set of guidelines has been created that identifies the types of matters that must be briefed to the Solicitor-General. Events demonstrate, however, that even in these jurisdictions, such matters may still not be briefed to the Solicitor-General. Further, the documents demonstrate the difficulty in attempting to identify and define the types of matters that require the advice of the Solicitor-General. Because of these difficulties, many Solicitors-General emphasised the desirability for the Crown Solicitor (or equivalent) to act as a more sensitive and flexible 'filter' for requests to the Solicitor-General. However, simply relying on personal relationships can be dangerous, as personal tensions may cause Solicitors-General to be deliberately 'frozen out' of work.

The lack of any requirement to ensure that the Solicitor-General is engaged by government raises the immediate concern that government can avoid obtaining high quality, independent legal advice before pursuing important policy. The involvement of the Solicitor-General may also provide an additional benefit to policy development: review of government action against a broader public policy framework informed by the Solicitor-General's conceptions of the 'core government principles'. More subtly, the ability of the government to avoid involving the Solicitor-General may have an impact upon the office's independence, and also aggravates a risk that, by choosing not to engage with a fiercely independent Solicitor-General, the government is obtaining legal services from less robust sources.

IV. Independence

Underpinning the statutory office of Solicitor-General in Australia is an assumption that the design of the office will protect the officeholder's professional independence. The legislation's drafters hoped that incorporating similar statutory guarantees of tenure as are enjoyed by the Judiciary would place the legal work of government beyond reproach. However, the large majority of participants believed that the independence of the office rested not on the statutory guarantees of tenure, but on an individual's professional competence and commitment to ethical behaviour. My interviews revealed that most participants thought that independence is protected by an individual's fortitude in the face of implied or express pressures. Without this internal fortitude, structural guarantees will not deliver independence. While statutory provisions can be important normative statements, may affect public perceptions and may create an environment in which internal capacity can be exercised, without individual integrity, statutory guarantees are easily undermined by subtle pressures and individual actions.[6]

A. The Value of Individual Independence and Structural Guarantees

James Madison wrote in 'Federalist No 10' that '[e]nlightened Statesmen will not always be at the helm'.[7] Neither will enlightened lawyers. Relying upon individuals' fortitude highlights the utmost importance of the robustness of the process for appointing Solicitors-General. Without the appointment of candidates well-established within the legal profession, who have exhibited a strong and ongoing sense of ethical purpose throughout their careers, the role may be manipulated and its ability to fill the important function of maintaining the legal integrity of government action will be reduced.

In most Australian jurisdictions, the appointment process is a closed one. This is similar to that traditionally associated with judicial appointment. It is retained as the privilege of the incumbent government. This brings with it advantages, but its closed nature also carries a greater potential for abuse.

Governments have not always been able to attract their preferred candidate as Solicitor-General. Given the emphasis on the integrity of the individual in upholding the independence of the office, these trends give cause for concern. In some cases, the government has struggled to appoint an officeholder at all. In 2012, to attract an eminent candidate, Western Australia substantially changed the structure of its office by allowing private practice.

In a system where structural protections of independence are not paramount, independence does not simply rest upon the officeholders' character but on the integrity of those in government. There was at least one participant who recalled an incident involving inappropriate pressure from government officials. Others

[6] The same conclusion is drawn in relation to in-house counsel in S Le Mire, 'Testing Times: In-House Counsel and Independence' (2011) 14(1) *Legal Ethics* 21, 38, see also 29, 35, 38.

[7] J Madison, 'Federalist No 10' in C Rossiter (ed), *The Federalism Papers* (Signet Classic, 1787, 2003 reprint) 71, 75.

recalled inappropriate requests for advice being made. In many of those instances, the Solicitor-General perceived that such events were not consciously improper overtures but motivated by misunderstandings of the Solicitor-General's role by those in government. Already, there is evidence of some formal and informal processes and mechanisms that have been instituted to combat this.

Different views have arisen in the US literature about the desirability of formal, structural guarantees of independence as against relying on the strength of an individual's commitment to independence. Delivering on the ideal of an independent Solicitor-General is far from facile. The independence of the Australian Solicitor-General remains, somewhat fragilely, protected by the probity of individuals, despite attempts to strengthen independence through the statutory framework. This is not necessarily an entirely negative outcome. The Solicitor-General is accountable through the government and exists to assist the government in achieving its constitutional mandate. Political considerations are, in many cases, legitimately taken into account by the Solicitor-General. Reliance upon the individual's commitment to independence means that these influences can be balanced against the necessity of maintaining independence in legal reasoning, and, when relevant, in providing advice on the congruence between government action and the public interest.

B. 'Autonomous Experts' and 'Team Members'

The conclusion that the protection of the Solicitor-General's independence rests predominantly upon the individual underscores the need for greater analysis of the approach of individuals in the role. This book has revealed two dominant, contrasting approaches. I have called these the 'team member' and the 'autonomous expert'. The two approaches represent either end of a spectrum, with emphasis on independence at one end and engagement with government at the other. Each approach represents a different balance that an individual might achieve between the importance of distance to maintain independence and the desirability of incorporating the Solicitor-General more integrally within policy development. The 'autonomous expert' demonstrates a preference for rigid structures and objectively, externally assessable independence; whereas the 'team member' demonstrates a preference for a flexible structure that prioritises government engagement, but it may be perceived to operate less independently.

Participants were divided about the normative desirability of one approach over the other, and which approach best achieved the office's constitutional role of ensuring integrity. Several reasons were apparent as to why individuals might prefer one approach over the other. A perceived need to reassert the independence of the Solicitor-General from politics after a period of intimate engagement between the Solicitor-General and the political Executive drove one individual towards the 'autonomous expert' approach. In another example, an individual was appointed after a period in which the Solicitor-General had not been engaged by government at all. To avoid over-engagement, or inappropriate engagement, caused by ignorance about the role, the individual adopted an 'autonomous expert' approach. During periods of constitutional transition (such as after self-government in the Northern Territory) or the pursuit of wide-ranging legal reform agendas, Solicitors-General tended to adopt a 'team member' approach, closely engaged in innovative policy development. In Queensland, the introduction of the Solicitor-General's right to private practice has necessitated a more removed approach to the role.

Unsurprisingly given the institutional context in which a Solicitor-General works, the view of those in government, and particularly the Attorney-General, also influences the degree of engagement with the development of policy, as does the strength of individual relationships with others in government.

It would be unwise to advocate that one of the approaches is better designed, in all circumstances, to govern the Solicitor-General's behaviour within government. Knowledge of both models, their benefits and disadvantages, will provide a useful guide for individuals in the office. The models should not be used as definitive norms but to inform difficult decisions about the appropriate conduct of the office.[8] It is likely that an individual Solicitor-General will move between the approaches at different periods and in different functions.

The identification of these two approaches, and the implications they may have for the intimacy of the Solicitor-General's involvement in development of policy, have wider application than simply this office, or even government lawyers more generally. Arnoud Boot and Jonathan Macey have already considered the roles of objectivity and proximity in relation to corporate governance monitors.[9] Other offices in which it might be useful to consider the applicability of the two models include the many institutional mechanisms that have been identified as fulfilling an 'integrity' function within government, including, for example, the Auditor-General and the Ombudsman.[10]

[8] For similar conclusions in relation to officers in the Department of Justice, see JR Harvey III, 'Loyalty of Government Litigation: Department of Justice Representation of Agency Claims' (1996) 37 *William and Mary Law Review* 1569, 1573, 1616.

[9] AWA Boot and JR Macey, 'Monitoring Corporate Performance: The Role of Objectivity, Proximity, and Adaptability in Corporate Governance' (2004) 89 *Cornell Law Review* 356.

[10] See, eg, JJ Spigelman, 'The Integrity Branch of Government' (2004) 78 *Australian Law Journal* 724; J McMillan, 'Rethinking the Separation of Powers' (2010) 38 *Federal Law Review* 423. Already in the scholarship on the Ombudsman, there is recognition that establishing and maintaining a 'good working relationship with executive agencies' is key to the office's effectiveness (see, J McMillan, 'The expanding Ombudsman role—what fits and what doesn't fit' (Paper presented at the 24th Australasian and Pacific Ombudsman Region Conference, Melbourne 2008), 6). Dedicated research into the operation of the two approaches, however, remains lacking.

C. Adviser and Advocate

The Australian statutes require the Solicitor-General to act as counsel for the Crown, a role that combines advisory and advocacy functions familiar to practising barristers. The two functions import different levels of independence. As an adviser, the Solicitor-General must provide a robust and independent assessment of the best interpretation of a legal rule or principle to ensure the integrity of government actions. In contrast, as an advocate, the Solicitor-General may draw upon legally available arguments to protect government action that has already been taken. These distinct ethical frameworks illustrate a unique aspect of the Solicitor-General's role: the combination within the same office of two distinct functions, one that is internally focused and designed to improve the legality and integrity of government action, and the other that defends the actions of the government against external attack. Other integrity mechanisms are singularly internally focused, investigating and reporting upon the integrity of government action.[11]

The functions of the office were, prima facie, perceived by participants to be fundamentally different, governed by different ethical frameworks that accept different levels of direction from the political Executive. However, a more detailed analysis of the functions reveals greater complexity. Some of the participants saw the duty to assist the government achieve its policies as a legitimate part of the office's advisory function. In many respects, this is at odds with the regulatory, integrity-driven aspect of the role. Providing advice to the government on consistency of policies and actions with 'core government principles' adds further complexities if the adviser function is seen as a neutral expositor of legal principles. In the advocacy function, the Solicitor-General's large discretion in setting the position for the government, or advising the government of the appropriate position for the Crown to adopt having regard to consistency of position and balancing of at times competing 'core government principles', particularly in constitutional litigation, encompassed a large degree of *de facto* independence not usually associated with this function.

The US literature raises the potential for the office's two functions to contaminate each other inappropriately, or cause confusion in government. In this way, the independence of the Solicitor-General's advice may be challenged. However, these potential negative implications flowing from the current Australian structure must be considered against the benefits of retaining the functions in the one individual, particularly in light of the significant overlap in the nature of the functions in practice. What the US literature reveals is that the Solicitor-General, and those within government interacting with the office, should be aware of the different nature of the functions and attempt to avoid any confusion and contamination, including the perception of such.

[11] Spigelman, above n 10, 728, points out that Auditor-General considers both probity and merits, so has dual function, but my point here is that both of these functions are internal review roles.

V. Concluding Reflections on the Australian Model

Chapter two introduced the two major inquiries into the English Law Officers that were conducted in 2007–08, one by the House of Commons Constitutional Affairs Select Committee[12] and the other by the Government[13] (the House of Lords Select Committee on the Constitution also conducted a smaller-scale inquiry into the role of the Attorney-General).[14] The House of Commons Committee proposed substantial reform to the office of Attorney-General: the splitting of the political and non-political functions between a political minister and a non-political officer. Ultimately this model, which so closely resembles the Australian one, was rejected in favour of the status quo. The British Government had several concerns about how a non-political Law Officer could be realised in practice. In drawing its conclusions, the British Government's inquiry failed to engage with the structural nuances and practice in those jurisdictions that have adopted a non-political model, including Australia.[15]

What this book has demonstrated is that the non-political grounding of Australia's Solicitors-General has in many respects removed the office from the immediate tensions between the public interest, the law and politics that face a Solicitor-General holding a ministerial post. However, the office's continuing relationship with democratic government means that these tensions, appropriately, remain and must be negotiated by individual officeholders. Thus the Australian model has *not* managed to cleanly cleave the legal and political functions of the Law Officers between the Solicitor-General and Attorney-General, even if this may have been the naive aim behind some of the legislation when introduced. Through the relationship between the political Attorney-General and the non-political legal specialist Solicitor-General, greater experience and strength is brought to all aspects of the Law Officers' roles, without breaking the important and necessary links between them.

The Australian position reinforces the conclusions of John Edwards and Neil Walker in relation to the English Law Officers: that the appropriately independent exercise of the Law Officers' functions rests not on the particular constitutional

[12] House of Commons Constitutional Affairs Committee, *Constitutional Role of the Attorney General*, Fifth Report of Session 2006–07 (HC306).

[13] See *The Governance of Britain: A Consultation on the Role of the Attorney General* (The Stationery Office Limited, 2007); and Ministry of Justice, *The Governance of Britain: Constitutional Renewal* (March 2008).

[14] House of Lords Constitution Committee, *Reform of the Office of Attorney General* (HL 2007–08, 93), available at <http://www.publications.parliament.uk/pa/ld200708/ldselect/ldconst/93/93.pdf>.

[15] See, eg, the overly brief description of comparative jurisdictions in *The Governance of Britain: A Consultation on the Role of the Attorney General*, above n 13, Annex B. Although it should be noted that some more detailed comparative analysis was provided in the submissions to the government inquiry. See, eg, P Bogal et al, *Report of a Working Group of the Bar of the Chairman, Geoffrey Vos QC: The Governance of Britain: Role of the Attorney-General* (November 2007) (on file with author) 7–10.

arrangements but on the integrity and capacity of an individual officeholder. The Australian position does provide, however, a strong normative statement of the government's commitment to appointing independent and highly qualified legal professionals to take up the position as Solicitor-General. The Australian position provides a framework within which good officeholders can negotiate the law, politics and the public interest, a normative statement they can rely upon in times of trouble, and a powerful tool for fostering public confidence in the role.

APPENDIX A—QUALITATIVE RESEARCH DESIGN

The empirical research in this book relies on a series of semi-structured interviews, supported by documentary research.[1] The latter included biographies and biographic dictionaries, memoirs, oral histories, personal manuscript collections, newspaper reports, government reports and other documents (such as Cabinet documents and legal opinions), the writings of officeholders and newspaper reports. Where it has been possible, the views of participants have been substantiated by examples from case law, written opinions and other data.[2] The purpose of this appendix is to provide a fuller explanation of the methodology employed to ensure adequate transparency and therefore the integrity of the research process.

Forty-seven interviews were conducted from June 2010 to June 2015. Of these, two interview participants requested that the information they provided, and their names, not be included in the final work other than for background purposes. A full list of the remaining 45 interview participants and the details of the interviews are provided in Appendix B. The interviewing process was preceded by obtaining the necessary ethical clearance from the University of Adelaide and University of New South Wales Human Research Ethics Committees, although the research was categorised as low risk.

I. Selection of Interview Participants

The primary research group for the interviews comprised current and former Solicitors-General. Also included were individuals from groups that operated closely with the office. These groups were current and former Attorneys-General, members of the Judiciary (some of whom had previously held office as either Solicitor- or Attorney-General) and members of the government solicitor's offices

[1] Interviews and documentary analysis are very common qualitative techniques, and have been identified as two of the three main methods of data collection for qualitative researching in law in a handbook on the topic: L Webley, 'Qualitative Approaches to Empirical Legal Research' in P Cane and HM Kritzer (eds), *The Oxford Handbook of Empirical Legal Research* (Oxford University Press, 2010) 926, 928.

[2] In this way, many of the interview data findings have been triangulated (that is, supported by independent measures): MB Miles and AM Huberman, *Qualitative Data Analysis: An Expanded Sourcebook* (Sage Publications, 3rd edn, 1994) 266.

or Attorney-General's Departments. These additional groups were included on the basis that 'their views, experiences and so on would bring contrasting and complementary insights to the enquiry'.[3] The groups were chosen because it is within these relationships—with the Executive, the Judiciary and the public service—that the Solicitor-General operates, and therefore these actors' expectations and interactions with the office would offer insight into the role from different vantage points. I had, in my early formulation of my research, anticipated that I would also approach Governors, Governors-General, Administrators and important parliamentary actors (including speakers, presidents and clerks), as I was interested in the relationship between these officeholders and the Solicitor-General. However, as I started my research, I found that I was able to gain sufficient information through interviews with the initial groups, and independently verify this through publicly available documents.[4] I was conscious to ensure that my sampling was directed towards the 'meatiest, most study-relevant sources'.[5]

The time period to which the research was confined varied across jurisdictions, as I was concerned only with interview participants who had operated under the modern model of a statutory Solicitor-General (see chapter three, section III.).

Participants were not sampled through a representative selection. This was for two reasons. Practically, the pool of potential participants was simply too small for this to be achieved, and access to some members of it was necessarily limited (by age, ill-health or distance). Secondly, it was not intended that the sample would reflect with any great probability the conduct of the group as a whole.[6] I was not measuring the frequency of any particular idea, but rather identifying that the idea existed, or did not, within the data.[7] My aim of developing a description of the 'social practice'[8] of the Solicitor-General rested on consideration and comparison of *individuals'* perceptions and experiences:

> When the aim is to describe and understand a complex, shifting reality in some depth, when one is working with the sheer messiness of human reality, it has to be recognized that the apparently 'unrepresentative' individual is expressing something vital.[9]

[3] J Ritchie, J Lewis and G Elam, 'Designing and Selecting Samples' in J Ritchie and J Lewis (eds), *Qualitative Research Practice: A Guide for Social Science Students and Researchers* (Sage Publications, 2003) 78, 86–87; HJ Rubin and IS Rubin, *Qualitative Interviewing: The Art of Hearing Data* (Sage Publications, 1995) 69.

[4] I did interview one Administrator of the Northern Territory, but this was on the basis that he was a former Solicitor-General as opposed to the holder of a Vice-regal office.

[5] Miles and Huberman, above n 2, 34.

[6] SN Hesse-Biber, 'The Practice of Feminist In-Depth Interviewing' in SN Hesse-Biber and PL Leavy (eds), *Feminist Research Practice: A Primer* (Sage Publications, 2007) 111, 119.

[7] See the comparison between qualitative and quantitative research: J Kirk and ML Miller, *Reliability and Validity in Qualitative Research* (Sage Publications, 1986) 9.

[8] B Flyvbjerg, *Making Social Science Matter: Why Social Inquiry Fails and How it can Succeed Again* (Cambridge University Press, 2001) 2.

[9] CH Evans, *Language People: the experience of teaching and learning modern languages in British universities* (Open University Press, 1988) 5, extracted in F Cownie, *Legal Academics: Culture and Identities* (Hart Publishing, 2004) 20. See also Webley, above n 1, 934.

While I was not aiming for a representative sample, the selection of participants was not random. 'Strategic',[10] 'purposive' or 'criterion based',[11] sampling was employed to allow for a comparison of persons of different backgrounds with different attributes to be considered, as well as focusing on the groups that I had identified as having a great deal of contact with the Solicitor-General, and thus were 'data-rich'. A 'pool' of potential participants was compiled, composed of current and former Solicitors-General, Attorneys-General and those in government legal services with close and regular contact with the Solicitor-General, such as Crown Solicitors, or Crown Advocates. Within this pool, those whose contact details were not readily available were removed; also removed were those who it was known were not geographically accessible.

My strategic sampling focused on obtaining participants with a cross-section of the attributes I had identified. I did this on the basis that these attributes would allow me to draw strategic, cross-contextual comparisons amongst my data. Within the sample, as far as possible, a combination of male and female participants were approached, although the number of women holding offices that fell within those groups being interviewed were few (female participants n=3). Sampling was also done to ensure that a combination of conservative and liberal appointees were interviewed (note, while Solicitors-General are not (usually) members of a political party, it is meant by this that the officeholder was appointed by a conservative or liberal government, although some officeholders had been appointed by both). Other attributes differed between participants including tenure experiences and backgrounds, for example a Solicitor-General who served governments of a single political persuasion only, and those who served and were appointed under governments of different political persuasions; and Solicitors-General who were appointed from the Bar or from within the government. This influenced my sampling as I selected invitees in an attempt to obtain the viewpoints of those with different attributes.

As my interviews progressed, my sampling became more targeted. This was for three reasons. First, it became clear that particular individuals were involved in the relations between the Solicitor-General and the government and would offer a unique view. Secondly, it was mentioned to me that a particular officeholder held a novel or outlying view regarding the office, and that my research would benefit from including that officeholder in it. Lastly, a particular event became of interest to my research, and to verify or expand on my data I needed to interview others involved in it. I also became interested in obtaining the perspectives from a number of different players in the same era; so I sought to include a number of sub-sets in my data of, for example, a Solicitor-General, Attorney-General and Crown Solicitor who all held office together. While time and cost meant that

[10] J Mason, *Qualitative Researching* (Sage Publications, 2002) 123–24.

[11] BL Berg, *Qualitative Research Methods for the Social Sciences* (Allyn & Bacon, 7th edn, 2009) 50; Ritchie, Lewis and Elam, above n 3, 78.

I was not able to follow all leads that materialised in this way, they offered valuable direction in participant selection.

The sample included those operating in the federal jurisdiction and those operating in state and territory jurisdictions. The interviews were collected and analysed across jurisdictions, because to a large extent, and as demonstrated in the history and legal chapters in the book, the jurisdictions are so similar that the constructs in one jurisdiction will inform the other. However, where the jurisdictions do differ, these points of distinction could be used to better understand each jurisdiction, and had to be borne in mind in the subsequent analysis.

There were limitations within my sample that were caused predominantly by fiscal and time constraints. There is, for example, a lack of breadth in the participants interviewed in some jurisdictions. This was predominantly because of time constraints, as I only visited some jurisdictions briefly. However, rather than seeing these sampling limitations as detracting from the study, they offer the opportunity to further test the findings drawn in future research.

Despite these acknowledged limitations in the sample size, I was confident in the sufficiency of the sample in outlining my findings of different practices of the office. Once I had conducted approximately 10 interviews and started to transcribe and code the data, it became clear to me that a number of recurrent themes, relationships and patterns were emerging. These were starting to repeat themselves in the succeeding interviews. I was reasonably confident by the end of my interviews that I had reached a satisfactory level of saturation with my data; that is, I was not gaining any significant new or novel insights in the interviews. That is not to say that the subsequent interviews were not extremely important for the research: many of my preliminary findings were being reinforced through further views, and additional examples arose as the interviews continued. As is explained further in section VI.c. below, I was able to verify and confirm my findings with these additional data, giving greater depth to their integrity.

II. Recruitment of Interview Participants

The recruitment of participants was done using publicly available information (including government directories, *Who's Who*, university directories (as many former officeholders are now adjunct professors) and the Internet). They were approached by telephone, e-mail or mail. The response of participants invited to be involved in the study was very encouraging: only two of the participants approached did not respond positively to the request;[12] and seven interviews failed to materialise because of an inability to coordinate a mutually suitable time. One

[12] And in both of these instances no response was received, rather than a negative response.

interviewee asked whether the interview could be conducted with a colleague, as they worked closely in the area and believed my research would be more complete with the two of them. In three interviews with current and former Attorneys-General, an adviser was also present.

Overall, I had little trouble gaining access to my participants and my response rate was very high. A number of likely reasons underlie this. Many participants indicated that they were highly interested in the topic, and noted that little research had been done in the area. This general interest helped them to understand the purpose and importance of the interviews. The nature of the topic also meant that for many participants it was an opportunity to talk about their own professional careers and reflect on them. The professional nature of the research meant that there was little reluctance on the basis of privacy or sensitivity. Many participants also knew me, or knew one or other of my doctoral supervisors. I believe that this generated a level of trustworthiness in the research that ensured a high rate of participation.[13]

This level of trust in the research was largely reflected in participants' approaches to confidentiality and anonymity (this is explained below in section VII.), and in the level of candour that all participants displayed. At the end of the interviews, a number of participants expressed how much they had enjoyed the interview: an opportunity to reflect on their experiences, and some of the larger concepts that touch on their role, with an interested third party. Many indicated that if I required anything further, I simply needed to get in touch. A number also provided me with additional documentary sources during, or after, the interview to assist me with my research.

This high response rate is critical to understanding the veracity of the data: the high participation rate meant that participants were less likely to be self-selecting, and therefore conclusions were less likely to be influenced by the suggestion that the participants had a particular interest or agenda in relation to the study's subject matter.

Participants were initially provided with an overview of the project and its goals, together with a copy of my CV. Once I received a response from them expressing an interest in being involved in my research, I forwarded the additional material for the interview and arranged a time and place for it. Most interviews lasted approximately an hour. Interviews were conducted at the place most convenient to the participant: this was largely in participants' workplaces, although a small number were conducted elsewhere.

The additional material forwarded to participants included:

1. A three page sheet of Explanatory Notes that explained in more depth the purpose and scope of the research, the intent of the interviews in the larger

[13] D Buchanan, D Boddy and J McCalman, 'Getting in, getting on, getting out and getting back' in A Brymer (ed), *Doing Research in Organisations* (Routledge, 1988) 53, 59.

project and the conditions that would surround the interview (particularly in relation to consent and confidentiality). This also provided participants with a list of subjects around which the interview would be conducted. These were:

- — the appointment of the Solicitor-General
- — the constitutional importance of the office
- — the Solicitor-General's client
- — the independence of the Solicitor-General
- — the processes of the office
- — the broader bureaucratic setting in which the office operates
- — the accountability of the Solicitor-General
- — the different functions of the Solicitor-General
- — the relationship between Solicitors-General
- — the relationship between the Solicitor-General and the Court
- — the role of the Solicitor-General in interventions before the High Court.

2. A consent form, that included an optional box regarding:
   (a) confidentiality and anonymity; and
   (b) tape recording.
3. Information on the relevant human research ethics independent complaints procedure.

III. Development of Interview Topics

The interview topics were initially developed during the comparative research into the British, US and New Zealand offices,[14] the historical research on the Australian office and the analysis of the Australian legal position. The focus of the interviews was the perceptions and experiences of the office regarding the key characteristics that divided the literature as to how the Law Officers ought to resolve the political, legal and public interest tensions inherent in their constitutional roles. Thus the attitudes towards the questions of client, function, independence and accountability were key themes explored in each interview. Also relevant in analysing the position was the participants' view on the relationship between the office and the three arms of government—the Executive, the Legislature and the Judiciary—and any perceptions about public interest obligations the office continued to fulfil.

The interviews also sought to understand better the processes of the office, and so questions regarding the appointment, everyday processes (including

[14] Ch 2.

relationship with the Attorney-General, ministers and other government legal officers), the broader bureaucratic setting in which the office operates and the relationship between Solicitors-General as a collective (particularly involving the SCSG) were explored.

The initial five interviews (which included current and former Solicitors-General, two judges and a former Attorney-General) were used as a pilot study to test the interview schedule and to gain an insight into issues of concern to participants. Following these interviews, the interview schedule was slightly modified.

IV. Conduct of Interviews

The interviews took between 25 minutes and two and a half hours. They were conducted in a semi-structured manner around those topics that had been provided to the participants in the Explanatory Notes. Solicitors-General (current and former) were asked about their perspectives on the role, any difficulties they had faced that demonstrated a perceived tension in the role, and whether they had been confronted by particular issues that highlighted such tensions. Those in the other groups—Attorneys-General, judges and members of the government legal service—were asked about their perspective of the role in the broader government context, particularly as it influenced their own role, together with their observations of, relationship with and interactions with the office. For each individual interview, research was conducted regarding the participant's current and former professional positions, political affiliations, events of significance during their time in office, previous writings (particularly on the topic of the Law Officers) and previous interviews or oral histories the participant may have given. This allowed the interviews to be tailored to individuals' experiences and opinions.

For my first five interviews, I arranged an informal meeting with the participant to discuss my project, the purpose of the interview and its general content. This allowed me to develop a rapport with the participant, and to ensure that the subsequent interview was tailored to the individual and that I could use the time allocated for the interview as effectively as possible. I was able to do this with these participants as I was living in the city in which their interviews were conducted, and thus access to them was relatively easily facilitated. As I grew more comfortable with my interview technique and preparation, I found this initial, informal meeting was unnecessary (and in many of my subsequent interviews, it was impractical to arrange two meetings with the participant). One of these initial interviews was with one of my PhD supervisors who is a former Solicitor-General. This was an important interview, as after it he provided me with feedback that allowed me to improve my technique, the flow of questions and the content of questions.

Three interviews were conducted over the telephone. This was not ideal, as it did not allow for the same level of rapport to be built between the interview participant and me as is achievable in an interview face to face. However, I did not feel that these interviews were prejudiced because of this method, for two reasons. First, the nature of the roles of the participants (each participant I interviewed over the telephone was an incumbent Solicitor-General) is such that they would often be required to conduct lengthy teleconferences. Further, I had met two of the participants on a number of occasions prior to the interview, which meant there was an existing level of rapport.

Seven interviews were conducted after my doctoral thesis had been completed. At least one of these interviewees had seen a copy of this manuscript and the arguments that had been advanced in it. This meant that this participant was aware of the previous responses of other participants in the project, and also how the responses had been analysed and the argument developed. This may have, at least initially, placed this participant in a position different from that of others, although (as I explain below) all participants were given copies of the final drafts of the relevant chapters of the manuscript and invited to make further comment.

The choice of a semi-structured interview for my methodology was necessary for a number of reasons. It allowed the interview to explore a topic in more depth if it was one on which the participant had extensive views, or with which the participant had had controversial experiences, while ensuring that there was sufficient similarity across subject areas that data could be collated and compared across relevant variables. Where time did not permit, it allowed the interview to focus on those areas that were of particular interest because of the character or characteristics of the participant. The semi-structured format also allowed participants to be asked about specific events and views that they had expressed publicly that related to the interview topics. Lastly, the order of the interview was able to be changed, depending on how a participant responded to the questions and the topics that naturally arose during the course of the interview.

Throughout the interview, funnel questioning was used to ensure that the participant's views on a topic were explored first, before I made suggestions about issues in the questions. This allowed the data, as far as possible, to be collected from the participant uninfluenced by particular propositions I wanted to put to him or her. As I conducted more interviews, the propositions that I put to the participants changed and expanded as I engaged in my preliminary data analysis and tested the conclusions I had drawn from it.

In the course of the interviews, I also pressed participants for illustrative examples of any broad generalisations or principles they provided. This ensured that the data I received were grounded in practical experience rather than idealised theory. It also enabled me to check accounts against other factual records to verify the validity of the data.

V. Situating Myself in the Interview Process

To some degree, the use of semi-structured interviewing that flowed as a conversation around pre-set topics placed me *within* my methodology.[15] Therefore some explanation of my perspective and background is necessary to provide a greater level of transparency, allowing for the discovery and understanding of any unintended influences and presuppositions.

I came to this research as somewhat of an 'insider', as a legal academic and having previously practised in the public law field in Queensland (as an articled clerk to the Queensland Crown Solicitor and then as an associate to a judge of the Supreme Court) and Victoria (as a Senior Lawyer at the Victorian Government Solicitor's Office). As such, I was, or my writings were, likely to have been known to a number of my participants (the likelihood of this dramatically increased in those jurisdictions where I had worked—indeed I interviewed previous colleagues and bosses—and because I provided participants with a copy of my CV when I invited them to be part of the project).

The advantage of bringing a legal perspective to the interview was that it gave me a shared language and knowledge with the participants.[16] At one level, this shared culture enabled me to decode answers more accurately.[17] However, I had to be additionally vigilant that I was not making assumptions based on any preconceived conclusions as to meaning in the gathering and subsequent analysis of the data.[18]

VI. Data Analysis

Interpreting data is 'an art it is not formulaic or mechanical'.[19] Nonetheless, I approached my data interrogation and interpretation on the basis that it must be systematic, rigorous and reliable without being too rigid. In my analysis of the data I relied extensively on the framework outlined in *Qualitative Data Analysis: An Expanded Sourcebook* by Matthew B Miles and A Michael Huberman.[20] It is a seminal and heavily relied-upon work in the social sciences. The approach of Miles and Huberman can be outlined as consisting of three concurrent 'flows of activity': data reduction (coding, writing summaries and memos, etc); data display

[15] S Roseneil, 'Greenham Revisited: researching myself and my sisters' in D Hobbs and T May (eds), *Interpreting the Field* (Oxford University Press, 1993) 180, referred to in Cownie, above n 9, 21.

[16] Rubin and Rubin, above n 3, 22; SN Hesse-Biber and P Leavy, *The Practice of Qualitative Research* (Sage Publications, 2006) 136.

[17] W Foddy, *Constructing Questions for Interviews and Questionaires: Theory and Practice in Social Research* (Cambridge University Press, 1993) 17.

[18] J Riemer, 'Varieties of Opportunistic Research' (1977) 5(4) *Urban Life* 467.

[19] NK Denzin, 'The Art and Politics of Interpretation' in NK Denzin and YS Lincoln (eds), *Handbook of Qualitative Research* (Sage, 2000) 317.

[20] Miles and Huberman, above n 2.

(organising, comparing data to further understanding and facilitate analysis); and conclusion drawing and verification (noting regularities, patterns, explanations, possible configurations, causal flows and propositions).[21]

A. Data Reduction: Transcription, Coding and Memoing

i. Transcription

All but five of my interviews were tape-recorded with the permission of the participant (including those conducted by telephone).[22] Where participants requested that certain information be kept confidential, this was generally flagged while the tape was still recording. The tape recorder was small and inconspicuous, and I do not believe it compromised the rapport or frankness of the interviews in any way.

The use of a recording device enabled the data to retain their richness through direct quotation. Where possible in the presentation of the analysis, these quotations have been used. All interviews were transcribed by me with the assistance of contemporaneous notes that I had made.[23] I made these notes as general 'post-interview memos' that noted any number of things that occurred to me during the interview or in my immediate reflection; these included ideas on the main themes of the research; relationships with previous interviews, or thoughts that I had had; any queries relating to demeanour, candour and frankness; ideas about where I might find further information on particular examples provided by the participant; and further avenues of research.[24]

Transcription was an invaluable part of my data reduction and analysis, and during it I not only became more immersed in the data, but I also developed codes and started to think and note down relationships and patterns that struck me at this early stage of the process.

ii. Coding and Memoing

The data were then reduced through an exercise in coding and memoing. I commenced coding my interviews when I had completed approximately 10 interviews. I had developed a series of codes based on my literature review and historical and legal analysis; but was also very open to allowing codes to develop from within the data, thus on the ideas underpinning a grounded theory methodology.[25] I was

[21] For an overview of these three flows, see ibid, 10–12.

[22] Of those that were not tape-recorded, two were at the request of the participant and one because the surroundings were too noisy to allow for a tape recorder to be used.

[23] Notes during the interview itself were avoided as far as possible, to ensure that the participant followed the answers and was able to develop probing questions to better understand them, and to ensure that open and receptive body language was maintained.

[24] I used the example 'Contact Summary Form' in Miles and Huberman, above n 2, 53.

[25] In this respect, I found the short memos I wrote after conducting each interview particularly helpful in the creation of new codes as, in these memos, I often wrote anything that had struck me as fresh in the interview.

very conscious that, as I had conducted my historical and legal analysis in the main prior to conducting my interviews and analysis, I brought to the exercise a number of ideas about how, in theory, the office should operate. This prior research had also alerted me to areas in which the theory was imperfect or lacked specificity for practical application. In these areas the office was little understood, highlighting the need for empirical research particularly acutely. In this sense, I was not rigidly testing preconceived hypotheses, but neither was I conducting entirely open-minded, grounded research.[26] In coding, I was identifying excerpts in the text that were either themselves perspectives on the particular code (for example perspectives on the code 'independence'), practical explanations of the code or illustrations of the code. When I came back to each code, the relationships between these different combinations would provide a rich cross-section of data for analysis.

As I developed new codes, I reviewed the earlier interview data. I also found that some of my codes collapsed, that is, I found two or more codes were capturing the same material. I was also able to start grouping my codes into thematic groups and hierarchies that I could use later to assist in the data display and analysis. These groupings, as they were refined, would also form my headings and subheadings when it came to setting out my interview findings in the final book.

During this coding process, I commenced a series of memos on those codes that I perceived from the outset to be fundamental (particularly client, independence and public interest) and also those that I was surprised to see rising in prominence (particularly the office's position within the larger bureaucracy). These memos noted 'typical' answers that were emerging from the data (that is, recurrent themes in relation to perspectives on the code, and relationships and patterns that I could start to see emerging from the data); 'negative' or 'disconfirming' instances in relation to these answers; and 'exceptional' and 'discrepant' instances (that is, particular novel ways of looking at the idea).[27]

For my initial 10 interviews, I also wrote summaries of each interview after I had completed my coding (I called these my 'interview memos'). These summaries helped me identify patterns and themes and develop the subsequent memos. As I progressed through the interviews, the need for these summaries lessened, as my codes stabilised and I developed a greater sense of the themes and relationships for which I was looking. After the first 10 interviews, it was no longer necessary to conduct such a rigorous analysis for each individual interview.

Approximately half-way through my data collection, I made the decision to change from manual coding and memoing to using NVivo software for this task. This decision was made predominantly on the basis that I needed to organise the growing data; but later I was very pleased with the manner in which the software allowed me to retrieve, search and display my coded data. I entered my codes (to date) and imported my interview transcripts. Within the software I was able to

[26] Miles and Huberman, above n 2, 17.
[27] ibid, 34.

group my codes and add the key 'attributes' of each participant (these were largely the attributes on which I had sampled my participants): position, jurisdiction, gender, years in office, subsequent position and political persuasion. This allowed for highly particularised searching and comparison of the data later on.

When I imported my interview data into NVivo, I decided to recode all of my interviews without reference to my original, manual coding. This allowed me to 'test' the accuracy of my original coding and increase its consistency across the data set. Once I completed coding my interviews, I also added into my data set a number of documentary sources and coded these. These were therefore able to be part of the data displays I would generate around the codes.

I conducted 11 of my interviews after I had largely completed the coding and analysis process. Rather than importing this data into Nvivo and coding the transcripts, I manually coded the transcripts and entered any additional material into my analysis. I was able to do this predominantly because the interviews did not provide a large number of new themes and findings but rather generally provided support and illustrations for findings I had already drawn and written up.

B. Data Display: Reconceptualising the Data

This part of my analysis was pivotal. Its purpose was to allow me to reconceptualise the data and thus understand relationships and themes that may not have been immediately apparent in the data's raw form (that is, in the interview transcripts themselves). The displays would facilitate comparisons and contrasts that would hold the key to drawing my conclusions.

I commenced my analysis by displaying the coded data (that is, excerpts from the interviews that had been coded—the huge advantage of this was it allowed me to look at the actual interview data, not simply summaries of them) using matrix tables collating different variables to allow for the systematic comparison of responses across the whole data set, but also within jurisdictions and time periods, and across groups of participants sharing the same attributes. In this way, I could see relationships across the data. This analysis commenced before all of the interviews had been completed.

As my data grew, my matrices became larger and unwieldy. My change from manual coding to NVivo allowed these matrices to be more easily created and viewed, and I was able to retrieve and search the data in a highly particularised manner (including using codes, grouped codes and attributes of participants).

C. Conclusion Drawing and Verification

The data displays and memoing that I had conducted to this point were the tools I then used to draw conclusions. I also returned to some of the pivotal interview transcripts and reread them to check that I was not taking data out of context.

The matrix displays were vital for my interpretation, as they allowed me to find patterns and relationships that formed the core of my conclusions and then verify these through providing substantiating examples and repetition.[28] My conclusion drawing and verification was an interactive and iterative process: the data spoke to additional issues requiring further research in the interviews, and conclusions could be verified and modified as required in the course of additional data being added. In this way, the coding and analysis paradigm that I used was neither truly 'inductive' nor 'deductive', but a combination of both.

It was at this point in my data analysis that I started to corroborate the validity of some of the data where they related to historical events. I was able to compare data within the interviews and other documents regarding the same incident to check veracity; and I also conducted research to externally verify statements and assertions. This included, for example, using case law, court transcripts, written opinions and Cabinet documents to verify, and at times further exemplify, claims made in the interviews.

By the end of my analysis I was confident that while there were limitations in my study (see below), my descriptions of the various role perceptions that emerged were reliable and sound. There was sufficient repetition and enough examples that substantiated my conclusions to demonstrate that they were valid representations of the individual interviews conducted and provided valuable insights into the operation of the office more generally. While I was, at a number of points, tempted to try to draw 'representative' conclusions about the Solicitor-General, I had to remind myself that I was not looking for 'representative' conclusions but rather conclusions that represented valuable insights and broad ranges of experiences of individuals in regard to the office of Solicitor-General.[29] In accordance with my methodology, therefore, I had to guard against overly broad generalisations in drawing conclusions.

VII. Participant Review

In accordance with my ethics approval, once I had a complete and almost final draft, I had to provide any extracts from interviews or information attributed to a participant (either expressly or anonymously) to each participant for comment. To do this, I decided to provide my participants with the full chapters in which these extracts or information appeared. In this way participants would gain an understanding of the context in which they were quoted. This gave rise to some difficulty—because I was providing all participants with the full chapter at the same time, I had to de-identify all references. I provided each participant with

[28] I used many of the 'tactics' for generating meaning outlined in ibid, ch 10, throughout this process.

[29] CH Evans, *English People: the experience of teaching and learning English in British universities* (Open University Press, 1993) x, extracted in Cownie, above n 9, 17; Webley, above n 1, 934.

an anonymous number, only informing the individuals themselves what number they had been allocated and drawing their attention to references to their interview (through electronic highlighting). At this stage, I also drew their attention to any parts of other interviews where comments had been made about their office, themselves or their jurisdiction, thus providing them with a further opportunity to comment.

This was a very rewarding exercise. Participants responded with interest to my research, and many provided additional comments and insights that developed the accuracy, depth and breadth of my research. There were only a small number of occasions on which participants requested that incidents they had referred to be removed or anonymised. In most instances, I was able to agree with the participant on alternative wording that sufficiently anonymised them, or the incident. This allowed me to continue to rely on their views and experience in my analysis. On a number of occasions in their responses, participants provided me with further data that I was able to, with their permission, incorporate into the draft.

VIII. Limitations of Study

The sample size for the interviews was not small for a qualitative study of this kind. However, as has already been noted, limited funding and time meant that within some jurisdictions, participants possessing different attributes were not represented in the data. This is particularly the case in Tasmania, Northern Territory and the Australian Capital Territory. It is therefore difficult to make larger generalisations from the data regarding these jurisdictions without analysing a broader cross-section of data that represents it. Although it should be added that such a limitation does not mean that commonalities that have been identified across the data will not still hold relevance in these jurisdictions.

Qualitative research that relies upon interviews always raises the possibility of a degree of (even sub-conscious) self-regulation by participants. Participants are informed that they will be involved in a study about how the office operates in practice, and there is a human tendency to paint the most 'proper' picture—whether that be in accordance with professional ethical standards, their own idealised self-image or attempts to 'please' the researcher, who may be giving subconscious clues as to the answers he or she is seeking.[30] As has already been noted, the large response rate to the interview requests in this study tends to mitigate somewhat against this concern: while participants might have consciously or subconsciously self-regulated, as a general rule they have not self-selected. The cross-section therefore is not limited to those with strong views, or who have considered the office, in the past.

[30] N Fielding and H Thomas, 'Qualitative Interviewing' in N Gilbert (ed), *Researching Social Life* (Sage Publications, 2001) 126.

There were a number of telling factors in the interviews that demonstrated the frankness of the information being obtained. All of the participants were very senior, established professionals, with great confidence in their professional and ethical opinions. As such, the likelihood was remote that they were tailoring answers to accord with any conception of the answer that they thought I was seeking. It was also known to the participants (as I explained to them at the start of the interview) that I would be interviewing a number of their contemporaries; this provided them with a subconscious reminder that any information they provided to me would be referenced against the recollections and views of others who might have been involved in any particular event. Lastly, a large number of participants disclosed instances where there was less than ideal behaviour: as any good evidence lawyer understands, self-incriminating testimony is taken as being particularly reliable.[31]

A further limitation of all qualitative research conducted with interviews is the recognition that people's views are 'constructed and reconstructed'.[32] The validity of the data obtained in all the interviews must be assessed, therefore, against a recognised fallibility in construction and recollection. There were a number of instances in the interviews, for example, where the detail of recollection was mistaken. Rather than completely undermining the validity of the data, however, it should be acknowledged that the intention of the interviews was to develop an understanding of the views of officeholders (and others); and that therefore imprecise recollection of historical events did not necessarily undermine the data. In the presentation of the data, any omissions of detail, or errors of fact made by participants, have been noted.

In the interviews, I often encountered reluctance from participants to comment directly on other individuals, particularly when they worked, or had worked, closely with them. At times participants declined to make comments about individuals but were happy to make general statements. These comments lacked some strength because I was not able to obtain details of the actual events or individuals that evidenced them.

One constraint of all interviews was the operation of legal professional privilege. This limited, to some extent, the degree to which participants could provide examples in practice of their views. However, most participants were happy to provide general references within the confines of professional obligations. Legal professional privilege was one of the underlying reasons why interviewing was such an appropriate methodology for the book. Most of the legal opinions and other written work of the Solicitor-General are not publicly available, and therefore interviews provide a way of accessing attitudes about the roles without infringing on privilege.

[31] On this basis confessions form an exception to the rule against hearsay.

[32] Mason, above n 10, 64.

APPENDIX B—INTERVIEW PARTICIPANTS

Forty-seven interviews were conducted in total. Two interviews were conducted in which the participants requested that the information they provided was used as background material and that they not be identified. Below is a list of 45 interview participants who agreed to be identified, grouped by jurisdiction and position. The date and place of interview is also included. Where participants held a number of relevant offices (for example, if they were Solicitors-General but subsequently appointed to the bench), this has been indicated in a footnote. Incumbent officeholders (as at July 2015) are marked with an asterisk (*).

Commonwealth

Solicitors-General

Sir Anthony Mason AC KBE QC[1]
Sydney
16 February 2011

The Hon Robert Ellicott QC[2]
Sydney
23 June 2011

Dr Gavan Griffith AO QC
Gold Coast
14 April 2011

Dr David Bennett AC QC
Sydney
27 June 2011

Stephen Gageler SC[4]
Sydney
17 February 2011

Attorneys-General

The Hon Thomas Hughes AO QC
Sydney
16 February 2011

The Hon Gareth Evans AO QC
Melbourne
27 June 2011

The Hon Duncan Kerr SC[3]
Hobart
21 December 2010

The Hon Professor Michael Lavarch AO
Brisbane
13 August 2010

The Hon Philip Ruddock MP
Sydney
17 February 2011

[1] Anthony Mason was subsequently appointed as a Justice of the New South Wales Court of Appeal, then Puisne Judge of the High Court of Australia and later Chief Justice of that Court.
[2] Robert Ellicott was elected to the House of Representatives and served as Attorney-General and subsequently as a Judge of the Federal Court of Australia before returning to the private Bar.
[3] Duncan Kerr was appointed a Federal Court Judge in 2012, after my interview with him.
[4] Stephen Gageler was appointed a High Court Justice in 2012, after my interview with him.

Justin Gleeson SC*
Sydney
30 June 2015

The Hon Robert McClelland MP
Sydney
15 February 2011

The Hon Mark Dreyfus QC MP
Sydney
19 June 2015

Judiciary

Sir Gerard Brennan AC KBE QC
Sydney
23 June 2011

The Hon Ian Callinan AC QC
Brisbane
1 November 2010

New South Wales

Solicitors-General

The Hon Keith Mason AC QC[5]
Sydney
16 February 2011

Michael Sexton SC*
Sydney
15 February 2011

Attorneys-General

The Hon Terence Sheahan AO[6]
Sydney
14 February 2011

Queensland

Solicitors-General

The Hon Geoffrey Davies AO QC[7]
Brisbane
3 August 2010

Chief Justice Patrick Keane[8]
Brisbane
6 September 2010

Walter Sofronoff QC
Brisbane
26 August 2010

Attorneys-General

The Hon Rodney Welford
Brisbane
2 February 2012

The Hon Linda Lavarch
Brisbane
24 September 2010

The Hon Dean Wells
Brisbane
23 September 2010

[5] Keith Mason was subsequently appointed President of the New South Wales Court of Appeal.

[6] Terence Sheahan was subsequently appointed as a Judge of the New South Wales Land and Environment Court.

[7] Geoffrey Davies was subsequently appointed as a Justice of the Queensland Court of Appeal.

[8] Patrick Keane was subsequently appointed as a Justice of the Queensland Court of Appeal before being appointed Chief Justice of the Federal Court of Australia. Keane was appointed a High Court Justice in 2013, after my interview with him.

Other

Barry Dunphy (Queensland Crown Solicitor)
Brisbane
15 October 2010

Greg Cooper (Queensland Crown Solicitor)*
Brisbane
12 October 2010

South Australia

Solicitors-General

The Hon John Doyle AC[9]
Adelaide
20 September 2010

Chief Justice Chris Kourakis[10]
Adelaide
16 September 2010

Martin Hinton QC*
Adelaide
24 June 2010

Other

The Hon Catherine Branson QC[11]
(South Australian Crown Solicitor)
Adelaide
2 April 2012

Greg Parker (South Australian Crown Solicitor)[12]
Adelaide
30 June 2010

Attorneys-General

The Hon Trevor Griffin
Adelaide
11 July 2010

Tasmania

Solicitors-General

William Bale QC
Hobart
21 December 2010

Leigh Sealy SC
Hobart/Adelaide (phone interview)
13 March 2012

[9] John Doyle was subsequently appointed as Chief Justice of the Supreme Court of South Australia.

[10] Chris Kourakis was subsequently appointed to the Supreme Court of South Australia, and then Chief Justice of the Supreme Court of South Australia.

[11] Catherine Branson was subsequently appointed to the Federal Court of Australia and then as President of the Human Rights Commission.

[12] Greg Parker was appointed to the Supreme Court of South Australia after my interview with him.

Victoria

Solicitors-General

Sir Daryl Dawson AC KBE CB QC[13]
Melbourne
28 June 2011

Justice Pamela Tate[14]
Melbourne
30 June 2011

Stephen McLeish SC[15]
Melbourne/Adelaide (phone interview)
27 February 2012

Western Australia

Solicitors-General

Rob Mitchell (acting)[16]
Perth
7 November 2014

Grant Donaldson QC*
Perth
7 November 2014

Attorneys-General

The Hon Jim McGinty
Perth
7 November 2014

The Hon Christian Porter MP
Perth
6 November 2014

The Hon Michael Mischin MLC*
Perth
6 November 2014

Australian Capital Territory

Solicitors-General

Peter Garrisson SC*
Canberra/Adelaide (phone interview)
5 March 2012

[13] Daryl Dawson was subsequently appointed to the High Court of Australia.
[14] Pamela Tate was subsequently appointed as a Justice of the Victorian Court of Appeal.
[15] Stephen McLeish was appointed as a Justice of the Victorian Court of Appeal in 2015 after my interview with him.
[16] Rob Mitchell was subsequently appointed to the Supreme Court of Western Australia.

Northern Territory

Solicitors-General

The Hon Thomas Pauling AO QC[17]
Darwin
10 June 2011

Michael Grant QC*
Darwin
10 June 2011

[17] Thomas Pauling was subsequently appointed as Administrator for the Northern Territory.

APPENDIX C—LIST OF OFFICEHOLDERS

Commonwealth Solicitors-General

Year	**Solicitor-General**
'Public Service Period'	
1916–32	Sir Robert Garran
1932–46	Sir George Knowles
1946–64	Sir Kenneth Bailey QC
'Modern Period'	
1964–69	Sir Anthony Mason AC KBE QC
1969–73	Robert Ellicott QC
1973–83	Sir Maurice Byers Kt CBE QC
1984–97	Dr Gavan Griffith AO QC
1997	Henry Burmester QC (acting)
1998–2008	Dr David Bennett AC QC
2008–12	Stephen Gageler SC
2012–	Justin Gleeson SC

New South Wales Solicitors-General

Year	**Solicitor-General**
'British Colonial Period'	
1824–25	John Stephen
1826 (appointed but never sworn in)	James Holland
1827	William Foster
1828	John Sampson
1830 (appointed but lost position for failing to take up duties)	Edward MacDowell
1831–36	John Hubert Plunkett QC

1836–41	VACANT
1841–44	William a'Beckett (acting)
1844–48	Sir William Montagu Manning QC
1848–49	William John Forster MLC (acting)
1849–56	Sir William Montagu Manning QC
1856	Sir John Bayley Darvall QC
1856	Alfred James Peter Lutwyche
1856–57	Sir John Bayley Darvall QC
1857	Edward Wise MLC
1857–58	Alfred James Peter Lutwyche
1858–59	William Bede Dalley
1859–60	John Fletcher Hargrave QC
1863	John Fletcher Hargrave QC
1863–65	Peter Faucett MLC
1865	John Fletcher Hargrave QC
1866–68	Robert Macintosh Isaacs
1868–69	Joshua Frey Josephson
1869–70	Sir Julian Emanuel Salomons QC
1870–72	Sir William Charles Windeyer
1872–73	Sir Joseph George Long Innes
1873–1901	VACANT*
1901–04	Hugh Pollock
1909–10	John Garland KC
1911–12	Walter Bevan
1912–15	David Robert Hall
1915	William Arthur Holman
1916–19	John Garland KC
1919–20	John Daniel Fitzgerald
1920–22	Robert Sproule

* During this period, Richard Edward O'Connor MLC and George Houston Reid QC MLA held the office for short periods. As is explained in ch 3, this was simply to allow these individuals to deputise for the Attorney-General during his absence, rather than a permanent appointment and reinstatement of the office of Solicitor-General.

'Public Service Period'	
1922–53	Cecil Edward Weigall QC
1953–69	Harold Alfred Rush Snelling QC
'Modern Period'	
1969–74	Harold Alfred Rush Snelling QC
1974–78	Reginald Joseph Marr QC
1979–81	Gregory Thomas Aloysius Sullivan QC
1981–87	Mary Genevieve Gaudron QC
1987–97	Keith Mason AC QC
1997–98	Leslie Katz SC (acting)
1998–	Michael Sexton SC

Queensland Solicitors-General

Year	Solicitor-General
'British Colonial Period'	
1890–93	Thomas Joseph Byrnes
'Public Service Period'	
1922–25	Sir William Flood Webb
1925–37	VACANT
1937–45	Hubert James Henchman KC
1946–54	William Graham Hamilton QC
1955–70	William Edmond Ryan
1971–80	Thomas Parslow QC
1980–84	Denis Vincent Galligan QC
1985–89	Kenneth George Mackenzie QC
'Modern Period'	
1989–91	Geoffrey Lance Davies QC
1992–2005	Patrick Keane QC
2005–14	Walter Sofronoff QC
2014–	Peter Dunning QC

South Australian Solicitors-General

Year	Solicitor-General
'British Colonial Period'	
1857	John Tuthill Bagot
'Public Service Period'	
1969–70	Andrew Wells QC
1970–72	Brian Cox QC
'Modern Period'	
1972–78	Brian Cox QC
1978–86	Malcolm Gray QC
1986–95	John Doyle AC QC
1995–2002	Bradley Selway QC
2003–08	Chris Kourakis QC
2008–	Martin Hinton QC

Tasmanian Solicitors-General

Year	Solicitor-General
'British Colonial Period'	
1825–32	Alfred Stephen
1832–33	Hugh Cokeley Ross (acting)
1833–37	Edward MacDowell
1838–41	Herbert C Jones
1841–44	Thomas William Horne
1844–48	Sir Valentine Fleming KC
1848–51	Alban Charles Stonor**
1851–54	Sir Francis Villeneuve Smith
1854–55	Edward McDowell (acting)
1855–57	John Warrington Rogers
1857–60	TJ Knight
1860	Sir William Lambert Dobson
1861	VACANT
1862	Robert Byron Miller MHA

** Resigned in 1854, but had taken sick leave from 1851.

'Public Service Period'	
1864–67	John Compton Gregson
1867–87	Robert Patten Adams
1887	Edward David Dobbie KC
1887–1901	Alfred Dobson KC
1902–13	Edward David Dobbie KC
1914–30	Sir Lloyd Eldon Chambers KC
1930–38	Philip Lewis Griffiths KC
1939–44	Rudyard Noel Kipling Beedham KC
1944–46	Marcus George Gibson KC (acting)
1946–51	Marcus George Gibson KC
1951–52	Sir Malcolm Peter Crisp KC
1952–56	Stanley Charles Burbury QC
1956–68	David Montagu Chambers QC
1968–84	Roger Christie Jennings QC
'Modern Period'	
1984–86	Christopher Reginald Wright QC
1986–2007	William Christopher Robin Bale QC
2007–08	Francis Counsel Neasey (acting)
2008–14	Geoffrey Leigh Sealy SC
2014	Francis Counsel Neasey (acting)
2014 –	Michael Ernest O'Farrell SC

Victorian Solicitors-General

Year	**Solicitor-General**
'British Colonial Period'	
1851–52	Sir Redmond Barry
1852	Sir Edward Eyre Williams
1852	James Croke
1854–55	Sir Robert Molesworth (acting)
November 1855–56	Sir Robert Molesworth
1856–57	Thomas Howard Fellows
1857	Robert Sacheverell Wilmot Sitwell
1857	John Dennistoun Wood

1857–58	Thomas Howard Fellows
1858–59	Richard Davies Ireland
1859–60	Travers Adamson
1860	James F Martley
1860–61	VACANT
1861 (Minister for Justice)	John Dennistoun Wood
1863 (Minister for Justice)	Sir Archibald Michie
1866 (Minister for Justice)	Samuel Henry Bindon
1869	James Joseph Casey
1870	Butler Cole Aspinall
1870–71	Sir Henry John Wrixon
1871–72	Howard Spensley
1872–74	George Briscoe Kerferd
1875	James Macpherson Grant
1875	Dr John Madden
1877	James Macpherson Grant
1880	Dr John Madden
1881–83	Frank Stanley Dobson
1883 (Minister for Justice)	Robert Stirling Hore Anderson
1883	Alfred Deakin
1892–93	Sir George Turner
1893	Sir Isaac Isaacs
1893–94	Agar Wynne
1894–99	Sir Henry Cuthbert
1899–1900	Sir John Mark Davies
1900–02	Agar Wynne
1902–03	Sir John Mark Davies
1903	Sir William Hill Irvine
1904–08	Sir John Mark Davies
1908	Sir John Emanuel Mackey
1908–09	Sir John Mark Davies
1909–13	James Drysdale Brown
1913	W J Evans
1913–15	Donald Mackinnon
1915–17	Sir Harry Sutherland Wightman Lawson

1917–18	Agar Wynne
1918–20	Sir Arthur Robinson
1920	Sir Harry Sutherland Wightman Lawson
1920	Sir Arthur Robinson
1924–24	Isaac Henry Cohen
1924	William Slater
1924–27	Sir Frederic William Eggleston
1927	John Allan
1927–28	William Slater
1928–29	Ian Macfarlan
1929–32	William Slater
1932–34	Robert Gordon Menzies
1934–35	Ian Macfarlan
1935	Harold Edward Cohen
1935–38	Sir Albert Louis Bussau
1938–43	Sir Albert Dunstan
1943	William Slater
1943–45	Ian Macfarlan
1945–47	William Slater
1947–50	Trevor Donald Oldham
1950–51	Thomas Walter Mitchell
'Modern Period'	
1951–64	Sir Henry Winneke KC
1964–74	Tony Murray QC
1974–82	Sir Daryl Dawson QC
1982–92	Hartog Berkeley QC
1992	Raymond Finkelstein QC (acting)
1992–2002	Douglas Graham QC
2003–10	Pamela Tate SC
2011–15	Stephen McLeish SC
2015–	Richard Niall QC

Western Australian Solicitors-General

Year	Solicitor-General
'Public Service Period'	
1902–30	William Frederick Sayer KC
1930–35	VACANT
1935–46	James L Walker KC
1946–69	Sydney H Good QC
'Modern Period'	
1969–79	Sir Ronald Wilson QC
1979–94	Kevin H Parker AC QC
1994–2011	Robert Meadows QC
2011–12	Rob Mitchell SC (acting)
2012–	Grant Donaldson SC

Australian Capital Territory Solicitors-General

Year	Solicitor-General
'Modern Period'	
2011–	Peter Garrisson SC

Northern Territory Solicitors-General

Year	Solicitor-General
'Public Service Period'	
1978–80	Ian McClelland Barker QC
1981–87	Brian Frank Martin QC
'Modern Period'	
1988–2007	Thomas Ian Pauling QC
2007–	Michael Patrick Grant QC

INDEX

All references concern the post of Solicitor-General in Australia and the jurisdictions of Australia, unless otherwise specified.

www.ingramcontent.com/pod-product-compliance
Lightning Source LLC
LaVergne TN
LVHW052241200926
848481LV00002B/234